The Meaning of
Superhero Comic Books

ALSO EDITED BY TERRENCE R. WANDTKE

The Amazing Transforming Superhero! Essays on the Revision of Characters in Comic Books, Film and Television (McFarland, 2007)

The Meaning of Superhero Comic Books

Terrence R. Wandtke

McFarland & Company, Inc., Publishers
Jefferson, North Carolina, and London

LIBRARY OF CONGRESS CATALOGUING-IN-PUBLICATION DATA

Wandtke, Terrence R.
The meaning of superhero comic books / Terrence R. Wandtke.
      p.   cm.
Includes bibliographical references and index.

ISBN 978-0-7864-6491-3
softcover : acid free paper ∞

1. Comic books, strips, etc. — History and
criticism. 2. Superheroes in literature. I. Title.
PN6710.W36 2012   741.5'9 — dc23   2012017518

British Library cataloguing data are available

© 2012 Terrence R. Wandtke. All rights reserved

*No part of this book may be reproduced or transmitted in any form
or by any means, electronic or mechanical, including photocopying
or recording, or by any information storage and retrieval system,
without permission in writing from the publisher.*

Cover illustration © 2012 Digitalvision

Manufactured in the United States of America

*McFarland & Company, Inc., Publishers
Box 611, Jefferson, North Carolina 28640
www.mcfarlandpub.com*

For Griffin and Reuben, my wonder twins
(with their joyous smiles, unaware of their positive effect on me)

For Walter, one of my mentors
(with his kind smile, unaware of his positive influence on me)

Acknowledgments

I give special thanks to: Anna Wandtke (for your encouragement), Bella and Ripley Wandtke (for your inspiration), Adam Davis and John Walter (for your expertise), the department of Communication Arts at Judson University (for your support), and book stores around the world (for your uncanny knack for always having something I desperately need).

Table of Contents

Acknowledgments vi

Introduction: How Comic Books Speak to Me and What I've Heard About Superheroes 1

1. Moving Beyond the Standard Arguments: The Superhero Revised (Again) 7
2. The Emergence of Orality: When Industry Becomes Epic 28
3. Orality and a New Medium: The History of the Man of Tomorrow 53
4. Amplification Through Simplification: The Traditional Basis for Superhero Iconography 80
5. The Persistence of Traditionality: When Industry Workers Become Artisans 105
6. The Failed Attempt to Impose High Culture: Literacy in Crisis 133
7. More Than Service to the Publishers: Artists Aware of Technology (and the Audience) 161
8. Eternal, Self-Conscious Recurrence (or More Revision): The Aesthetes of New Traditionality 191

Conclusion: Everything Old Is New Again (and Again and...): An Open Invitation to an Open Ending 221

Chapter Notes 225

Works Cited 251

Index 259

Introduction

*How Comic Books Speak to Me and
What I've Heard About Superheroes*

The stories of superhero comic book collectors are often like stories of fishermen who simultaneously cast a nostalgic eye on the naive days of youth and lament the ones that got away. Setting aside the melodramatic haze of memory as much as possible, I can say that I initially relied on my parents for the gift of new four-color reading material and was never quite sure when I might receive that gift. Even once I started to earn a regular allowance, it would never be enough to follow all the superheroes that I knew and loved on a monthly basis. In addition, I had established a pattern of choosing my comic books more on the basis of flashy cover art or the quick skim of the interior splash pages, something done in front of the disapproving local drug store owner. (He used classic lines like "This is not a library!" or "If you read it, you buy it!") My comic books would (sometimes literally) be thrown into an old cardboard box, ill-suited to its comic-book-carrying purpose, as it allowed the comic books to slide around as I carried them to my best friend's house. I had no organizational schema that took into account alphabetical order or issue number; instead, the comic book at the top of the pile would necessarily be the comic book most recently read and the majority of those on top were the most well loved. I can't say that I cared about the condition of the disposable pamphlets called comic books any more than the average comic book consumer of the 1970s and most of my comic books became yellowed and tattered at the edges. Even though I could not be properly called a collector or investor until sometime later, I was very invested in the fantastic worlds owned and produced by DC, Marvel, and other comic book publishers. I traded my comic books with my friends for other comic books with little regard for the condition but great attention paid to finding the conclusion of a three-issue story arc in which the Fantastic Four teamed up with the Silver Surfer. Based on some sort of arcane formulation to which only comic readers were fully privy, an issue in which Batman matches wits with a major villain like the Joker couldn't be traded for anything less than three comic books of the same size. Even with the formulas in place and the dramatic yield from a trade in mind, there were those specific comic books from which certain readers would never part due to whatever idiosyncratic reason made them love them so.

I'm not exactly sure when I moved from being an avid reader of superhero comic books to being an obsessive collector but I have pretty good idea. While the transition from occasional reader to the obsessive collector took place for many reasons, I know for certain that the foremost was my new found teenage ability to earn what many adults envied and called "disposable income." However, several other reasons were equally important, and these had less to do with my own situation and more to do with the state of the industry in general. In the 1980s, video games did what the medium of television was not able to do in the past to superhero comic books by stealing away the youth consumer. Comic book marketing was thereafter aimed at an older consumer with more money, and, consequently, the stories became longer, more complex, and more mature. As multi-issue stories became the norm, so did crossover events in which a story tied together most of the superheroes in a particular comic book universe (and required that you buy all those titles for months in order to fully comprehend the segments of the story in your regular titles). And the slender, stapled pamphlets on low-quality newsprint became large, square bound books on glossy paper, no longer sold at newsstands and drug stores but in direct market stores that specialized in comic books. Usually owned by men not entirely unlike the comic book storeowner on *The Simpsons*, these stores featured not only the most recent comic book publications but also bagged and boarded "back" issues of comic books. With the older comics sold at costs determined by annually published comic book price guides, the new breed of comic book buyer gladly paid well over twenty times the current cover price to get the issue of *Spider-Man* in which Gwen Stacy dies. I gladly participated in this cultural shift because it seemed as if superheroes were growing up with me, and this is what growing up required of me as a superhero comic book reader. I reveled in the complex and radical revisions of superheroes such as those enacted by Alan Moore on previously minor characters such as Swamp Thing. And I regularly bagged all of my comics (before reading them), bought multiple versions of the same comic (for the sake of alternate covers), and never once again considered trading a comic book (no matter what I thought of the story); after all, who knew what sort of minutiae within the plot might someday make that issue worth hundreds of dollars?

Many other people who grew up reading superhero comic books at roughly the same time have lamented the loss of days before the direct market, when story was full of innocent action and not stuffed with self-conscious reflection, when story seemed more important than investment. Although I believe the experience of comic book stories is different in these two eras, I don't know that one is definitively better than the other (or even that the first was more innocent). Instead, I simply believe them to be different and feel this is important to stress considering how I have previously understood my personal experience. Years after I had forsaken comic books as far too expensive for a relatively poor university undergraduate, I had studied literary history in a rudimentary fashion and characterized my early experience of superhero stories as similar to that of oral culture and my latter experience as similar to that of literate culture. After all, in the first case, I carefully chose story portions to satisfy my interests with little regard for the larger framework of the story and readily exchanged other stories with a community that did the same. In the second case, I was obsessed with precedent and chronology and I saw collecting all the issues within a serial story as a means to establish historical continuity (and therefore, a means to access the truth). However, even then, I recognized that the rudimentary description of the above mentioned shift was hardly universal; if it described anyone's experience other than my own, I would have said it was largely representative of the experience of those already part of the superhero comic book consumer marketplace. The public at large still seemed to maintain their nostalgic notions of Superman, unencumbered by the implications of his marriage to Lois Lane, his most recent costume change, or his death and rebirth. In addition, even for those participating in the superhero comic book consumer marketplace, the direct market stores provided a new superhero comic book community very like the one I knew as a youth. Recommending favorite titles and searching for hard-to-find issues, the relative safety of this community brought forth someone's declaration of love for the shapely disco superhero Dazzler, regardless of what anyone else had to say (including the disembodied authority of the price guide). Reflecting on this personal experience led me in some rudimentary way to the important claims about orality and literacy made by Walter Ong: not only is literate culture not an inevitable improvement on oral culture, but also, the oral culture will never be wholly absent from literate culture. In fact, what seems to be literate may be a façade hiding the new, secondary orality of the electronic age.

As I look back at my interpretation of my own experience and toward the thesis of this book, I have to reveal yet another problem in my youthful ideas without meaning to be too hard on the person I was at that time (because I still like him quite a bit). During my period of intense comic book reading with my newfound passion for literature in high school in the mid–1980s, I would argue vehemently against the suggestion that the *X-Men*'s Jean Grey should be brought back from the dead. Working with what was a rudimentary sense of literary rightness (tied to storytelling practices of the literate world), I felt that the *Dark Phoenix Saga* possessed a sort of integrity: a story structure that resulted in a climax where Jean Grey committed suicide in order to save the universe from her own uncontrollable power. To bring Jean Grey and the phoenix power back (regardless of how much fans missed her) would soften the original story by subtracting the drama of finality from her sacrifice. However, what I couldn't apprehend then is that while superhero fanboys are often sticklers for continuity within their stories, they also are sticklers for the formula of their stories. While the new readership of superhero comic books may have been older and more educated, they wanted what fans always wanted: formulaic stories (even the *Dark Phoenix Saga* as a reworking of formula became the new norm). As a consequence, almost every story within the "official continuity" of the *X-Men* universe that brings back Jean Grey has had her die once again but in ways that are probably more relevant to the current cultural situation

Jean Grey sacrifices herself to protect the universe from Dark Phoenix (a moment I'd remember very well because I'd see variations on it again and again) (from *X-Men* #137, p. 34).

of the most recent readers. Nevertheless, I now firmly believe that, on the whole, superhero comic books work with a sort of linear non-time connected to the standard storytelling practices of oral culture (in which the story of Odysseus can be endlessly updated). And even if the changes in 1980s superhero comic books could be considered the emergence of something like literate culture in the midst of something like oral culture (which I contend, in this book, that it should), it would be essential to acknowledge that those changes have been far from permanent. The rapidly swelling bubble of the 1980s collector market burst in the 1990s as many investors eventually found too little turn-around value in what they were buying; comic book buying traveled too far from comic book reading. Superhero comic book profits have now shifted from sales of individual issues, in direct market stores, to sales of collections of issues called graphic novels, in large chain bookstores. With decades of issues now bound or available on your computer, back issues are no longer essential—and not entirely desirable as graphic novels are supposedly self-contained; however, that is hardly the case as they still draw upon the readers' collective knowledge of superheroes. Both of the "big two" comic book publishers have established continuity-free series with their major superheroes that nevertheless make frequent allusions to the continuity-bound series. As superhero films have become ever more essential as tentpoles in Hollywood's annual lineup as summer blockbusters, the discussions about superheroes and their histories have become subject to even more mainstream "experts" featured on news shows and in the blogosphere. Herein I will demonstrate how this is a result of the way in which the psychological predispositions of oral culture have now become an integral part of digital culture.

Now, everyone seems to have a sense of what should be done to develop a good Superman story (or a good Spider-Man story, a good Iron Man story, etc.). This phenomenon isn't just part of my own experience as member of a subculture (although it is that as well); this phenomenon is part of the current cultural experience that I would describe as new media driven variation on oral culture (or more appropriately, "traditional" culture). I'm happy to have the opportunity to revisit superhero comic books as a cultural critic in a world that seems to not only be embracing superheroes but also identifying with the storytelling practices associated with superheroes. As I began to write this monograph, my working title was "From Beowulf to Batman," something that satisfied me because it is alliterative and generally captures the historical sweep that I had in mind. However, I do not discuss Beowulf so much as I discuss Batman and I felt that it might read a bit like the titles of so many other studies whose overly simple claim is that superhero stories resemble mythic stories of the past. Moreover, it does not wholly capture what motivates an American culture driven forcefully by technology to act in ways that are so notably traditional. With this stated, I should mention that I'll be following superhero comic books into the 21st century and exploring how the genre has paved the way for the traditionalism now seen in digital culture. In general, chapters 1 through 4 apply scholarship to critical histories of superhero comic books to reveal how the superhero industry operates as an oral/traditional culture and encourages the practices of traditional culture through the stories it produces; chapters 5 through 8 are case studies that begin with the traditional practice of the Silver Age and proceed to the "graphic literature" of the Modern Age, explaining why the practices of traditional culture persist (despite changes in the industry) within a digital culture. In chapter 1, I give a brief overview of superhero comic book history to demonstrate the complexity of revisionism at work throughout that history. Then, I show how the superhero's mythic stories have thus far been explained with academic theories that are incomplete and suggest that the reemergence of something like traditional culture is the best way to account for the characteristics of superhero revisionism. In chapter 2, I examine the specifics of the early comic book industry and how it gave rise to the superhero. Then, I demonstrate how the storytelling culture of the superhero industry works like an oral culture in its practices and overall audience sensitivity. In chapter 3, I look more specifically at Superman, the longest-lived and many-lived superhero, as a means to exemplify the unconscious practice of traditional culture in the 20th century. In chapter 4, I make a significant switch in terms, from "oral" to "traditional," as I explain how a visually-based print medium works in terms of traditional art. In chapter 5, I survey the unintended influence of Fredric Wertham on the superhero industry, leading to the Marvel comics revolution of the 1960s. Then, I argue that Stan Lee and Jack Kirby straddle various types of approaches, synthesizing traditionality with the ideals of literacy and the emerging ideals of postmodernism. In chapter 6, I show how the traditional practices of superhero comic books become more self-conscious with Gardner Fox's "Flash of Two Worlds." Then, I demonstrate how Marv Wolfman's *Crisis on Infinite Earths* fails to impose literacy on superhero comics, then based largely on a self-conscious love of variation (what I call new traditionality). In chapter 7, I discuss Frank Miller's *The Dark Knight Returns* and Alan Moore's *Watchmen* as texts that analyze basic tensions between traditionality and literacy, ultimately leading to each creator's future creative and critical choices. In chapter 8, I demonstrate how new traditionality describes the deeply related cultures of the digital age and postmodernism. Then, I argue that the most influential superhero creators of the 21st century, such as Geoff Johns and Warren Ellis, embrace the postmodern aesthetics previously considered to be the low art of superhero comic books.

As I make this turn toward the formal topics to be discussed in this book, I should now make some disclaimers to address the areas of interest (and concern) for readers who might come from a background in any of the following areas of study: (1) comic books and graphic literature, (2) superhero stories, (3) oral tradition and culture, and (4) digital communication and culture. Comic books and graphic literature are not merely a means to an end as a bridge between oral and digital cultures, a medium that has served its purpose and can now be relegated to a footnote in the history of the artistic world. While derivative of some artforms that historically preceded them, comic books and graphic novels have profound integrity unto themselves that justify their study, and that I think I intuitively recognized even as a young reader. While such a description of the medium may satisfy many scholars in this area of study, I have other things to argue that I know will not. I will identify certain characteristics of the medium that predispose it to present stories similar to what we identify as oral epics — or to stories very much like superhero stories. (For decades, scholars of graphic literature have been arguing that comic books are more than just superhero stories and that superhero stories are not synonymous with the medium.) In addition, I will argue that basic tenets of oral culture should be recognized as an important, if not essential, part of this print medium of a corporate culture that is in part determined by economic concerns. (For decades, scholars of oral culture have been arguing that a pure oral culture is largely separate from the power dynamics of the post-printing press world in which the individual takes precedence over the community.) And I will argue that digital culture seems to be a self-conscious product of a community trying to reactivate the experience of a traditional culture that they don't fully recognize or understand. (For at least a decade, scholars of digital culture have been arguing that digital culture proceeds from or revolutionizes the literature culture of the post-printing press modern world that immediately preceded it.)

In short, this introduction is designed in part to connect my old experience as a naive reader to my new experience as scholar and also to acknowledge that I understand trends in the fields touched by this study. Even though I don't mean to be cantankerous as a cultural critic and go against dominant trends in order to generate controversy, I do mean to pursue feasible arguments to their logical ends; Marshall McLuhan regularly engaged in such a practice, stretching conventional ideas with his unconventional arguments and revolutionizing media studies in the process. I mention McLuhan because I am inspired by his practice but not because I consider my work to necessarily be revolutionary and not because I believe that McLuhan was always exactly on target with his arguments. Nevertheless, he was always interesting in ways that still captivate us. In his career as a speaker, he was known to offer a variation on a Groucho Marx maxim: "Oh, you don't like those ideas? Well, then, how about these..." (Levinson 24–25). I'd like to begin my work with something like this sentiment; I am committed to the ideas that I present in the following pages but know that they might initially be off-putting and are certainly not the final word on many of the subjects covered. So, I'm inviting you to look into something like the old cardboard box that once held a wonderful collection of comic books available to trade, to look without preconceptions and to understand this as the beginning of an exchange that could result in exciting new discoveries for us both.

CHAPTER 1

Moving Beyond the Standard Arguments

The Superhero Revised (Again)

Nearly a century old, the superhero seems as vibrant as ever, extremely prominent within the culture of the world, identified alternately as the best representative of modern mythology and as the most flexible commodity within a capitalist world. While the superhero's status as myth and/or commodity might be the driver for it vibrancy, the simplistic reason the superhero seems as vibrant as ever is due to the fact that Spider-Man hardly ever looks a day over 20 and only rarely makes it beyond high school.[1] For the most part, these superheroes are drawn with a youthful appearance in comic books, played by young actors on film, and written as barely adults within internet fanfiction. Each generation wants to claim particular superheroes as their own and clothe them with the trappings of their era, but the collective impulse is to keep them outside the ravages of time (or at least to broaden industrial age notions of time that might trap superheroes within a single timeline). In recent years, as superhero fans age, they are not completely abandoning the superhero for other interests as was always thought would be the case in the early 20th century; and yet, as their connection to superheroes continues, most still want their superheroes young, close to their point of origin, and full of possibilities. With the successful transitions of superheroes to other new media forms, such as television and video games, the fact that they are no longer as profitable within comic books, the medium with which they are primarily associated, is irrelevant. After all, comic books (or graphic novels as superhero collections are now more often called) are still being produced by major superhero publishers with no end in sight, and, like superhero films, they are marketed fairly successfully around the world (defying previous claims that the superhero only represents American interests). Comic books provide a low-cost means to test new story directions for major superhero characters with an audience that is highly critical but also notably forgiving (willing to allow fundamental retcons that take the characters back to the beginning of their stories). With creators adhering to a story canon and house style of the companies that own superheroes, the medium of comic books seems the most readily capable of keeping Spider-Man the same (and in his teens). Yet, with creators willing to experiment with the sacred stories and looks of superhero comics, the medium of comic books is inevitably set to produce the next best and most loved variation on any superhero.

The Reaction from My Readers:
The Audience Is Always a Fact(or)

To me, some sort of acknowledgment is necessary to explain the starting point for this book that in many ways follows the general reaction to some of my previous work with superheroes. Interested in the development of heroic narratives within contemporary culture, I became fascinated by the appropriation and revision of the superhero throughout the relatively short span of its history. Since the superhero remained at the forefront of many forms of discourse, these revisions, sometimes subtle and sometimes radical, have profound social implications and I explored this most notably in a collection that I edited entitled *The Amazing Transforming Superhero*. From people outside the fields of my studies (literature, visual art, and popular culture), I expected little true excitement but rather something feigned and more like tolerance; this is something that I've found comes part and parcel with academic forays into popular culture. However, some of the reaction I received to my studies (and to second-hand accounts of my studies) fascinated me and my explanation of that reaction is in part the basis for this book — although pieces of my explanation predate the reaction. Upon discovering that I analyzed the implications of revisions to the superhero over the course of time, many would bypass the idea that there were implications to address in the aforementioned revisions; in turn, those many people would, in tones ranging from bewildered to derisive, flatly state that the fact that the superhero has been revised is painfully obvious (as if I claimed this idea to be my own and very original observation).[2] Regardless, I was curious about how they were so confident in the phenomenon of revisionism that they would say it was obvious and yet they demonstrated very little knowledge of superhero history before some of the most recent incarnations of the most popular superheroes. Moreover, I was curious that these people considered the phenomenon of revisionism as ordinary, acceptable, and not strange in any regard.

Trying to determine their likely expectations for narrative storytelling, I initially situated them in the context of the literate world — a context that requires of everyone some knowledge of original sources for a person to feel confident in any authoritative statement. However, they made the claim about what is obvious without demonstrating a perceived need to support that claim. One explanation for making such an improperly supported claim is that they simply didn't care much about what takes place in the low culture of superhero comic books. However, this is unlikely for two reasons: (1) most people who hold low culture in disdain do not claim to have certain knowledge about its operation and perhaps more importantly (2) very few people actually identify anything as low culture anymore, as our postmodern world makes the distinction between high and low less meaningful. And so, I felt I was encountering people who had common knowledge of (and basic comfort with) the phenomenon of revisionism without any real comprehension of it. At one level, I supposed this might be some sort of reaction formation in which I was indicating that these "critics" were unlike me (the learned academic who exuded a unique mastery of the situation quite beyond them) and thus, disrespecting the people who had shown some disrespect for my work. However, upon reflection, I truly believe that the phenomenon of superhero revisionism is much like the phenomenon of film as described by Christian Metz: "Film is difficult to explain because it is easy to understand" (69). In essence, the revision of superheroes is all around us because superheroes are escapable parts of our cultural zeitgeist, and revisionism has been built into the system that produces superheroes. In turn, the reason that superhero stories are now not generally regarded as low culture is not due to the tolerance of our so-called postmodern world; it is due to a larger shift within the aesthetic cultures of the world that had previously been identified via the characteristics of literacy. With this in mind, if we do live in an era of secondary orality as claimed by Walter Ong and Marshall McLuhan, an era in which the most current adaptation supersedes the authority of the original source, people might be rightly comfortable with the revisionism inherent within the genre of the superhero story (in recent years, continuing to expand to other media forms). Therefore, the revisionist practices and the general workings of superhero stories indicate larger trends within society. With this possibility in mind, it becomes very important not only to articulate that superheroes are being revised but also to explain how comic books represent the rebirth of orality (or traditionalism) in contemporary culture.

I contend that comic readers became accustomed to narrative revisionism much sooner than people who did not read comic books within the timeline of new media development. However, even from the point that marks the "invention" of the superhero, the comic book reading audience was never as discrete as the stereotype of the socially outcast, weakling comic book reader might have us believe. With the first superheroes (such as Superman and Batman) developed in the late 1930s, the target audience would undoubtedly be adolescents, but they would not be the only readers; the most famous exception in the early history would be soldiers to whom comic books were sent, because lightweight reading material more easily shipped in large quantities. Regardless of whether or not the audience was a subcultural youth demographic, the narrative experience was one that was often characterized as adolescent because the stories never developed beyond a certain point. Despite the fact that they were published serially throughout the 1940s, there seemed to be no larger story arc, and every segment within the series seemed to be a self-contained story that repeated the same story elements established in previous issues. For instance, Clark Kent, reporter, would receive a Daily Planet assignment and uncover some nefarious villain with a world-threatening plot; Lois Lane, fellow reporter, would become embroiled in the same investigation and find herself in a compromising situation that required Clark to quickly become Superman, defeat the villain, and rescue Lois; they would return to the *Daily Planet*, and Lois would rebuff some romantic overture made by Clark because Lois was truly in love with Superman. This repetition with slight differences represents the early comic book experience of the superhero. In addition to crafting short-action stories that would seem to satisfy only the most basic pleasure principle of adolescent boys, the comic books would sometimes create particular settings and develop certain traits in characters only to radically revise or erase them in subsequent stories of the superheroes. For instance, the expressionist landscape of Batman's New York would become a less paranoid and more brightly lit Gotham City, and the willingness of Superman to kill villains would become a pledge to never take a human life with no narrative explanation to account for such changes. Usually these changes were dictated to creators by editors who wanted to enhance the viability to a saleable product, but sometimes they resulted from the simple fact that various creators worked with the same character and reinterpreted that character within broad editorial boundaries. In fact, this reference to "various creators" would also have to include creators (in other media forms like radio and film) working for companies that had licensed the characters for their use. Sometimes, those creators used other existing tropes for the characters and developed the characters in unforeseen ways. For instance, the Batman serial took the character far from his roots as a dark vigilante and made him into a government agent working against the apish Japanese during World War II (Daniels, *Batman* 58–59). While Batman did encourage the purchase of war bonds on the cover of his comic book, this treatment of the character never completely took hold. However, the serial was the first place in which the Batcave was introduced, and this element has become an essential component of all subsequent renderings of Batman, demonstrating the organic relationship between the various (and sometimes logically inconsistent) treatments of Batman.

As Superman and Batman's origin stories were told and retold with significant revisions and additions throughout the 1950s, the most recent version (with a similarly young superhero in updated surroundings) became more widely recognized than the first version. Some of the simple explanations for the ready acceptance of these revisions is that (1) the adolescent audience represents an unsophisticated and uncritical readership, and (2) the audience has changed dramatically since the inception of Superman (with the original readers of Superman no longer reading comic books in preference of other more sophisticated reading material). Both of those explanations have some merit, but neither can fully explain the development of fan favorite trends in the 1950s and 1960s. For instance, the Batman stories of the 1950s transplanted Batman into situations very different from those situations typically associated with the standard tropes of Batman (i.e., Batman in the jungle wearing his mask together with a Tarzan-like loin cloth in "The Jungle Cat-Queen" and Batman battling the threat of otherworldly aliens in "Prisoners of Three Worlds"). While this may draw on other popular comic book traditions, part of the pleasure for readers is undoubtedly drawn from seeing the well-known character of Batman radically out of place (a sort of self-conscious variation that predates the camp of the Adam West television series). And the Superman stories of the 1960s included not only additions such as Supergirl, Superman's lost cousin from Krypton, that revised the sense of the series as a whole. The most well remembered stories of the time are the ones that are clearly identified as "imaginary" and outside the regular continuity of the series. Among others, these famously include "The Death of Superman" and "The Story of Superman-Red and Superman-Blue"; in the latter story, Superman's experiment with Kryptonite divides him into two beings who work together to make the world into a paradise and who (as two separate selves) marry childhood sweetheart Lana Lang and adult love interest Lois Lane. As these imaginary stories are predicated on the ability to apprehend the imaginary stories' differences from the "canonical" stories in order to fully

The superhero genre meets the jungle adventure story, Batman puts on something more comfortable, and superhero comic books become lighter in the 1950s (from *Detective Comics* #211, p. 9).

appreciate them, a question of the reality of Superman would have to come into play; even more allowances were required of the Superman fans of the 1950s who consumed various story lines from Superman comic books and the George Reeves's television series. And with these imaginary stories, variations were recognized as imaginary and yet were seen as significant and often preferred to the previous version (most often told). This type of appreciation redresses the idea that readers are unsophisticated and necessarily leave behind their superhero stories for other, more complex literary pursuits. After all, this process entails accepting certain fantastic premises and then embarking on a variation on those premises that plays with the conventions of the story and genre in general.

I also contend that participants in culture at large have become accustomed to the narrative revisionism of superheroes, even though they are not completely aware of its significance in general or within the timeline of new media development in particular. Even if the audience for comic books could once be represented as a subcultural youth demographic, it cannot be said to be so any longer. With the advent of the "grim and gritty" superhero of the 1980s, superhero comic books have been read by an increasingly older demographic, although still predominantly male. However, this male bias within the demographic cannot be said to significantly be present within the audiences for other media presentations of superheroes. In order to realize that the above-mentioned appreciation of revisionism and variation exists within the mainstream audience, we should look no further than recent manifestations of the above-mentioned standards, Superman and Batman. The television series *Smallville* takes a look at Clark Kent's youth and imagines that Clark may have grown up with Lex Luther as his best friend. In addition to requiring a surprising amount of knowledge about Superman's mythos from its viewers, the series also asks its viewers to willingly suspend what they know in order to reimagine the story, deconstructing and reconstructing the narrative.

The great emotional resonance of the series comes from knowing that Clark will one day be Superman; Lex will one day be his arch-enemy; and that Clark will not stay with his high school sweetheart, Lana Lang. In *Superman Returns*, a film released in 2006 during the run of *Smallville*, a story is constructed that cannot work in conjunction with *Smallville* (in part, the film retells the origin that the series is currently retelling with significant differences and presents a Superman and Lex Luthor separated in age by many more years). In addition to allowing different stories to exist side by side, the film also presents a possible continuation of 1980s *Superman II* that quite intentionally ignores the existence of *Superman III* and *IV* (very similar to the premise of many internet fanfictions which for instance, will tell the story of *Buffy the Vampire Slayer* from the end of season 3 as if season 4 did not exist). In order to retcon a fantasy world that should be based on unalterable facts, this move requires quite a bit of audience's willing participation (in an age of cable television, inexpensive DVDs, and streaming video services that keep alternative incarnations of Superman "alive"). Although it would not be well supported by demographic data, it could be argued that consumers simply care less, because people who saw *Superman Returns* have not seen *Smallville*. Even if this assertion could be convincingly made, it should be stressed that a general awareness of the intersections does take shape, and people are comfortable with the coexistence of these divergent narratives; they do not privilege an original source (with most not knowing what to call an original source for Superman) and often, regard the most recent incarnation as canonical (or disregard the idea of canon entirely).

The return of Batman to the big screen with director Tim Burton in the late 1980s was built on the bleak atmosphere and hard boiled storytelling of Frank Miller's *The Dark*

The superhero genre meets the crime story (again), Batman is a threatening anti-hero, and superhero comic books become "grim and gritty" in the 1980s (from *The Dark Knight Returns*, p. 70).

Knight Returns. Within that 1986 comic book series, Miller seemed to break many of the rules for superhero stories by making Batman 50 and retired, seriously unbalanced and hyper-violent, and at ideological odds with Superman. Curiously but not surprising (upon looking at the revisionism inherent within superhero stories), *The Dark Knight Returns* set the new standard ("grim and gritty") for Batman and also aimed superhero comic books primarily toward an adult audience. And yet Tim Burton's *Batman* also retained a love of spectacle associated with campy superhero stories. In addition, while both of Burton's Batman films (*Batman* and *Batman Returns*) stood on their own, they also played with tropes established in the sources such as other comic books, the serials, and the television series and seemed to require an audience aware of past differences to fully appreciate the present incarnation. When Burton left the franchise, the tone of the films became notably lighter (closer to the self-parody of the television series) and that one-tone approach seemed to bother the movie-going public more than the fact that they saw three different actors portray Batman in four Batman films (those films separated from one another by less than two years each). Later, when Warner Bros. decided it was likely that Batman might again be a huge hit at the box office, they entrusted Batman to the film noir director, Christopher Nolan, who chose yet another actor to play Batman and retold the origin story covered by Burton's *Batman*. And once Nolan's *Batman Begins* did succeed in monetary terms, plans were set in motion to rewrite Batman's first encounter with the Joker (also covered by Burton's *Batman*). In that sequel, *The Dark Knight*, Heath Ledger has been hailed for his performance as the Joker; the exact reason for this fairly unanimous adulation is unclear, but Ledger not only creates a post–9/11 enigma for the audience but also synthesizes highly divergent past performances of the Joker including that of Cesar Romero (in the television series) and Jack Nicholson (in Burton's *Batman*).

Again, in a world in which cable television, inexpensive DVDs, and streaming video services do not allow past superhero media spectacles to ever be truly forgotten, it's inconceivable that the public at large is interested in a retelling of Batman's story because they have forgotten the past telling (or that critics applaud the stories because they mistakenly see them as original). Both of these situations seem to imply that a certain psychology is at work in the mind of the recipient of these stories, a psychology that departs from the conventions of realistic storytelling and embraces some sort of bricolage. Moreover, it seems to be a worldview that departs from the ideas characteristic of modernism and approximates the ideas characteristic of premodernism (and also postmodernism). It should also be noted, that Warner Bros. (who owns the rights to Superman and Batman) believes that the audience is part of this storytelling sensibility that allows and appreciates the variations in their cultural icons. If the pre-production hadn't been disrupted by the writer's strike of 2007, Warner Bros. would have made a "Justice League" film starring two new actors as Superman and Batman despite the fact that they currently had active Superman and Batman film franchises starring other actors ("Justice League"). All of these big-budget successes and hopes for success suggest that most people feel the synthesis of elements from variations is the "best" outcome, regarding the current variation often more highly than the undiluted and simple original.[3]

As opposed to the things held dear by literate cultures (original sources, fixed facts, and the authority of the text), this sort of revisionism is taking us into a socially determined arrangement of information that is much more similar to that of oral cultures; it is oriented toward current development and performance, the interaction of fact and fiction (where fiction is not untruth), and authority as something that is shared and redeveloped by each telling of the story. In terms of this study, since the use of superheroes in forms of media other than comic books most clearly indicates the widespread reemergence of storytelling practices related to oral tradition, it may seem that this should be the express purview of my book. After all, in an era where other corporately owned characters operate in similar ways through various revisionings (like James Bond, the Terminator, and Hannibal Lecter), the phenomenon has relevance that extends beyond the comic book industry. It is certainly true that this phenomenon does extend beyond the comic book industry, but I assert that the superhero comic book industry is ground zero for this phenomenon. Within the early years of this industry, we can recognize the relative power to reshape cultural identity held by those outside the corridors of political and economic power (such as low-paid creators of pulp material who are generally held in low esteem); they are not wholly unlike current blog writers and makers of YouTube's amateur films.

While our society might be stratified in socio-economic terms, information and stories are being held in more of a common trust, thanks to the conventions of new media (especially as represented in the early 20th century by the low cost of the superhero comic book). People have a sense of shared investment and collective ownership of superheroes, and, as a consequence, individuals have the power to redesign stories for the self, the immediate community, and the world at large. In addition, if we can agree that the superhero should be the locus of this sort of study because we see more variation within these corporately owned characters than any other characters, the history of the superhero comic book industry will need to be assessed in a way that it hasn't previously. Nevertheless, although superhero comic books are the primary concern of this study, it's important to reinforce that the basic types of revision take place not only within superhero comic books but also within superhero stories in general. This second component of "superhero stories in general" is added because superhero comic books certainly do not exist in isolation from other media forms that feature superheroes. For instance, Spider-Man's story may be told in three Marvel comic books titles (one of which takes place in the completely different "Ultimate" superhero universe) while also being featured in a film in theaters and an animated series on television. While everything but the first two comic book titles take place in imaginary worlds theoretically independent, they often borrow from one another and operate in an organic way (as mentioned previously with the permanent borrowing of the Batcave from the Batman serial).

Although well-known for his reluctant feelings for superheroes and for sometimes arguing that their presence undermined the critical esteem that might otherwise have been afforded to comic books, Will Eisner, the "inventor" of the graphic novel, revised the superhero with his very own *The Spirit*. Understanding superheroes as an unavoidable force and admiring superhero works by creators such as Frank Miller,[4] he commented on what he considered to be their essential nature by saying, "I don't think that superheroes will disappear or go away. I think they'll just mutate forever."[5] Although completely speculative and therefore, ultimately unverifiable, this statement has the gravitas that his reputation brings with it (and thus far, it has proven to be true). With my general thesis in mind, I gravitate toward this statement because the idea of superheroes mutating implies that they have their own existence, independent of their creators, something that often seems the case in stories transmitted via oral tradition. Regardless, my genuine goal for this book is to provide a thorough explanation, accessible and yet nuanced, for the continued presence and continued change of the superhero: a narrative trope that powerfully connects with the common and uncommon reader.

From the Multimedia Superhero to the Comic Book Superhero (or, From the Big Picture to the Splash Page)

I would be remiss at the very start of my book to not mention the current parameters of the field of study through a brief description of the comic book medium, its overall development, and its critical study. Even though the history of comic books and the superhero industry is a story that has often been told and therefore, revised, it is a story that should be told again. While not wanting to burden this study with baggage of the infighting between postmodernism's prominent theorists, the idea that it should be told again is propelled by a valid assertion typically made within context of the theories of new historicism: that histories are constructed by the current dominant order and histories must be reconstructed in order to make them more complex and therefore, more true. In addition, my goals of reviewing the history of superhero comic books are multiple. Even while I acknowledge DC and Marvel's importance to superhero comic books, I want to move beyond the history of superhero comic books and superheroes in general as written by the "big two" superhero comic book publishers. While this may seem unnecessary as an act that had been previously undertaken, both DC and Marvel are dominant market forces and thus continue to jockey for position by reinscribing their notions of themselves on the culture at large. While this may seem necessary as an act that undermines the power of media conglomerates to obscure the truth, both DC and Marvel have served as significant participants in the oral culture I seek to reveal (rather than simply being copyright-obsessed, opponents to it)[6]; in short, they are not the supervillains in this comic book scenario. Beyond the history itself, I want to deal with prominent interpretations for that history; and I want to revisit past scholarship on the superhero, because the work has not dealt with the phenomenon of the superhero, its industry and media, in a wholly comprehensive manner. While I will identify trends within past scholarship to deal with essential traits within that scholarship, I will also demonstrate the complexity of the field and show how previous work relates to my notion of the comic industry as an oral/traditional culture. Before moving onto the business that I have set before myself, one final note should be made; I must acknowledge my bias and admit what follows serves my idea of American comic book and superhero history, narrowly focusing on the superhero and stressing patterns of revisionism that will be referred to more extensively in other parts of the book.[7] What immediately follows is in no way intended as an exhaustive history of comic books, American comic books, or even superhero comic books, but rather it will provide a context for examples already used thus far and a point of reference for the extended examples used throughout the book (and the book, as a whole, gives a fairly representative sampling of major trends within the history of the superhero).[8]

Bypassing the historically long and anthropologically debatable view that includes Egyptian hieroglyphics, Medieval tapestries, and William Hogarth lithographs as precedents for the comic book (Duncan 21; McCloud; *Understanding* 10–16),[9] I will identify the general starting point for my brief overview in the 19th century with a technological revolution that changed the notion of print media. The advent of the comic book is based in the use of the lithographic press, capable of reproducing pictorial matter on a vast scale (and thus changing notions of literacy created by the much earlier advent of the movable type printing press) (Duncan 22).[10] From photographs to drawn illustrations, the lithographic press could reproduce pictorial matter cheaply enough for publishers to feature it in magazines and newspapers. Through the comics pages of *Punch* in England and *The World* and *The Morning*

Journal in the United States, the basic formulas for the single panel joke (with a picture and a caption) and the multi-panel joke (with a series of pictures utilizing in-panel narration and word balloons) were firmly established and widely embraced by the reading public (Sabin 14–20; Wright 2).[11] As the popularity of newspaper comic strips soared, they featured many variations on the basic multi-panel joke. However, the strips also represented sophisticated art in the comedy of *Krazy Kat* and the surrealism of *Little Nemo in Slumberland*, and quickly evolved into narrative serials that represented many different genres: mystery with *Dick Tracy*, jungle adventure with *Tarzan*, science fiction with *Flash Gordon*, fantasy and historical fiction with *Prince Valiant*, and jungle adventure and proto-superheroism with *The Phantom* (Sabin 53–54; Wright 3–4). With devoted followings for these serial strips with color illustration, print technology even more readily available in the 1930s; American publishers collected the series in inexpensive "books" that actually resembled thick, stapled, four color pamphlets more than books (Duncan 29–30; Wright 2–4). Affordable to a new segment of buyers within the general population (young readers), they were generally regarded as disposable, not only because of their soft paper covers and their newsprint interiors but also because of the supposedly juvenile nature of its content. Because of the obvious problem with reprints, that their quick cliffhanger structure didn't work well with multiple strips on a single page, publishers began soliciting new material for their comic books similar to the genre material drawn from the strips. (As many people have already noted, *comic book* is hardly an adequate term to describe these books that were based largely in the adventure stories of pulp fiction and that lacked a distinctive comic element; nevertheless, the name stuck.)

As part of the new material developed for comic books, the characters of Superman (debuting in 1938) and Batman (soon to follow in 1939) created a sensation within the burgeoning industry, and both were quickly featured in multiple titles published by National Allied Publications (later simply named DC Comics after one of their best-selling titles: *Detective Comics*) (Sabin 57–62; Wright 13–18). These "superheroes" were distinguished from other comic book characters, as vigilantes who wore flashy costumes as they fought for justice beyond the limitations of the law (Duncan 31–32); usually orphans possessing extraordinary powers or means, they appealed to the ideals of the American reading audience in this post–Depression, pre–World War II era.[12] The titles in which they were featured sold exceedingly well, primarily to adolescents but also to a wider swathe of readers than is usually implied by supposedly simplistic, action-driven plots of the superhero power fantasy.[13] Nevertheless, in recognition of that prominent younger audience and to cement the appeal to them, writers often gained adolescent sidekicks (such as Batman's Robin) and the presence of the sidekicks represented an editorial mandate to soften the social criticism and violence present in some earlier superhero stories. In what would be standard practice with all comic publishers of the time, creators sold rights to their characters that excluded them from future profits associated with those characters (such as Jerry Siegel and Joe Shuster with Superman and Bob Kane with Batman).[14] Very much in line with this practice, the creators who produced the comic books (within an industrial model which separated the roles of writer, penciler, inker, colorist, and letterer) received no credit for their work within the comic books themselves (keeping the focus on the trademarked characters) (Duncan 33–34). In order to produce the vast amount of material to satisfy the consumer, a wide variety of creators worked on the most popular superhero characters, preventing one particular treatment of the superhero from being regarded as authoritative. With National Allied Publications turning an impressive profit by selling out print runs and licensing their superhero characters to merchandisers and other media producers, superhero characters were quickly developed by competitors such as All American Publications, featuring Wonder Woman, the Flash, and the Green Lantern, among others.[15] Fiercely protective of their profit potential with Superman, National Allied Publications filed suit against Fox Publications for developing Wonderman, a blatant copy of Superman and against Fawcett Publications for developing Captain Marvel, a less clear-cut imitation that outsold Superman. The other challenge to Superman's market dominance would be the patriotic superhero subtly represented through characters like Wonder Woman but overtly seen via the superhero most popular during World War II: Timely Comics' Captain America (Wright 35–36). With this super-patriot the clear preference of comic book buyers, publishers not only imitated this hero in new creations but also revised current characters such as Superman, so that he no longer threatened but now upheld the status quo implied by U.S. law.[16] Regardless of the competition and trends in consumption, superheroes came to dominate the American comic book market during its early years; however, that dominance would not have lasted without "help" from an unexpected source.

Shortly after the end of World War II, comic book publishers began to return to the genre diversity seen in strips before the superhero boom, in large part due to the growing interest in war, crime, and horror comic books.[17] As a consequence, superheroes like Batman lost some of their initial popularity but remained in continuous publication by stressing new aspects of the story line drawn from other popular comic book genres, such as the unlikely matches of jungle adventure and science fiction.[18] However, the rise of crime and horror comic books (produced very successfully by the newly prominent EC Comics) was brought to a halt through the efforts of the psychologist Fredric Wertham, a self-described expert on adolescent psychology and media (Duncan 38–39); some would also go so far as to suggest that the development of comic books as a diverse, adult medium was brought to a halt thanks to Wertham's very public and ill-founded campaign. Predicated on the notion that comic books were an inherently juvenile medium (an assertion that only wholly made sense to adults who did not understand the appeal of a new medium), Wertham would argue that reading comic books caused juvenile delinquency. Despite his simplistic one-to-one theorem and his scattershot research (later published in 1954 as *Seduction of the Innocent*), Wertham served as the single most important motivation for congressional hearings on the dangers posed by comic books to adolescents. With many politicians siding with Wertham's moralism (if not his research), the comic book publishers fared poorly during the hearings. Comic book burnings would follow, as would the financial failure of many comic book publishers; the surviving comic book publishers agreed to self-regulate on the basis of "Comics Code" rules that made the material safe for children (Duncan 39–40; Wright 88–98).[19] Since superheroes had received only a little of Wertham's ire, they continued to be published and enjoyed renewed attention from publishers as stories editors identified as easily revised to fit within the Comics Code requirements (Duncan 42). Through the Wertham's efforts, in the 1950s at least, comic books not only became more "wholesome" for children but also came to be understood as a child's medium; concomitantly, superheroes not only became more "wholesome" for children but also were brought back from waning interest from the comic book buying consumer.[20]

New stories emphasized comedy within barely plausible fantasy situations (like Superman trying to trick the multi-dimensional magician, Mr. Mxyzptlk, to say his name backwards) and deemphasized violence and romantic entanglements (like Batman and Robin conspicuously avoiding kisses promised to them by Batwoman and Batgirl). The eventual outcome of these revisions would be one of the most prominent superhero television adaptations of the 1960s: the brightly colored, self-parodying *Batman* starring Adam West. Unlike Superman and Batman who had been in uninterrupted publication from their inception, other superhero titles had been cancelled, and DC Comics took the opportunity to remake classic superhero characters that they had acquired. Characters like the Flash and the Green Lantern were reintroduced with new alter egos, new costumes, and new origin stories that borrowed more from science fiction (eschewing the more clearly magical explanations given to superhero powers in the past). Moreover, as superhero crossovers and superhero teams had been very popular with fans in the past, DC Comics wanted these revised characters to exist in the same world as Superman and Batman. In order to account for newly remade superheroes alongside superheroes in continuous publication, DC Comics suggested that there were past versions of most superheroes in another world; separate dimensions existed in which the heroes of the current and previous age lived, and they were identified as Earth-1 and Earth-2, respectively (the most curious aspect, this being that the current age was given primacy as Earth-1). Other publishers again recognized the success of DC Comics with superhero comics and Atlas Comics (previously Timely, the publisher of *Captain America* and subsequently, Marvel) sought to develop superheroes titles. Primarily through the efforts of Stan Lee and Jack Kirby, a world was populated with superheroes that may have been inspired by DC Comics but stretched basic tenets for the superhero's character and extended the framework of the superhero's narrative. With the Fantastic Four, the Hulk, and Spider-Man, superheroes respectively lacked secret identities, the ability to control their powers, and their revered place as champions to their world.[21] Incorporating unexpected genre influences such as the romance in unobtrusive ways, Marvel superhero stories stressed the ordinary lives of the characters out of their costumes, something that seemed to appeal to older readers (teenagers and beyond) who became very involved with the serial narrative. Rather than cultivate stories for the occasional reader, Marvel tended to develop multi-part stories "to be continued" in the next issue and made references to issues published years earlier (Sabin 69–74; Duncan 45–48).[22] In many ways, this was an appeal to the continuity-obsessed fans who poured over superhero minutia in chatty letters published and responded to by editors in the comic books' "letters pages." Probably the result of a letter to Marvel Comics, the designation of the first age of superheroes and this 1950s/1960s resurgence in the superhero became known as

With a story that adheres strictly to the Comics Code, Batman avoids Batwoman's affections and appears more gay than he had before Fredric Wertham (from *Batman* #153, p.25).

the Golden Age and the Silver Age, respectively. The sense of community and ownership created by Marvel's letters pages probably led to the earliest versions of comic book conventions and fanzines.[23] In appeals seemingly tailor-made for high school and college readers (but that may also tap into American ethos), Marvel editors described themselves as intellectual rebels throwing off the silly juvenile vision of the monolithic source of superheroes: DC Comics (Wright 204–222).

Eventually a financial rival for DC Comics, Marvel's narrative and visual storytelling, in part, became part of DC's style as well. Part of this transition was due to the fact that writers and illustrators would move from one publisher to the other for short periods (but aside from now receiving credit for their work on the title page, they rarely received a better deal from either, with both companies devoted to corporate ownership of stories and art). With extended story lines and continuity as one the new hallmarks, the invention of Earth-1 and Earth-2 became irrelevant in the 1970s (at least for the practical purposes of supplying a reason why superheroes never aged); superheroes remained eternally young despite the fact that time passed and circumstances changed (for instance, in the 1970s, in his alter ego as Clark Kent, Superman becomes a television journalist). Perhaps most importantly, superheroes inherit decades of their own history connected to historical circumstances accepted as the truth of their stories but which could not have been realistically experienced by characters as young as they were supposed to be. With this contradiction willfully overlooked, the more significant consequence of the Earth-1/Earth-2 split would be the invention of countless new worlds in the DC "multiverse," which the superheroes of Earth-1 usually encountered under strange circumstances. Exploring the endless possibilities of the various superhero stories (for instance, Earth-3 knows the superheroes of Earth-1 as supervillains and vice versa), DC titles featured an incredible number of stories (beginning in the 1960s) with superheroes crossing over to alternate realities. Taking this point of inspiration from DC Comics, Marvel developed *What If*, a series that explored alternate possibilities within the Marvel universe (an exercise presided over by the Watcher, a being charged with recording all events not only in the Marvel universe but in all parallel universes as well).[24] With many seeking to carry over the designations of the Golden and Silver Ages, the 1970s were dubbed the Bronze Age, but few things fundamentally separate it from the Silver Age that preceded it. Superheroes remained dominant as did the "big two" publishers of superhero comics, focusing more on its more narrowly defined audience: males in their teens and early twenties. While some genre comic books generally fell out of publication (such as romance and war stories), the Comics Code became less relevant to most people, and, within the DC and Marvel, superhero frameworks and genres that would have previously been controversial were revived or borrowed from other mediums (such as horror, sword and sorcery, and kung fu stories).[25] Minority superheroes began to make an appearance (the Black Panther and Luke Cage), but their stories were often drawn from tenuous points of inspiration such as blaxploitation films (Wright 249). In what many have identified as film effects developing to the point that it could almost represent superheroes as well as comic books, *Superman: The Movie* was released to decent reviews and an incredible box office return. In terms of the superhero story represented, it mixed many different sensibilities ranging from the nostalgic coming-of-age story of Clark Kent to the exciting action adventure of Superman to the broadly humorous slapstick of Lex Luthor. Few new superheroes were developed in comic books during this time that fundamentally changed the DC and Marvel frameworks, excepting the updates of Marvel's *X-Men* and DC's *Teen Titans* that would pave the way for the Modern Age of comics.

Several major market changes took place during the 1980s, a time that would inaugurate the designation currently associated with superhero comic books: the Modern Age. Primarily based on an even less complex kill-or-be-killed variation of the adolescent power fantasy, video games enticed the young consumer traditionally considered to be the bulwark of the comic book industry. This loss was not the blow it might have been in another time, as the audience had already begun to skew older with prominent titles such as the *X-Men*, which used its outcast mutant characters not only as metaphors for teenage experience but also as means to engage social issues (Sabin 158–160; Wright 263–266). Nevertheless, as a consequence of the en masse loss of its youth audience, comic book companies were relying even more on existing readers and began exploiting them in various ways, such as with crossover events. *X-Men* titles proliferated with the story in one *X-Men* title only fully understood by reading all the *X-Men* titles. In addition to continuing stories from one title to another (requiring that comic books be purchased in addition to the ones regularly purchased on a monthly basis), DC and Marvel created other limited-run series with enormous casts drawn from their entire superhero line-ups. Although Marvel would claim to invent the idea with *Contest of Champions* and *Secret Wars*, the most significant of the large crossover series would be DC's *Crisis on Infinite Earths*, working with the ulterior motive of "cleaning up" the DC multiverse; it featured a villain who traveled between dimensions and devoured all universes until only one was left. Subsequently, major character titles were restarted with new origin stories that placed them as adults in the 1980s; however, many of those origins only reinstated the complicated mythology of their past versions. Another factor indicative of the transition to the Modern Age was the locus of purchase moving from the newsstand and drug store to direct market specialty stores (which then served as a more discrete community-gathering place for fans). When print technology improved, cost for printing decreased and quality increased, making possible the rise in independent comic book publications sold directly to specialty stores. Working without fear of jeopardizing cultural icons with their controversial story choices, the independent publishers tried to produce innovative new conceptual takes on the superhero but often retained both Golden and Silver Age rules with sex and violence added to the mix. The big two comic book publishers responded to this new competition in two ways. On one hand, they separated themselves from the black and white publishers and they pleased an ever more demanding consumer by embracing Will Eisner's notion of the graphic novel, publishing books with high-quality paper, and reproducing high-quality artwork with a complex color palate. On the other hand, they aligned themselves with the goals of the supposedly innovative upstart publishers: they allowed creators like Frank Miller and Alan Moore to "push the envelope" further with publications such as *The Dark Knight Returns* and *Watchmen*. Profound contemplations of the superhero as a cultural centerpiece, these texts supposedly sought to be bid goodbye to the genre (Duncan 71–73; Wright 271–273); instead, they reinvigorated it with stories that are often described as "grim and gritty," filled with hyper-violent nihilistic protagonists.

In the late 1980s and early 1990s, thanks primarily to these two watershed works, the names used to sell superhero comic books would no longer be limited to the superheroes but would also include the writers and illustrators. This sort of recognition led to newly founded fan websites featuring discussions of Frank Miller's Batman versus Jim Starlin's Batman (thus mitigating the strict notion of continuity that the big two publishers were trying to maintain). Encouraged by the moderate success of independent publishers in the 1980s and their newfound celebrity status, creators agitated for creator rights within the current superhero industry. With DC and Marvel unwilling to change their policies in any significant way, major names went to smaller publishers and even started their own companies based on creator rights; this would most notably be represented by Jim Lee's Wildstorm Comics and Todd McFarlane's Image Comics, seeming like the wave of the future until Wildstorm was sold to DC Comics, and Image Comics began claiming trademark ownership in ways very similar to the big two (Sabin 174–175). In reference to the notion of continuity that DC Comics was trying to create with *Crisis on Infinite Earths*, editors were unable to keep writers from unintentionally referring back to the older timeline outside the new continuity. In less than five years, apparently unable to stem the tide, the editors allowed intentional references back to the older timeline and multiple earths in playful self-conscious superhero stories. As the purchase of superhero comic books became the art of collecting (with cost of back issues skyrocketing), superhero publishers would use this to increase sales, producing variant covers for the same issue (encouraging collectors to buy every one). Eventually, this practice exhausted the market and the collector's bubble burst. Despite sales that dropped dramatically, the big two managed to thrive by licensing of their superheroes, important from their inception but then vitally important. Cornerstone titles continued to be published, and Marvel in particular came to regard their publications as a testing ground for stories that might be featured in films or television series. The increasingly adult readership was held via the creation of separate imprints (Vertigo for DC and MAX for Marvel),which featured stories supposedly within their superhero universes but focused on new, alternative characters in stories with mature themes, the most notable being Neil Gaiman's *Sandman* (Sabin 168–170).

As the superhero comic book industry floundered, both the comic book and the superhero were growing as an area of academic interest, seen through the proliferation of scholarly study and the development of university classes focused on comic books. The big two worked with this new sensibility by largely bypassing the now meager direct market and binding long runs of their series as high-quality graphic novels for chain bookstores. Many of the oldest series were bound as high-priced hardcover books affordable only to libraries and adults with a sizable income (artifacts of popular culture as well as popular culture itself and folk art). In addition, the big two invited celebrity artists to work on their series with much greater freedom from editorial interference, and many of these stories are set outside normal continuity (such as Neil Gaiman's *1602*, which transplants the Marvel universe to 17th-century England). With the success of the *X-Men* and *Spider-Man* films, Marvel sought to market graphic novels tied to their films more effectively than DC had with the *Batman* films years earlier (the problem being that many superhero comic book collections were still mired in years of continuity). The solution was the creation of the "Ultimate" universe in which Marvel characters are rewritten from the beginning of their stories in contemporary times (Duncan 79). Soon to run into a similar problem that all runs of superhero comic books had previously, the Ultimate line of titles has been read more by current comic book readers than new ones (and creators are including references that only previous readers would understand), suggesting that the superhero comic book audience might be shrinking and becoming more insular. Rather than regard this as threatening, DC Comics seems to have embraced this multi-faceted reading experience for its readers, which could be characterized as quintessentially postmodern; in addition to officially reinstating the multiverse, they have developed the "All Star" line which utilizes major artists to tell stories of their major characters completely free from continuity (unlike the "Ultimate" line that is trying to create a new but coherent universe).

Despite all the changes to the superhero over the course of time, few within our American culture feel completely estranged from even the oldest of superheroes (such as Superman and Batman), because revisions make the superhero current and relevant. As the superhero has such a dynamic and immediate presence based mostly on the most recent version, all people who assert that they really know the story of Captain America or Spider-Man are in some sense right. Superheroes have a strangely transhistorical presence thanks to the way the most recent stories supplant (but do not erase) the previous stories. Based on the above history lesson, we can assert that in response to various factors that include the related areas of individual creativity, cultural development, and market pressures, the superhero has changed dramatically throughout its short existence. The superhero has been revised in ways that simultaneously seem to take these characters into uncharted ideological territory and yet also seem to reorganize elements already in play. After reading stories of the original Captain America inspiring the troops, stories of Spider-Man hunted by the police may seem unprecedented. However, they may not be so very different than the early stories of Superman, who exercised punishment on those unfairly protected by the law, such as slum landlords and wife beaters. After reading stories of the Silver Age's Green Lantern and his pure heart, stories of Image's Spawn and his selfish soul-selling may seem revolutionary. However, they may not be so different than the early stories of Batman, who sought revenge by inducing fear in the "cowardly lot" of criminals in Gotham City. After reading stories of the Justice Society of America, a superhero team patriotic and unified, stories of the Authority, a superhero team undermining major political powers and torn apart by their celebrity status, may seem shocking. However, they may not be so different from the early stories of the Uncanny X-Men, a superhero team hated by the powers that be and constantly disagreeing over their mission to protect people who consider them freaks.[26] This short list is not meant to suggest that revisions to the superhero only bring to the forefront elements already in place but is meant to demonstrate that the superhero hasn't evolved in a linear way. The path to the current incarnation is not straight, and the current incarnation doesn't cover up vestiges of the past; revisions borrow from earlier incarnations of the superhero, reshuffling the deck in a way that makes the development circle back on itself.

Superheroes as Mythology: Back to the Future of an Illusion

In *The Amazing Transforming Superhero*, my collection on the revisionism that is inherent in the superhero story, I offered a critical paradigm that described several different degrees and sources of revision; regardless, all types of revision refer back to the original in an implicit and unintentional way (unintentional in that current creators may not have any direct knowledge of the original, whatever "the original" might be).[27] In turn, I presented several texts that I considered to be central in the study of superhero revisionism, including Jules Feiffer's *The Great Comic Book Heroes*, Umberto Eco's "The Myth of Superman," Richard Reynolds's *Superheroes: A Modern Mythology*, and Geoff Klock's *How to Read Superhero Comics and Why*. Since I was narrowly focused on revisionism, this was not meant to be an exhaustive list describing the history of scholarship devoted to scholarship on superhero comic books. Nevertheless, it is a good place to begin, as I describe why studies of traditional art are helpful in understanding superhero comic books that I believe have now fully realized their potential in the digital age. All of these works deal with the way superheroes represent mythology, variations on ancient and modern folktales connected to the culture of its audience in ways more direct than other mediums. While Feiffer's very personal work is not academic in a traditional way, he approximates a cultural studies approach and identifies comic books as "junk" (low culture) that serves particular social needs (Feiffer 78). In an essay contained within *The Role of the Reader*, Eco examines Superman's design as consumable and yet inconsumable, possessing the illusion of development but never truly changing (Eco 111). In the work that dramatically spurred superhero studies forward, Reynolds compares the dynamics of classic superhero stories to that of classic mythology and analyzes how landmark texts like *The Dark Knight Returns* and *Watchmen* fit into those dynamics. And in a work that is very academic is its rigorous use of theory, Klock applies Harold Bloom's ideas to the evolution of the Modern Age superhero. When looking at superheroes as a sort of mythology, each work is indebted to popular notions of archetypal psychology and Marxist philosophy in varying degrees. Reynolds tends to see superhero mythology as a natural function of human psychology, and Eco identifies superhero mythology as a functional product of a society that disguises its own workings; without demonstrating an awareness of archetypal psychology or Marxist philosophy, Feiffer straddles the line between the two and with an acute awareness of literary theory, Klock chooses the Freudian anxiety of influence over the Jungian archetypal psychology.

Sometimes acknowledging these key texts and sometimes not, others have entered the fray to discuss the nature of superhero mythology such as Thomas Andrae ("From Menace to Messiah"),[28] Neil Harris ("Who Owns Our Myths?"),[29] and John Lawrence and Robert Jewett (*The Myth of the American Superhero*),[30] among others. And the debate about the source and influence of superhero comic book mythology extends further back in time to fanzine work in collections like *All in Color for a Dime* and even further to the Frankfurt school influenced critics that Jeet Heer and Kent Worchester identify as "the New York intellectuals." This debate about the nature of superhero mythology is important especially in the way that it identifies the cultural dynamic that accounts for the reader in more immediate ways than other print media, like the novel. Regardless, what interests me most is the way that the superhero has been identified as mythology: the fact that the superhero seems to change and yet reactivates a supposedly transcendent mythic sensibility. Despite the fact that superhero comic books are a print medium, the dynamics of their stories and their treatment of the audience resemble what takes place with epics in oral cultures. If we can determine why they operate like stories in an oral culture and not a literate culture, the debate about the natural or unnatural shape of superhero mythology is necessarily recharacterized; within the context of traditional aesthetics, mythology is something that naturally grows from the means by which stories are shared but that varies from culture to culture. In other words, the mythology of superhero comic books should then be understood as both natural and unnatural, thus adding more depth to the discussion about mythology already in progress. The idea of the superhero industry as an oral culture demonstrates how comic book superheroes function as both myth and commodity, and how the two ideas are not as diametrically opposed as they purport to be. However, in order to determine how superhero comic books operate like stories in an oral culture, I need to provide some basic groundwork for studies in oral/traditional cultures.

Although I have used the terms orality, oral culture, and oral tradition rather freely in the introduction and this chapter, specific definitions of these terms are necessary to proceed effectively. Orality is the most extensive of the above-mentioned terms, referring to not just verbal expression and comprehension and also thought in societies predating the advent of writing and print matter. Therefore, orality is often set in contrast to literacy as literacy is understood in a more historical and academic sense of the word; literacy refers to written expression and comprehension and also thought in societies postdating the advent of writing and print matter. An oral culture is a culture living in the midst of orality and the modes of thinking associated with orality. Oral tradition is the verbal and auditory means by which information is transmitted and received in an oral culture; the transmission of information is enacted within a specific social group, over the course of generations, and through a complex set of rules that govern the organization and reception of that information. Before proceeding further, I will address what may seem to be crucially important conceptual impediments to my study (to which I've already briefly alluded). Comic books are produced within a literate culture, are the product of print technology (which is a characteristic of literate culture's language-based transmission of information), and contain visual information (which seems far outside the boundaries of any sort of verbal transmission of information). However, orality and literacy are not opposites, and more recent work in the field of oral culture has stressed this (often examining their coexistence). While orality and literacy imply radically different modes of consciousness and social organization, identifying the two states as opposed to one another is not wholly accurate as orality always precedes literacy (leaving residual traces of orality and the opportunity to study orality within a literate culture).[31] In addition, new media technologies have often been understood as technologies that add something new to the cultural mix, returning us to an era more like that of orality, synthesizing orality and literacy, or inaugurating an era completely different from those preceding it.[32] And orality has been broadened in many studies to also indicate a set of related practices (that may include different sorts of image transmission) and referred to as traditionality.[33] Perhaps most important for the sake of this study, I want to make clear that I am identifying the ideals of oral culture as being enacted in certain terms within the culture of superhero industry. However, I am also using orality as a metaphor to describe the dynamics of comic book narrative and illustration.

In the 20th century, the prominent scholars who initiated the study of orality were Milman Parry and his student, Albert Lord.[34] In a series of articles,[35] Parry would make several groundbreaking claims about the nature of epic poetry (later made cohesive by Lord's *The Singer of Tales* in 1960). In a very general sense, epic poetry is a long narrative poem usually containing a heroic journey, and important cultural information is connected to that journey; regularly produced within oral cultures (Homer's *Odyssey* and *Beowulf* are known as primary epics), epic poetry is also self-consciously produced within literate cultures (Milton's *Paradise Lost* and Pound's *Cantos* are known as secondary epics). Interested in the dynamics of oral culture in general (and Homer's *Odyssey* in particular) and working with the notion that oral composition results in specific sorts of narratives, Parry would study performances of oral poetry in Yugoslavia. Based upon Parry's field research, Parry would contend that Homer's composition was based upon the skillful arrangement of formulae, fixed expressions usually adapted in performance of a narrative to suit metrical conditions. Therefore, this meant a classic such as Homer's *Odyssey* was the end result of generations of performers leading to Homer (and that it only ended its development by virtue of being fixed in writing) (Foley, *The Theory* 31–35). Lord would clarify that this written text was the product of a listening experience by the scribes and didn't accurately represent the epic poem that changed with every performance (despite the typical assertions of performers that they were performing the poem as originally intended). Among other things, the reason that Parry and Lord's work was considered so revolutionary (and controversial at first) is that they worked to refute certain conventions of art that were held as universal within the mindset of literate culture, such as fixity, originality, and primacy. Within the context of oral culture, the greatest version of an epic poem was not the original source (as no sense of originality existed) but the most recent variation. Fixity, originality, and primacy were luxuries of a culture that could fix their ideas in print. The larger implications of their writing were that there was a definite difference between thought in oral cultures and thought in literate cultures (36–44).

The most significant of the scholars to articulate this difference is Walter Ong, who also applied his ideas to visual culture and electronic media.[36] Significant works such as *The Presence of the Word* would lead to summative classic *Orality and Literacy*, in which oral culture is described as valuing: (1) repetition rather than innovation, (2) aggregation rather than analysis, (3) participation rather than objectivity, (4) the situational rather than the abstract, and (5) addition to rather than advancement beyond existing ideas (Ong, *Orality* 37–57). In essence, participants in an oral culture turn outward to group thought rather than inward to individual thought, and the innovation of writing and print culture "restructures consciousness" (77), fundamentally altering the values just mentioned. However, Ong would always be quick to acknowledge that, despite the sweeping influence of writing and print, such change would never be as uniform as one might think (based on the vehemence with which literate culture defends its values) (Ong, *The Presence* 18).[37] Arguments of fixity, originality, and primacy became especially important in the 20th century, and new media forms seemed to violate those tenets and often provided the basis for the division identified by some cultural critics between high culture (literature) and low culture (comic books).[38] As noted by Walter Ong and prominent media theorists such as Marshall McLuhan, new media contains elements of oral culture in a prominent way that extends beyond the residues in print matter.[39] In order to account for the reemergence of orality in an "electronic" age, Ong would develop the idea of secondary orality (with attention paid primarily to new media like film and television that actually contained audio elements). Like primary orality, this phenomenon generates a strong group identity, but, unlike primary orality, this group identity is not the result of an inability to think in terms of the self; instead, it is a more self-conscious choice (Ong, *Orality* 134). Thus with Ong's sense of secondary orality, the new media experience may require the label of postmodern to better explain the self-conscious creation of oral culture.

Inheriting and refining the work of Parry, Lord, and Ong, John Miles Foley would turn his interests to the comparative study of oral traditions (his interests shaped in part by his rejection of scholars' tendency to ignore the unique contexts and practices of individual oral traditions). Influenced by cultural studies, his works would explore the richness of individual oral traditions, in comparison and contrast, in *Immanent Art* and *The Singer of Tales in Performance*. In addition to establishing the field of study with a comprehensive bibliography and guide to teaching oral tradition, Foley has made connections between the practices of oral cultures and those of digital cultures in ways that may begin to explain how and why tendencies of oral epics are resurfacing in precursors to digital culture like comics books. In an essay that opens the collection *Teaching Oral Traditions*, Foley suggests that oral tradition is not something that can be contained within the confines of the literary canon or the museum, both constructs of power developed in literate cultures that uphold the "illusion of the object" and the "illusion of stasis" (Foley, "The Impossibility" 17). Oral performance changes every time it is performed for a variety of reasons and this makes oral epics multidimensional, unable to be confined on a static page. Rather than serve as information complete in itself, oral tradition provides pathways to information, much like the internet. As an open-ended, ever-expanding system, the internet serves as a better means to conceptualize (and actualize) oral tradition, something that exists only in its multiformity (22). Represented now in his web-based *Pathways Project*, this speculation about the nature of oral culture not only explains the resurfacing of oral culture tendencies in contemporary culture but also builds a bridge between oral culture studies and digital culture studies.

With this rudimentary overview of the foundational concepts in the studies of orality, the connections between superhero revisionism and the concerns of superhero scholars are hopefully already becoming clear. If we agree the general definition of an epic is a heroic journey with broad characters that are integrally tied to the culture, superhero comic books would seem to belong in this category. Together with Lord's assertion that the epic is developed in segments that make use of formulaic repetition over long stretches of time, the stories of superheroes seem especially well designed as epics. Staying with this discussion of the superhero narrative in abstract terms, this provides an explanation for the acceptance of the most recent version of a superhero story as the authoritative story (Earth-1 versus Earth-2). Through the policy of corporate ownership, the industry erased the individual author (and past versions of the superhero's story) and created a sense of collective ownership that stresses currency over primacy. In fact, even when variations are recognized as such, they are often valued by the public as much as the "official" version (with "imaginary" stories of superheroes in the 1960s culminating in the Ultimate and All Star lines of comic books). Consumers of comic book stories demonstrate tendencies characteristic of people within an oral culture through their almost pathological desire to return to the superhero's origin; repetition is privileged and this repetition reinforces the basic truths of the story and the fan community. Without even fully considering the fact that the basic superhero narrative is known throughout the world, topping the international box office in their film form, a focus on avid superhero readers suggests that they have a devotion that leads to their participation with the ongoing story (via letters pages, costumes at conventions, and internet fanficton). These extreme forms of participation (similar to the active participation in storytelling within oral culture) are continued within all age groups despite the general sentiment that identifies superhero comic books as juvenile reading material.[40] If we're tentatively willing to accept superhero comic books as an oral culture experience that has reawakened residual tendencies of oral culture, it could be argued that the direct market consumer of comic books might have a sensibility and community that refutes that sentiment (focused on continuity, creators, and collecting). But secondary orality describes the self-conscious deployment of traditional variations in a post-oral culture seen in the Modern Age of superheroes, with self-aware revisers like Frank Miller and Alan Moore. Despite lacking a genuine oral component, comic books seem to be that new media form that stimulates an orally based intellectual response that in turn activates a state of mind largely structured in traditional terms within a digital age. As seen in the works of Warren Ellis (*The Authority* and *Planetary*), superhero stories do not exist in an authoritative form but as a multidimensional, endlessly retconned situation that employs a digital culture sensibility and undermines the idea of a master narrative.

Whether or not practitioners are aware of the revisionism that occurs within the continually repeated superhero narrative (and the level of awareness does vary), the idea of the superhero industry as oral culture does account for all degrees of revisionism, as well audience-based critical participation in revisionism. In addition, this approach begins to explain why such different interpretations of the superhero phenomenon exist, from the assertion of archetypal mythology (that the superhero always remains the same) to the assertion of

Marxist interpretation (that the superhero always changes). The likely reason that the superhero continues to exist is not that the superhero is beyond our conscious understanding as a figure with essential content or no real content whatsoever (either as part of the collective unconscious or part of the ideology from which we can never be free). Instead, the mode of storytelling initiated by superhero comic books requires a distinctive sort of repetition that is only beyond the conscious understanding of the literate mind (that thinks only in terms of literacy). This is why the cultural studies approach to the superhero has asserted that the superhero is very significant to our culture: because the superhero is both the sign of something new and something old. While some may question the application of oral culture studies to superhero comic books, it circumvents the tendency to argue on behalf of a theory without fully considering the subject matter in question: superhero comic books, themselves. In his general description of orality and literacy, Walter Ong ambitiously states:

> There is no "school" of orality and literacy, nothing that would be the equivalent of Formalism or New Criticism or Structuralism or Deconstructionism, although awareness of the interrelationship of orality and literacy can affect what is done in these as well as various other "schools" or "movements" all through the humanities and social sciences. Knowledge of orality-literacy contrasts and relationships does not normally generate impassioned allegiances to theories but rather encourages reflection on aspects of the human condition far too numerous ever to be enumerated [Ong, *Orality* 1–2].

My argument probably still leaves what might seem like some insurmountable barriers for a scholar of oral culture regarding the field in the strictest sense. After all, comic books are print matter and comic books have no oral performance per se; in addition, they also seem indelibly connected to a visual culture that is understood as antithetical to the mind of oral culture.[41] Even if I only chose to identify superhero comic books as a manifestation of secondary orality, these ideas would be problems. Returning to my description of orality in the industry as metaphor would be an easy way to avoid these problems, but nevertheless, I do in fact see this type of culture reawakening, emerging in our digital age. The goal of this study is to argue that the characteristics of the industry and this visual medium work together to activate the sensibilities of orality (or traditionality), reawakening traditional culture in a form experienced more fully in America and the postindustrial world than it has been in centuries.

Considering my subject matter, I feel it is wholly appropriate to build up the suspense and direct you to my subsequent work in this book by saying this is all "to be continued!" in subsequent chapters. In an era in which superhero comics have changed radically and are no longer subject to the burden of popularity associated with their pulpy heyday, the time has come to understand what superheroes have been doing in cultural terms as a media force within the United States and the world. While I am not suggesting that my book will become the germinal history of superheroes or the academic work that ties together all the loose ends of superhero scholarship, I earnestly believe that it is another decisive step in the right direction. In short, this new approach addresses some of the deficiencies of previous work by using studies in orality to provide an overarching explanation of the historical development of the superhero.

CHAPTER 2

The Emergence of Orality
When Industry Becomes Epic

In *The Presence of the Word*, Walter Ong argues that the most significant problem with studies of oral culture lies with the terminology used to describe oral culture. According to Ong, critics had been describing the phenomenon of oral culture via ideas unique to the literate culture that, in historical reckoning, followed but did not supersede oral culture: "We tend ... to think of early oral cultures before the invention of script as simply illiterate or pre-literate, that is, as cultures without writing or before writing. How much do we say when we thus define cultures in terms of things which we have and they do not?" (Ong, *The Presence* 19). In order to more fully establish this point, Ong used a metaphor with oral culture as a horse that has been identified by people within the era of the automobile as "a four-legged automobile without wheels" (21). In some ways, this works to describe the treatment of the medium of comic books in general, which has been subjected to various forms of analysis by those who see it inaccurately and reductively through the framework of theories of literature and related areas of visual art. Some scholars have argued that there is a significant problem with the inability to recognize comic books as a true art form with unique conventions that work beyond its resemblances to other mediums.[1] As much as I agree with these scholars in principle, I want to do something more unconventional by identifying superhero comic books as an oral tradition (admittedly, a strange variation of Ong's complaint on behalf of oral culture). I want to discuss superhero comic books in oral culture terms—recognizing that superhero comic books have not yet been identified as a four-legged automobile without wheels. Also, it is important to recognize a second and concomitant emphasis within Ong's statement: that literacy is not superior to orality. My intention is to describe comic books not as a primitive form of high literature but as something other than a product of literate culture. In an era shaped in part by cultural studies that suggest there can be no single yardstick to measure art, there needs to be and is less of an apology made in recent years for the study of superhero comic books. More importantly, the characterization of this genre as something shaped by an oral sensibility helps to explain the general sentiment against it, going beyond the now cliché characterizations of comic books as kids' stuff or shockingly new. As noted in chapter 1, the history of the American comic book is largely recognized as the history of the superhero comic book, and the continued and growing popularity of the superhero in other media justifies further study. The scholarship of orality, oral tradition, and oral culture offers the best possibility of reorienting this field of study in a way that accounts for its problems and provides a means for understanding the field in a fuller light. The connections now being drawn between oral culture and digital culture suggests that the comic book superhero represents a paradigm shift in contemporary culture. With this in mind, there are several goals for this chapter and these foundational goals are multifaceted. To begin, it is important to develop an overall sense of the study of orality in order to identify the sociology and psychodynamics of oral culture. Thereafter, I will work to alleviate the hesitancy one might have to address the comic book (a product of the printing press) as an artifact that represents a new orality; the most important step in this chapter is describing the history of the American superhero comic book industry in a way that demonstrates that the industry serves as the instigator of a new sort of oral culture (one that might be called synthetic). Through studies of the evolution of oral culture, the dynamics of transmitting the story, the audience participation in the story, and the growing regard for the story, I will show the comic book industry and its superhero product to be the stuff of a new oral culture.

Oral Culture Studies and the Secret Origins of the Superhero Comic Book

As mentioned in chapter 1, the true founders of contemporary oral culture studies are Milman Parry and Albert Lord, despite the fact that many before them had studied oral culture. Although their ideas were anticipated in limited ways by others (most notably Robert Wood and Antoine Meillet), Parry and Lord worked against several prevalent ideas about orality. Although most sociological studies of the 20th century were decidedly anti-imperialist and took a stand against the stereotyping of oral cultures, many of the linguistic studies of the 20th century took an approach that established literate culture as decidedly superior; since literacy is the product of technology (a yardstick of the development of civilization) and allows for the study of orality and literacy, oral cultures were often identified as primitive (Foley, *The Theory* 3; Ong, *The Presence* 19; *Orality* 28–29). As Lord states, even the reference to such cultures as folk cultures carried with it a connotation that implied that these groups were backward tribes and quaint peasantry (Lord, *The Singer of Tales* 6–7).[2] At the same time, there was a curious sort of romanticism in the treatment of cultures that were relatively untouched by writing, a sentiment not unexpected nor outside the frame of reference associated with studies of "primitive" cultures; however, that sort of romanticism still existed alongside desires and expectations born of a literate culture. In addition to searching for the urtext that gave rise to distinguished oral traditions, these studies intended at least at an implicit level to uncover the singular genius behind the *Odyssey* or *Beowulf* (Parry x–xiv; Foley, *The Theory* 2–6).[3] And despite the aforementioned broad-mindedness of sociological studies of oral cultures, such studies were not particularly useful to the literary scholar because of their devotion to the specifics of living cultures and their often-demonstrated lack of knowledge in regard to oral tradition. In order to redress the deficiencies in previous studies, Parry used the oral poets of Yugoslavia as an instance of oral tradition in order to better understand Homer's epics in particular and oral tradition in general. "[In anthropology,] Parry found a model for his comparative investigations, and especially for the fieldwork expeditions undertaken in Yugoslavia" (Foley, *The Theory* 1). Although he was never able to assemble his work in a long published form due to his unexpected death, Albert Lord would use Parry's published and unpublished research as the basis for one of the foundational texts in the field: *The Singer of Tales*. Consisting of ideas drawn from Parry's field research and their application to classical epic and medieval epics, the text set forth ideas about orality that reoriented the study of oral tradition.

Oral cultures produce the epic poem cooperatively and incrementally through the process of oral tradition. With the epic poem being an accumulation of poetry sung over the course of generations, the epic poem is performed and therefore subject to the specific ideals associated with performance. The singer may belong to any class within society but has two common characteristics: illiteracy and the desire to learn epic poetry (Lord, *The Singer of Tales* 21). The singer performs in various circumstances but is always subject to the limitations of the audience, the attentions of the audience, and the ability to reproduce the poem with integrity (131–132). Delivery of the song is extremely fast with complex musical components reassembled from memory; often familiar with the songs themselves, the audience interacts with the singer through their participation and their opinion of the singer's arrangement (16–17). Incredibly important in Parry and Lord's work is the idea that every epic poem does not have an original point of composition but that every performance is the composition of the poem.

> [I]f the reader interprets oral learning as listening to something repeated in exactly the same form many times, if he equates it with oral memorization by rote, then he will fail to grasp the particular process involved in learning oral epic.... If we equate it with improvisation in a broad sense, we are again in error.... With oral poetry we are dealing with a particular and distinctive process in which oral learning, oral composition, and oral transmission almost merge; they seem to be different facets of the same process [Lord, *The Singer of Tales* 5].

Every song consists of formulae that represent content and form and every song is subject to rearrangement and development over the course of time for various reasons. "The singer never stops in the process of accumulating, recombining, and remodeling formulas and themes, thus perfecting and enriching his art" (26). This should not be misunderstood as a conscious intention to revise previous material; Parry and Lord discovered the singers and their audience were motivated by the conservative impulse to maintain the song as previously performed (120). And everyone is roughly aware of the content of epic poetry and that includes an awareness of the broadly drawn hero who addresses the violation of a cultural norm, moving the plot forward toward a conclusion that extols cultural values.

Nevertheless, this conscious intention does not prevent the rearrangement of elements that include the settings, characters, plot parts, and commentaries within the song; as the songs migrate throughout a society, significant variations are often produced. However, these variations are subsequently seen as integral to the story, and it is crucial to note that variants would never be recognized as such, because there is neither a concept of the original story nor of the original storyteller. "In oral tradition the idea of an original is illogical. It follows, then, that we cannot correctly speak of a 'variant,' since there is no 'original' to be varied!" (101). Although the story may have been encountered previously, the experience of the story is always immediate, drawn from the current performance; the memory of the story is thus based on the abstract sense of the story rather than the fact of the story as established at some sort of fixed starting point. The aural experience of the epic poem results in a sense of immediacy that is simultaneously gone once the last word is uttered and yet forever present as a consequence of its existence within the memory (Ong, *The Presence* 112). The freedom of the story results from its relevance; dependent upon its performance through all levels of society, its continued vibrancy is only threatened by the control that one person might exert on the story. Although the singers are professionals of a sort and perform the story, they do not understand themselves to be the owner of the story or to be in control of the story that predates their learning of it. The true threat comes from someone in a position of power who is seeking to fix the meaning of the story in a certain way, such as the king to control the message, the profiteer to make money, or the scholar to build a body of knowledge. Although the writers who record the oral epic do not necessarily fall into the above categories, it does take the story outside the creative tradition in which it thrives (making it into something else entirely) (Lord, *The Singer of Tales* 130).

In terms of the fundamental differences between orality and literacy, Walter Ong has developed lines of research that made plain the psychic shift between orality and literacy (working at the same time as Parry and Lord and in response to their work).[4] As indicated in his summative work *Orality and Literacy*,[5] the memorization of orally transmitted material (very significant to the maintenance of the oral culture) causes the oral mind, as well as the language material, to be structured differently from the literate mind. Oral cultures construct their traditional communication and storytelling in such a way that new information adds to previously established schemas (rather than creates new schemas or pushes "beyond" those established schemas); therefore; oral tradition produces a psychology that works in terms that are additive, aggregative, and redundant (Ong, *Orality* 37–41). As indicated by the specificity of situational detail and the participatory nature of performance, oral epics focus on the immediate with particular relevance to the human lifeworld (42–43). Stories are filled with broad characters known now as epic heroes that express themselves through action that reasserts the dominance of cultural values (69–70). As a consequence, a sense of the self outside the group does not exist in the same sense that it does within the literate world. Written records do not necessitate the internalization of cultural information in story form (or any form for that matter) and as a consequence, literate culture no longer has the need to maintain its outward orientation emphasizing culture and turns inward to create the individual.[6] Writer-centered thought understands the audience as a fiction and therefore thought is abstracted from the human lifeworld; this mindset allows the individual to think in terms of progression, an analytical approach that designs logical proofs with a clear beginning, middle, and end. Concomitantly, the literate mind values primary sources, systematic development of ideas, and closure (95–100). Stories are filled with complex characters who contemplate events so that the characters might order them in ways that often question the dominance of culture: characters best represented by the detective.

> Oral poets commonly plunged the reader *in media res* not because of any grand design but perforce. They had no choice, no alternative. Having heard scores of singers singing hundreds of songs of variable lengths about the Trojan War, Homer had a huge repertoire of episodes to string together but, without writing, absolutely no way to organize them in strict chronological order.... Because of increased conscious control [in literate culture], the story line develops tighter and tighter climactic structures in place of the old oral episodic plot.... Detective-story plots are deeply interior in that a full closure is commonly achieved inside the mind of one of the characters first and then diffused to the reader and the other fictional characters [140, 145, 146].

In addition, with aural sensitivity no longer a necessity in the acquisition of knowledge, literate culture develops a greater sensitivity and general preference for the visual (and the development of visual culture marks a decisive move away from orality) (115–121). However, in regard to these two states of mind, the oral world can be described as free of an awareness shaped by characteristics of literacy, but the literate world will always be haunted by an awareness shaped by characteristics of orality: "In all the wonderful worlds that writing opens, the spoken word still resides and lives ... writing can never dispense with orality" (8).[7] Ong makes the claim that literacy can never exist without some residual sense of orality and thus, the two are not mutually exclusive within the literate world.[8] Furthermore, to address the advent of new media such as film and television, Ong develops the idea of secondary orality, an experience of something like primary orality and yet unlike it in that secondary orality describes a mind conscious of its participation in oral culture (134); he suggested this concept might also apply to new manifestations of the written word as represented within electronic (or digital) contexts.

There have been various criticisms of the work done by Parry, Lord, and Ong that are important to take into account, as the criticisms do not necessarily invalidate their work so much as broaden the possible means by which we can understand them[9]; in addition, these criticisms may broaden orality in ways that make it even more relevant to identifying the superhero industry as an oral culture. In terms of reconstructing oral culture in all of its complexity, several aspects of the reconstruction must be acknowledged; however, it should be made clear that none of these aspects of the reconstruction were kept secret by the scholars but on the contrary, were foregrounded. Although it may seem terribly obvious in some regard, orality and literacy are conditions of culture, and orality only becomes an object of study through the advent of literacy. This claim is made with the idea that literacy is a point of contrast for orality that only people living in a self-conscious literate culture could experience. Paradoxically, the way that "pure" oral cultures transmit information about themselves is made obscure by the mindset of literate culture.[10] As a consequence, pure orality can only be known and studied in a way that is reconstructive at best and speculative at worst — usually based upon the knowledge of orality that exists alongside literacy. This is seen in two approaches, both of which are represented in *The Singer of Tales*: to study epic poetry from past cultures where orality and literacy coexist (producing written texts such as the *Odyssey* and *Beowulf*) and to perform research on living cultures where orality persists in a largely literate world (such as Serbo-Croatia). In quick response to *The Singer of Tales*, G.S. Kirk would set forth his ideas about orality and the Homeric epic in *The Songs of Homer*. Among other nuanced departures from Lord's work, Kirk would suggest that applying observations about Serbo-Croatian epic poetry to Greek epic poetry creates a false sense of Homer's work; it implies that less variation took place than actually did in Greek oral composition (or recomposition as we might understand it in literary terms) (Kirk 91–95). Larry Benson would also demonstrate the ways tendencies of orality profoundly influence the early traditions of Anglo-Saxon writing, implicitly arguing a strict division of orality and literacy was too schematic; some would later suggest this clear division unduly encourages the creation of binary opposites in scholarship that rise from studies of orality and literacy (such as Marshall McLuhan's notion of hot and cold media).

In regard to the basic historical schema used to situate orality and literacy in relationship with one another, orality doesn't always precede literacy in the sense that strict historical development is hard to chart. For instance, the literate society of Rome may have had direct influence and control over the culture of Germany, but oral culture persisted outside the ruling class, and upon the fall of the Roman Empire, Germany returned to orality as a primary means of communicating all forms of knowledge. Thus, the notion of a pure oral culture is made problematic. In addition, some scholars argue that the shift from written to printed material needs to be dealt with as another distinct shift and not lumped together in the general category of "literacy." In *Traditional Oral Epic*, John Miles Foley has convincingly argued that orality should not be understood monolithically, as the orality of one culture is often remarkably different from the orality of another. According to Brain Stock, orality and literacy are not as free from political interests of critical schools of thought as Ong implies. Seeing as literacy exists in the Western world for centuries, he understands it as more than a coincidence that orality is identified as a force decentering the author so soon after the advent of semiotics and the Frankfurt school (Stock 16–17). But as noted above, none of these arguments disavow the work of Parry, Lord, and Ong, and, for that reason, they may reinforce the strength of their central ideas. Along the lines of this work, the primary points of contention open up the study of orality in ways that allow orality to become even more applicable to broader situations: further outside the confines of traditionally defined oral culture and within the boundaries of not only literate culture but a "mixed" cultural situation that may be anchored in new media innovations of the 20th century. Since orality can only be recognized via the advent of literacy, then the understanding of orality (if not also the practice of orality alongside literacy) implies a certain level of introspection and self-consciousness. Among other things, if critical theory is not wholly separate from the subject of criticism, then the case for comic books as a sort of oral tradition would necessarily be very sound. After all, comic books are a media formation that takes place within the time period that gives birth to the work of Parry, Lord, and Ong, who all suggest that the readings of written texts can be similar to that of the listening of oral poems.

Why It Seems the Superhero Industry Would Not Work Like an Oral Culture (or, Are You Out of Your Literate Mind?)

With the fundamentals of orality in mind, I will profile the early history of the superhero comic book industry and explain how this American industry unintentionally creates an oral culture for us in the midst of the 20th-century literate (and visual) culture. However, I will begin by acknowledging why this seems as if this should not work. As previously mentioned, and as Bradford Wright directly states, "The American comic book industry is a 20th century phenomenon with origins in the late nineteenth century" (Wright 2). Although the technology to reproduce images on a mass scale predates the 19th century, advances in print technology allowed for the inexpensive reproduction of images, eventually images in color. With the conventions of the speech balloon and narrative text used with images in 19th-century pamphlets and political cartoons, the comic strip was born. Encouraged by England's *Punch* magazine, the comic strip was a short narrative that employed written text and drawn images in panels placed in sequence to set up the final panel: a verbal and/or visual gag (hence "comic" strips).[11] From its earliest inception in America with "The Yellow Kid," the comic strip was a popular sensation, increasing the circulation of the newspaper in which it was printed (Duncan 27). Originally, this newspaper was Joseph Pulitzer's *The World*, but the creator of the strip was hired at a much higher salary to produce the Yellow Kid strips for William Randolph Hearst's *The Journal American*. Part of the cutthroat competition between these two publishers later to be called "yellow journalism," the comic book character and concept clearly existed not only as narrative elements but also as marketable commodities. With the Yellow Kid appearing simultaneously in *The Journal American* (produced by his creator) and in *The World* (produced by an imitator), questions of copyright ownership of comic strips were articulated for the first time. In addition to the other characteristics of the medium already mentioned, comic strips began to develop a series of visual conventions such as lines used to indicate movement in a still image and symbols indicating state of being rather than a real part of the scene (the stars surrounding a character's head signifying wooziness). Although the comic strip maintained the title of "comic" strip (and would eventually transfer that name to its extended form book), the newspaper strip would begin to demonstrate diversity in subject matter that took the strip beyond the set-up and punchline formula. This would include experiments such as *Little Nemo in Slumberland*, which followed the dream life of its main character with no conventional plot and artistically borrowing from the ideals of surrealism. However, even more important to the comic book would be the extended stories presented in strips and continued from day to day and week to week. Most of these strips were inspired by pulp fiction, inexpensive fiction of the period that specialized in genre stories emphasizing action and adventure; they included *Dick Tracy, Tarzan, Flash Gordon, Prince Valiant,* and *The Phantom*, among others. Because of the success of the strips and the ability to produce them in book form at a low cost, Max Gaines convinced Dell Publishing to take its lead from the multipage comic inserts in newspapers and produce *Famous Funnies* (essentially a collection of comic strips that was wildly successful in the newspapers). With "little interest in the aesthetics of the medium" (Wright 4) Gaines produced vast amounts of comic book material from old newspaper strips, convinced of its ability to sell; other publishers soon joined the fray.[12] By the late 1930s, newspaper syndicates were no longer selling rights to their comic strip material but, instead, worked to publish their own collections. As would be the case with characters later created as original material for comic books, the syndicates, not their creators, owned their comic strip characters: a standard practice of those companies.

Unwilling to pay rising licensing fees to publish syndicate characters, Malcolm Wheeler-Nicholson, head of National Allied Publishing, worked with creators to produce original material for his comic books. However, the titles sold poorly, and it wasn't until Wheeler-Nicholson entered into a partnership with Harry Donenfeld and Jack Liebowitz, founders of the distribution company to which National Allied was in debt, that National Allied became successful. With Donenfeld and Liebowitz providing the money to create a new title, National Allied published *Detective Comics*, a collection of original work that differed greatly from the humorous material and reprints in most competing comic books. This would become the comic book after which the entire publishing line would be named: DC (Wright 3–7). As this book, filled with six-page comic book short stories, realized success together with others like it, publishers found themselves in need of new material to fill comic books that they wanted to produce for a growing, consumer demographic (from all walks of life but generally younger and male). In order to capitalize on the perceived needs of these publishers, comic book art shops formed to provide filler material for a variety of publishers (the most famous of these shops being Eisner-Iger studios, where Will Eisner first became part of the industry[13]). While the medium attracted readers, the invention of the superhero made it widely popular and focused its content in unforeseen ways; after Superman's 1938 introduction in DC's *Action Comics*, the comic book industry revolved largely around this new type of hero. Initially considered to too fantastic to gain serious attention from consumers (the Superman proposal had been rejected by Max Gaines), Superman's stories became so popular that he merited his own title by the next year. Often identified as a variation on the American frontier hero blended with a post–Depression era wish-fulfillment, Superman is an alien who has superpowers (such as incredible strength and near invulnerability[14]) and wears a colorful costume with a cape; identifying world-threatening crises as Clark Kent, Superman uses his powers to enact justice beyond the confines of human laws (both natural and legal). Superman sold phenomenally, and DC and other publishers developed many other superheroes. The most significant of these would be DC's Batman, a darker, costumed crimefighter with no superpowers whose world did much less to encourage a hope of change than the world of Superman's stories. In short order, the reality of Superman and Batman's marketability became apparent to publishers and to others in related industries. Superman had his own fan club and was licensed to toy manufacturers and producers of radio programs and animated films. In order to protect that earning potential, publishers required their creators to relinquish their rights to their creations to the company; in turn, the publishers filed and aggressively pursued copyright infringement lawsuits against any other publishers who tried to market characters that seemed to resemble the characters that were quickly becoming the cornerstones of their publishing enterprise. In regard to Superman, DC's most famous suits were filed against Fox Feature Syndicate for Wonderman (created by Will Eisner) and against Fawcett Publications for Captain Marvel (whose popularity overcame Superman's likely because Captain Marvel's adolescent alter ego connected so well with the youth readership). Various other superheroes were developed outside the confines of what DC might prosecute but still clearly within the boundaries of what made a superhero a superhero (the most notable of these were the proto-feminist Wonder Woman and the nationalistic Captain America). However, all seemed to incite protests from conservative watchdog groups who were concerned about the violent and (ironically labeled) "illiterate" stories being purchased primarily by adolescents.

Captain Marvel would free himself from the tentacles of this octopus more easily than Fawcett Comics would free themselves from DC Comics' copyright attorneys (from *The Marvel Family* #10, p. 16).

In many ways, this overview of superhero comic book history given up to this point is meant to acknowledge what seem to be inherent difficulties with regarding comic books as a manifestation of oral culture. In addition to being an product of print technology and containing printed information, comic books are the end result of printing innovations such as Alois Senefelder's lithography and the four color printing process (famously associated with comic books in the form of benday dots); this would seem to develop a visual sensibility that has the potential to further the literate mind's desensitization to the aural. Although identified as a new media form, it is unlike the new media forms of film and television that have a recorded oral component or live broadcast oral component experienced at the time of performance. Comic books have text and images that are sometimes intended to be naturalistic and sometimes intended to be symbols (and, therefore, act as language). Once printed, comic books are artifacts and occupy a space more material than subsequently developed digital communication in the form of email or text messages. Like other print matter, the author would seem to be removed from the audience making the audience, a fiction, rather than a real presence.[15] Perhaps most significant is that comic book publishers are motivated by a desire destructive to oral culture that exists prominently in literate culture: the desire to control the story for the good of the self (or the limited few) at the expense of others. For the sake of greater wealth, stories are treated as commodities to be sold and become portable, private experiences like all other books. Since the unconscionable treatment of superhero creators at the hands of their publishers has been well recorded and often described, I will not reiterate this here except to say it did often occur to the great detriment of the creators. Regardless, such a case would have little relevance to this argument since the fact of the matter is that some*one* holds the copyright to this story material. While copyright may work to protect individual interests within the context of literate culture, it conceptually works against the wide dissemination of story that takes place in oral cultures. Nevertheless, although I still assert that comic books are a manifestation of the oral mind, I will concede that this is not entirely manifest with the invention of the comic strip. Instead, the orality of comic books is something that grows incrementally and dramatically over time, successfully fighting off attempts by literate culture that birthed it to reassert oral culture.

In order to set forth my argument with subsequent and significant events in the history of comic books, I want to clarify what I consider to be the most important aspect of oral culture. Outside the scholarly study of oral culture, orality is often identified as a set of practices and only secondarily as a state of mind. In addition to this leading to a oversimplification of oral tradition (represented as an ancient world version of the children's game of telephone), oral cultures are a collection of traits grouped around pre-technological civilization, an uncritical encounter with ideas, and an acceptance of stories as truth. Parry and Lord have demonstrated that a culture's set of practices and state of mind are integrally related, and Ong, especially, has stressed the oral state of mind, perhaps as a measure to correct past misunderstandings and oversimplifications. In *Orality and Literacy*, he argues that the oral state of mind is complex but complex in ways foreign to the literate state of mind. One of the reasons for this complexity is that orality is a common experience across cultures whose practices are radically different from one another. One of the consequences of this recognition is that orality must be discussed more as a state of mind than a set of practices. However, I do not want to misrepresent Ong, who regularly refers to the needs to put the shift from orality to literacy within an historical context (approaching it diachronically rather than just synchronically, as might be the temptation in a structuralist era). Nevertheless, he suggests that the oral state of mind presents itself with oral cultural practices and within residual orality and secondary orality; it can also present itself in relation to literate cultural practices. My suggestion is that the oral state of mind presents itself in response to the practices of the superhero comic book industry. Along these lines, I want to make reference to another scholar who is not regularly associated with studies of orality and literacy (although to omit him would be a rather significant snub and perhaps an outright mistake): Marshall McLuhan.[16]

Although he is primarily regarded as a media critic with a scatological writing style (trying to imitate information transmission in a media age), McLuhan considers one of his most significant works, *The Gutenberg Galaxy*, to be a companion piece to *The Singer of Tales* (*The Gutenberg* 1).[17] His interest in media in relation to orality and literacy makes him an appropriate reference point in this study of comic books.[18] I will be analyzing McLuhan's ideas in great depth in subsequent chapters but here want to establish a few of his basic ideas. In McLuhan's estimation, even though new media may be nonverbal, new media reactivates the psychology of oral tradition. Using phrases such as "the global village" to describe the contemporary reappearance of preliterate community (a phrase Ong uses in his description of secondary orality), McLuhan would make a case for the reemergence of orality in the media age in a way much less restrictive than Ong: "In the electronic age which succeeds the typographic and mechanical era of the past five hundred years, we encounter new shapes and structures of human interdependence and of expression which are 'oral' in form even when the components of the situation may be non-verbal" (3). As valuable as I consider the distinction between orality and literacy and as much as it points beyond a simplistic understanding of oral culture, it can lead to a new problem: a schematic understanding of orality *versus* literacy. As implied by McLuhan and important to this study, communication technology and visual sensibilities existed in oral culture, but they were employed differently. Human beings have always been toolmakers but human beings didn't always have the printing press; human beings have always experienced the world in visual terms but human beings didn't always favor the visual to the near exclusion of the aural. Most clearly stated in *The Gutenberg Galaxy*, one of McLuhan's recurrent themes is that technology and media are the extension of human senses (4–5), and a modification of this concept is useful in this discussion of comic books. While McLuhan's argument for "extension" may work exactly when referring to the microphone or a zoom lens, it doesn't completely describe the experience of an audio recording or a film; these products of technology may reproduce and represent an extension of the senses but these products are certainly not the sense experience itself.[19] Instead, these products are representations of a state of mind in which the senses are extended and thought is shaped by its basis in the aural or visual. Despite this distinction that I develop in a way that McLuhan did not, he had an insight embedded within his "extension of the senses" argument that describes the new media state mind in relation to the oral state of mind. McLuhan would argue that "the contemporary student" doesn't find conventional book-based means of teaching compelling, because they find themselves unable to separate themselves from the subject matter being taught (*The Medium* 100–101). This description of the contemporary student connects the lack of self-consciousness associated with oral culture with the lack of linearity in new media (linearity being something heavily associated with the order of printed texts) (44–45). Again, my case is that superhero comic books in their early forms are not part of a secondary oral culture but are initially a manifestation of something much more like primary orality; only in more recent decades has superhero comics developed into something representing secondary orality. Despite the ways that early practices of the superhero industry may seem to point to a different conclusion, superhero comic books create a fundamentally oral state of mind. With McLuhan's contentions in mind alongside those of Parry, Lord, and Ong, I will show how the industry practices work to create sensibilities typically associated with orality (and in McLuhan's estimation, with new media[20]).

Why the Superhero Industry Does Work Like an Oral Culture (or, You'll Hear Me in the Funny Pages)

In Lord's profile of the typical singer in oral culture, he made careful note that performance is composition, and that the delivery of the epic poem is extremely fast, thereby suggesting that the singers are either geniuses or masters of some sort of composition foreign to the literate world (*The Singer of Tales* 13, 17). Although the production of superhero comic books cannot be construed as performance, the environment in which those books were produced highly resembles oral performance for epic poets. Everyone involved with superhero comic books understood the necessity of quick production to satisfy the incredibly hungry consumer, and, consequently, writers and illustrators worked to produce dozens, if not over a hundred pages every month (editors were certainly at work on hundreds). With most creators working on multiple titles, they were required to quickly master information relevant to a wide variety of stories (whether that be Superman's origin story or what happened last week with the Green Lantern). Concomitantly, comic books were based in part on the strips that favored conflict at the height of action over extended exposition (so that every strip was considered exciting); the plot worked outside the conventions of high literature, which favored gradual, linear development. Instead, superhero comic books were filled with flashbacks and always ended with the promise of more story to follow. Similarly, Ong suggests that the oral poet was working with a large catalogue of past information that caused them to structure stories in a way uniformly different from those of the literate world:

> The poet will report a situation and only much later explain, often in detail, how it came to be.... Homer had a huge repertoire of episodes to string together but ... no way to organize them in chronological order.... What made a good epic poet was, among other things of course, first, tacit acceptance of the fact that episodic structure was the only way and the totally natural way of imagining and handling lengthy narrative, and, second, possession of supreme skill in managing flashbacks and other episodic techniques [*Orality* 139, 141].

Therefore, comic book stories of superheroes often seemed to defy the conventional logic of storytelling as defined by Aristotle[21] but did so in order to reinstate elements in previous stories and, therefore, was expected by readers (at least in variation) within subsequent stories. Writers worked to craft stories that were quintessentially Superman or Green Lantern, repeating the story at the same time they were expanding it to become a lengthy narrative.

For instance, retellings of the origin story of Batman demonstrate how writers may add substantially to a basic narrative framework and yet do so in such a way that subsequent stories seem a necessary outgrowth of the initial framework; the subtle additions enlarge the backstory and yet preserve the overall themes and the narrative devotion to the height of action.[22] In the very first Batman story presented in *Detective Comics* #27, the rich and lazy Bruce Wayne rides with his friend, Commissioner Gordon, to a murder. Quickly bored with the routine nature of the investigation, the ineffectual Wayne leaves only to be replaced in the narrative by the costumed crimefighter Batman on the trail of the serial murderer who threatens the city's business elite. This leads to Batman solving the crimes and the "surprise" revelation that Batman is really Bruce Wayne. Although it reads more as a contemporary variation on the story of Zorro and lacks the traumatic origin now so famously associated with Batman, the story establishes several formulae readily associated with Batman: his outsider status relative to officers of the law, his violent form of justice, and his inscrutable dual identity. Once Batman was recognized as a commercial success, he earned his own title, but the first issue only featured a mere two pages of origin story to set up more hard-boiled Batman action. Regardless, the origin story hardly read as a surprise, as it simply rearranged the above-mentioned tropes in the flashback to Wayne's youth. An anonymous thief killed Wayne's parents (demonstrating the failure of the system), Wayne devoted himself to fighting crime (making himself a vigilante), and put on a disguise to frighten the cowardly lot of criminals (establishing a strange dynamic between Wayne and his alter ego, Batman).[23] In superhero comic books, this backward looping to the origin happens in a consistent way despite the fact that the story supposedly continues from issue to issue, thereby disrupting the conventional linear flow of time established in the literate world. A return to the origin point like this was often greeted with pleasure by readers, and revisions of the origin story were readily accepted not because new readers were unfamiliar with the origin; even if earlier issues were missed, they had sources such as other readers to fill in the details. Instead, they understood the backward looping as natural and saw the revisions not so much as revisions but as a natural outgrowth of the essential truth of the story. Producers of superhero comic books quickly rearranged tropes associated with the superhero and their character in particular in order to make a monthly deadline, and their on-the-fly composition prevented a self-conscious examination of their material. Thus, while change occurred, the changes resulted as a consequence of episodic return to the beginning, in order to more fully explain it and add relevance to the current story line.

Much of the same thing can be stated about some of the most famous Golden Age retellings of Batman's story in "The Origin of Batman" in *Batman* #47 and "The First Batman" in *Detective Comics* #235.[24] In "The Origin of the Batman," Batman becomes embroiled in an investigation that leads him to discover that Joe Chill, the murderer of his parents, is still alive and active as a criminal. During an elaborate sting to capture Chill, Batman reveals himself to Chill as Bruce Wayne. When Chill describes this turn of events to his associates, they kill him for inadvertently creating Batman, the greatest impediment to their criminal enterprises. In "The First Batman," Batman discovers that his father wore a similar bat costume to a costume ball at which his father encountered and brought to justice a criminal named Lew Moxon; however, Moxon subsequently hired Joe Chill to kill the Waynes. Again, Moxon was still active and Batman sought to capture him but was frustrated in his pursuit when Moxon ran in front of a truck and to his death (away from the sight of Bruce Wayne in his father's costume). In addition to working with the above-mentioned tropes and the forever-unsatisfied desire to avenge his parents, these treatments of Batman's origin merely expand the origin, changing one's sense of Batman only in additive ways. This sort of repetition is the express concern of Umberto Eco in "The Myth of Superman," placing the "problem" of Superman and all superheroes within the context of a "consumer" culture — what he describes as an oneiric climate. Despite the fact that Superman seems mythic and inconsumable (so that he might exist within the next variation on his adventure), he is consumed by virtue of being written as if part of a current time and place. After using a philosophic overview of time and narrative dating back to Aris-

When Batman confronts his parents' murderer, he reveals his secret identity as Bruce Wayne (but that secret is kept thanks to the plot mechanics) (from *Batman* #47, p. 10).

totle to describe a subject in time becoming self aware (as well as a character in relation to the reader), Eco posits that the double-play of superhero stories creates for the reader a hazy sense of the character's past (114); this allows the reader to continue every superhero story with the same enthusiasm as similar stories that have been previously read. Moreover, Eco concludes that the superhero sets forth an "immobilizing metaphysics" for the reader in which the superhero is "never achieving total awareness" (a sense of virtue represented only in partial acts that do not move the plot forward to a point of irretrievability) (124). The implied anxiety of not moving forward is notably Aristotelian and firmly connected to the ideals of the literate world. However, within the context of oral culture, such stories do not create a sense of the past that is hazy so much as create a sense of the past that is ever-present. And within the experience of orality, a wholly original story would not be required as the evidence of progress, an ideal that is neither desired nor even considered.

    The above mentioned mastery of past information about characters isn't the same sort one would expect from a writer devoted to the conventions of literacy, because the stories repeated rather than developed the plot (development being something privileged by the conscious awareness of the literate world). In addition to the superheroes never moving toward a particular conclusion (aside from righting the wrong committed in the most current episode), characters existed outside a strict historicity, within a frame relatively unconcerned with the "facts" of the past. Therefore, superhero comic book readers become willing to do something easily seen within oral culture but considered to be wholly unacceptable within literate culture (with written records always providing a point of reference and verification); these readers will allow not only repetitions but also "corrections" to the story already told. In the case of the incredibly popular Superman, who lived his life in multiple comic books and other forms of media, it was impossible from the start for DC editors to manage and restrict all story line developments. In one of the early Jerry Siegel newspaper stories of Superman, the hero tore the wings from a plane filled with the villains he pursued, and he watched them plummet to their death (Daniels, *Superman* 41). As editors sought to craft a hero that would be acceptable for young adults (their most significant consumer group), they made a pronouncement against Superman committing murder and the incident was willingly forgotten — because it was not repeated. In a more dramatic departure, the comic strip featured the marriage of Superman to Lois Lane in 1949 (only to later manufacture a just-a-dream explanation and rewrite the incident at the insistence of DC editors). But as it turned out, managing and restricting all story line developments was not always desirable. Many of the essential and now indisputable characteristics of Superman's story were not developed with the original comic book stories but were nevertheless absorbed from later versions of the comic book stories or from the versions of the stories produced in other media forms. Some of the most famous of these revisions would be introduced on the Superman radio show, including Perry White, the editor of the Daily Planet, and Kryptonite, pieces of Superman's homeworld now deadly to him (Daniels, *Superman* 54). To a large extent, the editors only managed stories as much as it made sense within the framework of reader opinion, and readers had a sense of what was true that operated outside of the original telling of the story. It's also worth noting that Superman stories in recent decades have featured him married to Lois Lane and killing the Doomsday monster, events in line with previously forbidden story ideas. As indicated by G.S. Kirk on the subject of oral tradition, the audience always served as a sort of corrective for the singer, working to ensure that the stories remained authentic (and yet this work did not result in the verbatim repetition of the tales) (319–320).

It has now become common for scholars to identify how World War II's super-powerful Superman departs from the vision of Superman in Siegel and Shuster's early stories.[25] Initially portrayed as a post–Depression era "super-reformer" (Wright 12), Superman would concoct elaborate schemes to sensitize the callous political and business sectors of society to crimes they committed under the auspices of what was legal. He reduced immoral stockbrokers to poverty so they might experience the life of those to whom they sold worthless stocks; he trapped a greedy mine owner inside a mine that the owner had secured with faulty safety measures that allowed previous cave-ins. However, during the war, Superman more clearly represented the establishment by hocking war bonds and generally supporting the efforts of the U.S. government. His adventures were less clearly grounded in the social problems of everyday America, and instead, he fought against fantasy opponents such as Bizarro (a character supposedly opposite to Superman in every way but still as powerful). With an ever-enlarging list of god-like superpowers, the resolution of Superman stories had less to do with sending a message to the powers-that-be and more to do with evoking humor from impossibly convoluted solutions. Often, this difference is ascribed to the general patriotic-toned sentiment of a country at war that preferred, in their entertainment media, to experience an escape from the questions of government authority rather than encounter a politically motivated social criticism. Despite what seems like a drastic change to scholars, Siegel would protest that the light-hearted and wholesome humor was there from the start: "There was a spirit of fun in the thing. As a matter of fact, Joe [Shuster] and I, when we first started going into comics, had intended to do a comedy strip. So we were very comedy oriented, and that's why Superman did have this comic flair to it." (qtd. in Daniels, *Superman* 67). In many ways, this proclamation could be understood as an indication that the changes made to Superman were not just catering to the audience; it seems as if Siegel was unable to separate himself from the crowd and the collective will that drove the content of Superman stories. Ultimately, writers of superhero comic books would make some changes to their retellings of superhero stories but would regularly do so with the idea that they brought forth what was present in the stories from the start (setting them in parallel with the epic poets of oral culture):

> [A]lthough singers are aware that two different singers never sing the same song exactly alike, nevertheless a singer will protest that he can do his own version of a song line for line and word for word.... When, however, their purported verbatim renditions are recorded and compared, they turn out to be never the same, though the songs are recognizable versions of the same story [Ong, *Orality* 60].

While oral culture does not concern itself with linear, logical argument and thereby creates a sense of openness within the narrative, oral poets are genuinely concerned with remaining true to tradition (even if that tradition has been unconsciously modified by new developments within the culture).

If the circumstances of production explain how superhero comic book creators think like oral poets, the specific material nature of early comic books at least adds to our understanding of why comic book readers think like an audience listening to an oral poem. One of the foremost reasons for the popularity of comic books among young readers was that comic books were inexpensive. Like the pulps, comic books were printed on low-quality paper stock with a low-resolution printing process (separating it from the "respectable" treatment given to reproductions of the literature and visual art part of the literate world's high culture). In many ways, its material nature works against a sense of investment in the material object on the part of consumer. With a design more like a pamphlet or a tabloid newspaper, comic books were considered disposable because of their initial cost and the associations that they had with the other disposable print mediums. While this does not mean that some readers did not keep their comic books for a while, those readers were as likely to share or trade their comic books as keep them for themselves.[26] "[In 1942, P]ublishers assumed a generous 'pass-along value' of five readers per comic book" (Wright 31). With these aspects of the medium in mind, comic books have another link to epic poetry in that they are considered to be practically immaterial ("sound exists only when it is going out of existence" [Ong, *Orality* 12]) and part of a community sharing process — thereby, like the oral word and unlike the permanence and privatization associated with conventional texts of literate culture. And since most of the comic books published between the 1930s and 1970s were thrown away (the number of disposed comic books increasing as we move backward in time),[27] the stories of superheroes from those times often live more vibrantly in the readers' memories than in the actuality of well-referenced comic book pages; this is a foreign experience in a literate world not predisposed to the memorization of stories.

In terms of the structure and development of the superhero comic book industry, it would seem that one of the most significant impediments to an oral-culture sensibility would be the idea of intellectual property in general and copyright in particular. However, the way in which major publishers enforced their claim to intellectual property led to not only another way in which oral culture was recreated but also possibly to the most significant way. McLuhan argues that the typographic press and the mass production of fixed-print manuscript lead to the mass production of literary art as commodity (*The Gutenberg* 124–125): a claim generally accepted and understood by most scholars of orality and literacy. The implications of his claim create a sense of story in the literate world that is uniformly opposed to the sense of story in the oral world. In addition to identifying a story with its "original" author, the story itself is a fixed reference point, and, therefore, the original assumes precedence over any subsequent renditions (with subsequent renditions regarded negatively as derivative). Moreover, a story in print is not profitable in performance but profitable because the story is a series of printed pages bound in a particular sequence and known as a text; it is an object to be sold by the producer and bought by the consumer, an object with monetary value because individuals want to purchase it for the experience it promises. Since an author's story may be reproduced as a text just as easily by others as by the author, the idea of intellectual property was developed in order to protect the profit potential of an author's "creation" (preventing others from replicating the work in exact or even approximate form). Of course, the motivation for intellectual property is the result of a cultural development associated with literacy (money and one's rights to it), and the claim to intellectual property is made possible by yet another cultural development also associated with literacy (a legal system based on written rules and precedent law). The most prominently known form of intellectual property is copyright, a notion that has been interpreted variously in different contexts throughout the years. In most countries, copyright extends throughout an author's lifetime and for a set amount of time beyond the author's death (belonging to the author's estate during that extended period). However, with the author's immaterial creation (and the rights to it) regarded as material, the author is free to do commercial things with the creation (and the rights to it), just as the author might with any material object, such as selling it. This describes the economic situation of not just the early 20th-century comic book publishing industry but also the long history of publishing since the early years of the printing press. Since those early years, not everyone with a marketable creation had a printing press or a means to distributed printed texts for widespread sale. Therefore, many creators relied on publishers to produce their stories for consumption, and that put the creators at an economic disadvantage that often resulted in the sale of not only a story but also the rights to that story.[28]

As previously mentioned, I will not delve too deeply into the inequity of this practice in the superhero industry of the 20th and 21st centuries because it has been documented so thoroughly in other places. Most feel the deep sympathy with Jerry Siegel and Joe Shuster who sold Superman to the company soon to be known as DC Comics for $130, only to see their creation earn millions for the company in comic books and other licensed forms. Most people feel some indignation over the failure of the legal suit set forth by Siegel and Shuster to earn more than wages as writer and illustrator and to regain their rights to Superman. After the suit, they were blacklisted and only worked on comic books in relative secrecy with lesser-known publishers.[29] The personal toll of this loss of creative control is dramatized in great detail in Gerard Jones's *Men of Tomorrow*, and their situation is paralleled with that of many other creators in the industry, most notably with Jack Kirby in contest with Marvel Comics.[30] Regardless of what most people feel about this situation, this forfeiture of personal rights to one's creations is still a standard part of the business practices of DC and Marvel. I do not wish to gloss over it or justify the position of the publishers, but at the same time, I want to regard these practices objectively in terms of their implications to particular culture (of the comic book creators and readers) and general culture. Along these lines, most of the superhero creators entering the industry were initially grateful to publishers for giving their creation a chance within one of their publications; with only slight reservation, Joel Siegel said, "At least this way we'll see him [Superman] in print" (qtd. In Daniels, *Superman* 41), and, even years later, professionals working in those early years like Will Eisner, who became advocates of creator's rights, indicated that creators knew what they were doing, and that publishers did not hide their business practices.[31] While this attitude is part of the big-business era of the United States in the early 20th century, it nevertheless establishes a general outlook conducive to an oral sensibility. I mention this to indicate a different sensibility possessed by the creators who understood themselves less as individuals and more as part of a system — a system that would ultimately cause many to think that their stories were just stories and not texts. Oftentimes, creators felt that publishers had justifiable rights to their creations for giving those creations a chance and for allowing creators to continue working in the field. While creators certainly did not consider publishers to be wholly benevolent, they also did not regard them as malevolent, and the notion that rights to ideas reside within a company changes one's attitude toward those ideas as well as to the self. As Ong has suggested, the sense of authority differs significantly within oral and literate cultures, with oral cultures regarding authority in ways that are much more favorable and conducive to sound thought.

> This is not simply because someone at the top is peremptorily imposing his views on those below. Such will be the later caricature of authority when it is under attack. The actuality is more complex. A personality structure built up in an oral society, feeling knowledge as essentially something communicated, will be relatively more concerned with what others say and relatively less concerned with its relationship to observation. In such as society, knowledge is a tribal possession, not a matter of individual speculation.... Oral culture does not produce a Descartes or Newton or Einstein [Ong, *The Presence* 231].

McLuhan makes a similar statement in regard to oral and literate cultures and adds, "as new technologies come into play, people are less and less convinced of the importance of self-expression. Teamwork succeeds private effort" (*The Medium* 123). This began with publishers' attempts to preserve their property at the expense of creators. Yet, while initially artificial, their practices became an organic part of the culture in short order, making the publishers' assuredly greedy intentions beside the point.

As a curious consequence of the standard practices of superhero comic book publishers, superheroes came to be regarded as collectively owned, and the story of the superhero transcended the individual writers and illustrators currently working on the superhero titles. Most of the comic book publishers had a policy of not providing credit within the comic books themselves to the creators who produced any of the work therein to keep from having any one story too closely associated with one creator.[32] In this way, the titles and the comic book characters themselves became more important than the people who produced their stories; this made for good sales with Batman fans buying all Batman stories regardless of writer or illustrator. In order to sustain the quick pace of production (that resulted in staggered weekly publication), publishers would divide up the labor necessary to produce comic book stories into its smallest component pieces, like an assembly line, and superhero stories would regularly have a separate writer, penciler, inker, colorist, and letterer. "'We made comic book features pretty much the way Ford made cars,' Eisner recalled. 'I would write and design the characters, somebody else would pencil them in, somebody else would ink, somebody else would letter.' This process contributed to the visual sameness and formulaic stories of many early comic books" (Wright 6). The motivation for this act was the practical need for speed but served the same functions as not providing credit. Since each of the workers contributing to the finished product was a skilled worker, there was no sense of singular genius but rather a sense of shared enterprise; someone on the assembly line could be replaced without disrupting the product as a whole. With the desire to quickly expand comic book offerings clearly a motivating factor for publishers, this idea allowed publishers to "farm out" work to production houses such as Eisner-Iger. Eisner's own testament to drawing in a few basic styles was meant to suggest to publishers that their staff was limited; however, his efforts were probably unnecessary in a system that encouraged the individual to work in ways that represented community standards.

Quite significantly, Ong would argue that such a process is not the opposite of art, just the opposite of the literate world's sense of art:

> Homer stitched together prefabricated parts. Instead of a creator, you had an assembly line worker. This idea was particularly threatening to far-gone literates. For literates are educated to never use clichés, in principle. How to live with the fact that Homeric poems, more and more, appeared to be made up of clichés, or elements very like clichés? [*Orality* 22].

Encouraged to work within the boundaries set for them, writers, illustrators and creators adhered to the ethic of "house style," and great lengths were often taken to preserve the cliché. For instance, when Jack Kirby made his surprising switch from Marvel to DC and worked on the *Jimmy Olsen* title, his renderings of Superman were redrawn to make them look less like something Kirby drew (representing Marvel culture) and more like Superman (part of the DC culture).[33] Since the motivation was to earn greater profit for the company at the expense of the individual, this work environment could certainly be understood as oppressive by a Marxist critic. In turn, the internalization of the ideas generated within a cultural construct could also be seen as a response to the system's hail (which obviates individual needs). However, such critiques must be recognized as decidedly post-orality in that community designs that obviate individual needs are always in place within oral cultures. Such critiques also do not work entirely, as the distinction is not between supporting the superstructure and supporting the base; the distinction is more clearly between individualized artistic production and more clearly community-based artistic production. And the community-based artistic production often signals changes to individual character that are quite radical to a literate culture. While most creators worked feverishly to make ends meet from the 1930s through the 1970s (hardly a worker's paradise), the only thing that tended to separate the publishers and creators from one another were issues of profit, an intrusion of the literate world. Aside from the money that publishers made thanks to star superheroes, preserving the integrity of the story became more important to the editors and creators than anything else.

If we shift our perspective away from a Marxist critique of capitalism, this business practice can be recognized as something that initiated a fairly remarkable trend in the midst of the literate culture of the 20th century. Within oral cultures, even if one were to trace a song back to its creator and first performance, that creator would have had no special rights to the song, and that first performance would have no claim to authority as the original.

> [J]ust as the first singing could not be called the "original," so the first man to sing a song cannot be considered its "author," because of the peculiar relationship, already discussed, between his singing and all subsequent singings. From that point of view a song has no "author" but a multiplicity of authors, each singing being a creation, each singing having its own single "author" [Lord, *The Singer of Tales* 102].

While this idea should not romanticize unfair business practices, it begins to point toward the essential consequences of the aforementioned company policies in regard to the superhero comic book industry. In order to ensure the near omnipresence of its product, publishers such as DC would have multiple creators working with the same superhero, beginning as early as the first issue of Superman, when Joe Shuster recognized that he was incapable of producing all the artwork required by DC; the Superman illustrator staff growing to include John Sikela, Paul Cassidy, Ed Dobrotka, Ira Yarbrough, and Wayne Boring (Daniels, *Superman* 44). Despite the mandate to replicate the agreed upon vision of Superman determined by the corporate culture of the publisher, these teams crafted stories that presented slight narrative and visual variants of the characters. Despite the fact that these variations were fairly invisible to the creators (who saw their work as living up to the publisher's mandate), future variations in the characters were then based upon past variations (thus making the changes over time almost imperceptible). With their long historical view of characters, publishers officially held the line in preserving the integrity of the superhero as previously written, but they understood the incompatibility of simultaneously maintaining the character exactly and wanting no one creator to be too closely associated with the work. In addition, certain leeway was afforded by the idea that there was a general turnover in the core readership of young adults, presumably moving onto other reading material as they matured; this was not always true, and, even when it was, certain superheroes like Superman and Batman were enormous commercial presences beyond comic books with their stories told in other mediums and their images used to sell countless products.[34] Therefore, maintaining too tight of control on copyrighted characters would have, to some extent, been counterproductive to a publisher looking to make money by licensing that character to other media outlets seeking to tell their own stories based on that character.

In this way, the interlocking circles of influence on the character grew in number and size, and the only true guide used to limit proliferation would be whether the public would still accept a variation as true to the popular original. Therefore, variations often came to be seen as strangely compatible with one another by the public at large who read Superman comic books and comic strips, watched Superman films and cartoons, and bought countless Superman products; artwork from two different eras of Superman could be displayed side-

Although Wayne Boring's depictions of Superman are more well known, Joe Shuster's style (*top*) built the foundation of Boring's style as an illustrator for Superman (*above*) (from *Superman* #13, p. 8 and *Superman* #53, p. 10).

by-side on products with little sense of cognitive dissonance. Perhaps the best example of this can be seen with the eventual difference between the original style of Joe Shuster's illustration of Superman and the later style of Wayne Boring's illustration of Superman. With Boring originally part of Shuster's staff, his style was initially fashioned to resemble the basic look of the Joe Shuster Superman: square-jawed, somewhat lean, and unimpressive in height. Due mostly to time constraints and the traditions of the medium, Superman was drawn in a simple, iconographic style, with a face rendered in just a few pen strokes. However, when Shuster was removed from his role as Superman's illustrator, Boring's variations became more prominent, influenced not only Superman's past but also his own sense of Superman informed by other artists and portrayals of Superman in other mediums. As a consequence, Superman became barrel-chested, muscular, and more realistic (in terms of overall design, with more elaborate backgrounds and lighting). Although set alongside one another, Shuster's Superman differs significantly from Boring's Superman, the change barely registered with Superman fans who considered Boring's variation to be the "classic" Superman (Daniels, *Superman* 74). In addition to the variation in Superman's image, variation existed in the telling and retelling of the same Superman story (mentioned earlier with the variation between Superman vigilante and patriot); the myth of Superman grew with the advent of the adventures of Superboy: Superman in his young life as a superhero (extending the story in significant ways within the "past" of Superman, making the story more "epic," and creating yet another public sensation). If we are willing to understand Lord's reference to the song of oral culture in a broader sense, his description of the variations within the songs applies well to the willingness to accept changes in superhero stories (indicating that the culture sees variations merely as realizations of the potential inherent within the stories).

> To the superficial observer, changes in oral tradition may seem chaotic or arbitrary. In reality, this is not so. It cannot be said that "anything goes." Nor are these changes due in the ordinary sense to failure of memory of a fixed text, first, of course, because there is no fixed text, second, because there is no concept among singers of memorization as we know it, and third, because at a number of points in any song there are forces in several directions, any one of which the singer may take [Lord, *The Singer of Tales* 120].

Although I could speculate how Boring's image of Superman and Superboy's story were within the potential of Superman's song, this speculation would ultimately be irrelevant. Since these variations were accepted, the implication is that those genuinely invested in the story understood them as already there. Ultimately, the changes made to Superman in particular and superheroes in general in the Golden Age cannot be understood as a truly conscious desire for change or an imperative for change dictated from the top down, from publishers to creators. Instead, this process is part of the organic change of epic heroes that the public allows, participates in, and is implicated with. Moreover, this situation not only resembles the typical change seen within the stories told within an oral culture, but comic books accelerate the rate of change to such a degree that it is remarkable that such variations are still accepted by the public at large. The subtle changes that take place over centuries in a traditional oral culture take place over decades in this new media culture.

Continuing this discussion, another way that publishers sought to protect the earning potential of their characters would seem to be the worst impediment to creating the highly potent oral culture situation thus far described: legal cases brought against rival companies for their supposed copyright infringement. However, much like other above-mentioned practices, these suits had unintended consequences that furthered the dynamic of the burgeoning oral culture. As previously mentioned, the character most aggressively protected by these legal means was Superman. While some characters like Fox Publications' Wonder Man were obvious copies and easy to legally squash, other characters, like Fawcett Publications' Captain Marvel, were not so obvious as copies. Captain Marvel was much more threatening to DC, outselling Superman by more effectively targeting the youth market; rather than simply feature a young sidekick, the story featured Billy Batson, an adolescent who transformed into the adult superhero Captain Marvel by saying the magical word, "Shazam!" During litigation, and a court case which lasted eleven years, discussions of the idea/expression dichotomy (based on the balancing act between the first amendment and copyright) set forth several important distinctions of the superhero as a general concept (available to everyone) and Superman as a specific character (owned by DC). In addition to concluding that DC did not own the concept, the judge declared that only certain acts committed by Superman within his stories were owned by DC. While this was enough to declare that Fawcett had indeed committed infringement, it also suggested that Superman wasn't the starting point for all superheroes and that Superman was neither the first nor the final word on superheroics. Although the outcome of the case was of little consequence to the public at large, it seemed to make DC more fully committed to an alternative strategy for dealing with competition: acquisition. They began buying competitors, their characters, and all rights associated with them. By adopting a business strategy that enlarged the base of superheroes within the DC "universe," the publishers pleased fans who wanted to see more of their heroes not only alongside one another on the newsstand but also within the same fictional universe. The porous nature of the worlds of individual superheroes was already well established with team-ups between Superman and Batman (who seemed ill-suited to compliment one another, but whose partnership excited fans). In the early history of the comic book industry, the superhero partnership is best represented by the highly successful Justice Society of America, a joint publication that featured a team comprised of DC and All American superheroes. However, when the joint publication of the title fell apart and some of the major heroes dropped out of the line-up, popularity suffered and seemed to serve as an indicator of the desires of the buying public. As just noted, after the Captain Marvel case, DC became more committed to acquiring competing heroes (eventually even including Captain Marvel) seeing them as elements that ultimately would benefit the DC "universe" by expanding it endlessly. In many ways, this corporate strategy (and aesthetic practice) works to approximate a singer culture willing to refine their art by recombining existing materials in a more satisfying way: "The singer never stops in the process of accumulating, recombining, and remodeling formulas and themes, thus perfecting his singing and enriching his art. He proceeds in two directions: he moves toward refining what he already knows and toward learning new songs" (Lord, *The Singer of Tales* 26). Thus, what might initially seem to satisfy the immature desire to throw together all on one's favorite fictional characters potentially becomes a work that clarifies the individual characters by virtue of comparison and contrast (seen in years to come, in debates between radically different superheroes such as Superman and Batman).[35]

Responding to consumer opinion is undoubtedly a good strategy for any business seeking to sell product, and the comic book industry did this exceedingly well, but there are distinctive consequences to marketing stories in this way—consequences that ultimately create widespread community dynamics consistent with orality. The foremost reason that the superhero industry responded so well to audience reaction is that comic books are serial publications that extend and repeat stories, tracking sales on a monthly basis. Able to quickly respond to the audience opinion, the producer of stories validates the audience in ways slower but still similar to the performer; while this response is somewhat delayed, it suggests the audience is something more than a fiction to superhero creators.[36] Since it is narrative material produced by the industry, the consumers have an attitude toward the product that is unlike the attitude toward other artistic products. In addition to the validation that the audience receives from the influence it exerts, the audience is naturally inclined to participate in the worlds of superheroes via imaginative engagement with the characters. Part of this may be due to the previously mentioned consumable aspect of the superhero (always written as part of a contemporaneous time) but also has to do with licensing and multimedia production that allows greater choice and interaction. For instance, the Batman's audience can choose to read one version of Batman but not another (comic strip versus comic book). Moreover, an audience comes to be invested in their version of Batman and more forcibly exerts their opinions (like the actually present audience of oral culture) because they are invited to live in Batman's world through coloring books, costumes, and dolls (items which require decisions to be made within the imaginary world of Batman). Again, although not wanting to stray far from the Golden Age, it is absolutely essential to note the way that the serial publication model was refined in years to come, with innovations such as the letters page. With the letters page, superhero comic books readers interacted with editors and creators in a surprising, informal way; gaffs were revealed, suggestions were accepted, and something like a genuine creative relationship developed. In addition comic book fan(atics) were part of the rapidly developing fan culture of the 20th century that thrived because of new communication technologies that encouraged their tribal organizations in the form of fan conventions. In addition to bringing the creators and audience together in situations that often resulted in spontaneous performance (from live panel discussions to impromptu sketches made by illustrators for their fans), comic book conventions saw the advent of fanzines and fanfiction (allowing the audience to work like professionals in the field).[37] With dynamics of superhero comic books ranging from the industry practices to the reading experiences to the culture at large, many readers lack the objective distance considered to be essential within literate culture.

Why Jules Feiffer Regards Superhero Comic Books as Junk (and Why He's Right)

Since I have chosen to remain largely within the framework of the Golden Age in this chapter, I feel it is important to make a concession in this regard. The case made thus far is not intended to suggest that the producers of Golden Age superhero comic books refined the form to the level of great epic poetry produced by Homer but to suggest that they worked within confines of the great epic poets. At the same time, these producers, generally misunderstood by the critics devoted to the principles of the literate world, established the phrases that would become the formulae of great superhero comic book "epics" in years to come. As they did so, they were establishing a form that, by and large, contradicted the basic tenets of artistic standards established by the literate world. When discussing the technical meaning of literacy, McLuhan complains about the common usage of the term literacy: "[W]e live at a time when literacy itself has become so diluted that it can scarcely be invoked as an esthetic criterion" (*The Gutenberg* 2). Although the word didn't have the exact meaning it would for a scholar of orality and literacy, it is important to recognize that superhero comic books were regularly dubbed products of an illiterate age (and the common definition of literacy is nevertheless based upon an idea of education and knowledge that privileges certain forms of the written word). Working with the standards set by high culture that portrayed the artist as one who transcends culture, critics of comic books certainly didn't like what they considered to be the slavish way that publishers responded to their audience. Seeming to violate the purity of inspiration, the source of the originality, and the litmus test for high art in a literate culture, comic books presented clichés from second-rate artists at best. One of the central ideas revealed by Parry and Lord was that the high art of Homer was essentially based upon the repetition, rearrangement, and redeployment of clichés. In reference to Parry's work, Ong states the explicit threat that such studies posed to the literate estimation of art:

> How could any poetry that was so unabashedly formulary, so constituted of prefabricated parts, still be good? ... There was no use denying the now known fact that the Homeric poems valued and somehow made capital of what later readers had been trained to disvalue, namely, the set phrase, the formula, the expected qualifier — to put it more bluntly, the cliché. [*Orality* 23].

While clichés are repeated bits of proverbial knowledge, such repetition in literate culture indicated meaninglessness (but in oral culture meant quite the opposite). Featuring men who always saved the day, superhero comic books always reestablished basic cultural values through violent confrontation between superheroes and villains. Decrying the violence in comic strips, Ralph Bergengren would write, "physical pain is the most glaringly omnipresent of these motifs; it is counted upon invariably to amuse the average humanity of our so-called Christian civilization" (11). Invoking the higher values to which Christian civilization should aspire, Bergengren uses a Platonic framework that privileges literacy with an emphasis on the progress toward the truth provided by abstract thought. However, what "far-gone literates" call cliché is often proverbial knowledge related to the human lifeworld and basic needs of the tribe; within the practice of oral tradition, there was never a perceived need to rise above culture, and, instead, the stories vilified those things which threatened culture. "In technological society today, the world has mostly left behind the old polemic and feudal oral-aural culture which had polarized knowledge, and with it the word, around struggles of heroic figures and thus (by today's standards) had overcharged man's life-world with virtue and vice" (Ong, *The Presence* 255).[38] As a consequence, portrayals of heroes, not self-conscious or troubled by their acts of violence, often fed the widespread fears of parents as well intelligencia in years to come that culminated in part with the Fredric Wertham campaign and Congressional hearings on comic books. These fervent reactions serve to indicate how comic books occupy the position of low art and primal expression within a literature culture (and yet are widely accepted to the point that superhero stories persist and grow more vibrant).

In *The Great Comic Book Heroes*, the widespread acceptance of superhero stories is captured well by Jules Feiffer's recounting of his own experience with sarcasm: "My interest in comics began at the most sophisticated of levels, the daily newspaper strip, and thereafter proceeded downhill" (2–3).[39] With Fieffer's notion that "our reaction [to superheroes] was less 'How original!' than 'But, of course!'" (9) in mind, we should carefully evaluate his subsequent description of superhero comic books as "junk." Even though junk may be an inexact critical term, his general description of superhero comic books makes it a release from the expectations of industrial culture and allowed one to easily distinguish hero from villain. Implicated within the idea of literate culture, he calls comic book stories a lie but also identifies something central to the oral culture mentality of comic books in a literate world:

> Children hungry for reasons, are seldom given convincing ones. They are bombarded with hard work labeled education.... It should come as no surprise, then, that within this shifting hodgepodge of external pressures, a child, simply to save his sanity, must go underground. Have a place to hide where he cannot be got at by grownups. A place that implies, if only obliquely, that *they're* not so much; that *they* don't know everything.... And the basic sustenance of this relief was, in my day, comic books. With them we were able to roam free, disguised in costume, committing the greatest of feats — and the worst of sins.... Psychically renewed, we could then return above ground and put up with another couple of days of victimization [Feiffer 76–77].

Ultimately, Feiffer is limited by his decision to not use critical language and by his ignorance of the literacy of the culture he resents, making his ironic humor even more bitter. Ostensibly, he yearns for rarified childhood but he really wants something other than the industrial age of literate culture. As Ong notes, the distinction between the storytelling and learning as work would only come in place with the advent of literacy:

> In an oral culture, verbalized learning takes place quite normally in an atmosphere of celebration or play. As events, words are more celebrations and less tools than in literate cul-

tures. Only with the invention of writing and the isolation of the individual from the tribe will verbal learning and understanding itself become "work" as distinct from play, and the pleasure principle be downgraded as a principle of verbalized cultural continuity [*The Presence* 29–30].

Although Feiffer places the tension between that of youth and adult culture, his descriptions work to describe the tension between that of oral and literate culture (with youth searching for an experience, not objective knowledge, that makes sense).[40]

While my claims may be true and superhero comic book culture leads to a new oral culture, there are two significant issues left to address (the proverbial elephants in the room — please forgive the wholly appropriate use of a *cliché*). The first issue is the content of superhero comic books in the form of the superhero, itself. Although the popularity of other genres of comic books has begun to grow in United States (with comix in the 1960s and the black and white art comic book boom of the 1980s), the growth has been slow and the superhero is still dominant (in United States and around the world).[41] Even though this popularity could be explained through the continued success of a "known brand," there was a point at which the superhero was the unknown and catapulted the medium to wild success.[42] Regardless of the reasons why the superhero story is the most popular genre of comic books, it would be worth studying superhero comic books as the most prominent representation of this resurgence in oral culture. Nevertheless, although the superhero is not the sole protagonist in all comic books in the world (with diverse genres represented in the Franco-Belgian and Manga traditions), I believe that the superhero story is more closely tied to oral nature of the medium than any other genre; the industrial basis for the proliferation of comic books differed in other major comic producing centers like France and Japan, and their major movements post-date the boom of the comic books and the superhero in the United States. Therefore, I would suggest that each of these movements are more clearly part of a secondary phase of comic book development (covered in the later chapters of this book) that allows for greater freedom of content. Regardless, based on the history covered in this chapter, I contend that form and content are integrally related and the superhero is the epic hero with some modern trappings. There is much more to be said on this topic, but I will reserve this for an in-depth discussion in chapter 3 on Superman's continuing life as epic hero throughout the long run of his publication.[43] As mentioned, there are two significant issues to address, and the content of superhero comic books was only the first proverbial elephant in the room. The second issue is perhaps the most significant objection that could be leveled at superhero comic books: the visual orientation required by the print matter of the medium. Within my discussion of this issue, I will make a transition from the term *orality* to *traditionality*, in order to describe a set of recent practices related to the practices and thought of oral culture. I want to clarify that this is done to more accurately reflect the substance of what is being analyzed and not to avoid the salient issues that make the visual experience of superhero comic books part of an oral sensibility. In addition to demonstrating how the use of illustration invokes thought processes characteristic of oral culture, I will examine the various visual clichés that grow from the narrative clichés and formulae of superhero comic book illustrators. Since this discussion is very significant, it will be the exclusive purview of chapter 4. Finally, an important note should be added to clarify the focus on Golden Age comic books in this chapter; as already noted, I do not feel that the Golden Age represents the height of superhero stories, their maturity as epics. However, even before the innovative work of Parry and Lord, the general idea existed that less sophisticated folk stories of oral culture lead to epic poetry, the height of oral tradition achievement.[44] Homer's *Odyssey* would not exist without centuries of storytelling, elements that Homer repeated in performance. While much of what is produced in the Golden Age is crude, it also possesses great innovation as a type of oral art struggling to emerge within a literate culture (and therefore received sharper criticism than it should have). Moreover, it possesses great potential that led Silver Age creators, such as Stan Lee and Jack Kirby, to refine the "phrases" of this artform in more readily employed formulae; this will be dealt with in chapter 5.

The primary goal of this chapter has been to identify the parallels between the oral culture and the conventions of the superhero comic book industry (and the culture it produced). Paradoxically, this is something that can be accomplished because of the existence of a literate culture that records the history of the industry in which this new form of primary oral culture emerges. While it would be much easier to regard it as a phenomenon of secondary orality, I want to again make clear that the early years of the comic book industry should be understood as something very like primary orality. As I will show in chapters 6, 7, and 8, the industry and art seem to enter the world of secondary orality only much later in the long life of the superhero, beginning in the 1960s and only wholeheartedly in the 1980s, because of changes in technology and the marketplace. Consequently, this chapter is exclusively about the industry and culture that leads to the Golden Age superhero. Because of the performance constraints of the creators, the practices and attitudes of the creators, and the corporate ownership of their creations that spins outward, the development of superheroes takes place in a culture remarkably like that of primary orality. As a consequence, superhero stories are not commodities driven solely by a 20th-century industry that is shaped by executives basing their ideas on surveys of popular culture (although aside from the term "commodities," most of this statement is true). Instead, they are dynamic forces that interact with a commercial market and, more importantly, operate as a powerful voice that harkens to a different sort of community organization; superhero comic books interact with culture, mirroring and shaping culture within America and beyond, revealing itself not so much as an empty marketing vessel but as an evocation of the mechanics of the traditional epic poetry.

CHAPTER 3

Orality and a New Medium
The History of the Man of Tomorrow

Long before the 2007 release of Christopher Knowles's bombastically titled work, *Our Gods Wear Spandex*, people were referring to superheroes as modern representations of God or at least referring to superhero stories as "modern mythology" (Richard Reynolds's title for his famous superhero comic book study). While I'm not opposed to identifying common links between superheroes and mythic heroes of the past, doing so as an end in itself helps us very little to actually work with superheroes in a new and constructive way (this is not meant as a criticism of Reynolds's work). In fact, even the concept of the archetype, which has a distinctive history and critical use in 20th century literary scholarship, provides us with little more to do than identify those links. (For example, an archetypal criticism often just plugs characters into certain categories: as the *hero*, Batman finds his *shadow* in the evil *trickster* known as the Joker.) Although many defenders of superheroes assume that such a practice is the path to critical respectability for superheroes,[1] such a practice has dubious value at best. Since the existence of the collective unconscious is unverifiable, so then is the existence of literary motifs as expression of archetypes of the collective unconscious. Superheroes do resemble mythic heroes but I believe the reason for this has less to do with the pressure that archetypes exert on the unconscious and more to do with superhero comic books as a resurgence of an oral sensibility. As stated in chapter 2, the psychology of oral culture describes very well the social dynamic of the early superhero comic book industry. Due to trends within the comic book publishing world in the early 20th century and the related conventions of the medium, the American comic book industry artificially and unintentionally re-created the basic tenets of oral culture. Moreover, the orality of the culture manifests itself forcefully in the aesthetics of superhero stories in comic books (as well as other new mediums). After all, the shape of heroes in epic poetry is directly connected to the form of the oral epic, just as the form of the oral epic is directly connected to the culture of orality.

Pow! Bam! and the Power Fantasy:
The Tradition of the Super Man in Epics

Walter Ong makes a controversial argument based on the notion that the literate world stresses dialogue over dialectical opposition: "When something is wrong in the social or economic order, it is hard for technological man to believe that the cause reduces simply to individual's or some group's villainy" (*The Presence* 257). While acknowledging that violence has not disappeared from the human landscape, Ong nevertheless draws a sharp distinction between what he considers the dominant approaches to problem solving in uniformly different societies: on one hand, the antagonist approach in oral culture and, on the other, the peaceful protest approach in literate culture. While some historians and sociologists might take issue with his broad claims, it can safely be argued that the violent confrontation of epic heroism has now been relegated to genre fiction like horror, fantasy, and thriller fiction and is often called escapist (thus identifying a clear difference between reality and the story depicted). In this way, the dominant sensibility of literacy negatively judges superhero stories as an adolescent power fantasy on the basis of "reality" as defined by literate culture — and yet the superhero story continues to grow in prominence. With this in mind, it becomes vitally important to show how this residue of oral culture not only persists but flourishes in superhero stories. In addition to examining the explanations for the dominance of superhero stories within the medium of comic books and the general popularity of the superhero, this chapter will use comic books' longest-lived superhero to exemplify the reemergence of the epic heroic tradition. This extended study of Superman over the years of his "life" will demonstrate how "the man of tomorrow" is also the hero of oral culture in the sense of primary orality. Employing Ong's description of the oral epic, this overview of Superman will demonstrate how the superhero story (1) creates heavy heroes within mythic and literal circumstances, (2) uses formulaic materials and recombines elements of previous stories, (3) repeats stories with subtle differences within plot points, and (4) employs common knowledge to develop the variants later seen as sacred stories. Also, this analysis will illustrate how the epic heroic characteristics persist even as Superman stories are told in the post–1980s era of comic books characterized by secondary orality; the strong sense Superman as epic hero seems to cause him to be less affected by any of the later era's literate age self-awareness. In addition, this chapter will demonstrate one of the most notable aspects of our new orality: the quick development of Superman from a rough-hewn folk hero to a refined epic hero (a development always presumed to take much longer in orthodox oral cultures).

To be thorough, it must be acknowledged that many other explanations have already been offered to identify the reasons why the superhero was and is a success, taking into account both the medium and the culture of the United States and the world.[2] With the potential to relegate comic books as a second-class, transitional medium, a popular explanation of the success of superhero comic books is that comics serve as a forerunner for the visual spectacle of film. Although William W. Savage, Jr., refers generally to the heroes of comic books in his version of this argument, Bradford Wright applies Savage's words exclusively to "costumed superheroes": "[Comic books] could show whatever the artist could draw, their lines and colors directing the imagination, their balloon-held texts defining time and space. Comic book artists and writers could produce that which could be conceived, which was more than the creators of motion pictures and radio programs could claim" (qtd. in Wright 14). Although Savage doesn't fully take into account the imaginative leaps needed to make iconographic art[3] realistic or to fill in the gaps between panels, he is wise to generally apply this description to comic book heroes; without Wright's application of the quotation, Savage's ideas would apply to science fiction or fantasy stories that also had fantastic elements. In addition, it would also apply to all other genres as any location or wardrobe could be drawn and thus potentially enhance the historical drama or even the romance.[4] In addition to seeming like common sense, it works to explain the success of comic book superheroes only in a very limited way. Another popular explanation of the success of superheroes lies in the idea that they satisfy increasingly widespread adolescent fantasies. According to Wright:

> While echoes of ... mid–twentieth century controversy resonate into the twenty-first century in debates over the link between violent images in popular culture and a rash of especially horrific juvenile crimes, the youth market has actually grown more expansive and influential — to the point where American culture itself has arguably become "juvenilized." The cultural history of comic books thus helps to trace the emergence, challenge, and triumph of adolescence as both a market and cultural obsession [xvi].

The basic premise and arc of the superhero story is often characterized as adolescent in the desire for amazing powers that defy the rules of the "real" world and in the fantasy of overpowering your enemies through your strength or guile. Likewise, in *The Mechanical Bride* (a work that predates *The Gutenberg Galaxy* by over a decade), Marshall McLuhan would interpret Superman in a similar way as a power fantasy, an expression of a youthful desire for the emotional satisfaction offered by the groupthink of totalitarian regimes: "The attitudes of Superman to current social problems likewise reflect the strong-arm totalitarian methods of the immature and barbaric mind" (*The Mechanical* 105).[5] However, these explanations (and arguments against the respectability of the superhero), which rely upon the "power fantasy" as an expression of a juvenilized and/or fascist culture, too conveniently ignore that very similar heroes exist in the long history of world mythology in oral epics.[6]

In many ways, the superhero does resemble the heroes in the stories of "barbaric" oral cultures, distinguished more by exaggerated characteristics and action than by extended introspection (as Ong notes, something much more difficult to memorize) (*Orality* 69). Their stories begin with some sort of violation of the self and culture that calls the hero to action and the often violent resolution reinstitutes cultural values. For Odysseus, those cultural values might be hospitality and rightful pride and for Superman, those values might be service and egalitarianism. Nevertheless, they occupy very similar moral universes that rhetorically pit the just position against the evil of the world and repeatedly identify the hero within the just position through the use of epithets. For Odysseus, those epithets might be "lion-hearted," "wily," or "favorite of Zeus" and for Superman, those epithets might be "the man of steel," "the man of tomorrow," or "faster than a speeding bullet"[7] (with Superman's epithets putting him in line with the futurist sensibility of an industrial age). As has been noted by Richard Reynolds and many others, the superpowers of superheroes are not a reliable means to identify the characters known as superheroes (although amazing powers do continue to put the superhero in line with the epic hero); one only has to consider the other prototype for all superheroes that almost immediately follows Superman in historical reckoning: Batman, a non-powered detective. However, the non-powered superheroes share with the powered superheroes certain characteristics, previously mentioned: seeking justice outside the law, experiencing an orphan status, wearing a disguise that leads to a dual identity. Both seeking justice and an orphan status can be seen prominently not only superhero comic books but also in the American pulps (often acknowledged as material and narrative predecessors of comic books) and in some radio and film productions:

> Superman and the superhero emerged at the end of the Great Depression and during the run-up to the outbreak of the European wars. Millions of Americans had experienced poverty and unemployment, millions more had had their faith in the notion of uninterrupted economic progress seriously undermined. Avenging "Lone Wolf" heroes abounded

in popular narrative of the 1930s and '40s on both sides of the Atlantic: From Doc Savage to Philip Marlowe, from Hannay in Hitchcock's *39 Steps* to the Green Hornet, from Rick Blaine in *Casablanca* to Captain Midnight of the radio serials [Reynolds 18].

However, seeking justice outside the law and experiencing an orphan status can also be seen in the longer history of American heroic mythology. Heroes ranging from Benjamin Franklin in his autobiography and Natty Bumpo in James Fennimore Cooper's "Leatherstocking Tales" are recognized as an almost essential outgrowth of the ideas central to American identity of natural law and revolution (that leave Americans without a "mother" country).[8]

Nevertheless, as satisfying as it might be for Americans to focus on these characteristics and make the superhero quintessentially American, these traits are also part of the standards of epic heroism and can be seen in the epic hero already mentioned: Odysseus. Hospitality, Zeus' gold standard for morality, is not enforced through the legal recourse taken by Odysseus' son before his departure to find his father; Odysseus not only relearns its value through his journey but also punishes the violators of this higher law upon his return to Ithaca. And while not a completely a literal orphan, Odysseus does lose his mother during and perhaps as a consequence of his journey and becomes estranged from the world around him for reasons just mentioned. In terms established by studies like Joseph Campbell's *Hero with a Thousand Faces*, the hero must always prove himself and to do so, must separate himself from his culture (a process by which one is willfully orphaned). Very similar things could be said about the epithets and themes of other epic heroes even when widely different cultures produce epic heroes such as Beowulf. (Beowulf, "the Geat," realizes a Christian imperative by working outside the false cultural ethic of personal revenge to save those unrelated to him; although known as "son of Ecgetheow," the presence of his father is only known through his father's pledge to Hrothgar.) This is not to deny the American values embodied within the stories of the superheroes as epic heroes always do embody the values of their culture (even though those values often seem on the verge of complete disappearance within the framework of the story). In many ways, this is the strength of this explanation of superheroes, as it does not deny previous explanations of the superhero based upon specific cultural values; if anything, the idea of the superhero as epic hero further asserts the validity of such explanations.

This leaves what may be the trait that many consider to be most distinctive in the overall characterization of the superhero: wearing the disguise that leads to a dual identity. After all, this duality within one's identity is emphasized and reinforced by a technical innovation readily associated with comic books: the word balloon and the thought balloon. Many consider it unlikely to be traced backward to a point not American or not part of the literate world. Like the other traits, the disguise and dual identity can be interpreted as something distinctly American and in this case, related even more particularly to the time of the superhero's inception in America. To some, the split represents the post–Depression era in which despair was felt but hope was desired, with the secret identity representing the reality of the common man (an ineffective Clark Kent) and the superhero representing the fantasy of the common man (a world-changing Superman). Wright articulates this idea very well in his historical analysis of Superman:

> From Depression-era popular culture, there came a passionate celebration of the common man. The idea that virtue resided within regular, unassuming Americans found expression ... [But] Superman's America was something of a paradox — a land where the virtue of the poor and weak towered over that of the wealthy and powerful. Yet the common man could

not expect to prevail on his own in this America, and neither could the progressive reformers who tried to fight for justice within the system. Only the righteous violence of Superman, it seemed could relieve deep social problems ... [10, 13].

However, the explanation could date back further and be tied to orphan status, with citizens of the revolutionary country known as the United States torn between the mother country and the new world. Or in a way that places the dual identity within a larger context, the split could represent the popularization of Sigmund Freud's notion of the split between conscious and unconscious: the dominant model of the mind in the early 20th century. Within the context of this study that finds superhero comic books so closely tied to orality in which form and content are inseparable, I again suggest that the Americanist reading of the superhero is too narrow (but not invalid). In addition, I will take what may seem an unexpected stand in limited favor of the second reading of the disguise and dual identity, not so much to affirm the reality of Freud's model of the mind in certain terms but to affirm the development of interior thought in literate culture. While this line of argument may seem to place the foremost trait of the superhero outside the confines of oral culture, it actually suggests that the superhero is an epic hero who works not only within an oral framework but also within a literate framework. The tension developed in the dual identity of the superhero is not the result of thinking about thought characteristic of psychoanalysis but rather the anxious desire to bring order to the world and self (to avoid the alienation from self Ong suggests is characteristic of literacy) (*Interfaces* 41–47)).

In his highly contested work, *The Origin of Consciousness in the Breakdown of the Bicameral Mind*, Julian Jaynes makes a speculative argument, suggesting the physical design of the primitive mind produced voices that were interpreted as the gods speaking. With the advent of writing, Jaynes argues that the "bicameral mind" begins to break down and reveal the voices as a component on one's self. Therefore, stories produced before the advent of writing contain remarkably unself-conscious characters and stories produced after contain notably self-conscious characters of which he considers Odysseus an exemplar. McLuhan would generally agree with this idea, with the theory that the Homeric man becomes a "split-man as he assumes an individualized ego" (carefully employing language specific to psychoanalysis (*The Gutenberg* 51). As Ong notes, bicamerality may just be another word for orality (*Orality* 30) and Jaynes's ideas bring up questions of the historicity of Homer's *Odyssey* that can never be fully answered.[9] Whether or not the construction of the character has anything to do with a change in the physical design of the brain as Jaynes states, it is worthwhile to think of Odysseus as a hero formed by the intersection of oral heroics with encroaching concerns of the literate world. To say that the superhero does the same acknowledges a minor intersection of orality and literacy in comic books, but it is also lines up the superhero more squarely with Odysseus; he is one of the most indelible of epic heroes and just happens to have a penchant for disguises that reveal essential parts of who he is or should be (most notably, the supposedly humble beggar at the end of the story). This "begs" the question of whether he is truly an epic hero of pure orality because he appeals to our literate sensibilities. However, I prefer to think of this situation with two complimentary ideas in mind: that oral culture doesn't lack all sense of self-consciousness and that the superhero is popular because it reawakens orality in all its complexity within a literate culture. When Ong cautions those who study orality and literacy to not be so schematic in the divisions between the two states, this could lead to the conclusion that the impulses toward literacy pre-dated the actual acts of writing. Nevertheless, as important as I consider this point, I do not wish to take it too far for several reasons: it has the potential to "break down" useful distinctions between the states of orality and literacy, and neither Odysseus or the Golden Age superheroes are truly self-conscious in the sense developed by psychoanalysis. Superman's early thoughts had very little to do with introspection and more to do with literal situations—even when those thoughts concerned his dual identity: "What a predicament!—I can't permit these thugs to get away with murder. Yet—if I act as Superman, I'll be forced to reveal my true identity" (Siegel, "The Machinations" 82). The disguises and role playing of these heroes merely serve as metaphors for self-consciousness and perhaps as an indicator of the things to come; in other words, they do not embody the conscious experience of modern man so much as the anxiety of heroes who straddle the worlds of orality and literacy.[10]

Regardless, at this point, it should be clear that the practices of the superhero comic book industry have created within that industry (and in turn, within the culture at large) characteristics more like that of primary orality. As has been argued in chapter 2, superhero comic books have been profoundly shaped by the practices of the industrial culture of the United States in the 20th century. From the factory driven division of labor (the comic book writer, penciler, inker, colorist, letterer, editor, etc.) to the public relations impetus of large corporations (branding superhero products with specific slogans), the basic aesthetics of superhero stories have grown from a shift in consciousness that accompanies the industrial world. The lawsuits designed to protect industry-owned properties of comic book companies would seem to limit the "ownership" that storytellers might have over superheroes and their stories. Yet, the regular rotation of creators on major superhero comic book titles and the large editorial boards that preside over those titles validate (at least superficially) the idea that everyone has a story to tell about every superhero. The ultimate intention of marketing superheroes is to reinforce and increase their popularity, the wide embrace of superheroes by popular consumer culture. We have inherited larger-than-life, mythic heroes who are larger-than-life and mythic because the culture has a sense of collective possession; not only do comic book artists and filmmakers have a story to tell about that superhero but so does everyone who has played with a superhero action figure, worn a superhero costume, or read superhero fanfiction. In this way, a larger awareness of cultural practice can show us how we move from cliché to archetype or as I suggest, from a pop culture hero to a cultural standard. Again, from a cultural studies standpoint, the idea of superheroes as the product of an oral culture society gives a more accurate way to evaluate their purpose and value.

The overview of the superhero as an epic hero should not be seen as a characterization that necessarily bolsters the archetypal psychology's approach to superhero comic book studies. Moreover, the previously mentioned attempt that is often made within that approach—to validate superheroes by connecting them to mythic heroes of past times—is highly ironic. To begin, this is not an incisive observation about the irresistible force of the collective unconscious on a new literary form; rudimentary research reveals that early superheroes were consciously based on mythical figures (Siegel and Shuster based Superman on Samson, Hercules, and many others;[11] Beck and Parker created the Superman look-a-like Captain Marvel, whose magic word "Shazam" indicated he was drawing his powers from Solomon, Hercules, Atlas, Zeus, Achilles, and Mercury; Marston identifies Wonder Woman as an Amazon, living in a world in which Greek gods exist). Moreover, even without these considerations,[12] recommending superheroes by using parallels to the "mythic characters" of oral cultures merely points out the problematic idea of validating popular folk art with popular folk art of the past (which has gained respectability only through the passage of time) (Zumthor 13).[13] To compound the ways that this claim is separate from the unconscious as a source of mythic archetypes, McLuhan argues that the unconscious is merely a representation of the interior thought developed in the literate world: "Since print allowed only a narrow segment of sense to dominate the other senses, the refugees had to discover another home for themselves.... The unconscious is a direct creation of print technology, the ever mounting slag-heap of rejected awareness" (*The Gutenberg* 245). While he overstates his case in a way in line with his sometimes excessive style,[14] McLuhan effectively demonstrates one of the problematic areas in the idea of the collective unconscious: the inability to prove that it has always existed. Within *From Cliché to Archetype*, he would further this argument with the suggestion that the rarified space between the cliché and archetype is merely the result of how the literate world chooses to respectively disapprove or approve of repetition. The realm of myth is in no way a pure space (like the collective unconscious) from which all great things proceed. In fact, the cooperative construction of comic book stories that become comic book myths (multiple titles with the same characters, superhero "team-ups," and crossover events) forces us to recognize that the superhero industry enacts the corporate situation of orality in several fundamental ways.

From the Golden Age to the Modern Age: Superman Lives in Our (Oral) Traditions

In *The Singer of Tales*, Albert B. Lord identifies a sense of corporate identity as central to the formation of oral tradition, heroic epics such as *The Odyssey* and *Beowulf*.[15] In order to develop this study of Superman as a prototype for superheroes, I will revisit Lord's most significant precepts in order to set up Ong's overview of the content of epic poetry. As previously mentioned, the oral tale exists in a fluid state without the sense of originality as identified by the literate world:

> It follows, then, that we cannot correctly speak of a "variant," since there is no "original" to be varied! Yet songs are related to one another in varying degrees; not, however, in relationship of variant to original, in spite of the recourse so often made to an erroneous concept of "oral transmission"; for "oral transmission," "oral composition," "oral creation," and "oral performance" are all one and the same thing. Our greatest error is to attempt to make "scientifically" rigid a phenomenon that is fluid [101].

In contrast to the literate world's devotion to original sources, oral culture does not prioritize the first appearance of a character and does little to discover the "real" story (excepting the sense that the recent and the relevant constitutes the real); in general, minor changes and even major revisions are not recognized but if brought to the attention of a singer are thought to be part of the song from the start, enhancing rather than distorting (105). In *Orality and Literacy*, Ong would also describe the fundamental shift from orality to literacy as a profound cultural transformation but would spend more time describing the psychological implications of this shift, contending that literacy brought about a different sort of cultural consciousness. He demonstrates that literate culture's devotion to originality is hardly the ultimate goal of oral culture as the concept of "originality" does not exist; really, only variation exists but with little or no conscious awareness that identifies the variation in stories. Working with the simple notion that the transmission of oral texts requires different expectations and aptitudes than the transmission of written (or more accurately in the 20th century, printed) texts, Ong outlines many characteristics of oral tradition from which I am selecting some as the most important (and also emphasizing because they are most appropriate to the topic of superhero revisionism). Consequently, most of the characteristics listed hereafter are content-based rather than mnemonic in order to relate most directly to the construction of superhero comics.

Oral culture has very little use for nonformulaic thought, and knowledge is accumulated only by adding to existing patterns. Oral culture is based on learning rather than studying, and orally transmitted material reinforces ideas but cannot be referenced. "[Oral cultures] learn by apprenticeship ... by listening, by repeating what they hear, by mastering proverbs and ways of combining and recombining them, by assimilating other formulary materials, by participation in a kind of corporate retrospection" (Ong, *Orality* 9). Consequently, stories developed in oral culture contexts tend to have a timeless quality (as they seem to apply to all of history) that exists alongside a timely immediate relevancy, addressing the needs of the current group (whether those needs are practical or moral). This use of formulae is somewhat exceptional in literate culture: "[Oral] poets simply maximize, in often exquisite ways, processes of thought and discourse endemic to the entire culture. The point here is simply that the elements figuring in the discourse are basically formulary to an extent radically greater than what highly literate cultures can ordinarily tolerate" (Ong, Interfaces 19). Further, oral culture tends to deemphasize the storyteller and emphasize the society that shares the story, emphasizing traditions and points of origin already in existence with rather "flat" heroes who play the "heavy" roles:[16] "Colorless personalities cannot survive oral mnemonics. To assure weight and memorability, heroic figures tend to be type figures .... The same mnemonic or poetic economy enforces itself still where oral settings persist in literate cultures, as in the telling of fairy stories to children" (69). With its stress on shared knowledge and tendency toward the formulaic, oral culture always knows the heroes' point of origin and therefore, finds it unnecessary to begin stories at the beginning.

Moreover, this mode of storytelling (the mode of the epic poet) creates fundamentally alternative notions of the idea of plot. As previously mentioned, episodic structure was the not only the natural way but also the only way of structuring a lengthy narrative, with the storyteller preferring flashbacks to tight linear structures: "Starting 'in the middle of things' is not a consciously contrived ploy but the original, natural, inevitable way to proceed for an oral poet approaching a lengthy narrative.... If we take the climactic linear plot as the paradigm of plot, the epic has no plot" (Ong, *Orality* 141). In addition, oral culture lives with the expectation that any one hero's story will continue beyond its current telling, and conventional closure that precludes future retellings is rarely seen "We must not forget that episodic structure was the natural way to talk out a lengthy story line if only because the experience of real life is more like a string of episodes than it is like a Freytag pyramid" (Ong, *Orality* 145). In *The Presence of the Word*, Ong argues that electronic media is a harbinger of a new openness (298–301) (and although he does not, I would certainly include comic books within a similar category, perhaps as a forerunner for his and McLuhan's sense of electronic media). Quite clearly, the standards identified by Ong are the tenets not only for epic poetry but also for the type of storytelling to which Siegel and Shuster would refer in their development of Superman. However, two things are important to reinforce at this point. First, unlike Siegel and Shuster who looked back at the ancient heroes with longing, Ong resists the temptation to romanticize orality. Instead, oral culture is simply a culture that is different from literate (post printing press) culture. And yet, while *Orality and Literacy* is still criticized in some of the same ways as *The Singer of Tales* (as too schematic), Ong implies much cross-pollination can take place between the conscious experience of literacy and the traditions of orality within contemporary culture: "[While] oral expression can exist and mostly has existed without any writing at all, writing [can] never without orality" (*Orality* 8). Second and more important, while Siegel and Shuster may have had personal inclinations that led them to love mythic figures such as Hercules, their microcosm of the comic book industry would intensify the tendencies of those inclined to think in terms of orality.

The references to Siegel and Shuster are meant to be quite pointed, as their development of Superman marks a unique moment in the history of comic book industry (and perhaps even in the history of new media industries in general). "It is difficult to overstate the importance of the character. Superman established the essential vocabulary of comic books. As Sheldon Meyer later explained, "'Jerry [Siegel] was way ahead of us on what was right for comics'" (qtd. In Wright 14). And since the relationship between superhero comic books and other superhero media is quite porous, an overview of Superman cannot be fully accomplished without also referring to the development of the character in other media. In addition, since contemporary society works in ways literate as well as oral, I can do something in my analysis that would be impossible within an entirely oral culture: retrace the story to its historical point of origin.[17] Nevertheless, the loss of widespread awareness of the names of Siegel and Shuster paired with the omnipresence of Superman prove the way in which orality dominates the elements inside and outside superhero stories, with original authors an incidental concern at best.[18] The effacement of workers in the field has much to do with inserting one's self into the industrial model of the superhero comic book industry and the mastery of clichés already in place. By working from models already in place, comic book writers and artists tended to think in terms of comic strips (or more directly, what they could communicate in the course of a few panels). They relied on formulaic ideas of comedy, action, and/or shock and depended heavily on regular readers who neither needed nor desired much context in order to understand a story beginning at a fever pitch of excitement. From the conventional print world, predecessors included pulp fiction such as "The Shadow" and "Captain Satan"; on the popular rise in the early 20th century because of their affordability, the dime novels used the genres of science fiction, fantasy, and mystery (supposedly low culture entertainment that contained heavy heroes like those of epic poetry). While comic writers and artists offered readers enough variety to keep them interested, the scope was fairly limited, based on the formulas the readers learned through exposure to standard genres in other mediums (Wright 2–3). However, the claim that superhero stories are limited in scope and derivative of other storytelling mediums may be made in reference to the early development of any medium; therefore, an extended look at Superman will help to clearly establish the way primary orality is present within the industry's epic stories (and continues to persist well beyond the early development of superhero comic books). Coming into this environment, Siegel and Shuster would develop several ideas for various publishers. One of their works for the pulps would be "The Reign of the Superman," in Siegel's self-published, generically titled *Science Fiction #3*, a story that seems to only tangentially relate to their greatest creation as "The Reign of the Superman" is much more an exploration of the Nietzschean Overman.[19] Working with a variation on the Frankenstein theme, the Superman of the title was Bill Dunn, a homeless man enhanced by the experiments of an amoral scientist. With unlimited mental power, Dunn encourages warfare between nations in order to further a plan for world domination (until the effects of the experiment unexpectedly dissipate). The story borrowed from tropes of science fiction and yet featured emblematic characters that worked like the flat characters of action-oriented epics. While this Superman had little in common with the famous incarnation of Superman that served as a cornerstone for the comic book industry, it demonstrates Siegel and Shuster's connection to the concerns of their time and place, depicting the desperation of the disenfranchised suddenly endowed with power. In addition, the story includes aspects of Superman's character initially only implicit within the comic book form, such as Superman's position as an outsider, an orphan who possessed power to violently represent the position of the outsider.[20] Perhaps most significantly, it posited that there was no place "beyond" morality for this Superman, a counter to the argument Nietzsche could only make in a post-orality environment; within oral culture, there would be no conceivable place beyond the standards set by the group.

As the years passed a few opportunities presented themselves as a platform for releasing what became for them their favorite creation (the superhuman savior whom they also dubbed Superman), Siegel and Shuster remained hesitant, hoping to release "Superman" as a strip — well aware of the tenuous staying power of most comic book publishers (Wright 3); this also demonstrated their conservative desire to work within the framework of the form firmly established within their culture, because of their sense of the strip's successful nature and their not consciously seeking to expand the form in revolutionary ways. After staying financially solvent with other comic book stories such as "Slam Bradley" and "Dr. Occult,"[21] the duo would release their first Superman story in 1938 in *Action Comics* # 1, published by National Comics (later named after their premier title, *Detective Comics*, as DC). After two earlier rejections of their story, Siegel and Shuster both felt that the venture with DC represented the best opportunity to see Superman in print (Daniels, *Superman* 31–35; Wright 8–9). They had been experimenting with variant panel sizes and arrangements to present their hero in the comic book medium, developing a certain virtuosity within very specific limits. However, to suit the expectations of their "first gate" audience, the story presented in that issue was a truncated version of the same story that would only appear as intended later in Superman's own title (Daniels, *Superman* 35). On one hand, this experimentation with the possibilities of the comic book form demonstrates Siegel and Shuster's work with formulae (not unlike that of the storyteller in oral cultures), their sense of allowable variation within the confines of a few pages of fixed size. On the other, the success of Superman would serve as a commentary on the psychology of comic book readers who recognized an epic story in *Action Comics* #1, despite the story being placed within a truncated format (as the story worked within the previously mentioned "vocabulary" of the comic book known well by the audience). Based on Greco-Roman heroes such as Hercules and with a secret identity like Zorro and an outfit like a circus strongman, Superman was a popular sensation, with many essential characteristics of the superhero thereby put in place. In Siegel and Shuster's first story, Superman takes a thug along for a run on a telephone wire in order to frighten the evil-doer: "Birds sit on telephone wires and they aren't electrocuted — not unless they touch a telephone pole and are *grounded*! Oops!— Almost touched that pole!" (Siegel, "Superman" 36–37). Superman's run comes to an end as he threatens to drop a thug from the capitol building, immediately thereafter jumping far above it (symbolizing his love of a justice beyond the scope of the law). The dual identity was established through the use of Superman's costume (that still functioned as a "disguise" even though Superman's face was fully exposed); the costume was garishly colored, in part because of the limited color palate, but the design and colors were broad stokes that, like an epithet, made Superman unforgettable. Further along these lines, it's important to note that Superman's identity as Clark Kent was a means to a narrative end rather than a character-driven mechanism that led toward introspection about the split nature of man in modern society. Even before he was hired as a reporter, Superman eavesdropped on the editor in order to uncover news about the local, national, and global threats he would address as Superman. In fact, after preventing a hanging at the county courthouse, an officer asks Superman (in costume) "Who *are* you?" to which Superman replies, "A reporter" (23).

It soon became apparent to Superman's creators that the Superman sensation would not disappear, and, therefore, their publisher's support and publication would continue. Over the next few months, they worked in opposition to the linear development demanded of the stories in literate culture; they presented variations of the same story (episodes that would only be part of linear development if the reader assumed it was); they consistently brought the story to climax in short order and maintained that fever pitch throughout, only much later to present a more complete origin story (with details about why Superman was rocketed from a dying planet called Krypton). In addition, the masculine orientation of this "power fantasy" would quickly take shape with Superman as a consistent savior for Lois Lane (the precocious reporter and damsel in distress) and Superman as a muscular vigilante who beat up slum landlords protected by the law of a corrupt American society. Somewhat at odds with a feminist viewpoint more readily expressed in late 20th-century America, this orientation again puts Superman in line with the epic hero. One of the most famous early encounters for Superman takes place with a wife-beater whom Superman catches in the act; after breaking a knife on Superman's impenetrable skin, Superman declares, "And now you're going to get a lesson you'll never forget!," upon which the man faints (30). With this in mind, mild-mannered Clark Kent, a reporter regularly scooped by Lane, could be described as the disguise for the much more "real" Superman, thus giving hope to other ordinary male readers who felt emasculated by the social forces that caused the Depression. In a sequence immediately following Superman's encounter with the wife-beater, Clark refuses to fight a bully trying to take advantage of Lois; this allows readers to be privy to the real, quite good reason (protecting his secret) for this perceived impotency of the common man. Superman stories were always repetition with a difference (like the stories of oral tradition) and the idea behind the approach was the idea behind most similarly marketed narratives: to maintain the core of this simple character and provide only enough difference to keep readers interested. However, consumers seemed more than willing to return to ground already covered (like an oral culture) and Superman's origin unintentionally grew beyond the details supplied in its initial presentations. As described from his point of introduction, Superman was a character not completely revealed in the course of one story line. While he contained some essential characteristics, such as his alien heritage and his super powers (including strength and invulnera-

Certain conventions are repeated in Superman stories such as when the strong-willed Lois Lane becomes the damsel and distress (yet again) (from *Superman* #123, p. 2).

bility), the mythos of Superman was extremely and intentionally flexible in the creators' estimation, subject to endless addition and revision. Parts of his origin, such as Krypton's destruction and his adoptive parents on earth, were later considered to be canonical within the superhero industry and yet were revealed nearly a year after Superman's debut (because of the cuts in the first Superman story); and the tragic story of Jor-L and Lara, Superman's parents on Krypton, was only depicted a year after that in the comic strip spawned by the comic book feature (Daniels, *Superman* 42). Since the initial Superman story in *Action Comics* #1 was truncated, it could be argued that this expansion of an earlier story was not an expansion at all. However, within the oral culture of the comic book industry, such questions would be irrelevant (as any sort of change nor growth is regularly considered part of the essential story and neither change or growth); whether or not truly intended from the start, Siegel would claim that the mythos was in place from the start (much like an oral poet would).

Regardless, much more significant than the attitudes of the creators was the industry practice that created and reinforced such attitudes. Just as Superman's sketchy but soon-to-be elaborate background can be attributed to DC's wait-and-see approach, Superman's continued existence in these terms (as an epic hero of oral culture) can be attributed to the company's ownership of Superman. As was standard practice in that day (and continues today with major publishers such as DC and Marvel), creators signed over the rights to their creation to their publishing company. With this framework in place, companies retained creators in order to continue to turn out their product, but the creators were treated more as wage laborers than as creators. Of course, there would be no need to treat them as privileged creators who could make fundamental changes to their creations because all of those privileges belonged to their companies. In line with standard business practice, the ultimate goal of DC was to protect their market, increase the appeal of their product, and to maximize profitability. A related goal for DC would be to establish brand identities for their various "products" like Superman (i.e., maintain a common recognition of their characters by instituting equilibrium rather than development). As mentioned in chapter 2, when Siegel and Shuster were first presenting Superman and his method of operations as a superhero, they developed a story in which Superman tore the wings from a plane and allowed the villains inside to plummet to their deaths (Wright 9–11). Concerned about the public image of their highly marketable icon, DC would intervene not to prevent the publication of that story but to prohibit further stories in which Superman directly and maliciously caused the loss of life. Even if the creators didn't feel the same way (and most often they did, submitting to the authority of the community), the company instituted a policy of conservatism inherent within the practice of oral tradition — ensuring that new ideas adhered to old. After all, DC was selling their superhero to others seeking to employ Superman's popularity to sell other products in cross-marketing campaigns and more importantly, to use him in other storytelling mediums.

The most obvious means of selling Superman would be to companies seeking to sell products such as lunchboxes by associating those lunchboxes with Superman. At times, these market-driven associations seem to fundamentally disconnect Superman from his story (such as Daisy's Krytpo-Raygun), but they also demonstrated that the sense of Superman overwhelmed even the faulty connections of bad "storytellers." Regardless, superheroes did not exist exclusively within the medium of comic books but rather existed in a simultaneous and codependent way in other forms of media also developed in the 20th century. Within the decade following Superman's first appearance in *Action Comics*, Superman also was incarnated in radio, film, and animation (Daniels, *Superman* 47–58), potentially facilitating a larger community organized differently than that of literate society. Radio and film demonstrated a more consistent diversity in genre throughout its early history than comic books (with animation perhaps being an exception more in line with comic books, thanks to being downgraded by cultural forces from folk art to kid's stuff). Nevertheless, all of the above mentioned mediums were quick to embrace the superhero; although it is far beyond the scope of my study to comment on the oral characteristics of other new media, at the very least, it can be said that practitioners within these mediums were anxious to work with the epic and the episodic; this is a contrast to writers of conventional literature who have very rarely told superhero stories.[22] But more important would be the license given to companies seeking to develop Superman in other storytelling mediums such as radio and animation, as these other stories of Superman often worked in a dynamic and interrelated way with the comic book stories. In this way, DC would unintentionally develop a situation that artificially required the practices of orality from the creators of Superman and the culture at large. In this way, Superman belonged less to his creators and more to the culture that was DC. And DC's culture included not only the comic book company but all those who bought a piece of Superman; this could be done by those who licensed Superman for a television series or more abstractly by those who bought a comic and then put on a Superman costume to act out Superman's adventures. Since the development of superhero comic books serves as a locus for the rebirth of oral culture in the 20th century (probably one among many others), I do not wish to stray too far from the medium; nevertheless, I do want to show how the practices of orality were superimposed upon or further activated within other new media that both Ong and McLuhan associated with the rise of a new type of orality.

Ong suggests that oral culture has very little use for nonformulaic thought, and knowledge is accumulated only by adding to existing patterns. And oral culture is based on learning rather than studying, and orally transmitted material reinforces ideas but cannot be referenced. Several basic tropes of superheroism were reinforced in Superman stories: Superman is the vigilante, the orphan, and the split personality. The types of additions and revisions that did not affect core ideals of Superman regularly took place — particularly, if those additions and revisions were made by other outlets to which Superman had been licensed; Perry White and Kryptonite were story elements created for the Superman radio show and are now essential parts of the regularly accepted Superman mythology (Daniels, *Superman* 50). And decades later, when Jack Kirby defected from Marvel and began working on *Jimmy Olsen: Adventures*, his distinctive artistic style was corrected by his inker to make Superman and Jimmy Olsen look more like the company's standard representations of themselves (Evanier, "Introduction" 4). However, his still distinctive renditions of Superman and Jimmy Olsen are now considered classic, and the "Fourth World" stories he developed at that time are now inseparable from current Superman adventures. The point is that additions and revisions are so readily incorporated in existing schemas that they are no longer recognized as revisions or even additions; this demonstrates the organic flow of change in oral culture, which subsumes innovations as always present and identifies the present as part of the past. Hence, the easily reinforced formula and general idea of Superman becomes more important than the realism of Superman's character development. Related to this ready reconfiguration, Ong also suggests that oral culture tends to deemphasize the storyteller and emphasize the society that shares the story, in particular emphasizing traditions and points of origin already in existence. In another pointed way that follows how Siegel and Shuster fit themselves to the expectations of comic book culture, Superman's mythos not only addressed his time of creation but also effectively hid the unique culture of his creators. Despite Siegel and Shuster's Jewish background, the Superman story would be increasingly read as that of a Christ-figure, sent from above, to modest parents, in order to save a fallen and embattled people.[23] Whether this was an intentional self-effacement of their Jewishness or an alternate reading by a largely Christian culture is unclear but again is somewhat irrelevant; the meaning in the flexible stories within an oral culture tradition always represents the recipient and the larger culture more than the "original" storyteller.[24]

With the past and present readily intermingled and the values representing the culture at large, the newest Superman story would always be classic and yet have a sense of immediacy by connecting with the culture of the time. Superman stories would continue to serve as a means to comment upon society's preoccupations, ranging from World War II politics to homefront gender roles. As in oral poems, mixing the fantastic elements of epic poems with the recognizable in the human lifeworld was a paramount concern. Therefore, when support for the World War II effort was increasing, Clark Kent went to enlist but accidentally used his x-ray vision and read the eye chart in the next room; as a consequence, he was rejected by the enlistment officer on the ground of his poor vision, and Superman took this rejection as an indication he was meant to stay in the United States and continue his homefront mission. Even though this provided a partial excuse to not depict Superman inevitably defeating Nazis with his incredible powers (and offending those following the progress of the real war), this also upheld the essential conservatism of superhero comic book storytelling practice, keeping the stories essentially similar. Nevertheless, Superman readers were aware that if this superhero who represented the American way lived in their world, the conflict with the Axis powers would have been different. In a famous two-page story from 1943, Siegel and Shuster acknowledged this perspective and entertained the question "What If Superman Ended the War?" This story portrays Superman not only defeating Hitler and the Axis powers but bringing Hitler *and Stalin* to a trial conducted by the League of Nations (with Superman on our side, the league would no doubt have been a success, and the cold war a minor event in world history). While this may seem to defy the oral dynamic of Superman stories that folds all relevant variants back into the larger story, this practice establishes an important understanding of Superman's epic story.

Published in *Look* magazine, far from any of Superman's regular publications, this story qualifies as a musing along the lines of an extended joke based on common knowledge such as: "Wouldn't it be funny if Odysseus had been eaten by the Cyclops?" Of course, jokes are always based upon the knowledge of what is real and the thing that is placed alongside it, the thing recognized as absurdly incongruous. Most Superman stories are set in a world that looks very much like that of the reader's world, but some are set in a world fundamentally altered by the presence of a superhuman with god-like powers — but this story is clearly identified as not part of the "real" story line continuity of Superman and his world (by the creators and the audience who quickly assert that that never would happen). This sense of certain Superman (or Odysseus) stories as real is ironic since Superman (or Odysseus) stories seem absurdly incongruous with our real world — that is, the real world without a real Superman (or Odysseus). "What If Superman Ended the War?" is clearly identified as a fanciful and imaginary story, with a note reassuring readers that this did not happen within the real world of Superman. By doing so, several points are acknowledged: Superman is real to his readers in much the same way that epic heroes are real to an oral culture as literal embodiments of a group's hopes and dreams. Literate culture and its representatives (in the form of certain cultural critics) would be quick to establish a line that relegates all Superman stories as fiction opposed to the reality of the real world. However, literate culture is able to do so because it can regard stories as separate from the self, as "far-gone" literates do not have to internalize the stories as part of their own subjective experience. Ultimately, despite the desire to see Superman in a world very much like that of the reader's world, Superman would fundamentally alter the world in which he'd live and this would threaten to change a story that cannot change (in order for the world to still see Superman in a world very much like that of the reader's world). Therefore, the Superman stories will always contain a tension that encourages the extended joke, the "imaginary" permutations. Perhaps a story that is a bit less pointed but significant nonetheless is "Lois Lane, Superwoman," a 1946 story that featured Lois with superpowers and a costume much like that of Superman (preceding stories featuring the similarly derivative Supergirl, cousin of Superman). In many ways from the start, Lois had contained the tensions concerning women's roles in the United States. On one hand, she is plucky and independent as the quick-witted reporter and on the other hand, needy and dependent as the perennial damsel in distress in love with Superman. After being magically endowed with superpowers, Lois found herself just as powerful as Superman but less capable (lacking the intelligence and skill needed to control her powers). In succinct fashion, the story acknowledges the changing nature of female identity with the advent of Rosie the Riveter and reasserts the masculine desire for traditional gender roles as men return from the service to the jobs women temporarily held.[25] In this way, Lois's identity is not only consistent with her previous representations but her super-powered adventure turns out to be just a dream, an imaginary story that reasserts the reality of the Superman story as it was.

Even though it's safe to say Siegel and Shuster never separated themselves from their awareness of the larger community of their audience, they did try to separate themselves from the business practices of the smaller community known as DC Comics. This was done after they became frustrated by having no rights to the large sums of money DC Comics made with Superman (and thus, their separation would be practical and legal rather than aesthetic or ideological). After about a decade of writing Superman stories and seeing DC comics grow increasingly wealthy from the company's ownership of their character, Siegel and Shuster would sue DC in 1947 in order to win back at least some of the rights to their creation; in addition, they would sue to recover the five million dollars they said Superman had earned for DC. Unable to force their way out of the fairly strict language of a contract that clearly favored the company, Siegel and Shuster not only lost their case but also damaged their working relationship with DC (Wright 60). Convinced that the creators of Superman were not essential to the continued success of Superman as a comic series or a marketable product, DC would give the character from Joe Shuster to Wayne Boring who produced the muscle-bound version of Superman with which most people are now more familiar than Joe Shuster's rendering—again the more recent version is the truer version. (Of course, as mentioned in the chapter 2, Boring was one of a team working under Shuster, and thus his style would largely build on previous representations of Superman.) In 1948's "The Origin of Superman," Superman's origin would be retold, further expanding existing elements within the mythology (with the origin as a continuing point of obsession with all comic book characters, emphasized and reinterpreted but still retaining basic plot points). Weaving together various details of the origin story presented separately but which all influenced Superman as a whole, the origin was updated in a move characteristic of oral culture. Although Superman had become increasingly powerful throughout the years (not only stronger but now endowed with heat vision, x-ray vision, and the power to fly), the war years made him less of a vigilante and more of a patriot. The newly retold origin reinforced the tragic loss of his biological parents and his adopted parents more than the split between public and secret identities and much more than justice above the law. On his deathbed, Pa Kent states:

> There are evil men in this world.... Criminals and outlaws who prey on decent folk! You must fight them ... in cooperation with the law! To fight those criminals best, you must hide your true identity! They must never know that Clark Kent is a ... Superman! Remember because that's what you are ... a Superman! [Finger, "The Origin of Superman" 66].

The willingness of the public to accept this revision of the origin story with new emphasis given to some of the story's tropes over others suggests that DC's notion of the inconsequential nature of the creator was largely correct. While it's certain that editor Mort Weisinger initiated this retelling, it was unclear for some time who authored this story; although eventually credited to Bill Finger, it may actually have been (and probably was) a cooperative effort with a major property like Superman. The loss of the author reinforces the oral culture characteristics of the comic book industry. Within this context, not only did knowledge of the creators themselves become inconsequential but also did an awareness of their original intentions for Superman.

The Imaginary Becomes Real Again: Variation and the Very Conservative Dynamic of the Superman Story

In the early 1950s, the cultural anxieties that came to bear on the comic book industry were something that was born of concerns of the literate world about the oral culture; however, it also ensured that the comic book industry would more clearly carry on as an oral culture. As comic book material began to diversify further, superheroes were losing their market dominance (although Superman was one of the few superheroes who did maintain his popularity in several on-going titles). As EC horror comics became more popular, the comic book industry would move in other directions but ironically return to the emphasis on the superhero thanks to the influence of psychologist Fredric Wertham and his 1954 book, *Seduction of the Innocent* (Wright 157–161). Wertham would identify comics as a medium designed for the attention span of the adolescent (a dubious claim at best) that nevertheless contained material grossly inappropriate for the adolescent in the form of crime and horror comic books. While his emphasis was on graphic depictions of violence in crime and horror comics, he also suggested that Batman comics contained homosexual suggestiveness through the relationship between Bruce Wayne and his ward Dick Grayson. Developing a simplistic cause (comic books) and effect (adolescent delinquency) argument, Wertham's book had several unintended consequences. By arguing for the pervasive impact of comic books on behavior, he validated the cultural influence of the comic book industry as an institution (even though in his argument the institution was an evil empire). By taking his case to the public, he participated in the subsequent generation of new and supposedly moral stories and thereby, encouraged a certain kind of growth in the industry (not just marginalization and decline as some might suggest). One of the results of congressional hearings concerning comic books would be the industry's self-regulation in the form of the Comics Code (Duncan 39–40; Wright 88–98). These regulations seemed to concede to Wertham's claim that comic books were for adolescents and this was a problematic concession at best. However, it guaranteed that for the immediate future that comic books would remain subcultural and allowed the oral tendencies of the superhero story to continue in the midst of a literate culture. While eliminating graphic violence and sexual suggestiveness from comic books may have made Batman's male bonding with Robin seem more gay than before, the comic code was nevertheless applied more easily to the superhero story than to the horror genre. With Superman, story lines about the fantastic were encouraged as were story lines in which humor predominates. Again, this emphasis was not new to Superman and was considered essential as Superman grew increasingly powerful (there seeming to be less drama in violent confrontation) (Daniels, *Superman* 67–68). Covers featured various humorous comments or situations (such as Superman struck by lightning and saying "It tickles," a barber breaking a giant scissors on Superman's hair, and Chinese citizens surprised as Superman emerges from the ground after presumably digging to China). The perennial comic villain of Superman stories was the magical Mr. Mxyztplk whom Superman could only defeat by convincing Mr. Mxyztplk to say his own name backwards. In the Comics Code era, such humor made its way to the forefront of Superman stories and remained a very significant part of the idea of Superman during that era.

Even more significant than the emphasis on humor in the Comics Code era would be the larger presence of imaginary stories, thought to be fairly harmless, as they explored outlandish possibilities and had no consequence within the real world of Superman. As is the case in most oral cultures, stories of the past organically interact with stories of the present (seen in the on-going conceit of the superhero genre in which the superhero remains as young as when first introduced 40, 50, 60 years ago).[26] This framework should be applied to stories of the imaginary present or possible future. Exploring the ways in which the world would be altered with Superman in its midst, these imaginary stories took Superman's mythology very seriously and made particular conceptual demands upon the reader in order to enable their full appreciation. During Curt Swan's tenure as artist in the 1960s,[27] stories were written such as "The Death of Superman" and "The Amazing Story of Superman-Red and Superman-Blue." In "The Death of Superman," Jerry Siegel takes the time to further emphasize Lex Luthor, Superman's arch-nemesis. After obtaining certain privileges and work releases in prison, Luthor develops a cure for cancer. Eventually released from prison for his humanitarian efforts, he cuts ties with the criminal world and gains Superman's trust. Luthor then reveals these acts to all be part of a grand plan that allows him to not only kill Superman but also to enjoy the sadistic pleasure of watching Superman's loved ones see him linger. While Luthor is punished in the end, the world is notably vacant without Superman. Moreover, the story explores the potential influence of Superman on the world for good but also for evil, with his presence pushing a genius to focus exclusively on his destruction; in this case, great power invites great power to rise up as its rival. In the Superman-Red and Superman-Blue stories, Superman works to eliminate his vulnerability to Kryptonite, and, with a comic book pseudo-science explanation, his experiment divides him into two hyper-intelligent Supermen (one with a red costume and the other with a blue). Implementing Superman lore developed over many years, red Kryptonite (which had previously created an evil Superman) now interacted with other Kryptonite to this end. Subsequently, the split in Superman's identity was reworked as the Supermen abandoned their Clark Kent personas with one marrying Lois Lane and the other Lana Lang. With their hyper-intelligence, they created a utopia and eliminated the need for the old order of Superman who took violent action to save the world whenever the world's laws failed; even Lex Luthor began to live a productive life, developing a super-serum to cure all diseases (and baldness too). Both stories require a certain level of previous knowledge of the con-

The first of many "death of Superman" stories that are either imaginary or temporary but clearly popular and somehow resonant with fans (from *Superman* #149, p. 10).

ventions central to Superman, ranging from the specific psychology of Lex Luthor and the superhero power fantasy to the fundamental tropes of the superhero story, such as the split identity and justice found beyond the law. And both stories develop a playful and interactive way to investigate and question the basis for those conventions.

Various possible future histories of Superman would be created within various Modern Age stories, like Frank Miller's *Dark Knight Returns* (with Superman as a sell-out to a paternalistic and jingoistic USA) and Mark Waid's *Kingdom Come* (in which Superman rejects the UN and the earth in general because of their moral relativism and shabby treatment of superheroes). Again drawing upon the precedent of the "imaginary" stories of Superman, these series explored the implications of Superman's existence within the world in convincing ways and were identified as adult superhero stories. While this "adult" label may in some ways be accurate regarding the controversial content and complex themes, these stories ultimately cover ground similar to that of stories that preceded them. Therefore, the landmark status usually associated with these works becomes debatable. Incidentally, it should also be acknowledged that "landmarks" in storytelling history is a convention of literate culture. Moving across all Superman titles, the "Death of Superman" in the 1990s story line was regarded as a stunt by some and part of what drove the collectors' bubble to a point of bursting; after all, Superman really wasn't dead, and the story felt like a bit of a cheat. However, it was also an extension of the Superman mythology in its Christ-like readings. Even though harkening back to the 1961 "Death of Superman" story, the new "Death of Superman" story line would not be "imaginary." Coordinated between all of the Superman titles (with five writers, five pencilers, six inkers, and two colorists), Superman faced the muscle-bound monster dubbed Doomsday and only saved the world at the cost of his own life — or so it seemed (as the dead never stay dead in comics because their stories need to be told and retold). In the "World without a Superman" segment of the story line, the tomb that contained Superman was visited by a cult that believed he would rise again, and, not surprisingly, the tomb was found to be empty. In the time before Superman's resurrection, false or misguided saviors rose to take his place in a segment titled "The Reign of the Supermen" (a reference to the pulp story written by Siegel predating the creation of Superman).[28] With Bruce Timm's 2007 animated film, *Superman: Doomsday*, the story has been retold and streamlined in some ways by amplifying major characters such as Lex Luthor but more importantly, developed into a "classic" component of Superman's mythos to be revisited and revised.[29]

Ong suggests that oral culture always knows the heroes' point of origin and therefore, finds it unnecessary to begin stories at the beginning. However, the episodic structure of the epic encourages a continual return to that point of origin, presenting greater detail with that return. This is due to the fact that oral culture lives with the expectation that any one hero's story will continue beyond its current telling, and conventional closure that precludes future retellings is rarely seen. In part, because of the widespread exposure of the George Reeves television incarnation of Superman in the 1950s (although it would be best to regard the show as part of the incremental commercial process that represents Superman), the mythos of Superman (such as "truth, justice, the American way") would become part of the common knowledge of Superman's identity of America. From the simple special effects of the serial, the whistling of wind would forever be associated with what seemed at the time to be the "realistic" flight of Superman. More notable would be the lasting association of George Reeves with Superman; many people were shocked upon news of his suicide, not believing Superman could die.[30] Even today his image as Superman endures with people even though they have little conscious awareness of George Reeves as Superman. Alex Ross, the hyper-realistic Norman Rockwell of contemporary comic book illustration, paints Superman in a barrel-chested way clearly derived from George Reeves, and those renditions of Superman occupy high profile releases, such as the recent DC coffee-table book, *Mythology*. If not sooner, at least after George Reeves, the public at large responded enthusiastically to not only the continuing adventures of Superman but also the continued retelling of Superman's origin with more nuanced changes made for dramatic effect. As the number of comic book titles featuring Superman increased, more writers contributed to the Superman comics and various imaginative ideas were explored within the "real" world of Superman (what was regarded as "canonical" by official writers of Superman titles). For instance, the Superman family would be expanded with other survivors of Krypton such as Supergirl, Superdog, Supercat, and so on. A chief editor's position became essential, as it was necessary to keep Superman's stories consistent and in line with the company's vision of Superman. However, the editor could never completely contain the variations that developed because of the personal styles of different writers and artists. In 1978, again within a medium influenced by the corporate models of the 20th century, a virtual cooperative of writers[31] would develop a film in which Superman learned as a young man to be an outsider by hiding his power, and, consequently, he longed to be an ordinary human being. Particularly notable in this emphasis of split identity is Christopher Reeve's portrayal of Clark Kent, a caricature of weak humankind so extreme that no one would ever think him to be Superman. Scenes of the planet Krypton emphasize the many ways Superman's homeworld is unlike earth and introduces the shield on Superman's costume as not an "S" but the family crest of his long-dead biological father.³² And ultimately, the real enemy is not Lex Luthor, played in the film for buffoonish comic relief, but Clark's role as Superman. Superman's responsibility to save the world indirectly allows the death of Lois Lane, and the only way to save her is by defying nature and reversing time itself. Greeted with disdain at the time and ever since for its deus ex machina, this specific aspect of the story has not been reinforced to the same degree as all the other emphases in the film (although defying nature and playing with time in general is part of Superman's standard operations).

As noted in previous chapters, the growth in the adult readership and general respect of superhero comic books in the 1980s would initiate a change in superhero storytelling within the DC superhero universe destined never to completely take hold. DC company executives began thinking in a way they believed was more like fans obsessed with continuity, believing that the standards of storytelling within literature culture should be applied to comic books: round characters, linear plot structure, logic, and originality. As a consequence, DC developed the *Crisis on Infinite Earths* miniseries that gathered all of the superheroes in the DC universe together to fight against a force destroying all the variant earths created in nearly 50 years of superhero comic book publication. While perhaps the best of the super team-up miniseries from the 1980s, the series was flawed in that it was driven by an ulterior motive (cleaning up superhero mythologies) and that it fundamentally misunderstood the playful oral culture that is superhero comic books; identifying the failure of the series to bring superhero stories in line with the conventions of literate culture is more proof that those stories never were part of literate culture in any particular way.³³ In general, the premise of the series was flawed; the crisis would enable the origins of all major superheroes in the DC universe to be retold within the context of the 1980s and all things would then proceed from that point. And yet now, decades after the crisis, we are still dealing with superheroes who seemingly haven't aged a day. Moreover, characters are often written with reference to Golden and Silver Age selves that, according to the crisis, never existed. In fact, DC has allowed writers to bring back characters who died during the crisis in contradiction with the new mandate of "realism" and logic within the DC universe. (Much more will be discussed in chapter 6, wherein I cover the philosophical need for a "multiverse" within an oral culture framework.)

In specific reference to Superman, the "final" Superman story that preceded the crisis is regularly hailed as one of the greatest: Alan Moore's "Whatever Happened to the Man of Tomorrow." Making extensive reference to the elaborate mythology of Superman, Moore plays with expectations that could be shaped only by an oral culture's rich knowledge of the specific conventions of Superman; Superman shares a wrenching scene with Superdog, the silly Mr. Mxyztplk becomes the ultimate threat, and Superman intentionally robs himself of his powers by exposing himself to *gold* Kryptonite. This last Superman story would soon be considered imaginary or noncanonical by the presentation of the "new" origin story from John Byrne (and by that line of reasoning, all of Superman's history that preceded the crisis revamp should be understood as imaginary). In essence, DC gave Byrne the license to further the insignificance of storytellers who had preceded him. In Byrne's *The Man of Steel*, the post-crisis revision of the Superman mythology, Superman's powers would initially be lessened, Lex Luthor would be a corrupt businessman and politician, and the Superman "family" would be nonexistent. Ironically but not surprisingly, elements of the Superhero mythology were quickly revisited; the partnership with Batman, the Frankenstein-type other Superman (Bizarro), and Luthor's green and purple costume/exoskeleton were all part of *The Man of Steel* miniseries and soon thereafter John Byrne brought most familiar elements back to the three on-going Superman titles (including Mr. Mxyztplk and the various colors of Kryptonite). Byrne was allowed this creative retcon of Superman because he had revitalized many of the Marvel comic book series featuring "classic" Marvel characters, such as the Hulk and the Fantastic Four; however, his approach in revitalizing these had been to retool the series with what had worked well in the past for these classic characters (like most participating in the culture of the superhero comic book industry). No more likely to relegate past ideas of Superman to obsolescence than most in the industry, Byrne worked effectively as a creator participating in the epic process that shaped Superman up to that point.

In a seeming response to the television series *Lois and Clark* where Lois became well aware of Clark's other life (beginning in 1993), Lois and Clark were married within the comic book world (1996), demonstrating the continuing dynamic and organic relationship between superhero stories in various forms of media. In addition, Clark would marry Lois when Superman lost his powers (an echo of the film, *Superman II* in which Clark revealed himself as Superman and gave up his powers as Superman to live a "normal" life with her); this common link could be seen as a self-conscious homage but should also be understood as a thematic preoccupation in the Superman story concerning the masculine anxiety about domestication. This idea of domestic life has been played with in different ways, in various stories, with Superman as a father (most notably in *Superman Returns*) and with a married and super-powerless Superman avoiding his wife and pursuing Lex Luthor as Clark Kent, star reporter (in Kurt Busiek's *Up, Up, and Away*). The typical adherence to real world history has changed in recent years, with comic book story lines like the long-term tenure of "President Lex," but, again, Lex Luthor eventually reveals his power-mad self and loses his presidency. (And if willing to think beyond the "real" in a post–Enlightenment sense, the President Lex story line has been described by some as a real-world commentary on the Bush presidency.)

As becomes the case in most oral cultures, knowledge of the variations of the story is just as important as knowledge of an authoritative text. The most recent retelling of Superman's origins have been published as miniseries and are therefore separate from the regular "continuity" of the ongoing series; however, they are also often (ironically) identified as authoritative and centrally important to the continued survival of Superman stories, which must be as contemporary as they are classic. In Jeph Loeb's *A Superman for All Seasons*, the origin is told in four chapters, in rough sequential order, but from the perspectives of four central figures in Superman's life: Pa Kent, Lois Lane, Lex Luthor, and Lana Lang. Based primarily upon his connection to his Kansas farm-boy roots, Superman becomes more iconic as the quintessential American, the alien adopted by a foreign land and made strong through heartland values.[34] Consequently, despite the trappings of the modern world, such as the modern technology and attitudes of Metropolis, this rendition of Superman is terribly nostalgic, with his hometown of Smallville as the land that time seemingly forgot to update after 1938.[35] Another one of Superman's origin stories is Mark Waid's *Birthright*, in which Superman's origins are explored in a two-fold fashion. Within a story that again uses the Kents as a consistent reference point (and interestingly creates a closer bond between Clark and Ma Kent than Clark and Pa Kent), the loss of his birth parents is centrally haunting to Clark. While he is aware of his extraterrestrial origins (as in the Superman films), he has no practical means at his disposal to retrieve his heritage; he has a holographic book of Kryptonian history in a language he cannot understand. This loss of parentage is traumatic not only for him but also for those around him: his mother constantly searches the internet for descriptions of UFO sightings, and Lex Luthor uses his discovery of Superman's alien

The future of Superman (in *Kingdom Come*) looks like his past (in *Adventures of Superman*); Alex Ross's Superman bears much more than a passing resemblance to George Reeves (from *Kingdom Come*, p. 54).

origin to turn Metropolis against Superman. Featuring a Luthor not older than Clark (as is traditional within the Superman stories), Luthor does not serve as an evil Oedipal figure but a fatherless outsider like Clark.[36] In a commentary on the symbiotic relationship between the superhero and supervillain dealt with consistently in the Superman comic books, Luthor's evil quest to contact Krypton in the past results in Superman sending a message to his parents, giving Superman a fuller sense of himself.[37] The circularity of history is a pronounced idea within contemporary superhero epics and almost explicitly develops the idea that the canonical present informs variations in the "past" or "future" of superheroes. For instance, *The New Frontier* takes the grim and gritty paranoia of Superman's world in stories such as *The Dark Knight Returns* and applies it to a story of Superman and the Justice League set in the McCarthy era of the 1950s. Conversely, *Kingdom Come* charts a possible future for the DC universe overrun by nihilistic superheroes flourishing in the 1990s but finds its central ideas in the redemptive power of a stalwart Superman based upon the vision of George Reeves as the excessively honorable Superman.

With this in mind, the continuation of the Superman stories in this fashion after the collectors' bubble burst is particularly interesting. After the dramatic fall of comic book sales in the later 1990s, one of the arguments set forth in industry analysis has been that superhero stories have become increasingly self-reflexive, written for fanboys devoted to obscure inside jokes (Putz 141–143). While that may seem to be true, particularly in the case of other publishers (with Wildstorm's *The Authority* featuring the Superman look-alike as a gay partner to the Batman look-alike), DC has successfully created worldwide awareness of Superman in the form of his mythology in all its permutations.[38] The mythology of Superman has continued to grow and demonstrates the additive nature of oral tradition that contributes to the myth in a way that is simultaneously progressive and reactionary. This intense awareness of central motifs within the epics of Superman is not necessarily an insular movement (known only to detail-obsessed fanboys), as the epics always contain themes but not details known by the culture at large. Regardless, the details grow from the themes and seem familiar: again, recognizable as the tropes of superheroism even if they've never been previously encountered. "[Some] themes have a tendency to cling together, held by a kind of tension, and to form recurrent patterns of groups of themes" (Lord, *The Singer of Tales* 112).[39] Lord suggests that oral stories not only develop meaning through the story's growth over time but also contain meaning not apparent through a single telling of the story. His reference to Homer as the ultimate "singer of tales" is made in order to demonstrate how Homer worked with previous material to create stories expansive and mythic by discovering the expansiveness and mythical already within the stories. Perhaps more to the point of the self-consciousness and self-reflexiveness of the supposedly postmodern superhero story is McLuhan's claim that the Homeric hero is the split man.

> The hero has become a split man as he moves toward the possession of an individual ego ... that is to say, detribalization, individualization, and pictorialization are all one. The magical mode disappears in proportion as interior events are made visually manifest. But such manifestation is also reduction and distortion of complex relations which are more fully sensed when there is full interplay of all the senses at once [*The Gutenberg* 51].

Clearly, McLuhan sees Homer more as a stepping-stone toward literacy than Lord does. Regardless of those differences, McLuhan highlights a facet of the Homeric hero very applicable to the contemporary superhero, whose story exists as oral (or at least, secondarily oral) within a literate culture. He points out the inherent complexity of assembling discordant stories about one figure into a coherent mythology that accounts for the past but also paves a clear way for a self-contained story of the present. In *From Cliché to Archetype*, McLuhan would contend the cliché is incompatible with other clichés but the archetype (the supposedly unconscious residue of myth) opens up the storytelling field: "[The] archetype is extremely cohesive; other archetypes' residues adhere to it. When we consciously set out to retrieve one archetype, we unconsciously retrieve others; and this retrieval occurs in infinite regress" (McLuhan and Watson 21). When applied to the above examples of "All Seasons" and "Birthright," this could be seen as an argument that the oral complexity of these texts as a newfound phenomenon appeals only to the increasingly insular superhero comic book reading community. However, the multimedia phenomenon that is Superman continues to suggest otherwise, as the storytelling community becomes more aware of its own practices.

As previously mentioned, a more recent Superman film, *Superman Returns*, in 2006, requires knowledge of the first two Superman films (released in the 1978 and 1980) and a willful ignorance of *Superman III* and *Superman IV* (released in 1983 and 1987) to make complete sense, putting it in line with the flexibility of stories presented in oral cultures. Within *Superman Returns*, Superman has journeyed to the ruins of Krypton and returned to earth, six years after his romance with Lois Lane and his battle with General Zod; Superman finds Lois the single mother of a five-year-old son, and Lex Luthor once again hatching evil plans. In some ways, this device can be read as an extremely hackneyed attempt to preserve a comic book story for the sake of sequels that repeat material rather than develop new material.[40] At the same time, this device can be read as unintentionally allusive to the willful forgetfulness that takes place within oral culture (that the same story may be retold with some variation, resulting in a reliable sense of pleasure in its recipients).[41] This willful discounting of film continuity is much more characteristic of a media age in which the media recipient has the ability to shape stories as he or she sees fit. According to McLuhan, the advent of typography results in the general regard of stories as commodities to be consumed (*The Gutenberg* 161). This represents a clear difference as a member of an oral culture would never accept a role as a passive consumer (38). In addition to Paul Zumthor's claim that the oral story's participants are required to participate at many levels (183–184), Ong claims that oral stories are constructed in order to facilitate recall and enable the recipient as a storyteller (*Orality* 36). With superhero comic books, this selection was often part of the early tradition of trading comic books (the selection of favorite bits of superhero histories) before the practice was largely lost because of literate culture's notion of comic books as collectibles. But with postmodern culture becoming increasingly devoted to the selective storytelling practices of fanfiction (an outgrowth of the highly interactive letters page featured in most comics),[42] it seems the secondary orality of the electronic age will only complement the primary oral characteristics established by the superhero comic book industry. Within oral culture situations, there is a much less clear-cut distinction between fact and fiction, between life and story. One last comic book example will reinforce this point, drawn from an author who seems to recognize this idea at least at an unconscious but more likely on a conscious level). In *Secret Identity*, Kurt Busiek works from an idea established as part of the *Crisis on Infinite Earths* story line. In *DC Comics Presents*, Elliot S. Maggin would present one of the last stories of Earth-Prime (a world without superheroes, supposedly "our" world). A young boy named Clark Kent grew up hating his name because everyone teased him, identifying him as the nerd who really was Superman. Amazingly, during his high school years, he discovered that he had the powers of Superman and consequently, he did the only thing that seemed logical to him: he put on a Superman costume and fought crime. He would then participate in the crisis battle until the universe-eating force consumed his planet and him along with it.[43] Ironically, the series that was to "clean up" the DC universe produced a story of a planet's destruction that Kurt Busiek retells and expands in 2004 (minus the destruction of the planet). Regardless, what is most important is the concept behind the story that is completely in line with oral culture's precept that life shapes story and story shapes reality. The Clark Kent of Earth-Prime becomes Superman because Superman's name is Clark Kent; the character in the story works as a reader who chooses his story.

In a literate age of intellectual property, the creators' rights movement, instituted in the comic world by figures such as Dave Sim and Scott McCloud, has gained significant ground. Artists have insisted on ownership of their creations and have been accommodated more often than before by the big two comic book publishers. This has often been credited to a supposedly new and growing recognition that the creator is as important as the creation.[44] While this may seem to indicate a shift away from the orality I have described, two tangentially related examples provide reason to think this is unlikely to ever take place fully at the corporate or individual level within the media world of superheroes. Firstly, during the boom of the 1990s, the major challenge to the reign of the big two came in the form of Image and Wildstorm Comics, designed respectively by the extremely popular artists Todd McFarlane and Jim Lee; these new comic groups promised writers and artists complete ownership of their material. Leading with McFarlane's flagship title, *Spawn*, Image quickly realized direct market sales of its title that rivaled those of DC and Marvel. However, the idea of creators' rights became more complicated as artists argued over what part of the creation they owned within the industrial model that in some cases still included a division of labor. This problem reached its height after Neil Gaiman wrote an issue of *Spawn* that was drawn by McFarlane and introduced two new and subsequently popular characters: Medieval Spawn and Angela. When McFarlane marketed action figures based on these characters,[45] Gaiman brought suit against Image Comics for violating his rights as a creator. Despite the idealism that propelled the inception of the company, the popularity of characters had a life of its own and the profit potential of the characters reshaped the attitudes of the company's architects. While this case isn't necessarily descriptive of all corporate situations, it is highly representative of the turn most companies will take while publishing stories that walk the line between art and commodity. Incidentally, in the court case that ensued, McFarlane offered Gaiman ownership of *Marvelman* as part of his settlement. McFarlane had tried to acquire the British series written by Alan Moore and then by Gaiman (the series was known as *Miracleman* in the United States, because DC owned the rights to Captain Marvel and the Marvel family). Adding to McFarlane's attempt to acquire the creations of other artists (such as Gaiman) for the sake of profit, this serves as an interesting extension of Superman's revisionism: Marvelman was Great Britain's variation on Captain Marvel who is arguably a variation Superman. In addition, the section in Marvelman's history that McFarlane tried to acquire is Moore's 1980s reworking of Marvelman, considered to be a radical conceptual leap forward in the Modern Age of superheroes; it provides a glimpse of how the world would be fundamentally changed if a Superman lived in our midst. Gaiman wisely rejected McFarlane's offer, as McFarlane's claim to ownership was highly dubious ("Gaiman, Neil v. McFarlane, Todd"). In the end, this serves to demonstrate how hard it is to separate a corporate creation from corporate culture (greedy capitalists or others) and how hard it is to identify a discrete starting point for the origin point of any corporate creation.

Secondly, setting aside the psychology of the contemporary corporation, in this Modern Age of comic books in which artists have taken superheroes to their logical extremes, the likelihood of artists committed to this new vision of superheroes returning to tropes of the past would seem very unlikely. Nevertheless, major shapers of the contemporary comic book scene, Warren Ellis and Mark Millar, have done just that (demonstrating the way that the producers of superhero media are drawn to revisionism). Well known in the adult superhero comic book market as the first two writers to work on the previously mentioned series *The Authority*, Ellis and Millar crafted stories of superheroes who do not blithely accept the mandates of leaders of their country. In many ways a commentary on a Superman who too readily associated truth and justice with American leaders, the Authority recognizes that their superpowers place them in a realm far beyond the dictates of ordinary human beings and they seek to remake the world as they see fit. As mentioned earlier, a member of this superteam, Apollo, is intentionally similar to Superman in significant ways; however, he is gay and takes Superman far from the family values of American conservatism. However, while the series pushes conceptual boundaries of superhero stories (featuring a overman-themed story in which the Authority literally kills God), it also loves its own concept and superhero tropes in general. In "Transfer of Power," when new, less moral, and less capable superheroes displace the Authority, the stage is set for the triumphant return of the Authority and the restoration of what was once the new but now is the traditional order. In other words, the story line revises itself in ways that also incorporate typical Superman-type ideas the story line seemed to forsake. Subsequently, both Ellis and Millar have written for Marvels "Ultimate" line which seeks to retell the stories of classic superheroes from the start, and Millar has written for DC's "Elseworlds," which presents variations of classic superhero stories outside the boundaries of the mainstream DC universe continuity (thus allowing them to do something new and old simultaneously, as would be suggested by oral culture of the medium).[46]

I believe this oral culture framework could be used to describe the evolution of other superheroes throughout the 20th century and into the 21st in much more detail. With the dynamic relationship between the storyteller and story established as part of an oral culture framework, storytellers should be recognized as bringing many different elements to their stories that represent themselves and their cultural context and therefore necessitate a variety of different modes of analysis to properly describe the superhero story and how it transforms the act of reading. An important consideration for continuing this discussion is how we can move beyond orality as a term limited to the discussion of oral performance, live or recorded, and recognize the conventions of orality as a more pervasive aspect of traditional storytelling. Thus far, it has been retained so that I can connect with earlier pertinent scholarship regardless of the fact that referring to orality in printed works or oral literature will make many scholars of oral tradition a bit queasy. In limited ways, stories of superheroes exist in oral forms with orality defined in the stricter sense: the radio shows of the 1940s, which fundamentally contributed to the development of the superhero mythos; the participatory play of children with action figures and adults with role-playing games; the mostly oral and somewhat literate internet fanfiction that sets up a dialogue between the canonical superhero history and legions of fans surfing the web; and even the somewhat oral and mostly literate novelizations of superhero stories based on comic book, film, television, and animation versions of superheroes. Nevertheless, while the focus in this chapter has been on storytelling practices in the abstract (with Superman's stories exemplifying those practices), it would be more than remiss not to acknowledge the essential characteristics of the media that most often contains the stories of superheroes. They exist in media with orality defined in a much looser sense: comic books, film, and television (media forms that, like refined print matter, only exist because of innovations in technology ranging from the benday process to celluloid film to the reception of broadcast signal). Referring again to Ong, new media technologies shouldn't always be seen as a furtherance of literary culture, and McLuhan implies that new media technologies could result in a return to something like primary orality. The fundamental aspect of the most popular media for representing the superhero is the visual, and the question that must be addressed is whether the paradigm of orality can justifiably be applied to visual experience. This becomes very pertinent, as comic books, the primary medium in which superheroes have been featured, contain language but no oral performance (as could be said of the recorded performance for film or animation features). In the strictest sense, "oral" is a term used to describe the transmission of language units and could be understood as uniformly different from anything "visual." However, when regarding the conventions of orality in a general sense, its application to the visual renderings of comic books (and animation) becomes more acceptable with iconographic renderings of superheroes encouraging visual reinvention and variation. However, this discussion is the express purview of the next chapter, in which the connection between oral and visual culture will be explored with more help from the man of steel and his iconographic representation.

CHAPTER 4

Amplification Through Simplification
The Traditional Basis for Superhero Iconography

In *Ramus, Method, and the Decay of Dialogue*, Walter Ong would indicate that his work had come to be known as an "archeology of thought" (*Ramus* vii).[1] While I consider the term somewhat grandiose in application to my work, it is also somewhat appropriate, as I'm hoping to uncover how superhero comic books came to be, through their means of production. There is no aspect of superhero comic books that requires fuller explanation within my study than the way in which comic books exist within contemporary visual culture; Ong indicates in much of his work on orality that the visual culture of the literate age inevitably takes us away from orality. However, while all aspects of contemporary visual culture may sometimes be lumped together as a thing set in opposition to the psychology of oral culture, this is the result of an oversimplification of contemporary visual culture. In addition to arguing that many different types of visual culture exist, I would also suggest that the popular phrase, visual literacy (referring to the ability to "read" visual culture), implies a false paradigm. In the beginning, with comic books, there was the word but there was the image as well. And while this book has thus far dealt more with narrative aspects of comic books, I don't intend to avoid the essential synergy between the word and image in superhero comic books. Although the importance of each and their reliance upon one another will vary from one comic book work to another, they are inseparable within the medium; in fact, the coexistence/codependence of word and image in comic books is what usually forms the basis of the definitions that theorists use to distinguish comic books from other mediums. Rather than avoid it, I claim that superhero comic book stories work like an oral epic not despite its visual presentation but because of that presentation.

The Primitive Man and the Comic Book Reader: Why Superheroes Stories Do Make You Illiterate

As described in detail in chapter 2, superhero comic books are the product of various historical circumstances that in combination closely produce the thought and aesthetics of an oral culture. As I begin this chapter, it is essential to note what may seem obvious: that the visual components of superhero comic books are produced by these very same circumstances. This fact is noted because the orality of superhero stories might be readily accepted when comic books are discussed somewhat more abstractly as pure stories (as in chapter 3). After all, work has already been done on the persistence and reemergence of oral characteristics in written texts in various periods throughout human history (with practitioners who sometimes lack and sometimes possess an awareness of oral culture). Nevertheless, one of the most significant motivating factors in the excitement shared by creators, publishers, and the audience of comic books was the ability to easily reproduce images to accompany the text. Unavoidably, the visual art of comic books is the product of advanced printing technology, but it should be remembered that visual art can be produced with other technology and was often part of oral cultures; technology, in general, is not the opposite of orality and neither is advanced printing technology. The concerns expressed by scholars of oral culture about the visual have much to do with the way the emphasis on visual experience replaces the use of the other senses (especially the aural experience and the psychology tied to it). However, I intend to reveal that the general design of art within the early (and later) history of superhero comic books is traditional in the sense that it activates a psychology very much like that of primary orality (or at least an orality that still predates the widespread dominance of literacy). As technology, distribution, and audience sensibilities have allowed wider stylistic diversity in superhero comic book illustration, the traditional style of illustration not only has persisted but also has been advocated by many of the most well-respected practitioners in field. I believe that those creators recognize some sort of connection between the medium and this style of illustration, and, though they might not recognize it as such, this forms the oral-visual praxis of superhero comic books. Since orality and visuality are related in superhero stories and yet seem to represent different fields, another term would better serve the discussion in order to characterize the visuals that work in ways consistent with oral tradition. With this in mind, we will be referring to the traditionality of comic book illustration.[2] Such terminology is useful as this chapter is concerned with not only the illustration style but also the other elements within the illustrated content of superhero stories (and the way comic book visuals work to form certain formulae in line with oral tradition).

To begin, it is important to establish the reasons why visual culture (or a bias toward the visual) has been understood to necessarily work against the dynamic operation of oral culture. In a continuum of the human sensory experiences, Ong lines up touch, taste, smell, hearing, and sight in that order. Although we are primarily concerned with hearing and sight, it's worth noting that Ong states that the move from left to right on the continuum means a move from concreteness to abstraction, from subjectivity to objectivity, and from existence to idealism (*Interfaces* 136–137). Within the literate world, words are no longer "spoken things—writing transposes language to a spatial medium" (Ong, *The Presence* 3). The end result of this is what Ong refers to as a "hypervisualism," a tendency that is problematic because it ignores that language is an aural experience before it is a visual experience.[3] As words become increasingly understood as an alphabetic construction, individuals have more distance from what was "said," as language exists less as an experience immediately taken inside one's self and more as an abstraction that can be studied objectively.[4] "To become intelligible, what we see has to be mediated, in one way or another, through verbal formulation, which as such cannot be reduced to a visual presentation" (Ong, *Interfaces* 125). Within his extensive study of Peter Ramus, Ong is able to show how thought, in an age of literacy, became spatialized with schemas developed in visual terms of two and three-dimensional maps (the general evolution being from sounds to picture writing to alphabetic representation to diagrams and maps). The implication of Ong's observations is that the textual is the visual, and it exists in its own terms and serves as the preferred substitute for images of the human lifeworld; now that language is textual, sight is not used in the way it had been previously: "Primitive man has keen eyes, and in many ways observes more acutely than does technological man: a primitive hunter sees all sorts of things happening in the woods about him of which his urbanized visitor is completely unaware. But he cannot expiate them or describe them accurately to any appreciable extent" (*Interfaces* 129). In fact, after discussing George Berkley's refutation of René Descartes ("who had wholly abstracted the visual sense from the interaction of the other senses"), Marshall McLuhan would go so far as to suggest that "the suppression of the visual sense in favor of or the audile-tactile complex, produces distortions in tribal society" (*The Gutenberg* 53). Since the visual experience of the "human lifeworld" is deemed lesser by literate culture, this experience of the literal is downplayed, and illustrations typical in the hand-written manuscript begin to disappear in the printed text (Ong, *Orality* 116–119); the technology needed to represent the human lifeworld would be slow in coming, and illustration did not distract from the truly important visual: the words. From this overview, it should be evident that I consider the visual orientation that clearly precludes the thought characteristic of oral culture to not be a general consequence of the visual; instead, it is an orientation toward typographic representation that distances one's thought from the experience and processes associated with all other senses.

Moreover, oral cultures are not strangers to the process of image-making in either epic poetry or the visual arts. To be more specific on the image-making that takes places within oral culture, it is worth mentioning the visual references made extensively with oral epics. While I realize that these references are not the same as telling stories with materially reproduced pictures, it nevertheless reinforces the idea that oral storytelling is not the antithesis of pictorial storytelling. Oral storytelling tends to include exhaustive visual detail (intricate word-pictures) because corresponding visual media forms do not exist within most oral cultures to the same degree that they do within most literate cultures. Stories will focus on extensive details of a knight's armor and the intricate movements of a warrior in battle, and the stories will eschew discussions of abstract ideas that cannot be tied to literal plot points. The description of Achilles' shield in Homer's Iliad is one of the most famous examples of visual detail communicated in an oral poem: ekphrasis (or a description of the visual in another work of art). "Oral cultures tend to use concepts in situational, operational frames of reference that are minimally abstract in the sense that they remain close to the living human lifeworld" (Ong, *Orality* 49). In turn, Eric Havelock would suggest that the visual sensibility of the epic pushed the narrative of the epic forward, event to event (in my estimation, much like a comic book):

> [Act and events in the epic] had to be presented visually, or as visually as possible ... [a] method of suggestive leading-on of the memory could be supplied by visual resemblance between the items of record; that is if one agent looked something like another one or one performance looked something like another. The picture of an angry man leader to the picture of a man drawing his sword; but the drawing of a sword may link to the picture of someone else holding on to it from behind.... The Homeric epithet can be seen to have a double function. It fills in a portion of the rhythm by automatic reflex, and this saves the bard effort. But equally it visualizes the object more keenly [Havelock 187].

In addition to reinforcing the idea of the visual as paramount within the oral epics, Havelock identifies the visual as a necessary component that carries both the creator and the audience forward to the next event. Since this emphasizes narrative momentum, the visual serves as an element to close the gap between what is already said and what is later said. Thus, we have the sense that oral poetry works with what would come to be called the imaginary in order to fully activate and cement the story in the mind of the audience. Although language-based illustration would not cease in the language-based stories of literate culture, the attitude toward illustration would change significantly. As McLuhan suggests, "To the oral man the literal is inclusive, contains all possible meanings and levels.... But the visual man of the sixteenth century is impelled to separate level from level, and function from function, in a process of specialist exclusion" (*The Gutenberg* 111).[5] And as Ong indicated, illustrations (like diagrams) become a means to the end of more fully understanding the printed text and the concepts beyond the text (to which the text points).

The sort of image-making characteristic of epic poetry has been separated from the experience of the literate mind in the Western world (with only a few significant exceptions) even longer than might be implied by Ong's above-mentioned work. Within *Preface to Plato*, Havelock addresses one of the components of Plato's *Republic* that contemporary critics often find problematic: Plato's rejection of poetry and image-making. Based upon Plato's doctrine of the forms, art is an imperfect imitation of the real world and the real world is an imperfect imitation of the formal world (where all things exist in perfection). With this notion in mind, art takes thinkers in the wrong direction, away from an appreciation of the forms: all that is good and true. Havelock argues the crucial point in understanding Plato's vehemence against artists is to whom he refers in that those artists practice poetic mimesis; they are epic poets and epic poetry is separate from Plato's project.

> [J]ust as poetry itself, as long as it reigned supreme, constituted the chief obstacle to the achievement of effective prose, so there was a state of mind which we shall conveniently label the "poetic" of "Homeric" or "oral" state of mind, which constituted the chief obstacle to scientific rationalism, to the use of analysis, to the classification of experience, to its rearrangement in sequence of cause and effect. That is why the poetic state of mind is for Plato the arch-enemy and it is easy to see why he considered the enemy so formidable.... He asks of men that instead they should examine this experience and rearrange it, that they should think about what they say, instead of just saying it. And they should separate themselves from it instead of identifying with it; they themselves should become the "subject" who stands apart from the "object" and reconsiders it and analyzes it and elevates it, instead of just "imitating" it [Havelock 46–47].

As Havelock argues, the thought of oral culture is founded upon principles that work in ways nearly antithetical to Platonism (a highly refined version of the thought of literate culture). Where oral culture would seek to maintain culture through the immersive experience of epic poetry, Plato would seek to question culture through the systematic analysis of the individual mind (Havelock 102–103). In fact, Plato's most famous deployment of imagery, "The Allegory of the Cave," uses the visual as a metaphor, an abstracted means to an end (much like a diagram). The end would be to understand things in conceptual terms and leave behind the shadows cast on the wall; by extending Havelock's argument, it could be said that these were the things to which participants in oral culture had devoted themselves.

In estimating the influence of Platonism and literacy (which is undeniably extensive), one of the crucial elements to keep in mind is that Plato refers to mimesis and image-making as something done by epic poets.[6] However, in rough historical reckoning, the rise of Platonism and literacy in ancient Greece would coincide with what is often referred to as the Greek revolution in art: the movement away from the flattened representation of Grecian urns to the perspective-driven representation of Grecian realism. Consequently, what Plato called mimetic may not be what the literate world calls realism (the aesthetics that far-gone literates have in mind when thinking of how to represent the human lifeworld). In *Art and Illusion*, E.H. Gombrich makes a compelling case that cultures outside the reach of Platonism have a psychology that causes them to make art differently and subsequently, argues that an artist is always more influenced by what is known than what is seen. Since the distinction between these two categories may be slippery, Gombrich examines the ancient Egyptian art that preceded Platonic philosophy and the art of the Greek revolution and makes several points.[7] Despite having the intelligence and technical skill that allows artists to depict figures realistically, these artists chose to emphasize aspects of their culture much closer to the ideals of orality (my contention, not his); these include the use of narrative, stereotype (cliché), relative time line, and repetition (Gombrich 103–107); moreover, the art departs from rules that might govern the realistic depiction of objects in space in order to present the object holistically and connect the viewer with all aspects of the object. While acknowledging that every culture is different, certain generalizations can be made about traditional art, whether it is the visual arts of Paleolithic caves, ancient Egypt, or medieval Europe. Although subsequent civilizations have often tried to reduce such art to the level of the functional or decorative, it is rarely just one or the other. The images in these works are almost always tied to a story that may be made clear in the course of the work but usually does not need to be (as the story is a preexisting and indelible part of the culture). Selective exaggeration calls attention to details and emphasizes story points, and, sometimes, images will be set in sequence in order to indicate narrative development. In addition, the figures are drawn from the human lifeworld but are stylized in such a way as to avoid particulars that would fix the art within a limited time or place. Employing what may be rudimentary tools for image-making, these stylizations become standards by which characters within the works are readily known (visual clichés or stereotypes used to designate the king, the warrior, the enemy). Concomitantly, these stylizations also are suggestive beyond the representation itself, symbols known to the culture familiar with the general practices of art. By often working outside the strict rules of three-dimensional representation, this art avoids the limitations of surfaces; this allows the individual to experience the thing depicted as a whole, to penetrate the image in a way that some have speculated enables identification and participation. Ultimately, the recipient of the art is regularly participating in a reality of culture already well known and long taught and that experience of the art is additive rather than a suggestion for radical change. The stylistic tendencies of the artist are passed from one generation to the next (and with cave paintings, artists often trace over previous paintings) suggesting a worldview unlike that of Plato who wants to move beyond the status quo.

In addition to Gombrich's arguments, McLuhan would cite Kurt Seligman in his discussion of the mnemonic memory manifested in the manuscripts of the medieval period that contained appeals to oral culture in their illustrations (readable by illiterate and literate alike) (McLuhan, *The Gutenberg* 108–109).[8] Also, Ong's account serves well to indicate what shortly preceded the Renaissance and the rebirth of Platonic ideals in the Western world:

> The greater visualism initiated by script and the alphabet is given more and more play in the West through the Middle Ages and then suddenly is brought to a new intensity in the fifteenth century and thereafter with the invention of alphabetic typography ... for at approximately the same time that alphabetic typography appears, painting is being swept by a revolution in its treatment of perspective [Ong, *The Presence* 8].[9]

Similar to the other scholars already mentioned, Ong implies that there is a conceptual connection between the rise of print texts and not only the decline of book illustration but also the rise of realism and naturalism in the visual arts (*Orality* 116–119).[10] In any case, with the Greek revolution, the characteristics of realistic art would differ from the ideals of traditional art, (realistic art being nonnarrative, individual, grounded in time, and unique); moreover, realistic art adheres to rules that govern the realistic depiction of objects in space in order to present surfaces separate from the viewer, surfaces to be studied. Nevertheless, even though such art is much more clearly in line with Plato's vision of the world, Gombrich points out that pictures can't fit into a logical framework as true or false, fiction or nonfiction (59, 109); tied to the human lifeworld, realism is still something problematic (and may be used in the service of epic storytelling). Therefore, this necessitates Plato's extreme stance against all image-makers, as even realistic art is a disruption within the Plato's world. While visual art may not be banned from Plato's world, it occupies a status that is clearly secondary to that of the written word.

With this in mind, it is worth noting that the criticisms against early comic stories have much to do with its emphasis on the pictorial (for instance, Annie Russell Marble's "The Reign of the Spectacular"). In addition, those who argued against early comic stories did so with Platonic anxieties toward the psychology of oral culture at the forefront their arguments. Associating comic strips and comic books with other elements of "mass culture," Irving Howe would articulate fears that these new media experiences were leading to "the depersonalization of the individual" (44); comic stories promised diversion but merely reinforced the worker's "semi-robot status," and the ominous movie theater was "like a dark cavern, a neutral womb" (44, 45), a space like that of Plato's cave. Again, in their relatively uninformed ways, these early critics actually see some of the truth of the matter. Since oral culture in general and oral poetry in particular contain visual information that does not crowd out but furthers the oral sensibilities of the story, my goal then becomes to identify how we "see" this in superhero comic books as well. But before proceeding to my explanation of how superhero comic book illustration works in line with the practices of oral culture, I would like to modify the terms in play by reintroducing the term "traditionality." Traditionality is a term that has been used by some scholars of orality and literacy, such as John Miles Foley and Adam Davis (who sometimes use traditionality and textuality to replace orality and literacy).[11] The reason for the preference of these terms has much to do with the greater critical specificity in a culture that uses literacy in ways that have little to do with the typical parameters of orality and literacy. In addition, despite the best efforts of Ong and others, the two terms have come to be seen by many as antonyms. In the survey work that fully established the study of orality and literacy (*The Theory of Oral Composition*), Foley questions whether the oral and written literature "are still viable as opposite categories" (107).[12] Nevertheless, I have chosen to use orality thus far and will continue to do so in a limited degree in connection with traditionality because of its still more recognizable place within the scholarly discourse. Moreover, although I choose to avoid it because of its awkward and confusing implications, I consider "oral literature" to be a permissible means to describe literature that is written in the midst of an oral culture. However, for the sake of the discussion in this chapter, I want to begin using *traditionality* because traditionality can include many practices other than oral tradition related to the culture of orality. While I consider *oral literature* to be permissible, the term *oral illustration* just doesn't work. With this established, image-making and illustration within the confines of traditional culture include various related ideas. Images do not support the story but are an inseparable part of the story, not only in terms of content but also in terms of form, tied to the mechanics of storytelling. Tied to the human lifeworld, illustration serves a narrative role within the story and points to the story itself (rather than beyond the story and the culture to abstract concepts). The experience of oral culture leads to the creation of a certain style of visual art that is more compatible with the common experience of the oral epic: engaging the audience as a participant. This often means refusing to distance the visual art from the audience with excessive realism because such art is a depiction of objects in space so particular that it limits the audience's identification with those objects.

Although I do not wish to take this argument too far, Plato's attitude toward the visual has made its appearance generally in the age of new media (Ong's age of secondary orality). Even though this book is devoted to making its case about superhero comic books rather than new media in general, this sort of discussion is unavoidable (and potentially worthwhile in short) with the superhero as a multimedia phenomenon. Visual culture of new media is different from the visual culture of the literate world, something that activates the means of thinking within that oral mind. With comic books, film, and computer technologies, the visual has become a clearer counterpart to the textual, enacting a dynamic relationship between discourse elements much more indicative of oral culture. In *Writing Space*, Jay David Bolter identifies our postliterate shift as a return to a basic emphasis on images where images need not be occupy a secondary and supportive status relative to text in order to validate the those images. In *Understanding Media*, McLuhan divides media into what he referred to as hot media (such as traditional books and lectures) and cool media (such as comic books and television). Although many scholars including myself find significant problems with his choice of some mediums as hot and cool, the essential idea behind the division work is to set up a discussion of comic books as a new media form in line with oral culture; hot media requires less participation and thereby, engages one sense more than others, and cool media requires more participation and thereby, involves the senses more equally. If comic books can be seen as fundamentally related to film (as implied by McLuhan and Ian Gordon's *Film and Comic Books*), then it may be worth considering the anti–Platonic turn of much film criticism. The most notable critic in this vein would be Jean-Louis Baudry (despite his psychoanalytic and Marxist leanings). In his "apparatus" theory, he would suggest that film experience took people back to the quite contented experience of shadows in the cave; like Irving Howe, he would describe the movie theater as a womb, but, unlike Howe, Baudry's connotations would be largely positive. Christian Metz, one of film's most famous theoreticians, has declared, "A film is difficult to explain because it is easy to understand. The image impresses itself upon us, blocking everything that is not itself" (69). David Carrier describes comic strips in a similar way: "Comics [are] an art form almost all of us understand without theorizing ... slight popular images, art that everyone understands without need of any explanation" (2–3). These statements certainly harken back to the earlier mention of Ong's "primitive" man who can appreciate visual experiences of the human lifeworld better than literate man but who "cannot expiate them or describe them accurately to any appreciable extent" (Ong, *Interfaces* 129). But with or without this larger context, superhero comic books remain the best example of a resurgence of oral culture and the concomitant resurgence of traditionality in illustration.

The best point of departure to characterize superhero comic books in this way is a work almost as frustrating to me as it is remarkable: Scott McCloud's *Understanding Comics*.[13] Within the work, Scott McCloud offers a fairly comprehensive theoretical discussion of comic books in an attempt to establish comic books as an artform with unique conventions and possibilities. I'll begin my discussion with my frustration with *Understanding Comics* (and Scott McCloud in general), a frustration that is roughly the same as that of comic book scholar Thierry Groenstein[14]; McCloud does not work within the traditions of academia that require he place his ideas within a historical and theoretical context. At the same time, McCloud's approach is not entirely surprising as his background is as a comic book creator and not as an academic (and his intention is to connect more with a general comic book reading audience than a scholarly audience). *Understanding Comics* is remarkable not only because of strong (albeit quickly developed) ideas but also for the basic form of the book; McCloud engages the medium by putting his ideas within a nonnarrative comic book, in which he represents himself as a character and directly addresses the reader.[15] And I believe that the context that I have thus far provided with superhero comic books as part of the reemergence of oral culture works to validate McCloud's ideas. Despite being a product of the printing press, comic books are unlike the dominant print tradition in the literate world and pictures are not subordinated in the medium of comic books. While the typographic press reorganized culture in a way that it no longer worked wholly in terms of orality, the lithographic press reorganized culture (especially relative to the use of images in comic books) in a way that it no longer worked wholly in terms of literacy.[16] Since the printed image is no longer subordinated to the printed word (and McCloud effectively shows the relationship between the two is fundamentally related), narrative and illustration are codependent (McCloud, *Understanding* 153–154). Moreover, he connects comic books to ancient traditions that bring together word and image in storytelling practices and picture writing; these range from Egyptian hieroglyphics to the image-based manuscripts from the pre–Columbian period to word-image combinations in the Bayeux tapestry from the medieval period.

Interested in finding precedent for the "sequential art" of comic books,[17] McCloud immediately showcases hieroglyphics but acknowledges that hieroglyphics work very much as a predecessor to alphabetic construction (even though they do have narrative-like sequence) (*Understanding* 12–13). Recalling Ong's model of development from sounds to picture writing to alphabetic representation to diagrams and maps, it might be argued that comic books are at least some form of picture-writing and therefore closer to orality than the hypervisualism of far-gone literacy. However, comic books are much more than that, and McCloud notes that "pictures predate the written word by a large margin" (141), placing certain types of pictures within the category of traditionality. Moreover, returning to ancient Egyptian art, McCloud notes that Egyptian paintings (to which Gombrich also referred) work with flattened and stereotyped but symbolically rich figures set in a sequence to reveal a story (like both the pre–Columbian manuscripts and the Bayeux tapestry) (*Understanding* 13–14). Although he does not discuss them in depth, he also mentions early Greek painting and Trajan's column as potential predecessors for comic books (which I want to mention because they seem to work outside of a worldview influenced by Plato and literacy). Within this broad historical survey, McCloud then ventures into the world of print, mentioning only a smattering of examples by various artists like William Hogarth and Rodolphe Topffer that precede the explosion of sequential art and comic books in the 20th century. To account for this relative absence, he describes the advent of print in a way not entirely dissimilar to Ong:

> It didn't take long though — relatively speaking — before ancient writing started to become more abstract. Some written languages survive to this day, bearing traces of their ancient pictorial heritage. But in time, most modern writing would come to represent sound only

and lost any lingering resemblance to the visible world. With the invention of printing, the written word took a great leap forward — and all of humanity with it. But where had all the pictures gone? Words and pictures did coexist at this stage in Western civilization. But those instances were becoming the exception, not the rule.... The written word was becoming more specialized, more abstract, more elaborate — and less like pictures. Pictures, meanwhile, began to grow in the opposite direction: less abstract or symbolic, more representational and specific [*Understanding* 142–144].

All of this is not to suggest that McCloud completely anticipates the implications of my suggestion that comic books work in line with the conventions of orality and traditional illustration. Considering that my approach is directly informed by studies of orality and literacy, I find McCloud to sometimes misunderstand and be inconsistent with his own sense of comic books. While his project is to represent comic books as derivative in their 20th-century forms but thereafter quickly becoming distinctive, he at times lumps comic books together with other forms of new media and also other media innovations such as print (to the detriment of his own argument).[18]

> The art form of comics is many centuries old, but it's perceived as a recent invention and suffers the curse of all new media. The curse of being judged by the standards of the old. Ever since the invention of the written word, new media have been misunderstood. [A character in the ancient world says to a scribe:] "Careful, Jacob! If you keep doing this, you'll stop using your memory" [McCloud, *Understanding* 151].

The quotation ends with a supposed fallacy that is an important idea set forth in studies of orality and literacy (although the change in memory skills is regularly described with much more nuanced terms). Moreover, McCloud seems to suggest there is some sort of linear development from one new medium to the next, from writing to comic books (which doesn't work entirely). Despite mixing a traditional sense of the artform with a Platonic notion of moving beyond old media, McCloud continues his analysis of art history with a broad but fascinating claim. After centuries of moving in "opposite" directions (literary art toward abstraction and visual art toward realism), we see the two swing back toward one another in 20th century, in the center of a continuum ranging from abstraction to realism. Although he offers little in the way of a historical basis for this change, McCloud gives good examples (contrasting John Keats "Ode on a Grecian Urn" to Walt Whitman's "Facing West from California's Shores" and portraits by Rembrandt to portraits by Pablo Picasso) (*Understanding* 144–147). More important is that word and image are regarded with equal esteem and placed alongside one another in the medium of comic books (where image does not simply serve the word). While this explanation for the synthesis of word and images may or may not be persuasive to art historians, it does a fairly good job setting up the reemergence of traditional art, what McCloud would label the iconographic.

At the center of McCloud's discussion of comic books is the idea that comic book visuals are iconographic, pictures simplified to the point of having universal appeal.[19] While he uses the term "icon" in order to avoid the complications of the term "symbol," he doesn't fully acknowledge the rich history of the icon in the medieval period or the current use of the term within the realm of computer interfaces.[20] (The former works very well in relation to Gombrich's sense of traditional/universal artwork and the latter with the argument that new media in general brings back conventions of traditionality.) Regardless, when setting up an argument that advocates for the use of images that are general, pictures are described in specific terms:

In pictures ... meaning is fluid and variable according to appearance. They differ from "real-life" appearance to varying degrees. Words are totally abstract icons. That is, they bear no resemblance to the real McCoy. But in pictures the level of abstraction varies. Some, like the [highly realistic] face in the previous panel so closely resemble their real-life counterparts as to almost trick the eye! Other, like yours truly, are more abstract, and, in fact, are very much unlike any human face you've ever seen! [McCloud, *Understanding* 28].

The image of "yours truly" is a simple rendering of McCloud, a man with round glasses, drawn with just a few lines and not too dissimilar from the earliest representations of Clark Kent.

McCloud discusses comic books in a comic book format and presents his ideas about the icon through an iconographic representation of himself (from *Understanding Comics*, p. 27).

It is important to note that iconographic art is not the same as abstract art, in that iconographic art is always representational.[21] This approach agrees with the emphasis in traditional culture on a stereotyped depiction of the human lifeworld but disagrees with the emphasis in textual culture on a particularized depiction of the human lifeworld. While iconographic art has elements of abstraction, it never breaks down reality to the point that it becomes disconnected from or irrelevant to a narrative context. In McCloud's consideration of the ascendency of the iconographic image in the 20th century, the questions become: "Why are we so involved? Why would anyone, young or old, respond to a cartoon [image] as much or more than a realistic image? Why is our culture so in thrall of the simplified reality of the cartoon?" (*Understanding* 30). For McCloud, the answers to these questions lie in his doctrine of "amplification through simplification" that, quite appropriately, can be described rather simply. Less people are likely to identify with a realistic picture of a middle-aged white man than they are to identify with a smiley face (which lacks all markers of age, race, and gender and could conceivably represent anyone): "The more cartoony a face is ... the more people it could said to describe" (*Understanding* 31).

However, there is a psychology behind it that suggests the type of mental activity encouraged by the tradition of subjectivity in orality more than the objectivity of literacy.

> We humans are a self-centered race. We see ourselves in everything. We assign identities and emotions where none exist. And we make the world over in our image. Think of your face as a mask.... Seen by everyone you meet but never by you.... When two people interact, they usually look directly at one another, seeing their partner's features in vivid detail. Each one also sustains a constant awareness of his or her own face, but this mind-picture is not nearly so vivid; just a sketchy arrangement ... a sense of shape ... a sense of general placement. Something as simple and as basic — as a cartoon. Thus, when you look at a photo or realistic drawing of a face — you see it as the face of another. But when you enter the world of the cartoon — you see yourself.... We don't just observe the cartoon, we become it! [McCloud, *Understanding* 32–36].

And thus the iconographic representation that McCloud associates with comic books takes the individual far from a world shaped by Plato who wants to make the human being understand everything in its own terms. Far from being shaped by knowledge of the particulars of the objective observation, human beings, as described by 20th-century psychology, are more involved with those things that seemingly represent the self; they engage with art that activates one's subjectivity. As the "cartoony" representation of McCloud states, "It would never occur to you to wonder what my politics are, or what I had for lunch or where I got this silly outfit! I'm just a voice inside your head.... Who I am is irrelevant. I'm just a little piece of you" (*Understanding* 37). In essence, iconographic art is much more likely to work in an additive way, to reinforce the individual's sense of self as developed within the individual's community (rather than encouraging the individual to think beyond one's community). As suggested earlier by McLuhan's notion of comic books as a cool medium, comic books work with the reader to create something more like aural experience than conventional books. I do not mean to rest this argument on the ability of readers of comic books to "hear" characters speak in the midst of their reading experience; that could just as likely happen with readers of traditional books — and even McCloud makes the comic (humorous) point about his readers "hearing" him (*Understanding* 25). Instead, comic books' pictorial representation activates subjectivity and eschews objectivity in its narrative framework.

At this point, I'll note several aspects of McCloud's approach that might make it problematic as an unintentional descriptor of the traditional state of mind. The first aspect is less obvious as it is embedded within the definition of the icon (and this embedded portion also explains why McCloud insisted on the distance from the term symbol). The icon is a visual element that represents something else and he includes the American flag, the Nike swoosh, and a stop sign. The iconographic image as described above is really a subset of the icon: the picture (an image like the smiley face that actually resembles the thing depicted). Ultimately, such symbols are closer to the abstraction of alphabetic language that McCloud does include on the continuum of the icon; in doing so, McCloud seems to suggest that the language used in comic books also invites (if not requires) the same level of participation with the story. However, he doesn't do so directly, and his general definition of the icon could also bring up the idea of the icon as a sign in the sense created by Ferdinand de Saussure. Since Ong flatly states that the spoken word is not a sign (*Orality* 75–76), this could problematize an otherwise useful connection. However, it need not for other reasons: Ong's claim is debatable, and Ong's suggests that structuralist approaches to oral epics might bear fruit (*Orality* 161–162).[22] The second aspect is more obvious, as contemporary comic book illustration now ranges from the iconographic to the realistic to the abstract. For me, this is a much more significant problem with McCloud, as he fails to account for the significance of the industry to the development of this aesthetic approach. Rather than do this, he acknowledges the wide range of artistic styles represented in contemporary comics (*Understanding* 52–53) but implies that the simple iconographic style is the superior aesthetic choice (mentioning contemporary practitioners such as Dave Sim and Art Spiegelman). Part of McCloud's problem in this regard may be McCloud's bias against the mass-produced superhero comic books of the early 20th century, seen in his fiction work (like *Zot!* which rejects the flat characters and epic violence of superhero stories) and later nonfiction work (like *Reinventing Comics*, which nearly identifies superhero stories a bankrupt genre) (McCloud, *Reinventing* 114–115).[23] Curiously, he almost moves past this blindspot in his chapter on color in which he shows how certain combinations of color, in certain ratios work to represent superheroes (like blue, yellow, and grey for Batman and green and purple for the Hulk).

As comic book art (in the recent years of superhero stories and other comic books) has become widely varied (ranging from the iconographic to realistic to abstract),[24] McCloud's formulation could be read as an unacknowledged and romanticized perspective on the past of comics (in which artists drew in simple terms because of a lack of time rather than for a philosophical attachment to the general appeal of images). Even though McCloud tries to explain the flourishing of the comic book as an artform in the 20th century by saying that visual art is finally complimenting language (and can exist comfortably within the same space), he largely ignores the nature of 20th-century technology that first made comic books possible. As noted in previous chapters, the technological and industry-based limitations placed on creators resulted in large part in the creation of the superhero.[25] The iconographic style that McCloud advocates, for all its aesthetic worth, was in large part produced by these limitations. I would argue that on the whole, his advocacy is an appropriate prescription for the medium that (perhaps to his dismay) is predisposed to superhero comic books by its history. In addition, I have to acknowledge that referring to the "limitations" of the print technology may not only miss the point but also may reinstate the misbegotten notion that technological advancements produce better art. Technological advancements led to the increasing presence of naturalism and realism in visual arts in general, in various eras in world history; this is also true for comic books in particular (with advances made in the 1980s) but McCloud's advocacy of iconographic art shows us that this increasing presence of naturalism and realism isn't necessarily desirable. While many of the most well-regarded superhero comic book creators may not promote the idea of iconographic art in the same overt way, their practice implies that they operate with the same inclinations. Moreover, since the early technology and industry of the superhero comic book industry led to a reappearance of traditionality, it would be wrong to assume that future developments in graphic imaging and internet distribution will not continue the trend (with naturalism and realism being a temporary aberration rather than the ultimate end). Regardless, McCloud's iconographic art is in line with traditional art and is the product of the industrial model dominant in the comic book industry from the 1930s through the 1970s.

The Dynamic Icon of the Superhero: A New Reading Experience, Years in the Making

The earliest print technology of the comic book industry only allowed low-quality reproduction, and that necessitated the same broad lines and basic colors used at the turn of the century for poster art. Higher resolution print transfer was already possible when the first issue of Superman hit the newsstands, but publishers sought to balance the cost of production with what consumers were willing to pay. Low-quality printing in line with newspapers that featured comic strips ensured that publishers would continue to reach the widest audience possible, at what the audience considered to be a minor cost.[26] In addition, superhero comic book publishers were always producing the next installment in a favorite character's story for a hungry consumer, and, therefore, these installments were produced quickly. This necessitated the cooperative group of artists who worked on Superman in the style of Joe Shuster and the farming of work out to various independent creators expected to work within the confines of a very limited number of house styles. Despite the criticisms of the early superhero comic books publishers as purveyors of crude art produced by incompetent artists, the fact is that these artists worked within the style of the strips that was conditioned by the necessity of speed. But to say that illustrators were conditioned to produce material quickly is not the same as saying that their work lacked a distinctive style. Even though the talent of the artists would of course vary, many artists understood the tenets of realism but worked within the style established within the field.[27] Their iconographic style was not the opposite of realism but their style included things characteristic of comic strips such as caricature, exaggeration for impact, motion-related transitional effects, the regular use of visual clichés, and the absence of background detail.

Examining the early artwork produced by Joe Shuster in the first stories of Superman, the iconographic image that McCloud describes can easily be seen. With five to seven simple lines creating Superman's facial features, minimal detail to the background, and primary colors representing all characters, a sense of generality allows the reader to easily identify with the character with whom the reader spends the most time: Clark Kent and Superman. Although intended to take place in the real world, background details remain undrawn unless they are specifically required by the story itself; there is a flatness and general lack of attention paid to techniques that might create depth. While grounded in a specific time, the art itself seems to work in contrast with this aspect of setting, with generalized characters types and nondescript fashions repeated throughout the first decade of Superman comic books. In *Action Comics* #4, "Superman Versus Luthor" provides clear depiction of these features in panels 61 through 68 (as Superman answers Luthor's challenge of his superpowers). Before Luthor later became the evil genius Lex Luthor, he had hair, and, therefore, without the benefit of color and Superman's costume, the two figures would be practically indistinguishable (simply rendered in illustrations that approximate the same midrange spectator distance). However, as rendered with starkly different colors, they are strikingly separated from one another as the antagonist threatens Superman with one danger after another (a grenade, a mortar, and poison gas). The only significant details outside the characters themselves that are drawn are those dangers just mentioned and related to the challenge (and Luthor's plane, against which the triumphant Superman threatens to throw him). A horizon line is provided in only two of the eight panels, and background detail establishing relative size (a tree alongside Luthor's plane) is only provided in one. Instead, there are more lines devoted to the stylized convention of depicting movement within a static scene: the motion lines of (1) a thrown grenade, (2) an explosion, (3) a fired mortar, (4) dispersing gas, and (5) a flying plane. Although somewhat more oriented to realism than Egyptian painting (which mixes two-dimensional and three-dimensional representations by contorting human figures in impossible ways to reveal all fingers, etc.), this same Superman story uses a technique that is similar in effect. Both Gombrich and McLuhan have indicated that traditional cultures react with great anxiety to not being able to see a part of a figure that, in a realistic depiction, is blocked from view by another part of that same figure. Although slightly modified as sequentially arranged panels in time, "Superman Versus Luthor" provides the means to see Superman from every angle in short order; the five panels ranging from 80 through 84 provide five different perspectives of Superman in quick succession.[28] When encountered in film, the experience of seeing something from all perspectives is often identified as the experience of hyper-reality, something that seems more real than the experience of the real world. However, this could also be understood as a common phenomenon of traditional culture in which the audience is in the midst of the artistic event, feeling connected rather than separated (as they would if limited by the singular perspective of realism).

Many other examples could be drawn from the first decade of superhero comic books and lead to similar conclusions, whether those examples came from Bob Kane's Batman, C.C. Beck's Captain Marvel, or Harry Peter's Wonder Woman. Out of the three prominent superhero artists just mentioned, Peter might be the most interesting as an artist who had worked for about thirty years, illustrating periodicals with different standards for their images. Despite much work in his past that required three-dimensional perspective and intricate line work, Peter readily adapted to the culture of the superhero comic book industry and produced renderings much more in line with other superhero comic books. Maintaining my focus on Superman, it could be argued that a course could be charted from Joe Shuster (1930s and 1940s) to Wayne Boring (1950s) to Curt Swan (1960s and 1970s) that demonstrates a march toward realism and naturalism in superhero comic books. Each artist is incrementally more detailed in their representations of characters and backgrounds, and more complex colors are used to compliment their work. I would concede this argument to a certain extent, as Boring uses more definitive hatching to indicate the presence of light and dark, and Swan more regularly depicts Superman relative to other elements in a scene. Nevertheless, the change from Shuster isn't dramatic, and both artists retain relatively simple drawings of facial features and general outlines of human and architectural forms that are reinforced by a simplistic color palate. What should have been much more significant than this apparent incremental move away from traditionalism would be the introduction of Marvel superheroes in the Silver Age intended to rival well-established superheroes within the DC universe, such as Superman, Batman, and Wonder Woman. When Stan Lee received his first superhero assignment from Martin Goodman, he decided to experiment with the formula that required all superheroes to be ideologically perfect. Many critics involved with superhero scholarship see the Marvel universe created by Stan Lee, Jack Kirby, and Jack Kirby to be the end of the heavy and generally flat heroes of the Golden Age. As I will note in chapter 5, this perspective tends to be influenced by the desire of critics to find definitive historical turning points, but I will offer here what I consider to be some of the clearest support for the faulty basis of such historical revisionism; the illustration provided for Lee's stories by Jack Kirby and Steve Ditko continued to work in iconographic terms and avoid strict realism and naturalism.[29]

Although both Kirby and Ditko would work for years in the comic book industry, before the creation of Marvel superheroes, both would be best remembered for their contributions to that superhero universe.[30] And while Ditko spent his time working within other genres before the 1960s Marvel comics "revolution," Kirby would have a much more extensive background with superhero comics after working with the Fox Syndicate on various superhero titles. His most famous collaboration during that time would be with Joe Simon, resulting in the 1941 creation of Captain America (a character that captivated most superhero readers during the war years). With the exception of the famous cover of issue #1 (featuring Captain America punching Hitler) with its fairly detailed backgrounds, the interior art of *Captain America* worked in ways very similar to Joe Shuster's *Superman*. However, there are a few things worth mentioning that expand the traditionalism of Kirby's early work, such as the first page of issue #1, which presents Captain America fully costumed and disconnected from the story (in a way similar to the formal presentation of royal figures or heroes in a triptych). In addition, Kirby seems to indulge in the use of caricature and stereotyped images more freely than Shuster to represent villains (who are regularly ugly, disfigured, and primitive).[31] Beyond the tenets of traditionalism already mentioned in conjunction with ancient art, Kirby also works with the synergy McCloud establishes between word and

Although he experiments with several different approaches, Jack Kirby's style becomes increasingly simple and iconographic (from *Fantastic Four* #37, p. 11).

image. In the concluding pages of the story, Kirby combines two elements related by virtue of story but not realistic space or proportion, by placing a running Captain America in front of enlarged representations of newspapers sporting headlines about him: another collage-type arrangement. Throughout the story, Kirby uses the direction of movement within a single frame to carry the reader to the next frame and to involve the reader within the action itself (as Captain America steps out of the panel frame); while this technique accentuates the dimensionality to some extent, its overwhelming effect is to involve the reader as a subject connected to the story.

As the Silver Age superheroes of DC comics again became popular, Atlas (later renamed Marvel) joined the fray with the previously mentioned assignment to Lee to create their own version of DC's Justice League of America. Working with Kirby, Lee developed a superhero team influenced by other genres in which he had worked such as science fiction and romance. However, being a team that lacked the unity seen with the superheroes of the JLA, the team members still represented types and their famous bickering didn't depart from precedent set in oral epics like Homer's *Iliad* or in comic books like *The All Winners Squad*.[32] Likewise, Kirby didn't change his iconographic style to fit something more in line with literate culture (which Lee's writing was not) so much as to refine his iconographic style. As Kirby's characters became more block-like in their facial features, they became harder to distinguish from one another, excepting that they usually possessed wildly different and symbolic accessories (like the weapons of epic characters): the Mole Man's goggles, the Sub-Mariner's ears, or Medusa's hair. To further elaborate on the growing iconographic depiction of characters, two of Kirby's most famously designed creations appear in *Fantastic Four* #48, "The Coming of Galactus," and represent his overall aesthetic approach: the Silver Surfer and Galactus. While the hero, the Silver Surfer, is a sleek silver figure who is devoid of all distinctive characteristics (with no hair, clothes, or weapons excepting his surfboard), the indifferent god and villain, Galactus, is suited in garish and highly detailed armor that hides all potentially distinctive human features. (Speculation could be made on the attempt to create reader identification with certain figures in Lee and Kirby's tendency to put no masks (or readily removable masks) on the heroes and permanent masks on villains.) While backgrounds do become slightly more elaborate in Kirby's Marvel comics, there is no subsequent creation of realistic depth; instead, the backgrounds are more decorative and strangely abstract, suggesting elaborate pipework or circuitry that does not exist in the "real" world.[33] Even when Kirby utilized photomontage, as in issue #48, he did so to represent the strange and barely recognizable "testing machines" of the otherworldly Galactus, much more stylized than realistic. However, the dynamism of Kirby's artwork directs movement of the eye and becomes even more noticeable as an indicator of movement (such as with the opening sequence of issue #48, featuring the Inhumans). On page 2, the first panel reveals the Fantastic Four to be thrown across the room; the second panel focuses on the faces of Mr. Fantastic and the Invisible Girl; and the third panel moves outside to depict the shaking of the Inhumans' complex. Unlike the movement within the above-mentioned Superman story, the changes made from panel to panel involve not only changes in perspective on the same subject but also distance from that subject and other subjects as well. This sort of "cinematic" movement develops a sense of this story within an imagined world and involves the reader even more within the expanding scope of the story (as with an oral epic that regularly forsakes a singular perspective to include all relevant details).

In addition to the Fantastic Four, Kirby would co-create other superhero staples of the Marvel universe such as the X-Men, the Hulk, Iron Man, and Thor.[34] The other artist who provided the foundational ideas for the Marvel universe would be Steve Ditko in his work on Spider-Man and Dr. Strange. Ditko drew characters simply, reserved most of his detail work for elements such as the webbing on Spider-Man's costume, and allowed his elongated style to be more important than the idea that these characters existed in a real world. With an approach similar to Kirby's, Ditko would nevertheless often provide more detailed and realistic backgrounds, like the mechanical lab equipment seen on pages 15 and 16 of *Spider-Man* #3, but would balance this out with practically blank backgrounds on pages 18 and 19; again, details in the background are motivated by story emphases. In addition to Ditko's standard artistic elements, he would be noted for introducing abstract characters in *Dr. Strange*, such as Eternity (a personification of the universe), represented as the outlined figure of a human, filled with an image of outer space (stars, planets, etc.).[35] On one hand, such an illustration could be understood in modernist terms as surreal or on the other hand, in iconographic terms, as the negative space that either enables or resists identification. While I do not want to enter this debate at any length, I do bring this up to highlight the fact that identifying art as traditional is not an attempt to *over*simplify the work of these artists. While that may be the impression made by a reference to traditional art, that impression is likely the result of a literate culture's sense that nontraditional art is necessarily more complex and simply better. As in the study of orality and literacy, the study of traditional and nontraditional art should lead to the conclusion that neither is better but that the two are fundamentally different. If anything, I hope that describing superhero comic book art enlarges a discussion about it (with thoughts of how Kirby's photomontage or Ditko's so-called "surrealism" might be the result of traditional impulses as much as nontraditional impulses or how other "innovations," like Jim Steranko's use of Pop Art and Op Art, might be something other than a step forward). While some may be inclined to ascribe this iconographic approach to individual style, I would argue that the use of this iconographic style is too uniform in both the Golden and Silver Ages of superhero comic books to suggest that this style is not a community formation. In addition, the idea that people were copying the style of Shuster and Beck or Kirby and Ditko because it was popular is ultimately irrelevant, because that style was popular in superhero comic books for a reason. The fact that Kirby and Ditko were recognized as significant artists is not necessarily out of keeping with what would be the social dynamics of an oral culture. While the conventional story may have had a life long before the singer, there would undoubtedly have been favorite singers able to sing stories in ways within tradition and most preferred by the culture.[36]

The Modern Age Is Still Traditional: The Costume and a Panel of One's Own

Throughout the Golden and Silver Ages of superhero comics books (what I consider to be the primary orality), the artistic style is unquestionably traditional (or iconographic); however, there are different degrees of realism and naturalism represented in the work of each artist. The reason for this variation may be due to the fact that the traditional culture of comic books exists within a literate world but more likely, that different degrees of realism and naturalism are represented in traditional illustration. Again, it's important to remember that iconographic art is not the opposite of realistic art. Regardless, what can then be observed and hardly disputed in the general history of superhero comic books is a widespread shift toward realism and naturalism in the late 1970s and early 1980s. As in the previous chapter, I will not spend too long on work outside the era of comic books' primary orality (saving this attention for the second half of the book) but do want to offer some commentary on it at this point. The forerunners for this shift would be the superhero work of artists like John Romita and Neal Adams. When Romita took over illustration of *Daredevil* from Kirby and later *Spider-Man* from Ditko, his style was very similar to the artists that had preceded him but slowly morphed into a more realistic style. And when Adams reconceptualized *Batman* and the *Green Lantern/Green Arrow* series with Denny O'Neil, he consistently implemented distinctive physiognomy, complex shading, and detailed backgrounds that provided the illusion of real space. The influence of these artists spread as technology improved, distribution changed, timetables relaxed, and audience became more particularly interested in realistic representation. In the 1980s, improved print transfer became less costly for the publishers, and superhero comic books were being sold at specialty shops (and seeking to lose its low-cost association with newsprint). In wake of talks about creator ownership, publishers began to profit more and allowed illustrators to work on less titles (and sometimes just one title exclusively). Perhaps most importantly in the 1980s, superhero comic books began to lose the traditional young adult audience and sought to retain the adult audience. As the adult readers became increasingly exposed to literate culture bias against traditional art, they demanded "better" art from superhero comic books (eventually represented in the supposedly realistic depictions set forth by John Byrne, Arthur Adams, Jim Lee, and Bryan Hitch). This realism may be considered somewhat relative as it was accompanied by a new idealism of the human form as represented in superheroes, excessively muscled and generally beautiful. As superheroes were featured side-by-side in epic team-ups by supposedly realistic, detail-obsessed artists like George Perez, incredibly fit men with clearly defined abs and impossibly thin women with enormous breasts could be separated by only the uniqueness of their coloring or costumes. Moreover, despite the pressure that literacy exerted upon creators, the iconographic persists both as a style and as an idea in many different genres within comic book illustration but particularly within superhero comic books. In fact, certain aspects of the style, such as simplification, selective exaggeration, and caricature, have become more pronounced in the work of artists who have made the choice to work in this "rudimentary" form as compliment to the superhero genre. This can be seen in the increasingly popular "big-footed" style of artists, such as Joe Quesada and Ed McGuinness and with other prominent names within the industry. These other artists are often the most uniformly hailed by critics as innovators within the field but in fact may be recognizing a perceived need of the genre as it should be represented within the medium. Many of these artists, such as Frank Miller, Todd McFarlane, and Frank Quitely, started with the new house style in the 1980s of a pseudo-naturalism and realism but moved to something much more like McCloud's iconographic style.

At this point, I do not want to cover the implications of their styles within the Modern Age of superhero comic books (what I consider to be largely the experience of secondary orality) but I will make more extensive reference, especially, to Miller in forthcoming chapters. Also, I do not want to argue that traditionalism is represented in a certain critical percentage of post–1970s illustrations to demonstrate the continued importance or resurgence of traditionality. Within a culture of secondary orality, such choices will be made with much more self-awareness and could be motivated by more self-conscious impulses, such as an intentional nostalgia or kitsch. To me, what is most important is that the ideology of traditionalism persists as an aspect of the illustration nearly impossible to separate from superhero story: the iconography of the superhero itself, ranging from costumes to powers to fantasy situations. Much more important than artistic style is the iconographic images that consistently appear within superhero stories, such as that of Superman's costume, representing his role as a distinctive character; superhero stories have a large sense of their traditionality indelibly imbedded in almost every representation of the superhero: the costume as the emblem of the alter ego and symbol of much more. Superheroes and the trappings of their story serve as a check on the realistic representations of superheroes. Ultimately, realism and naturalism can never be completely part of the superhero comic book by virtue of its overall conventions, such as costumes, powers, and fantasy situations. These are simplified points of focus imprinted upon the characters in ways that circumvent the distance from characters that might be created by realistic depictions of a superhero's face or physiognomy. And even more than the iconographic facial features, costumes grew from the hasty production and delivery of superhero comic books, a visual shorthand and a marker of the superhero built on a limited color palate necessarily disconnected from realistic details. While the costume (at the forefront of these things) seems to not represent an aspect of the human lifeworld per se, it takes the idea of iconography a step further by representing a character via ultra-stylized symbols, such as a lightning bolt (Captain Marvel) or an eagle (Wonder Woman). These symbols do not immediately invite personal identification, but, if identification with characters who wear the symbols is encouraged by the story, these images can better place the audience in a subjective position (as these images carry even less unique characteristics than a simplified human face).

When McCloud introduces the idea of the icon, his working model is the smiley face, but he later refers to Superman's shield (the symbol on Superman's chest) as an icon. McCloud reinforces this idea upon referring to the iconic power of color. When McCloud refers to the colors of blue, yellow, and gray that represent Batman (*Understanding* 188), he could have just as easily referred to the colors of red, yellow, and blue that signify Superman, colors that work very similarly to the epithets of oral epics. Just as the symbols in medieval paintings have meaning grounded in their associations with stories and the human lifeworld (red worn by royalty, the dove flying above the mortal coil, and the cross of Christ's crucifixion and sacrifice), the symbols in superhero comics (like Superman's shield) are similarly grounded. Yet while the shield is a stylized "S" that abbreviates Superman's name and provides a centerpiece on his costume, the shield (like the above-mentioned medieval symbols) resonates with meaning beyond its role as a marker of language[37]; this greater meaning is drawn from the unfolding story of Superman. Although relatively little explanation was offered for his costume and shield early in the series, the costume has been consistently identified as an attempt to protect Clark Kent's identity (but it really reveals his identity as a super-powered being). One of the enduring clichés of Superman comics had been the way in which Clark Kent tears open his shirt to reveal the shield on his costume hidden beneath, his true identity and inner self rendered no less iconographically and even more abstractly than Golden and Silver Age renderings of his face. In addition, it has been alternately suggested to be his own design, his adoptive parents design, and a family crest and formal design from Krypton (often made with swaddling clothes from Krypton); however, as it is always vaguely tied to his identity and heritage, it is no less iconic as a consequence. In fact, it could be argued that such explanations, despite tying the origin of the costume to more specific details, make it more iconographic (making it the generalized self and the past of a character). This is much like the oral poets tendency to return to various simple starting point with the intention to describing them more elaborately. While Superman stories have delved into the specifics of his costume in a way not dissimilar to an oral poet's attention to a warrior's armor, the particulars and the variations never crowd out the generalities that enable widespread cross-cultural identification such as truth and justice, heroism and hope. Again, I am focusing primarily upon Superman as the first superhero but could just as easily focus on costumes and icons associated with other Golden Age superheroes, such as Batman or Silver Age superheroes, such as Spider-Man.[38] Even though their characters represent variations on the superhero themes (such as punishing criminals or the heavy burden of conscience), ultimately their symbology works in a similar way: to activate an even more generalized response to the heroes.[39] Even those Silver Age superheroes who might seem to present a problem to this idea, such as the Hulk (through metamorphosis) or Wolverine (through his changing costumes), have iconography associated with them that encourages people to imprint cultural values.[40]

With the superhero symbols like Superman's shield thus established as a general point of identification and general container of values held by all cultures, Superman's shield has been used to trigger reader connection and invite pathos in the Modern Era. Within Alan Moore's "For the Man Who Has Everything," Superman recognizes he is not his own man but the fantasy of every man, and, therefore, the shield design is distorted inside the replica of the last vestige of Krypton: the bottle city of Kandor. Within *The Dark Knight Returns*, the emblem becomes a representation of his adopted country, and, as the American flag morphs into the shield in the development of several panels, it indicates his compromised status as a one loyal to the misguided, paternalistic American government. In the "The Death of Superman" story line, after being killed by the Doomsday creature, Superman's cape (which bears the shield) has been torn from him and becomes a flag itself, flying only in a tattered form. Once reunited with Lois in "For Tomorrow," the narrative jumps forward to reveal her clad in nothing but Superman's cape, the shield lying across her breasts, indicating the forbidden fantasy of the story (a sexually satisfied Lois) alongside the conservative principle of the story (a Lois only in that position now that she is married to Superman). Although these examples from the Modern Age might seem to imply a cultural ability to self-consciously play with the past in a way unlike that of a traditional culture, the Modern Age will always be paying homage to that traditionality (adding to an existing schema). I would further argue that superhero comic books will never move far beyond the conventions of the oral epic as long as they employ the iconography of the costumed superhero. One of the best cases for this may be found with the work of Alex Ross, a fan-favorite realist painter who works from photographic models to produce painted pages with a realistic aesthetic like that of Norman Rockwell. With Superman rendered very much like George Reeves in works such as *Kingdom Come* and *Justice*, Ross's style seems to work in opposition to the amplification through simplification iconography described by McCloud.[41] However, the costume itself still enables general identification, as does the fantastic feats of Superman. Ultimately, Ross should be understood as a master of the superhero cliché, whether it is Superman in graceful flight, Captain America with bullets bouncing off his shield, or Spider-Man hunched on all fours and ready to pounce. And at this point, it should be unnecessary to clarify that becoming a master of cliché may be a vice in the literate world, but it is a virtue in the traditional world. Also, it's worth noting that Ross only attaches himself to projects that feature self-conscious heroes but ultimately reinstate the simplicity of the early superhero stories (with stark lines drawn between good and evil). (Ross's philosophy toward superheroes will be discussed more in chapter 6, with reference to his monumental work *Earth X*.) Regardless of what may sometimes be its self-consciousness use, the significance of the Superman's iconic shield has become more prominent in the Modern Age, curiously increasing in size on Superman's chest (compare Joe Shuster's rendering to that of John Byrne's to that of Ed McGuinness's).

In addition, his costumed presence has been reduced to perhaps its most basic form, as mere streaks of red, yellow, and blue, by many artists, such as Matt Wagner, Leinil Francis Yu, and Adam Kubert.[42] Of course, the streaks are the result of Superman moving at speeds supposedly beyond the ability of the human eye to register — and this brings up the artistic rendering of superpowers that works in a way similar to the iconography of superhero costumes. Although the exercise of superpowers would seem to separate superheroes from their non-superpowered reader, such depictions are the extension of basic human desires. "[W]hat boys or girls ... couldn't recognize themselves in these heroes, who are so much stronger and faster than they are? ... Whether or not athletic, what kid wouldn't desire Superman's ability to fly and lift heavy objects?" (Carrier 83). Many critics of the superhero story have emphasized an aspect of the preceding quotation and referred pejoratively to such desires as juvenile (McCloud included); however, these critics often gloss over the fact that the adult recognition of the limitations of reality does not eliminate such desires. This notion that we move beyond a previous state of ourselves (rather than simply add to it) relates to Platonic notions of the self and culture, at least in part. Regardless, the demonstration of power with which readers identify has been employed repeatedly, and certain demonstrations have become some of the most notable clichés of medium: whether it be Superman in flight or bending steel with his bare hands. One of the images of Superman that caused the most anxiety for publisher Harry Donnefeld would be the cover image of *Action Comics* #1 that featured Superman lifting a car over his head (feeling that it destroyed any "real world" credibility the title might develop) (Wright 9). However, that cover is now one of the most recognizable graphic images of the 20th century and has been placed in many contexts in the retellings of Superman's origin, including those in the Modern Age.[43] Within *A Superman for All Seasons*, the image is part of a video montage ironically used to brainwash a pawn of Lex Luthor. (It is accompanied by the "audio" clichés, "Look up in the sky! It's a bird! It's a plane! It's

Superman! Who can change the course of mighty rivers! Bend steel in his bare hands! He fights for truth, justice, and the American way!") Just as interesting is the use of the image in *Birthright*, in which a pre–Superman Clark Kent lifts a car over his head while on assignment in West Africa; surrounding Clark with African characters simultaneously shows the whiteness of the world in the original comic book and the universal applicability of the Superman story. Again, the intention of such use may be more self-conscious than repetitions of the same image in the Golden and Silver Ages, but it is simultaneously a derivative impulse such as that of traditional artists. Regardless, I include the Modern Age examples because the intention becomes less relevant than the end result: activating basic desire and enabling yet another means by which the superhero is identifiable in one's own terms.

A young Clark Kent fights against thugs in a variation of Superman's superheroic action on the famous cover of *Action Comics* #1 (from *Superman: Birthright*, p. 50).

4. Amplification Through Simplification

This reference to a specific cover and reconstituted panel image brings the general ideas set forth in this chapter to its most important point: the existence of the formulae in superhero comic books. This was already mentioned briefly in chapter 3, but the mention was intentionally brief, merely suggesting that narrative elements are repeated and rearranged. As Lord notes, "The most stable formulas will be those for the most common ideas in poetry. They will express the names of the actors, the main actions, time, and place" (*The Singer of Tales* 34). However, this idea is far from enough, as such a thing might be said to take place in a lesser degree within literate culture. While it is true that oral poets have a limited number of formulae that can be rearranged in a vast number of ways, we cannot forget that the arrangement is dictated by the meter of the song; Lord states:

> Precision was needed, and the work of Milman Parry was the culmination of that need. The result was a definition of the "formula" as "a group of words which is regularly employed under the same metrical conditions to express a given essential idea." ... The stress in Parry's definition on the metrical conditions of the formula led to the realization that the repeated phrases were useful not, as some have supposed, merely to the audience if at all, but also and even more to the singer in the rapid composition of his tale ... the formula is the offspring of the marriage of thought and sung verse. Whereas thought, in theory at least, may be free, sung verse imposes restrictions, varying in degree of rigidity from culture to culture, that shape the form of thought [*The Singer of Tales* 30–31].

With this definition of formulae in mind, we can return to one of Ong's consistent claims about oral literature. For the formulae of the oral epic, story is integrally related to the particulars of sound, and this relationship gives the story its immediacy. In turn, my overview of the illustration of superhero comic books will lead to a related idea that springs from traditional culture (but may not be obvious, because of the general ideas about the visual in many studies of orality and literacy). For the formulae of superhero comic books, story is integrally related to the particulars of illustration, and this relationship gives the story its immediacy.

At this point in the book, the separation between orality as a function of time and literacy as a function of space should no longer be wholly accepted. Nevertheless, I do want to become more specific in my description of the formulae of superhero comic books to identify how something like meter and rhythm dictate the presentation of story. From their very inception, superhero comic book creators were required to produce the latest episode within a certain definitively structured framework that begins with page limits. Although the books were larger overall at the outset in terms of pages, the expectation was that no individual story would exceed six pages; as characters became popular, their individual stories grew in length but were still limited to a set number of pages. In addition, the size of pages were consistent within each book and from book to book, necessitating an arrangement of panels that would completely fill up the pages. Since empty space was considered a cheat by readers and therefore unacceptable by editors of the comic book, creators had to make things fit and work in a way foreign to literate aesthetics (that allowed writers to end a chapter by adding just one line onto the next page). As panels contained both text and illustration, it became incumbent upon creators to limit elements of both, striking a balance between them in order to not crowd one or the other out for inartistic reasons. All of the above mentioned elements impinged upon one another and certainly, inexpert comic book creators could make narrative choices that were simplistic (keeping all panels the same size) or sloppy (wrapping up the numerous loose ends of the episode with an overly wordy summary, lacking an illustration, in the last panel of page six). However, the expert comic book creators make narrative choices that capitalize on the poetic form of the medium; in addition to the choices made about illustrative style and the composition of individual panels, creators may choose to enlarge an important panel, use adjacent panels to represent simultaneous action, and reserve a plot-driven surprise for the first panel of the newly turned page. Each choice made impinges upon other choices on the immediate page, on the two-page spread, in the issue, and in the series as a whole (and experienced creators understand this well).

For instance, in the first Superman story to feature "The Mysterious Mr. Mxyztplk," John Sikela uses circular panels to focus attention on certain events but must find ways to incorporate that within a rectangular page (still using most if not all of the page space and moreover, still enabling the audience to easily follow the story). In the issue #2 of Jack Kirby's *New Gods*, Kirby uses mostly large panels to indicate general significance of the "cosmic" story[44]; however, he does alternates sizes, using the largest to indicate the vastness of an entire world (New Genesis), the importance of a major character (Darkseid), and the significance of an action (Lightray's argument with the High-Father). As a consequence of these designs from the beginning of the issue, Kirby had to continue this design aesthetic throughout the entirety of the issue, if not the series, to maintain the rhythm created by the illustration. In issue #191 of *Daredevil*, Frank Miller uses several techniques to accentuate the narrative that moves from a current to a past timeframe. While the current timeframe in which he talks to Bullseye is lacking almost all background detail, the past timeframe in which he tries to rescue a boy from his damaged life is depicted with more background detail.[45] Also, as the story progresses, repetition is used extensively to create an internal rhythm by returning to the same story ideas (with Daredevil pointing a gun at Bullseye in exactly the same way in the central panel of page 11 and the first panels of pages 12, 14, 15, 16). All of these choices are similar to willful departures made in traditional art from the conventions of naturalism and realism: manipulations of presentation and size, employments of selective details and symbolic repetition. I realize that I'm dealing with these examples very briefly, and all deserve in depth analysis. However, these quick mentions serve the purpose of demonstrating the implicit complexity of mainstream superhero comic book design rarely noticed by the audience (just as the complexity of formulae is seldom apprehended by traditional culture). Working with Lord's ideas that such design is first (and perhaps foremost) a concern for the composer, there are innumerable "how to" manuals that address these issues, but the best are those written by practitioners and theorists, such as Will Eisner (*Comics and Sequential Art*) and Scott McCloud (*Making Comics*); although not necessarily written for practitioners, Robert Harvey's *The Art of the Comic Book* is a critical study that works like the two aforementioned works, addressing not only the *how* but also the *why*. Yet, while the *why* is of paramount interest to scholars like myself (and thus shapes my notion of the "best"), it should be acknowledged that the expert comic book creators of the Golden and Silver Ages worked without a fully conscious notion of why they did what they did; for instance, even the team of Stan Lee and Jack Kirby, often identified on the cusp of the Modern Age, regularly avoided discussions of the cultural or aesthetic implications of their work.[46] On one hand, this lack of self-awareness may reinforce the tirades of critics of the superheroes and comic books; with creators unable to articulate the higher principles at work, superhero comic books clearly do not live up to the standards of high art. On the other hand, this lack of self-awareness may reinforce the idea that superheroes and comic books are born of an impulse like that of the oral poets: "[The singer] does not 'memorize' formulas, any more than we as children 'memorize' language. He learns them by hearing them in other singers' songs, and by habitual usage they become part of his singing as well"

(Lord, *The Singer of Tales* 36). Even though no artform can ever be naturalized, some artforms are more a part of traditional practices than others, and comic books seem to fall into that category; as with the interaction with the environment that Ong's "primitive" can't describe, superhero comic books are something that many of the early creators only have an intuitive grasp of.[47]

In regard to the formulae of comic books, I'd like to make one final note to accentuate the traditionality of a medium that necessitates subjective involvement. In addition to choices that the creator must make to more effectively represent the story on a page, there is one more aspect of comic book formulae that harkens to the participatory ideals of oral performance. As previously mentioned, very important to McCloud is the idea that comic books are a succession of panels (or sequential art), but that leaves the "space" between the panels. According to McCloud, fundamental to the visual narrative of comic books is the "gutter," a term he uses to describe that space between the panels. In many ways requiring readers to fill in the narrative gap between the panels was an aspect of superhero comic book stories especially important in stories of the Comics Code era, in which violence needed to be obscured. McCloud uses two panels in sequence to represent the narrative requirement placed on recipients: the first with a man running from another man wielding an axe and yelling, "Now, you die!," and the second with the city scene from which the only sound heard is "Eeyaa!"

> Every act committed to paper by the comics artist is aided and abetted by a silent accomplice. An equal partner in crime known as the reader. I may have drawn an axe being raised in this example, but I'm not the one who let it drop or decided how hard the blow, or who screamed and why. That dear reader, was your special crime.... Participation is a powerful force in any medium [*Understanding* 68–69].

The emphasis in McCloud's formulation of comic books resides in the participation of the recipient in the visual narrative. Will Eisner concurs with this estimation of the medium: "[Comics] are a participatory medium.... The blank spaces between images, when properly employed are not blank. They are abstract elements of time and space in which imagined action connects the images" (Gorla). This is not to imply that the meaning of works is necessarily ambiguous, as the gaps to be filled in superhero comic books of the Golden and Silver Ages rarely require intuitive leaps that take the story in a radically different direction. However, in this way, these calls for participation are clearly connected to the narrative demand of oral tradition, requiring active participation of the recipient that reinforces (rather than overcomplicates) ideas central to story. For a multitude of reasons, it is unnecessary to give a profile of the many uses of the gutter and the functions of editing in superhero stories except to say that they exist. Returning to our standard of Superman, the variety is great throughout comic book history, ranging from picture book transitions between plot points in the earliest Siegel and Shuster stories to the dynamic action of splash page representations of Superman in Jack Kirby's *Jimmy Olsen* and *Forever People* stories to the interweaving of parallel plotlines in *Superman: Birthright*. All make particular demands on the recipient in terms of simple understanding and general storytelling, encouraging creative connections between narrative and thematic elements.[48]

In *The Singer Resumes the Tale*, Lord takes issue with Derek Pearsall's interpretation of Lord's previous work as suggesting "that literacy is the death-blow of oral tradition" (qtd. in Lord, *The Singer Resumes* 102). Although he doesn't completely disagree with that suggestion (a bit more extreme in his position than Ong), he is more measured than Pearsall and states that literacy merely "carries the seeds of the eventual demise of oral traditional composition" (102). Thereafter, Lord notes the ways in which orality has thrived in cultures where the majority of people were literate. However, with the notion of secondary orality, Ong suggests that orality should not be understood as in continual decline within literate societies; instead, orality is always present, although somewhat latent, and capable of being reactivated by media innovation. Moreover, in both *The Gutenberg Galaxy* and *Understanding Media*, McLuhan begins to move away from terms like *orality* and *literacy* as his own schema and suggests that the resurgence of a traditional outlook need not be modified by the term *secondary*. All of this is important to keep in mind as I again argue that visual culture in general is far from the death-blow of oral culture and traditionality. *Visual culture* is a term with which one must deal in a measured and nuanced way; the visual culture that develops as a consequence of literacy's orientation toward typography is very different from the visual culture of comic books (and perhaps new media in general). The approach to illustration practiced within the medium of superhero comic books proceeds upon, activates, and encourages a psychology in line with traditional culture. In fact, the content of superhero comic books causes this traditionality to persist even beyond the 1980s (when artwork is no longer uniformly traditional). Perhaps most important is the way that audience engagement is built into the formulae of superhero comic books, and, therefore, illustration provides an immediacy like that of the spoken word. The limitations of the comic book length and page size necessitate creative possibilities in illustration and panel arrangement, making the comic book even more clearly like the epic poem, a medium that necessarily contains an epic hero. Rather than work in ways that are somewhat like orality, as is the case of much European medieval literature, this traditional medium actually works in ways more purely in line with orality. Since *oral literature* is a widely acknowledged contradiction in terms, it makes more sense to refer to superhero comic books as a traditional artform, a medium that reconfigured literacy in a way not unlike the printed text's reconfiguration of orality. The following chapters will begin to chart a history beyond the rough shod epics of the Golden Age and suggest ways that the primary orality of superhero comic books is modified, challenged by literacy, and changed into something very like secondary orality.

Chapter 5

The Persistence of Traditionality

When Industry Workers Become Artisans

The first four chapters of this book are designed to establish a foundation for superhero comic books as a resurgence of the oral epic and traditional art that thrives in the midst of a literate culture oriented toward the textual and the realistic. As the result of a convergence of various intentional and unintentional acts, the medium of comic books operates in a way fundamentally unlike entirely text-based books produced by the conventional printing press; and the popularity of the superhero within comic books results from the resemblance of the medium to the narrative works of traditional culture. In an effort to show how the early state of the technology and industry had a lasting effect on the comic books, I focused on the earliest eras but extended the historical scope to include examples beyond the Golden Age. The next four chapters of this book are more strictly historical, examining the evolution of this unlikely traditional-culture phenomenon; by the end of the book, it will be apparent how this phenomenon quickly transitions to what Ong calls *secondary orality* (and what I call *new traditionality*) and reveals itself as a indicator of the dynamics of the digital age. In this chapter, I will be looking at the Silver Age and the way the rough phrases and formulae of the Golden Age become much more like the distinguished oral epics of the ancient and medieval worlds, with the Marvel superhero stories of Stan Lee, Jack Kirby, and Steve Ditko. In subsequent chapters on the Modern Age, I will examine the failure of the attempt to impose literacy in the DC multiverse; the self-conscious examination of the tension between the traditional and literary in the works of Frank Miller and Alan Moore; and the firm establishment of Modern Age superhero comic books as self-conscious purveyors of the aesthetics of the new traditional era, the digital age, and postmodernism. Ultimately, it will become apparent that superhero comic books have never and perhaps can never be completely separated from the methodologies, themes, and ideas growing from the sensibilities of traditional culture. To begin the second phase of this journey, I will be focusing on the Silver Age, Frederic Wertham, and Marvel's superhero comic books.

Fredric Wertham Loves Superhero Comic Books (or, How Gay Superheroes Are Not as Bad as Violent Monsters)

While there are several explanations of how the designations of the Golden and Silver Ages were developed for superhero comic books,[1] these designations have stuck as a means to separate the first decades of superhero comic books from the next few. The desire to do so is a result of a perceived separation between eras implied by one or both of the following conceptual shifts: (1) DC's classic superheroes and DC's reinvented superheroes and (2) DC's classic superheroes and Marvel's new superheroes. Both are significant as the first eventually leads to DC's Earth-1 and Earth-2 split and the second creates the other major universe in which superheroes relate to one another. Since the ramifications of the Earth-1 and Earth-2 split do not completely play out and become clear until the Modern Age, I will be focusing on this in chapter 6. Therefore, the events leading up to and including the Silver Age creation of the Marvel universe will be the express purview of this chapter. In order to fully appreciate the Silver Age and the Marvel universe, I must highlight the most interesting event that continues the above-mentioned "convergence of various intentional and unintentional acts," an event that not only prolongs the primary orality of superhero comic books but also allows it to flourish. Instigated by the general fear of new media and the paranoia of Cold War culture, the single event most important to enabling the maturation of this fledgling traditionality would be the congressional hearings initiated by Fredric Wertham (and the Comics Code they subsequently encouraged). On the surface, this seems like a very unlikely source of "help" for superhero comic books (even if that help can be characterized as inadvertent), as Wertham's unsupported attacks were not limited to crime and horror comics (his favorite targets). Instead, Wertham charged that comic books, a medium inherently juvenile, caused delinquency in many forms, extending beyond the violence clearly encouraged by crime and horror comic books. In Wertham's *Seduction of the Innocent*, he would charge that Superman also encouraged violence (and fascism) and that Batman and Robin encouraged homosexuality. The resultant public scare and self-regulation of the comic book industry via the Comics Code identified superhero stories as suitable only for juveniles, and it created an artificial authority that regulated the content of superhero stories; this works contrary to the dynamics that allow free flow of information and ideas within traditional culture. Many proponents of comic books have identified Fredric Wertham as the single most important figure in stagnating its artistic growth in America. However, at the same time, Wertham and the congressional hearings eliminated the comic book competition that seemed to be bringing the popularity of superhero comic books to an end in the 1950s, and, moreover, this also created a safe haven for the traditionality of superhero comic books to continue to develop (set apart from the literate principle of the adults' high-culture world). This chapter will examine how Wertham paved the way for the Silver Age of Marvel superheroes, an extension and refinement of the primary orality developed in Golden Age superhero comic books. While often dubbed the Marvel "revolution" by its creators, the Marvel superhero universe was much more of a realization, with creators like Stan Lee, Jack Kirby, and Steve Ditko working together to refine the raw material of the Golden Age. Thanks to the inept social consciousness of Wertham and the immense creative efforts of Lee, Kirby, and Ditko, the traditional approach of superhero comics would continue to be refined, making only gradual overtures toward literacy.

While I earlier identified the history of superhero comic books and their characteristics, it is important to clarify and perhaps reemphasize some aspects of the early history. To begin with the superheroes themselves, despite their uniform "heaviness," the prominent heroes were really quite diverse ranging from the justice-over-the-law vigilantes, such as Superman and Batman, to love-the-establishment heroes Green Lantern and the Flash. Concomitantly, Captain Marvel with his adolescent alter ego, Wonder Woman with her Amazonian background, and Captain America with his patriotic sentiment all hailed from different sensibilities and appealed to different demographics. In addition, despite the vast popularity of superhero comic books and their league of imitators, the diversity of genre initially seen in the comic strip also continued to a lesser degree within the late 1930s and early 1940s (the years of the superhero boom within the industry). Other genres that enjoyed decent sales included the genres of funny animal stories, such as Disney Comics, teen humor best exemplified by Archie Comics (and appealing strongly to teenage female readers),[2] and science fiction and fantasy that similarly adhered to many of the tenets of oral epics.[3] However, more important as an indicator of the shift in demographic targeting would be the growing success of "jungle comics," including many Fiction House titles such as *Sheena, Jungle Queen*. Like many other titles in many other genre categories seeking to bolster its consumer base of young male readers, the jungle tales featured scantily clad women in exotic settings. In a way that perhaps related to this content, these jungle tales were generally imperialist stories with overt racist caricatures that extended far beyond the imperialist fables of writers in the literary world, like Rudyard Kipling. In addition to proving the superiority of the white Western world, these stories often featured violence and sexuality in prurient ways, with implied scenes of torture and sadomasochism. One reason to make special mention of jungle tales is that their basic narrative shared some common links to the traditionality of superhero stories but for the most part borrowed ideas from the age of exploration (and the Enlightenment), rejecting the tribal in favor of the grand ideal of literate society. Even though the industry practices toward workers and ownership of intellectual property changed very little, it is inconceivable that comic books could forever remain an island of traditionality and creators would continue to resist the pressure of ideas set forth by the literate world. Another reason to mention the jungle tales is that the popularity of superheroes, while not challenged by jungle tales per se, would be challenged by another genre that utilized similar taboo themes and explicit content in an "adult" context, also working somewhat outside the epic tradition: crime stories. Working under the guise of the cautionary tale, titles like *Crime Does Not Pay* featured depictions of extreme violence, existing during the war years in the space between the pulps and popular comic books. However, after the end of World War II, crime comic books soared in popularity with an audience apparently willing to return to the post–Depression sensibility that created film noir and questioned the American dream.[4] In obvious ways, these subversive stories would undermine cultural ideals and work in ways generally contrary to the affirmations of community in the traditional superhero story.

> Whatever might be said about their moral virtues, these crime comic books marked an important stage in the evolution of the industry and youth culture. By demonstrating that successful comic books need not be confined to juvenile adventure stories, fatuous teen humor, and talking animals, they expanded the creative possibilities of the medium considerably. More significantly, they broke from the unwritten code that said comic books had to offer fulfillment, affirmation, and conflict resolution to their young audience on terms established by a supposedly virtuous and progressive society [Wright 84].

The negative connotations in Wright's descriptions of other genres is clear, but, nevertheless, he is very accurate in his representation of the change of target audience among publishers and in his understanding of the content of crime comic books. Ultimately, this new trend would pave the way for more explicit content to come and a controversy that would question the medium as a whole.

While crime comic books began to cause controversy and invite protest in many forms, the general popularity of their more gruesome images encouraged the publication of horror comic books, seen most clearly in the rise of Bill Gaines's EC line of horror titles, such as *Tales from the Crypt*.[5] Remembered well for featuring bloody dismemberments and titillating presentations of partially clad women, the EC horror titles characteristically turned on a surprise ending that reshaped the meaning of the story as a whole. Often cleverly following in the tradition of crime stories that exposed the dark underbelly of American ideals, these horror comic books were far from mindless entertainment but still were undeniably gratuitous (with highly detailed, realistic artwork). Wright characterizes the EC approach in the following way:

> EC offered young people a liberating alternative to ... culture. With a calculated editorial strategy that sought to demolish the myths, triumphalism, and half-truths that informed Cold War America, EC challenged prevailing assumptions about race, democracy, anti-communism, authority, warfare, the atom bomb, history, marriage, family, children, and ultimately, taste [Wright 152–153].

With this in mind, it is hardly a surprise that EC horror titles brought to a head the concerns incited by crime and horror comic books in general. Because of the fears of U.S. culture in the 1950s, a psychiatrist named Fredric Wertham would navigate cultural currents in a way that made him respectable at the time but quite infamous in years to come. "At this time America faced two primary fears: communism and juvenile delinquency. The axis on which these two met found Wertham, whose studies probed the social dynamic permitting the development of these fears and the underlying violence inflaming their intensity" (Reibman xxvi). Well-respected in his field for his research and general practice, Wertham was already the author of works on the psychology of murder and the role of psychiatrists in court cases by the time he entered this contentious discussion of comic books. Since the intricacies of the debates have been explored well by authors, such as Amy Nyberg in *Seal of Approval*, it is unnecessary to go into exhaustive detail, but a few specifics are important to include. As anxieties led to comic book burnings and eventually a hearing convened by the Senate Subcommittee on Juvenile Delinquency, support from prominent figures marshaled on both sides of the debate (with the Child Study Association and Dr. Benjamin Spock writing in support of comic book reading) (Wright 89). However, in the McCarthy era, hints of anti–Americanism were often tied to the specter of juvenile delinquency, leading to great support regardless of the case being made. While Wertham was not the only cultural critic who made this case, he was undoubtedly the most important in regard to comic books and fairly representative of the general sentiments against them.

After publishing several articles based on the dubious connections between comic book reading and juvenile delinquency, Wertham would write *Seduction of the Innocent*, his widely read condemnation of comic books in general; therein, he lumped together all comic books that featured crime (whether crime, horror, romance, science fiction, jungle, or superhero stories) as "crime comics" (Wertham 20). Based largely upon the self-reporting of the juvenile delinquents with whom he worked, Wertham cobbled together a case that suggested comic book reading led to the fundamental problems facing and caused by youth today. Appealing to the conspiratorial fears of 1950s Cold War culture, Wertham would regularly portray the comic book publishing industry as an indifferent and perhaps insidious elite, shaping American culture in unhealthy ways (Wright 162).[6] Although he would repeatedly reiterate that comic books were not the sole cause of juvenile delinquency, Wertham's book is filled with alarmist rhetoric that works against the establishment of a nuanced position. "Murder, crime and drug traffic are offered to children in literature which the defenders of comic books call the modern version of the stories of the Brothers Grimm, Han Christian Andersen or Mother Goose. But are there heroin addicts in Grimm, marihuana smokers in Anderson or dope peddlers in Mother Goose?" (Wertham 84). With dubious ability as a critic of literature and visual art, Wertham made vast generalizations, took examples out of context, and ignored the resolution and larger meaning of works. Although his primary target was crime and horror comic books, he did also aim invectives at superhero comic books as well, identifying the partnership of Batman and Robin as homosexual pederasty[7] and superheroes in general as fascists who glorified violence:

> The Superman type of comic books tends to force and superforce.... Actually, Superman (with the big S on his uniform — we should, I suppose, be thankful that it is not an S.S.) needs and endless stream of submen.... It is this feature that engenders in children either one or the other of two attitudes: either they fantasy themselves as supermen, with attendant prejudices against the submen, or it makes them submissive and receptive to the blandishments of strong men who will solve all their social problems for them — by force.... The superman conceit gives boys and girls the feeling that ruthless go-getting based on physical strength or the power of weapons or machines is the desirable way to behave.... In these children there is an exact parallel to the blunting of sensibilities in the direction of cruelty that has characterized a whole generation of central European youth fed in the Nietzsche-Nazi myth of the exceptional man who is beyond good and evil[8] [Wertham 34, 97].

Although it might be tempting to berate Wertham for all his missteps in literary interpretation (from the S.S. comment to making all of central European youth into sub-men), such a move is unnecessary with generations now soundly rejecting much of his work. Instead, I will simply point out the first part of this series of quotations where Wertham indulges in the sort of cause and effect argument that he repeatedly claimed his work avoided. This brief example is not intended to indict Wertham's faulty case any more than it has already been but to identify basic problems with his ideas that even some recent, more sympathetic readings cannot help but identify as a low point of his intellectual career.[9]

Wertham's ideas are useful to study as an example of a certain type of intellectual orientation toward comic books, and he is undeniably important as an activist who radically changed the direction of the industry (and unintentionally preserved the traditional culture of the superhero comic books). Wertham is the best representative of the cultural critics (some already quoted in this book) whose misgivings toward comic books have as much to do with misunderstanding the new medium as objecting to the content.

> The comic book was a new medium altogether, a medium that relied on the interaction of words and pictures to tell stories in a unique way.... Reading comic books was teaching young readers a whole new vocabulary, one that was largely foreign to adults, because adult readers did not immerse themselves deeply enough in this new cultural form to learn its language. The conflict over comic books became generational ... [Nyberg 5].

Recognizing Wertham's animosity toward superhero comic books and his inability to separate them from crime and horror comic books indicates not only his poor readership but also his anxiety toward the medium in general. As Matthew Pustz notes, Wertham was a quintessential outsider to the unusual culture of the comic book consumer: "[T]he few outsider perspectives on comic books — Wertham's *Seduction of the Innocent* is a classic example — are perhaps even more flawed by denying consumers the power to explain how they use their favored texts" (Pustz 202). In general, Wertham was motivated by his good intentions, "modern" psychiatric studies, overconfidence in his dubious interpretive skills, and a poorly articulated devotion to literate culture. Entrenched in the conventions of high literacy, Wertham's awkward commentary often indicates what this fledgling artform is as well as is not. Wertham's biographer, James Reibman, identifies Wertham's concerns as quintessentially Platonic, fearing that the influence of art will distort the mind. Something frequently lost in the summaries of *Seduction of the Innocent* is that Wertham identified several tiers in the negative consequences that he associated with comic books: (1) illiteracy, (2) juvenile delinquency, and (3) problems with psychosexual development. In order to set up the first of these three areas, Wertham stated: "Comic books are death on reading. The dawn of civilization was marked by the invention of writing. Reading, therefore, is not only one of the cornerstones of civilized life, it is also one of the main foundations of a child's adjustment to it" (121). Clearly articulating his bias toward the literate world and inability to completely apprehend or appreciate the experience of the comic book, Wertham would later demonstrate a literate sensibility with his description of the "inartistic" illustration of comic books.

> I know that quite a number of [comic book artists] are highly gifted; but they have to turn out an inartistic assembly-line product. That is what is essentially wrong with comic books: there are too many pictures. The mass effect of the stereotyped, standardized images is something totally different from and much inferior to the well-spaced illustrations in a good children's book. Instead of helping a child to develop his artistic imagination, they stifle it. Even if the drawing were good, which they are not, their numbers would kill their artistic effect [267].

In this quotation, Wertham manages to cover several of my major points within this book (but he is uniformly negative about them all). Implicit within this quotation is many of the central tenets of literate society: that pictures are inferior to text, that stereotype and cliché are wrong, and that realistic drawing is good; in addition, picture books are for children and text should be eventually preferred to pictures.

Regardless of the overall motivation behind his work, Wertham's book would be the primary mover toward the 1954 Senate hearings at which he was a star witness[10] and at which Bill Gaines became the scapegoat for the fears of adults facing the Red Menace, juvenile delinquency, and a medium that literate culture couldn't fully comprehend. Although Wertham claimed to not encourage censorship, this was essentially his aim and he used a convoluted argument about the majority in a democracy to justify it (Wertham 302). To satisfy an outraged public legally held in check by the first amendment, the industry agreed to regulate itself through the Comics Code. Modeled on the Hollywood production code and the unenforced code drafted earlier by the Association of Comics Publishers in 1948, the Comics Code contained rules primarily designed to eliminate depictions of sexuality, excessive violence, and drug use; some publishers like DC had long been an advocate of such self-regulation, in the hopes of staving off something like the 1954 hearings.[11] However, the code went further in its dictates; in concept, authority figures must always be portrayed with respect, and good must always defeat evil, and in literal fact, vampires, werewolves, and zombies must not be featured, and the words "horror" and "terror" must not be used in titles. As might be expected, the code brought to an end most of the crime and horror comic books being published at the time, as such stories under the Comic Code would be completely void of the content that had made them popular; within the year, all of the EC horror titles were cancelled, and Bill Gaines focused most of his energy on producing the subversive humor of *Mad* magazine (not so vulnerable to the code).[12] Wertham was dissatisfied with the Comics Code (identifying it as not directly addressing the problem):

> [T]he Senate Subcommittee ... stopped short of accepting Wertham's findings, concluding that further research of a broad and controlled nature was needed before the precise

influence of comic books could be determined.... Frederic Wertham found nothing to praise in comic book industry self-regulation. He dismissed the code as the latest attempt by publishers to whitewash their products and deceive the public [Wright 174–175].

Regardless of Wetham's opinion of it, the code forced the industry to capitulate to Wertham's insistent claim (that the content of comic books is inappropriate) but more significantly, his assumption (that only a certain type of content is appropriate to comic books). Perhaps due to the fact that so many young people read comic books, Wertham labeled comic books as "children's literature." In addition to limiting the artform to a particular audience, acknowledging the simple fact that it could or should be regulated potentially makes it something less than an artform: folk art at best and a commercial product at worst.

Responding to the dictates of Wertham and those like him is something that seemingly threatens the integrity of an artform that I have thus far identified as primarily traditional. Rather than grow from the diffused authority of the community, comic books were thereafter proceeding from the rules established by the few or one. A fixed point of reference for a story is a clear function of literacy as it has been identified by scholars of literacy (and in other contexts, by Michel Foucault and Roland Barthes who argue that such authority as an illusion). Nevertheless, I believe that even less than threaten, the code unintentionally preserved the oral culture of comic books expressed in what had, up to that point, been its most popular genre: superhero stories. As already mentioned in this chapter, superhero comic books were becoming less popular in the wake of other comic books that I believe were influenced much more clearly by the dominance of the literate culture around it (although they still existed in a space between those two cultures and may have had as many traditional as literate characteristics). Still, the trend seemed to be taking comic books further from their roots as a traditional artform, and the surprising result of Wertham's misguided protest is that it allowed superhero comic books to continue to thrive as a traditional artform. While there were certain genres that were relatively immune from the code's regulations, comic book publishers lost their latest popular sensations and superhero comic books would return to fill that gap. "While funny animal, teen, and romance comics performed adequately on the newsstands, the publishers were in search of a genre that would appeal to the baby-boom youngsters who were now teenagers. Their 'experiment' would be to resurrect the genre that started the industry, that of the superhero" (Nyberg 136). Considering the code regulations as a whole, the integrity of superhero stories were not threatened greatly by them, with the exception of the limitations on depictions of violence; but superheroes lent themselves to fantasy situations in which violence could still be depicted in relatively nonthreatening ways. In addition, as subversive as early stories of Superman and Batman were, more recent depictions had been featuring them as advocates of traditional authority; this would not be as radical a change as might be initially suspected, as both fought for traditional values from the start against the corruption of larger social forces (much like Odysseus fighting to reinstitute hospitality in the new world formed by the suitors). In essence, referring to comic books as children's literature undoubtedly limited the audience in a way unwelcome by writers such as Jerry Siegel and Bill Finger but had also been part of the formula for many superheroes for years (consider Captain Marvel's adolescent alter ego and the teenage sidekick phenomenon). Moreover, this characterization now given to comic books created a haven for the redevelopment of "folk art" separate from adult sensibilities much more clearly shaped by the ideas of literate culture. As will be shown, this persistence of superhero comic books in successive generations opens up opportunities for early readers to continue to read superhero comic books, informed and perhaps later entrenched in sensibilities in line with traditionality.[13]

With its own code established in 1941, DC was relatively unhurt by the Comics Code in terms of its lineup of publications; despite the general decline in the popularity of superheroes during the heyday of crime and horror comics, their standard heroes had continued to produce sales. In addition to the success of the television show, *The Adventures of Superman*, "the Superman comic books seemed immune from recession, consistently selling around a million copies per issue" (Wright 182). Actually, the connection between the television show and the comic books may have been the key element that saved the title from a recession generally caused by the growing popularity of the new medium of television.[14] Other superhero titles still being published were *Batman* and *Wonder Woman*, but, like Superman, both characters had been receiving less attention from publishers who were contemplating other directions for their comic book lines. However, as various superheroes like the *Flash* and *Green Lantern* were revived with great success, this encouraged DC and other publishers to again push the superhero to the center of their lineups. And as these titles again provided a commercial cornerstone for the comic book industry, more superhero titles were seen including the enormously successful update of the Justice Society of America (now called the Justice League of America). Many have commented on the advent of the scientist hero in this era with the Flash and the Atom and the blending of the superhero story with science fiction with Green Lantern and Hawkman — both as a step toward greater realism in the genre. However, the science is pseudo-science at best, ignoring the physical impossibilities of superspeed with the Flash and the ability to alter one's physical size with the Atom; superpowers were gained usually as the result of accidents or unexpected discoveries and thus, didn't question but set aside the Platonic ideal of scientific accuracy. In addition, the supernatural is still part of the larger body of superhero stories produced in the Silver Age, and the stories of Batman and Superman prefigure these Silver Age trends (science and science fiction) rather directly. Barry Allen's situation is only realistic as far as one might be willing to redefine the conventions of narrative realism; after he discovers that a lab accident gives him the ability to move at super-speed, he almost immediately dons a costume in order to fight crime.[15] More than anything, DC's new lineup of superhero titles was an extension of the previous conventions established by Golden Age superheroes. Taking into account my argument thus far, these habits were likely an easy, very "natural" fallback position; in addition to business practices and community ideals remaining the same, the controversies of the 1950s undoubtedly reinforced the idea that their material was not being produced for the "literate" culture at large. The exception to this simple continuation of previous stories would be what some saw as an impossible aspect of superhero stories: the idea that superheroes lived in the present timeframe of the "real" world. If that were the case with DC heroes like Superman and Batman now included in the Justice League of America, both would now practically be senior citizens and ready for retirement. In order to maintain the relative youth of their heroes, DC would develop an alternate earth (inspired by Gardner Fox's "Flash of Two Worlds") with current heroes living on Earth-1 and Golden Age heroes living on Earth-2. While this might be seen as an intrusion of literacy, it should be recognized as a somewhat permanent recognition of and perhaps desire for variation (that seems to indicate secondary orality much more than literacy).[16] Regardless, this phenomenon will be discussed at length in chapter 6.

The Marvel "Revolution" as a Fuller Realization of the Epic: Superheroes That Respect Your Intelligence

The express purview of this chapter is the reaction of Atlas comics (originally Timely and eventually Marvel) to the resurgence of superhero comic books in a comic book market that was devoid of any other clear prospects for extreme popularity. While Atlas was certainly not the only publisher to rethink their lineup and try to produce superhero stories (others include Dell, Charlton, Archie, and Tower), none of DC's competitors challenged their dominance in this field until the establishment of Atlas' Marvel universe.[17] At the beginning of the 1960s, chief editor Stan Lee was primarily producing science fiction comic books with a limited success that was bolstered by the newly hired artistic talents of Jack Kirby and Steve Ditko. The attitude of Lee's comics tended to differ from that presented in the platitudes of DC superheroes but still resulted in a community ethic similar to that represented in traditional art:

> The unknown in DC's comic books was something to be conquered through scientific progress. In Marvel's, it was something best left undisturbed.... While the moral thrust of these comic books ultimately affirms the individual's obligation to society, much like those of DC did, the important difference — and the key to Marvel's developing formula — lay in the grim endings and tragic qualities of the characters [Wright 202–203].

While Wright comments on work by Lee, Kirby, and Ditko that precedes the advent of Marvel superheroes, these ideas are important to keep in mind as the basis for the creation of their epic universe. The three creators worked with a similar worldview that would predispose their work to represent a perspective that in the modern world can be read as tribal (with a dubiousness about progress and a fear of the unknown).[18] Their characters were sympathetic and yet flawed and proud in ways that led to dramatic conflict and poignant ends not unlike the heavy heroes of oral epics. And their concerns lay with stories that worked outside the confines laid down by the explicit rules of the Comics Code, questioning that comic books were intended just for children. Although somewhat humorous in its obvious approach, Lee would retitle the Ditko-illustrated *Amazing Fantasy* as *Amazing Adult Fantasy: The Magazine that Respects Your Intelligence*, thus separating adult content from objectionable material. When they began to produce superhero comic books, this perspective would cause their work to be decidedly different — but not as literacy is different from orality. Instead, these creators would take the basic phrases and rudimentary formulas of superhero comic books established in the Golden Age and weave them into something more than DC's universe, haphazardly filled with epic happenings. They would serve as mature producers of superhero stories, much like Homer would serve as a mature producer of the oral epic; this is not to suggest that these creators have equivalent artistic accomplishments to Homer (as their mediums are somewhat dissimilar) but to suggest that their methodology is incredibly comparable. In identifying the early stories of Golden Age superheroes as produced by oral culture, I was not suggesting that each episode represented the greatest height of the oral epic.[19] The formulas that these artisans inherited were often rough-hewn because they were produced by predecessors reinventing the carriage wheel in a world that found the carriage wheel hopelessly outdated, perhaps suited only as a toy for youth. Nevertheless, informed by their knowledge of the craft, these subsequent artisans took the formulas and rearranged them in an effort to create a magnificent carriage, reiterating and reinventing at the same time. If this metaphor seems labored, let me explain that I'm playing with Ong's suggestion that literate culture defines the epic poem of primary oral cultures as "a four-legged automobile without wheels" (Ong, *The Presence* 21); the horse-drawn carriage is an extension of this metaphor to describe the height of the oral epic like Homer's *Iliad* or *Odyssey* that is realized shortly before the wide spread of literate culture.[20] As I begin to make this case about Marvel superheroes, I want to acknowledge that the work of Lee, Kirby, and Ditko serves as a bridge to a more literate concept of the superhero. However, the evidence doesn't wholly bear out that the Marvel "revolution" (as billed by the publishers themselves) was in fact a revolution but rather an evolution marked by the gradual encroachment of the ideals of the literate world (and perhaps the subtle emergence of secondary orality).

All this began with the suggestion of a publisher who had previously developed successful titles by mostly using material derivative and only varied enough to avoid potential lawsuits. Although there are several variations of the story about the creation of the first Marvel title, publisher Martin Goodman sought to resurrect his floundering comic book company by replicating the success of the *Justice League of America*; he would go so far as to suggest that Lee could recycle and team some of their now defunct superheroes such as Captain America, the Human Torch, and the Submariner (members of the short-lived *All Winners Squad*) (Lee, *Origins* 112). While Stan Lee responded affirmatively to Goodman, he wasn't willing to abandon his standard position that a discriminating, sophisticated reader would be attracted to something other than DC's representation of benevolent authority, happy affluence, and uniform characterization.[21] "DC's Comic books emphasized responsibility to the community over individualism, and the creators minimized the importance of the latter, perhaps unintentionally, by giving all their superheroes essentially the same personality" (Wright 185). Rather than use the previously created superheroes mentioned by Goodman, Lee invented a superteam consisting entirely of supposedly "new" characters but whose powers resulted from a freak accident that incited them to band together and serve the world at large (much like the majority of Silver Age superheroes). While I don't want to deny the artistic accomplishment of Marvel's *The Fantastic Four* (and I will describe this at greater length), I do want to place their story within the proper context, and that is the traditional culture of superhero comic books. To begin, Lee co-created the team, working closely with illustrator Jack Kirby (the co-creator of Captain America), developing in this process what would come to be known as the "Marvel method." Years after the basic patterns had been established and the Marvel method expanded beyond the small circle of Lee, Kirby, and Ditko, Lee would describe it in the following fashion:

> I usually get a rough plot ... who the villain will be, what the problem will be, and so forth. Then I call the artist in.... And we talk it out.... Then the artist goes home ... he draws the thing out, brings it back, and I put the copy in after he's drawn the story based on the plot I've given him. Now this varies with different artists. Some artists, of course, need a more detailed plot than others. Some artists, such as Jack Kirby, need no plot at all ... occasionally I'll give him a plot, but we're practically both writers on the things [McLaughlin 6].

At what point the Marvel method was fully formed is unclear, but the fact that it was initiated, developed, and refined by these creators is significant. The publishers of Marvel comic books would maintain many of the hallmark characteristics of publishers of the Golden Age, such as owning all created material and demanding incredibly speedy production; as described in chapter 2, these are elements that ultimately result in an oral culture dynamic that produces the traditional art of the superhero epic.[22] Again, in order to facilitate speedy production, division of labor was necessary, but in the case of the Marvel method,

5. The Persistence of Traditionality

Fantastic Four #1 begins in the middle of the action and requires a flashback to the origin of their superpowers (from *Fantastic Four* #1, p. 1).

creators have even more clearly internalized the dynamic with the production of the superhero story as a shared effort.[23] The Marvel method is less hierarchical than was the system with many Golden Age publishers (where power over the story didn't have to be shared and might simply trickle from publisher to editor to writer to penciler to inker and so on). In this way, the oral culture initiated by Golden Age practices becomes more genuine as the creators make it their own, less as workers within an industry and more as artisans within a traditional cultural system.[24]

It would be from this working relationship that the Fantastic Four, the first of the Marvel superheroes, would be born. Continuing the well-established tradition of grounding superhero stories in contemporary settings, the characters in this story are Reed Richards, Ben Grimm, Sue Storm, and Johnny Storm, New Yorkers living in the midst of anxieties about atomic war and the Red Scare. In the sequence that introduces our superheroes, Reed Richards shoots something like a flare into the sky that spells out "The Fantastic Four" in smoky letters. Three police officers see it and exchange these remarks, tied it to popular sentiments of the Cold War era: "Look! In the sky — what is blazes does it mean?" "I dunno but the crowds are getting panicky!" "Rumors are flyin' about an alien invasion!" (Lee, *The Fantastic* 1).[25] The tension of this setting and in particular, the fear of the atomic age and radiation would provide the basis for most of the superpowers in the Marvel superhero universe. After the other three members of the Fantastic Four respond to the summons of Reed Richards (Mr. Fantastic) and demonstrate their powers in the process, the narrator takes the reader back to their origin and the source of their superpowers. Despite the objections of Grimm, who fears the effect of "cosmic" radiation, the four make an unauthorized launch of the rocket designed by Richards in an effort to beat the "Commies" in the space race. The radiation penetrates the shielding of the rocket, incapacitates Grimm as the pilot, and sends the crew hurtling back to earth fundamentally changed; Richards' body becomes elastic, Sue Storm's becomes invisible, and Johnny Storm's becomes engulfed in flame. All these changes are subject to their will with the exception of Ben Grimm's transformation: his body permanently transforms into an organic rock. Also, continuing the well established tradition of altruism carried out in secrecy in superhero stories, the four make a decision almost immediately after their crash and respective transformations: REED: "Listen to me all of you! That means you too, Ben! Together we have more power than any humans have ever possessed!" BEN: "You don't have to make a speech, big shot! We understand! We've gotta use this power to help mankind, right?" And after the four quickly choose the code names of Mr. Fantastic, the Invisible Girl, the Human Torch, and the Thing, the narrator proclaims, "And so was born 'the Fantastic Four'!! And from that moment on, the world would never again be the same!!" (Lee, *The Fantastic* 13). Returning to the initial time frame, the story proceeded with the threat posed by the misfit explorer now known as the Mole Man (who threatened humankind with the prehistoric monsters he discovered and trained to do his bidding). Eventually, the team of superheroes defeats the Mole Man without costumes and despite the bickering between the team members. From this brief description, the Fantastic Four can read as superheroes for a new age, differing from the Justice League of America in that they are not part of the establishment; their personalities are far from uniform; and they have no costumes per se. However, while the reasons for that reading may seem obvious, these superheroes do not mark as fundamental a break from the past as some have suggested.

To begin, Lee and Kirby were part of the same industrial model that produced and influenced earlier superhero comic books and internalized it to an unprecedented degree via the Marvel Method. This working habit would be understood by its practitioners as means to more efficiently work with each other and turn out product with a limited staff; therefore, none of those involved would make what was done with the concept of the superhero an overly intellectual enterprise. In 1969, after the critical success of Marvel comic books, Kirby would state, "Nobody does anything by themselves. When a guy comes out and makes a statement like, 'I did this,' you can be sure 50 people helped him" (George, *Jack Kirby* 8). And as noted, almost apologetically in the foreword to *The Comic Journal* collection of interviews with Jack Kirby, "His natural inclination was to do, not to yap about doing. Kirby could turn out ten pages of inspired words and pictures while other artists spent time theorizing aloud about quality versus quantity.... He was a meat and potatoes man with a powerful work ethic, whose primary objective was paying the mortgage and putting food on the table" (George, *Jack Kirby* 1). This is squarely in line with artisans who produce traditional art, who do not engage in self-conscious review of what they do (not because they consider it unworthy but because they never consider it something that requires self-conscious review). Likewise, Lee would be enthusiastic in unbridled ways but would shy away from the politics and significance of his work; however, as a spokesperson he was often pushed into describing Marvel like a brand, new and different from DC comic books, in order to gain traction with and develop loyalty from superhero fans. Lee describes what he considers to be the innovations of the Fantastic Four and the Marvel universe, but, upon analysis, these innovations are hardly straightforward movements beyond formulae of traditional superheroism:

> I think our big policy was to avoid clichés. For example in the *Fantastic Four*, the first cliché was: all superheroes wore costumes. We soon learned that was a mistake because, much as the readers like offbeat things, there are certain basics that we must have, and apparently superhero fans do demand costumes as we learned in subsequent mail [McLaughlin 4].

Like most of comic book creators working in a traditional environment but living in a society with a literate worldview, Lee would feel the need to justify his work with literate rhetoric.[26] Therefore, Lee suggests that his project was to rid superheroes of clichés, unoriginal storytelling conventions understood as anathema to sophisticated storytelling in the literate world. However, still operating within an industry that responds directly to the consumer (much like a singer to his audience), Lee shows how he misjudges the audience for superhero comic books (shaped as much by the traditional conventions of the medium as by literate culture at large).[27] As much as an intelligent audience would, in his estimation, reject cliché (and "like offbeat things"), they demand that creators adhere to conventions seemingly inherent within the genre, such as the costume.[28] Also important is that Lee's description of the Fantastic Four neglects to mention that, with code names that imply an alter ego (if not secret identity), he preserved an essential part of the superhero and leads fans back to this idea himself.

Kirby would place the phenomenon of fan opinion in a commercial culture in a much grander, long-standing, and mythic context that suggests dynamics similar to that of an oral culture:

> If the readership responds, we use the characters and if the readership fades out, the character fades out. In other words, they're myths. Nobody worships Hercules today so there is no Hercules, and it's the same things with one of our characters. If people won't read Ant-Man, not *won't* read Ant-Man, but feel that not enough has been done on him, they won't respond [George, *Jack Kirby* 8–9].

Returning to the previously mentioned speech by Lee, he would continue to expand his notion of destroying clichés only for the interviewer to reveal yet another problem with his estimation of his superheroes.

> The other cliché ... was the cliché of all the superheroes being goody-goody and friendly with each other. If they're members of a team, they're nice and polite.... We had our Fantastic Four argue amongst themselves. [The interview cites the company precedent of the rivalry between the Human Torch and the Sub-Mariner with the Sub-Mariner as a sort of anti-hero.] Yes, I think you could say that ... he was a hero-villain. He was really more hero than villain ... but he wasn't 100 percent hero in the sense that heroes are today [McLaughlin 4].

Lee is forced to backtrack and modify the way that he supposedly demolishes the clichés of the past by the interviewer who identifies a precedent for the bickering superteam in the

All Winner's Squad. Even though traditional stories feature heavy characters and are community-oriented, this does not negate the possibility of disagreement within the community, the primary source of conflict in Homer's *Iliad*, regardless of the most recent shape of the Justice League of America.[29]

While Lee may have wanted to set his superheroes apart from past superheroes, the primary means by which Marvel superheroes were set apart was by more fully realizing the epic tradition in which he found them (and only by secondarily and unintentionally suggesting means by which they might be understood outside that tradition). Most of the rhetoric that suggests Marvel superheroes were a radical departure from superheroes of the past is the result of a retcon (retroactive configuration of meaning): looking at a more recent version of the Marvel universe developed after Lee, Kirby, and Ditko as the essence from the start and ignoring the incremental movement made in the Marvel universe to realize this "different" shape. In many ways, Lee and Kirby were masters of character type rather than creators endowing their superheroes with "previously unseen psychological complexity" (as proclaimed by the back cover blurb of Stan Lee's autobiography, *Excelsior!*). Much like Homer in the *Iliad*, Lee put together characters who would necessarily be in conflict with one another on the team called the Fantastic Four. From the start, Reed Richards is the scientist, always wanting to subject situations to the careful scrutiny of a cool head and often separated from the passions of the human lifeworld (drawn as unnaturally thin with bolts of grey hair indicative of his age).[30] Ben Grimm is the surly curmudgeon, loyal but gruff in a way that overpowers his intellect and activates his short temper and caustic humor (drawn as large, wide, and unkempt and in his permanent form as the Thing, rock-covered in a way that accentuates basic features). Sue Storm is the damsel, superpowered but an emotionally needy romantic interest, willing to fulfill secondary roles on the team as costume designer and mother figure — signified by the diminutive label of the "girl" in "Invisible Girl" (drawn as curvy and generally attractive, with a regularly changing hairstyle).[31] Johnny Storm is the impulsive teenager, interested in girls and cars but also desperate to prove himself and resistant to authority, represented most notably in the form of the other members of the team (drawn as athletic with tousled hair); in addition Johnny is endowed with a power that fits his unpredictable nature (just as it could be argued that the other powers fit the respective natures of the other characters: flexible, intractable, and obscured). Similar to the *Iliad*, which begins with the anger of Achilles and the tensions among the Greeks, the opening episodes of *The Fantastic Four* clearly indicate the problems inherent within the forced situation of cooperation between these types. In issue #2, the Thing lashes out at Reed who wants to more carefully investigate the imposters posing as the Fantastic Four and turning public opinion against them:

> THING: Talk! Talk! All you ever do is talk! But I'm not built that way! I want action!
>
> MR. FANTASTIC: I know you do, Thing! But we can't fly off the handle! We've got to wait till we know who's behind all this!
>
> THING: Wait? That all right for you, mister! At least you're human! But how would you like to be me? I won't wait any longer! I'm going out — to fight! — to smash!
>
> INVISIBLE GIRL: Reed, how much more of this can we take! Sooner or later, the Thing will run amok and none of us will be able to stop him! [Lee, "Skrulls" 6].

And in a move that is even more like Achilles in issue #3, Johnny flies away from the team with the words, "Relax Sis! They're not gonna argue about me any more! I had all the bossin' around I can take! I'm cuttin' out of this combo right now!" (Lee, "The Menace"

23). I am not trying to draw direct parallels between characters Achilles and the Thing or the Human Torch (an enterprise to be undertaken by a proponent of archetypal psychology) but I am identifying general parallels in order to show how similar situational dynamics are at work. Readers within literate culture often mistake the collision of two characters or ideas as demonstrating psychological depth when, as suggested by Peter Toohey in *Reading Epic*, such a collision is not uncommon within epic poetry. With one generation inheriting the work of the previous generation but inscribing it with the current generation's values, the superhero story is likely to be read in this way (i.e., the superhero can still be a type and yet not be "goody-goody and friendly").[32]

In this regard, it should also be mentioned that as Lee, Kirby, and Ditko began to develop other characters like the Hulk, Thor, Iron Man, and Dr. Strange, and other superteams like the Avengers and the X-Men, and, with their "offbeat" approach, they were creating an interactive universe. As opposed to DC who only allowed superheroes to inhabit the same world as they came to recognize the popularity of the idea, Marvel created a series of titles separated by the most porous of membranes (intending from the very start to have crossover stories).[33] In addition to encouraging the openness that invites the sort of participation associated with traditional culture,[34] these writers began to create a cosmology that also works in line with certain ideas or traditional culture. Since the dominant traditions of western Christianity were based on Platonic and Augustinian thought (especially in the post–printing press world), the dominant notion of God was conceptual and largely absent from the happenings in the human lifeworld. Although the exact representation of the gods differs throughout the history of ancient Greece, it is clear not only how Homer represented gods, but also how oral cultures would view the gods: as literally present to the people who recognize them. While the exact motivations for their choices are unclear, it seems that Lee, Kirby, and Ditko were interested in presenting a mythic world like this for their readers (albeit something superficially outside the Judeo-Christian framework of the immediate culture and invented for their superhero universe). The higher beings who interact with superheroes and play roles in their stories include characters such as Uatu (the super-intelligent alien "Watcher," who pledged to never interfere but helping humans in times of great need), Galactus (the otherworldly force that consumes entire planets and regards other life-forms as inconsequential), and Eternity (a personification of the universe that manifests himself in order to preserve the natural order of things). First appearing in *The Fantastic Four* and the "Dr. Strange" feature in *Strange Tales*, these figures are just a few among many others that exist at various celestial levels in the Marvel universe and act similar to the gods in many oral poems: powerful enough to guide human affairs but invariably tied to those affairs and acting as characters within the stories. Consider the Watcher's speech to the Fantastic Four in issue #13:

> We have seen once-noble races turn savage and warlike with the passing of time! A fate which your own foolish race seems headed for! But during all the ages we have done nothing but watch — never have we interfered! Never have we made our presence known! But now I have broken the silence of centuries, in order to save your people from savagery!" [Lee, "The Fantastic Four Versus" 13].

This mythic sensibility has some precedent in *Wonder Woman*, where the lead is featured as an Amazon created by Aphrodite, and in *Captain Marvel*, where the lead is created by the magician Shazam and endowed with the strengths of mythic figures. While the Marvel universe carries on this tradition, the Marvel gods do more than provide an excuse for the superhero characters and interact with the plot in ways fundamental to the outcome of the stories. For instance, Kirby intended to carry the story of Thor (a character seemingly like Wonder Woman with a literal basis in Norse mythology) to its ultimate end (Ragnarok) and introduce a new series based on god-like characters. (With Marvel unwilling to lose the character of Thor, this would eventually become Kirby's DC series *The New Gods*.) All of this is to demonstrate the engagement that the Marvel universe was willing to have with heavy god-like characters, usually flattened by their one central trait and yet part of the unfolding story of the Marvel epic.

Within *The Fantastic Four*, Lee and Kirby would maintain the high action of the superhero story through the episodic structure of past comic books that is very much related to traditional notions of narrative. As already indicated by the summary of issue #1, the story begins with the Fantastic Four called to action and their origin told in flashback; in turn, they encounter their adversary for the issue in the Mole Man, whose origin is also told in flashback. The beginning of issue #2 begins with the following narration: "What is happening here? What is the Thing doing, swimming miles offshore towards a lonely Texas tower? Why do his eyes gleam with a sinister, crafty light?" (Lee, "Skrulls" 1). While not quite the same in intent as Homer "tell us this story, goddess daughter of Zeus, beginning at whatever point you will," the sentiment and the effect are very similar, with the narrator supposedly excluded from the meaning and outcome of events unfolding. In addition to this, almost every issue returns to and recounts the origin story of the Fantastic Four for some character-related reason (such as Richards blaming himself for the accident that led to the Thing's permanent transformation). The structure of each issue may be tied to giving young fans what they want (high action from the start) and giving new fans necessary information (background that makes sense of the superpowered team); however, as already suggested, this habit still evokes a different narrative sensibility within the creators and audience. In addition, the epic purpose behind the repetitive, oneiric climate identified by Eco becomes even clearer with Marvel comic books in which characters refer back to episodes presented in previous issues and thereby, suggest something other than the a reader's forgetting (which Eco found threatening) is taking place. Just as character-driven themes return throughout the series (such as the Thing's perceived ugliness, Mr. Fantastic's coldness toward the Invisible Girl, and the Human Torch's resistance to adult authority), so do literal events, such as conflicts with past enemies like the Mole Man, Dr. Doom, and Annihilus. However, these events are predicated on the incremental building that takes place in epic poetry with repeated variations on themes and events; Kirby indicates past enemies (even those supposedly dead) return to "haunt" the superheroes even though each return ends with a recapitulation of the cliché associated with that character.

> We'll bring them back after three or four issues and maybe even longer than that. They'll come back. We may like to explore another aspect of their lives. For instance, I did this Mole Man story in *FF* where he had built a house.... It humanizes him, and then he retreats into his own insanity and goes underground. He's ready for another episode [George, *Jack Kirby* 11].

Although I've chosen to focus on the Fantastic Four as the first of the superheroes in Marvel's self-proclaimed revolution, much of the same things can be said about other superheroes created in the amazingly productive first few years of the Marvel universe; in roughly two years, Lee, Kirby, and Ditko would produce the Hulk, Thor, Iron Man, Dr. Strange, the X-Men, and the Avengers (with the Avengers being a diverse team of superhero stars held together by a loose premise, much more similar to the Justice League of America than the Fantastic Four were). All were filled with type characters and were informed by Marvel cosmology with stories told in episodic form. With all the above-mentioned superheroes, Marvel continued the tradition of epithets for the heroes, not only in visual forms, with signature costumes, but also in more traditional forms, with the *Incredible* Hulk, the *Invincible* Iron Man, or the X-Men, *the Strangest Superheroes of All* (and this is a fairly random sampling with many more used).[35] Lee's penchant for bombastic epithets and alliteration undoubtedly helped him as he worked within the Marvel method; he was provided with panels with space to fill by narration as well as dialogue (illustrated by artists who had pages to fill) — much like an oral poet needing to fill the space of a metrical framework.[36] As opposed to his colloquial dialogue, Lee's narration is often characterized as excessively formal with intentionally antiquated verbiage and inverted grammar that evoke a false pastness and establishes the gravity of the story; the opening narrative of the issue #1 of *The X-Men* reads: "Never within the memory of man was there a class such as this! Never was there a teacher such as Professor X! And never were there "students" such as the X-Men!" (*The X-Men* 1). Lee's narration sometimes harkened to the "dear reader" convention of the Victorian period (which signifies the creation of the author in literate culture), seen as the same narration continues: "And now prepare yourself for one of the most exciting reading experiences of your life! For you are about to enter the fascinating, unpredictable world of ... the X-Men!" (*The X-Men* 1). Nevertheless, the above-mentioned heaviness of his narration initially crowded out the most significant threat to the orality of superhero comic books: the interiority implied by the thought balloon. In the early history of Marvel superheroes, the characters were like the Golden Age superheroes in this regard with thoughts usually reinforcing plot points made by narration, speech balloons, and/or illustration. For instance, in issue #3 of *The Fantastic Four* within a panel that shows the Invisible Girl in the back of the Atomic Tank stolen by Miracle Man, she thinks, "The Miracle Man is driving off with the Atomic Tank! But this time he's got an unseen passenger!" (Lee, "The Menace" 13). This is not to completely ignore some thought about the self, but these thoughts are usually things that characters would be willing to speak aloud (as Achilles would concerning his choice to return or not return to battle).

Although Lee frequently addressed the reader in a way that may seem to violate tenets of the traditional storyteller, he walks a line as a narrator that mostly sets him apart from the "dear reader" narrator of high literacy. To maintain dramatic tension, he would separate himself from the superior knowledge of a narrator in control of the story and act much more like the oral poet responding to the muse. But more specifically, Lee's narration was connected to his approach to marketing Marvel comic books that emphasize an interactive relationship between the creators and their audience distinct from literate culture's objective distance between texts and their readers. As indicated by Bill Schelly's *The Golden Age of Comic Fandom*, this sense of interactivity began before the Silver Age and Marvel Comics incorporated the fan-clubs that created a virtual sense of community.[37] Nevertheless, Marvel began to takes decisive steps beyond this idea of fandom to not only gain readers from the old demographic base for superhero comic books but also to entice other sorts of readers to join the Marvel community. Two features were a regular part of Marvel comic books: an advertisement page for upcoming comic books and a letters page. While sometimes the advertisement page would be overwhelmed by images of the upcoming comic books with relatively little space for original text, other times this page would feature more extensive descriptions of Marvel titles written in an informal prose style that spoke directly to the fans. Even more important would be the letters page in which the letters of fans were printed and the editor responded in the same informal tone, validating the opinions of the fans and encouraging them to read the comic books critically. For instance, in issue #6 of *The Incredible Hulk*, following a letter on seemingly erratic rules governing Bruce Banner's transformation into the Hulk,[38] the response reads, "Those changes you refer to, Tom, are merely part of the character development. After our first issue was launched, we received many suggestions from our readers, and tried to comply with those which have merit" (Lee, "Vs." 19.2).[39] In addition to addressing the letter writer by name, the response indicates how seriously readers are taken and includes them in the creative process — after justifying the "changes." Later, on the same letters page, another fan notes an inconsistency that is acknowledged by the writer as an outright mistake and played off with humorous aplomb: "Judging by the letters we receive, Dick, if we had a dollar for every mistake we've made, we'd be loaded! But, we're glad you enjoy our efforts, and we'll try to be more careful from now on. (Come to think of it, we don't have a copy of the first issue on hand to double check...)" (Lee, "Vs." 19.2). In addition to acknowledging a misstep within the storytelling, they identify that storytelling is an on-going enterprise that is enhanced by the careful attention of the audience. In fact, the reader is placed in a superior position by indicating that the creators don't have a copy of the first issue handy. Ultimately, this invitation to find mistakes was somewhat institutionalized with the Marvel "no-prize" that basically only meant the error-hunter would receive his or her letter published. However, the simple fact that this no-prize worked as a motivating factor indicated a community ethic was at work among Marvel fans in a way previously unseen in comic book fandom.

Lee would accentuate the importance of fans to the creativity and integrity of their line in many different ways, at times suggesting that the community was really responsible for the stories within the comic books:

> [Receiving fan mail] was one of the most exciting things that ever happened to us. We found out that there were actually real live readers out there — readers who took the trouble to contact us, readers who wanted to talk to use about our characters, about our stories. With each new letter they got to know us better, and what was more important, we got to know them. We learned what they liked, what they didn't like, what they wanted to see more of ... and less of. After a while I began to feel I wasn't even an editor; I was just following orders — orders which came in the mail [*Origins* 73].

Extending far beyond votes cast by sales, Lee indicates that a personal connection exists between the creators and the fans that generates stories based on cultural values (i.e., likes and dislikes). Undoubtedly part of a sales pitch to the readers, Lee's comments can be understood as a type of populist sensibility that gave to fans what they wanted to hear more than it revealed the actual creative process (Pustz 167). "For the first ten to fifteen years of Marvel's existence, Lee and his company were selling ... a participatory world for the readers, a way of life for its true believers" (Pustz 56). Still, this sense of a participatory world is something that was generally extolled and propelled the creation of "Stan's Soapbox," a column which Lee wrote for Marvel comic books: "I initiated a column called 'Stan's Soapbox,' in which I discussed anything on my mind, mainly for the purpose of eliciting responses from the readers. I would write whatever came into my head, trying to avoid sales pitches; it was just me communicating with them" (Lee, *Excelsior!* 149–150). Even if we chose to cynically regard statements such as this as mere rhetoric, such rhetoric has consequences within the real world. And while the letters page and "Stan's Soapbox" represents the creation of a virtual community, Lee's descriptions remind us that it's connected to something more concrete with references to "real live readers out there." Although it's impossible to establish a one-to-one relationship, the 1960s rise of fan gatherings known as comic book conventions seems to coincide too closely with the rise of Marvel comic books to be coincidence. And the subsequent rise of other real communities' activities must be taken into account, with communities so deeply invested in Marvel superheroes that these communities produced creative and critical work such as the fanfiction and fanzines distributed at conventions. Much more clearly than in the Golden Age, the superhero comic book culture was working in traditional ways, with active engagement between creators and the audience and the development of traditions to be passed from one generation to the next.[40]

Marvel's Attempts to Be Literate and Realistic Finally Stick (with Spider-Man)

However, the rhetoric of Marvel also contained hints of the more literate shape of superhero comic books to come from Marvel in the 1970s. With a Comics Code established to supposedly make comic books safe children, Marvel did not seek to defy its rules per se[41] but did identify a different audience for its comic books. One of Lee's well-established strategies was to flatter his reader by crediting their intelligence as a factor that enabled creators to produce popular Marvel stories. As previously mentioned, Lee was selling Marvel superheroes as a new and improved product, as not your father's superheroes (or at least not the superheroes that you used to know).[42] The second half of the statement was vitally important because Marvel courted older readers, particularly a college crowd that may or may not have been familiar with DC superheroes.[43] Nevertheless, it would be impossible for Americans in general to not have some sort of knowledge of superheroes, and Marvel was looking to lose the kid's stuff association particularly reinforced by the Comics Code. The term to which Lee would often return would be realism, that, in any artform, does not mean true contact with the human lifeworld but artistic conventions used to represent reality. While *realism* is a term that certainly had the potential to appeal to the literate high-culture sensibilities of a college student who had never read superhero comic books, *realism* is also a somewhat ambiguous term. As the consummate salesman, Lee sometimes had difficulty sticking to it (sometimes identifying the appeal of comic books as being their ability to represent the fantastic).[44] With the medium, realism could also mean different things as a term applied to the narrative or the illustration (and as noted in chapter 4, neither Kirby or Ditko's style qualifies as truly realistic). Regardless, when Lee did elaborate upon the term, he would apply it to the narrative and argue that realism took shape in Marvel superhero comic books through continuity, consistency, and psychological complexity (Pustz 52). The first two of the these three items do not contradict the basic idea of traditional storytelling at all,[45] and the last item may not wholly, as a characters thoughts may sometimes be represented in limited degrees in epic poems. In addition, as discussed in chapter 3, the rudiments of self-conscious thought need not be seen as antithetical to traditional sensibilities.

However, when thoughts are represented in larger degrees in ways that contradict spoken words and/or become as important as actions, we are seeing an understanding of internal life foreign to traditional experience. This was always a potential (though not necessary) direction for comic books thanks to the thought balloon. Lee stated:

> I've always felt it was important to let our readers know what a character was thinking as often as possible. Remember how Shakespeare always had Hamlet soliloquizing through-

out that famous play? Well, if it was good enough for Shakespeare —! Now, picture Spider-Man crawling up a wall. There's no one with him, no one near him. Therefore, since he had no one to talk to, you have no dialogue. So, all you have is a costumed character moving on a wall. But by adding the thought balloons, by showing what he's actually thinking, you get inside his mind and add a whole additional dimension to the story [Lee, *Excelsior!* 135–136].

Again, characterizations of his own work presented retrospectively in an autobiography must be understood as subject to a sort of convenient revisionism, this being an aspect of Spider-Man that became more pronounced as years passed (and Lee is being very vague in this statement anyway). But even taken with the proverbial grain of salt, Lee's statement encapsulates much of what I believe does take place with Marvel superheroes. Part of Lee's quotation sets up the thought balloon as a practical device to fill up space as Spider-Man is "crawling up a wall," and this sets it in line with traditionality. However, using thoughts to provide "a whole additional dimension to the story" suggests as level of interiority unknown within the communal world of the epic poem; Lee even connects this convention of literacy to Hamlet, the quintessential example of self-consciousness out-of-step with the traditional world. Despite the initial typing of characters, Lee would begin to suggest a different sort of character that may retain some aspects of traditionality but clearly leans toward literacy. For instance, four or five years after the debut of the *Fantastic Four*, more thoughts that reveal the self in contrast to outer behavior would be seen (such as the Things long-standing doubts about his relationship with Alicia Masters). Thinking of Marvel superheroes as a bridge between the psychology of orality and the psychology of literacy, a quotation from Wright sets up their significance in this way: "The heroes' idiosyncrasies often impede their work as a team.... Despite their bickering and personality clashes, the Fantastic Four always prove to be a cohesive and formidable team in times of crisis.... These were heroes who reconciled the competing imperatives of individualism and communal responsibility" (Wright 204–205). This is one of the most remarkable facts about the rebirth of traditionality in the United States, in that the country is not only founded as a literate society but founded upon literate ideals that stress individualism.[46] And while individualism isn't the same thing as interiority, individualism nevertheless indicates a predisposition against the exteriority more frequently associated with community. Many of Marvel's superheroes worked in this way, as individuals set against community who nevertheless worked for the greater good of community (the Hulk perhaps being the most notable in this category, usually working to save the larger community by accident). Nevertheless, the most notable of Marvel's creations along these lines, who I have intentionally neglected to mention up to this point but whom Lee specifically mentioned above, is Spider-Man. This neglect has been intentional as this hero seems to be the one with the most notable leanings toward the literate world through his thoughts and more so through the self-conscious nature of the Spider-Man story.

Although the premise may have been a light outgrowth of Captain Marvel with his teenage alter ego, the story of Spider-Man had its own unique trappings that took into account much more carefully the experience of teenage life. Debuting in *Amazing Fantasy* #15,[47] Peter Parker, an insecure high school student, is raised by his elderly aunt and uncle whom he loves, but he is cast out of the popular social circles whose attention he craves. Upon attending a demonstration on "radioactive rays," Parker is bitten by an irradiated spider and soon realizes that he has gained spider-related superpowers: strength, speed, agility, and the ability to scale sheer surfaces. After "testing" his powers in an amateur fight for which he wins money, a promoter convinces Parker that his powers will make him a star. After designing a costume and constructing web-shooters, "Spider-Man" makes his first appearance on television. Upon leaving the studio, Parker ignores the a police officer who calls for help as he chases after a thief; the criminal escapes, and, when the officer turns on Parker, he responds by saying, "Sorry, pal! That's your job! I'm thru being pushed around — by anyone! From now on I just look out for number one — that means — me!" (Lee, "Spider-Man!" 8). However, Parker remains devoted to his aunt and uncle and is shocked to find another police officer at his home, reporting that his uncle had been shot and killed by a burglar. Donning his celebrity costume and using his superpowers to track the burglar, Spider-Man captures him only to discover that the burglar is the man he failed to stop earlier in the story. The narrator then ends Parker's story with what was a standard sentiment in superhero comics and in exact phraseology would become one of the enduring clichés for Marvel superheroes: "A lean silent figure slowly fades into the gathering darkness, aware at last in this world, *with great power there must also come — great responsibility*! [italics mine]" (Lee, "Spider-Man" 11). Within this story of Spider-Man, there is actually only one thought balloon used to indicate how Parker feels about his aunt and uncle, "They're the only ones who've ever been kind to me! I'll see to it they're always happy, but the rest of the world can go hang for all I care!" (8). Even though the number of thought bubbles and the thought itself is rather unremarkable, the story does set up a fuller basis for an interior life in a few others ways with Parker talking to himself (in what amounts to soliloquies). Upon creating his web-shooters, he says, "So [my classmates] laughed at me for being a bookworm, eh? Well, only a science major could have invented a device like this!" (6) and upon catching the burglar, he says, "My fault — all my fault! If only I had stopped him when I could have! But I didn't — and now — Uncle Ben — is dead..." (11). Again, this sort of introspection does not depart greatly from the obvious themes of the story, and the basic story had many of the trappings of the superhero story, from orphan status to an alter ego to justice above the law; specifically, the guilt that will motivate him as a costumed crime fighter is not too different from the revenge motive of Batman. Nevertheless, there are some notable departures from the superhero story that works together with Parker's slight but still present interior life, suggesting a more literate sense of self-consciousness. After all, Parker is a stereotype based not so much on past superheroes as on the stereotype of the typical comic book reader in his slight build, social awkwardness, and book-smart ways. In addition, he fails to do what so many people surprisingly endowed with extraordinary powers do so very naturally in superhero stories: put on a costume to fight crime for the greater good of humankind. On one hand, the argument could be made that Spider-Man is another variation on the traditional epic in the form of the superhero story, but, on the other hand, there are enough elements that it would be foolish to ignore the seeds of literacy planted within the story. Even though the first Spider-Man story is a far cry from a fully self-conscious analysis of the superhero story, comic book readers caught a glimpse of where superheroes would eventually go with self-conscious characters and self-consciously constructed narratives.

Over the course of years, Lee would make more extensive use of the thought balloon in many of the Marvel titles, but this use was undoubtedly most pronounced in Spider-Man, the most introspective of Marvel heroes (perhaps initially considered to be inclined to navel-gazing as a teenager). One of the most well-known of Parker's introspections would take place in the "Spider-Man No More" story presented in the numerically significant *Spider-Man* #50 (an issue, incidentally, written in 1967 after the departure of Steve Ditko and drawn in a more realistic style by John Romita). After beginning in the middle of Spider-

Man's fight with quickly dispatched thugs and Spider-Man's trademark humor, the people just saved from the thugs recoil with fear from Spider-Man. Initially, Spider-Man offer a soliloquy about the situation as he crawls a wall, trying unsuccessfully to shake off the public's regard for him as a criminal: "Well who cares what people think anyway? That's just the trouble — I care!" (Lee, "Spider-Man No More!" 4). This leads Parker to continue to contemplate the ways in which his life as Spider-Man disturbs his life as Peter Parker, often drawing him away from those things that he cares about most, such as his Aunt May. After being informed by the neighbor that his aunt had fallen ill, called out repeatedly for him, and fallen asleep only after the doctor administered a sedative, he thinks, "If I had been at home — like any other normal guy — they could have reached me fast! But no ... I was out ... flexing my muscles ... trying to help the very people who fear me!" (4). After finding out his grades are declining and having to turn down a date from Gwen Stacy (both because of his perceived responsibilities as Spider-Man), Parker begins to think even more about the negative public perception encouraged by newspaper publisher and now media personality, J. Jonah Jameson; in an alleyway, Parker thinks:

> Being Spider-Man has brought me nothing — but happiness! In order to satisfy my craving for excitement — I've sacrificed everything that matters — Aunt May — my friends — the girls in my life — and — for what...?? Can I be sure that my only motive was the conquest of crime? Or was it the heady thrill of battle — the precious taste of triumph — the paranoiac thirst for power that can never be quenched??... I was just a young, unthinking teenager ... when I became ... Spider-Man... Every boy — sooner or later ... must put away his toys ... and become ... a man! [7–8].

The last panel featuring these thoughts is a full-page panel that shows Parker in the background, walking away from a trash can in the foreground containing his Spider-Man costume: an excellent use of relative size to maintain a sense of realistic perspective and yet communicate the relative importance of Parker versus Spider-Man. In the subsequent panels, Spider-Man's "retirement" is revealed and publicized, becoming a subject of debate for pundits and causing a rise in crime throughout the city.

Although his personal life begins to improve (caring for his Aunt May, studying for his college classes, paying attention to romantic possibilities), Parker eventually can't resist the needs of those around him. After saving a security guard from some criminals without his costume, the resemblance between the guard and his Uncle Ben reminds Parker of the overriding reason for his life as Spider-Man: the failure to act that caused the tragedy of his uncle's death. After a quick recap of his origin, Parker soliloquizes:

> I can never renounce my Spider-Man identity! I can never

As usual, Peter Parker is thinking about his life (and as becomes increasingly apparent, his thoughts crowd out his image) (from *Spider-Man* #50, p. 4).

fail to use the mysterious powers which a mysterious destiny has seen fit to give me! No matter how unbearable the burden may be ... no matter how great my personal sacrifice — I can never permit one innocent being to come to harm ... because Spider-Man failed to act ... and I swear I never will! [18].

The story ends with Parker again donning the costume and in order to stand against the tide that caused him to doubt himself, he reveals to Jameson his intention to return to action. In some ways, this basic story frame could be seen as very similar to the standard practice of recapitulating superhero origins by adding to the significance of those origins with fresh narrative details (as described with Batman in chapter 2). The thing that causes Parker to return to his role as Spider-Man is an event, a new call to action in the form of the attack on an old security guard; he is much like Achilles, who is brought to introspection by a specific event and brought out of introspection by another event. And similarly, Parker's story does end with a reaffirmation of heroic values and a speech that affirms his responsibility to the community. However, with all of this stated, it is clear that the time he spends with his own thoughts is much more focused on the self and clearly divorced from the action that moves the plot forward; on pages 6 and 7, very little happens, and Romita fills panels with representations of Parker from multiple perspectives and with various expressions to continue some sort of movement within the visual narrative as Parker thinks and thinks. In addition, while he may be choosing between destinies, he is divided in many ways, not just between Parker and his costumed identity; Parker's future is unclear and frustrated, regardless of which path he chooses (and Spider-Man represents more than one thing to him as good humor and thrills on one hand and guilt and social consciousness on the other). This self-consciousness of literate culture is only intensified by a narrative that seems to be about the superhero story as well as being a superhero story: fighting crime in costume is not only a choice for Parker but fighting crime in costume is a subject of public debate and cultural division.

If this is one of the points at which Marvel superhero comic books became most fully realized as *literature*, its important to note that it was something to which Lee built, and, as I demonstrated, he did not begin with a clear intention to make superhero comic books literate or self-conscious. As already noted, Lee, Kirby, and Ditko initially set for themselves the rather modest goal of making superhero comic books different (even though they often implied that they were different in ways that they were not). Regardless, Lee began to think in terms of his own hype, and the creators who took the titles after these creators were often converts of his inaccurate but dynamic rhetoric, reading past stories in terms of self-conscious literacy. As the author of *Marvels* (a revisionist history of the Marvel universe), Kurt Busiek's introduction to that text is an excellent example of this sort of creative rereading of the early Marvel stories. After admitting that he was not a regular reader of Marvel superhero comic books as they were published, Busiek argues that everything he presents is part of the source material: "For all that *Marvels* has won praise for its humanity, for its perspective, for its depiction of a complex and mostly-believable world, and for all that I'm willing to accept credit for what I contributed to the project..., it ultimately boils down to this: If it wasn't there in the first place, it wouldn't have ended up here" (*Marvels* 261). But while a contemporary reader might choose to regard the Fantastic Four's first encounter with Galactus as a critique of the superhero power fantasy and an acknowledgment of the Nietzschian origin of the superman, the fact remains that Lee and Kirby were still part of a largely traditional system and were in the process of crafting a better epic, as much as they were crafting a superhero for a literate reader. While leaning toward literacy, the early stories of Marvel superheroes were far from fully committed to the precepts for literate culture, and their unique characteristics as literature only developed in Marvel superhero stories over the course of time.

Nevertheless, they did develop, and this can be seen in increasing degree with other creators in years to come, in the late 1960s and 1970s. With Marvels approach to the superhero finally becoming financially successful in 1965, the new and different rhetoric that Lee had crafted for Marvel was validated. In addition, the years immediately following that success would see the defection of Ditko and Kirby and the loss of Lee as a writer (devoting all of his time to his editorial responsibilities as the number of titles and their popularity grew). As Marvel titles began to grow in number, the staff also grew, initially with long-time industry professionals like Roy Thomas but also with creators relatively new to the field like Steve Englehart and Neal Adams. Whether old or new to the business, they seemed to be converts to Marvel's general ideas (either by inclination or by the necessity of their employment); these ideas included the related concepts of the rejection of cliché, the new outsider ideal for superheroes, and the anti-institutional stance (even though often taken in a way that was insistently apolitical). For instance, when Captain America was brought back from a frozen state he was placed in during World War II, he was the man out of time who questioned and tempered his super-patriotism in the new era of the 1960s. Yet, while this new Captain America was more in line with traditional American values, he read as being countercultural by not taking a political stance in line with institutional politics (as were other Marvel superheroes).

> A 1965 college poll conducted by *Esquire* revealed that student radicals racked Spider-Man and the Hulk alongside the likes of Bob Dylan and Che Guevara as their favorite revolutionary icons.... The outsider hero had arrived as the most celebrated figure in youth culture, and Marvel had him. Marvel's popularity among older readers also stemmed, at least in part, from revised assumptions about the virtues of popular culture in general [Wright 223].

In addition to participating in a fashionable anti-establishment ethos, Marvel superheroes could readily be considered alongside real (not fictional) cultural revolutionaries. And thus, Marvel continued its march forward toward literacy and general cultural respectability, but that general cultural respectability was not necessarily a result of its increasing literary nature. Instead, as Wright notes, the pop art of Andy Warhol and Roy Lichtenstein were forcing a reconsideration of the products of mass culture as art (and I would say, thereby, changing aesthetic values in such a way that traditional art might be appreciated).

Ultimately, Marvel superhero comic books remained tethered to traditional culture even when the new Marvel creators of the 1970s took Marvel titles in supposedly more self-conscious directions. For instance, the Roy Thomas/Neal Adams arc of *The Avengers* called "The Kree-Skrull War" (issues #89–97) placed the superteam in the midst of an intergalactic battle with the shape-changing alien Skrulls living on earth. With Cold War paranoia represented at a metaphoric level (more obvious than in the Skrulls first appearance in *The Fantastic Four* #2), the Avengers themselves become objects of the witch hunt conducted by H. Warren Craddock, head of the Alien Activities Commission. With superheroes frequently thinking over their role in fighting for the greater good, they are eventually called outside that frame of reference to settle the battle between the Skrulls and another alien race, the Kree. In the end, Rick Jones (teenage sidekick to the Hulk, Captain America, and the Avengers), who seemed increasingly superfluous, was elevated to a central role in ending the war. The self-consciousness of a story that examines the role of the superhero in the midst of conflict between superpowers is clear, and this in turn results in increasing introspection among the masked heroes under suspicion. Nevertheless, the structure is excessively episodic with almost every scene change entering into events in *media res* and with characters largely based on type: Vision as the dispassionate android, Goliath as the unsophisticated, physical power, etc. Similar stories from the same time period include "The Death of Gwen Stacy" issues of *Spider-Man*, in which Spider-Man intentionally turns against his family, friends, and conscience in an attempt to avenge his girlfriend, and "The Saga of the Nomad" issues of *Captain America*, in which Captain America finds his country unworthy of direct superheroic representation and decides to fight crime in a new costume as "a man without a country." With long stretches of time spent with the thoughts of characters as in "Spider-Man No More" and "The Kree-Skrull War," these stories make more overtures toward a literate worldview but remain grounded in many of the conventions of traditional storytelling. Although these stories could be discussed in more depth, such discussion is unnecessary to show what has already been acknowledged: with Marvel, superhero comic books make an incremental move toward the conventions of literacy but even in their second decade, Marvel superhero comic books represent a blended artform that retains many conventions of traditionality.

Even though I've described the thought balloon as a convention leading toward interiority, it has limitations that keep it from ever being completely suited to the self-consciousness of high literacy. In *The Aesthetics of Comics*, David Carrier teases out the implications of this convention in relation to the worldviews of philosophy dominant at various times in history.[48] These implications are useful because they unintentionally demonstrate that the thought balloon moves beyond the ideas of traditional culture but do not completely embody the objective analysis of consciousness characteristic of high literacy:

> According to Descartes, we cannot know another person's mind directly; we can only infer thoughts from their outward expression in words and gesture.... The possibility of skepticism arises, for there is a potential gap between the indirect ways in which I know your thoughts and the immediate intuition in which they are revealed to you. Balloons reveal what the philosopher of the mind might dream of, that another person's thoughts might be displayed indubitably and transparently.... Comics do not merely duplicate the functions of an older system of expression, but add to them in essentially new ways [Carrier 29–30].

Although the ultimate end of Carrier's discussion of comic strips is much different than my discussion of superhero comic books, he makes a good point that identifies the essential limitations of the thought balloon as a tool of literacy. On one hand, the thought balloon may expose the audience to the general idea of interiority and may skew the narrative away from action to thought (perhaps even thought that works in opposition to deed or thought that is divided against itself); yet, on the other hand, the thought balloon provides a sense of immediate presence and transparency of the thought to the audience in a way that will not allow the distance essential to a foundational premise of high literacy's Cartesian worldview: skepticism. While the aesthetic convention of the thought balloon may lean toward the conventions of literacy and may become more pronounced in the superhero comic books of the 1970s, it is a narrative convention that can never release the reader completely to enact an idea central to literacy and realistic art; with the thought balloon revealing "what the philosopher of the mind might [only] dream of," the thought balloon still holds out the promise that a genuine subjective connection might be realized, and, therefore, the audience never fully realizes the ability to objectively scrutinize impenetrable surfaces.

For reasons already mentioned in previous chapters, the comic book was created as part of an industry that worked in ways similar to oral culture, and, therefore, the conventions of the medium itself prevent it from ever fully embracing a literate worldview. If the thought balloon may not be as distinctively literate as one might first think, it would seem that the thought balloon's literate implications might still be somewhat realized by self-conscious storytelling techniques, such as the metanarrative. Yet, even when Lee and Kirby seem at their most self-conscious, it is usually in service of the larger paradigm of the heroic epic (whether they're fully aware of it or not). One of the most often mentioned moments of self-consciousness relative to the story itself within the early history of Marvel superheroes takes place in *The Fantastic Four* #10. The cover features two men facing away from the reader and toward the action on the page (although their relative size sets them outside standard rules governing the depiction of depth and proportion). One states, "How's that for a twist, Jack? We've got Doctor Doom as one of the Fantastic Four!" and the other replies, "...And Mister Fantastic himself is the villain! Our fans oughta flip over this yarn!" An arrow points to these two figures and the text inside the arrow reads, "In this epic issue: Surprise follows surprise as you actually meet Lee and Kirby!" (Lee, "The Return" cover). This attention to the existence of the author and the author's influence on the story as portrayed on the cover works very much beyond the role of the singer with epic poetry. However, the significance of the idea is muted to a large extent by the execution within the story that makes the story much more cliché than expected and keeps this issue of *The Fantastic Four* from becoming *Four Characters in Search of their Authors*. While the narrator interrupts the story with "And that dear reader, is as far as Jack Kirby and I got with our story before the unexpected happened!" (Lee, "The Return" 5). Like the cover, the narrator seems to be identifying the Fantastic Four and their world as a fiction to be manipulated, but, thereafter, Lee and Kirby become characters within the story. Used by Dr. Doom to trick Mr. Fantastic (with whom they discuss their stories), Lee and Kirby become as clearly fictitious as the Fantastic Four, and their appearance reads more like a stunt than an exploration of the nature of fiction and reality characteristic of modern literature. Thereafter, Dr. Doom switches places with Mr. Fantastic and tries to destroy the Fantastic Four from the inside as an imposter, but, as usual within traditional superhero stories, the supervillain's sinister plans are foiled. Certain moments within the Marvel "revolution" seem to decisively signal a break from the past of traditional superhero comic books but are sometimes unintentional steps toward

Stan Lee and Jack Kirby live in Marvel universe and discuss their next *Fantastic Four* story (but their presence is mostly a plot device that enable the return of Dr. Doom) (from *Fantastic Four* #10, p. 5).

the self-consciousness of literacy — or more likely, the self-consciousness of secondary orality. The self-consciousness of the storyteller could be said to not be completely foreign to oral epics such as Homer's *Odyssey* and *Beowulf*, in which singers fashion at least small parts for the storyteller in the story. Often, those storytellers will tell stories that reveal crucial information about the nature of the society within the story. In addition, Homer makes his role as singer part of the epic itself through the direct address of Eumaeus, and, in turn, the audience, all of which can be characterized in a way not totally different from the ideals of postmodernism. While postmodernism allows metafiction because everything is a fiction, traditional culture allows such intrusions because there is no separation between the self and the story (or everything is a reality of sorts). In any case, these moves are much more characteristic of the phenomenon of secondary orality to be discussed further in chapter 6.

The intrusions of literacy in comic books in the late 1940s and the early 1950s and the new found diversity of genre began to take comic books in another direction that the medium itself would never be able to fully accommodate but could nevertheless approximate. The most significant part of this other direction would be EC horror comics, significant because they contained content objectionable for young readers and unintentionally provoked a widespread debate about the content, audience, and essential nature of the comic book medium. As noted, Fredric Wertham may be generally reviled by all comic book enthusiasts including fans of superhero comic books, but Wertham's charge against comic books and the resulting Comics Code did much to save superhero comic books from their slow decline. However, while the Comics Code may have destroyed competition and created a safe space for the return of superhero comic books, the code formalized the idea that comic books are simply kids stuff (and this limitation does not allow epic poetry to reach everyone in culture as it should).[49] As Ong notes, the heavy heroes of epic poetry and folk tales and the operation of those heroes persist but only in limited, relatively unsophisticated ways:

> Contest between heavily laden type figures is a central operation in an oral culture's retention of its articulated knowledge and its sense of identity. The old oral world had to keep everything as formulaicly fixed as possible, and violent external conflict had been the principle ploy to make a story interesting. The old oral world will be recognized as the one in which little children still want their stories told: typed heroes and gore — though the sophistication of great epics is wanting in children's tales, as it is in the regressive Westerns and whodunits on television [*Interfaces* 210–211].

The code would ensure that gore would not be a part of superhero comic books, but, had it been otherwise, Ong probably would have included them with regressive Westerns and whodunits as relatively unsophisticated. That's not to say that conflict didn't continue as a central feature of Silver Age superhero stories but the conflict was based on fantastic situations that disguised the violence. Ultimately, the code not only paved the way for the return of DC superheroes but for the reinvention of the superhero at Marvel, a company that adhered to the code in letter but intended to sell their superheroes to a broader audience that included adults as well as children and adolescents. In addition, they were very effective at creating a sense of culture that shared essential "knowledge and its sense of identity." However, in order to retain such an audience, concessions were made toward literary thought within adult culture, in ways that had different levels of impact. Yet, while *The Fantastic Four* and *Spider-Man* (and other Marvel titles) introduce conventions that imply self-consciousness and inch toward literacy, the supposedly cliché-defying adult superhero stories of Marvel do not at any one point definitively move beyond traditionality. As the superhero story persists at Marvel in the 1960s, the move toward literacy in comic books is much slower than when other genres began to thrive in the post–World War II years. At best, we can say that the conventions of literacy are intrusions in superhero comic books and only have been seen as central to the Marvel revolution by readers conditioned by literate culture. Quite notably, in the years of Marvel's rise, DC would be unable to ignore the upstart superhero publisher and approximated Marvel's success by updating their superhero stories with the template established by Marvel's superheroes. In fact, in years to come (and as will be discussed in the next chapter), the most marked expression of literacy would be seen with DC in the mid–1980s, with a massive crossover series called *Crisis on Infinite Earths*. And yet, even though it was meant to remake the DC universe (and should theoretically appeal to a literate culture at large), that expression of literacy would have hardly any staying power — indicating that superhero comic books are a traditional phenomenon (whether primary or secondary) and cannot ever be fully co-opted by the mechanics of literacy.

CHAPTER 6

The Failed Attempt to Impose High Culture

Literacy in Crisis

As new mediums were developed in the first half of the 20th century, the ideals of literacy pervaded American culture and the degree to which these new mediums would incorporate those ideals had much to do with the design and production of the various mediums. As argued in chapter 5, the pressure of the larger culture was nearly irresistible, even to a medium like comic books that seems ill-suited to accommodate the ideals of literacy. This chapter will focus on an interesting development within the DC superhero universe that occurred in 1961, the same year as the debut of the Marvel superhero universe; this development seems to serves a similar function, building a bridge from traditionality to literacy. By suggesting that Silver Age superheroes live on Earth-1 and Golden Age superheroes live on the parallel world of Earth-2 (with each existing at "different frequencies"), the longest-standing company producing superhero comic books seemed to make a concession to literate notions of realistic storytelling that could not accept the continued youth of superheroes created over twenty years earlier. Whether this concession truly undermined the traditionality of superhero stories or simply was a narrative choice long in coming is debatable. On one hand, DC superheroes existed in fictitious cities such as Metropolis, Gotham, and Keystone, but, on the other, they also lived in the timeline of a world vaguely approximating that of the reader's world (with clear acknowledgments of World War II and other contemporaneous events). Regardless, this concept provided a science fiction explanation for the long lives of superheroes; this explanation is grounded in storytelling practices that in some ways, work beyond the episodic structure of traditional stories and are grounded in the linear historicity of literary culture.

Yeah, but What about the Earth-2 Way of Looking at Things? (or, How the Flash Is Too Quick for Just One World)

With this change, the imaginary space inhabited by DC superheroes could no longer be properly called a universe but eventually was called a multiverse (a title that became even more appropriate as parallel worlds proliferated in DC superhero comic books).[1] The multiverse concept validated the variation that is inherent within the practice of traditional storytelling, whether it is variation from one episode to the next episode (developed by one storyteller) or from telling to retelling (developed by one or more storytellers). Unavoidably, the medium of comic books is a print medium, and variations are often preserved and recognized in a way that they would not be recognized in an oral culture; print serves as a sort of prosthetic extension and refunctioning of the memory of oral cultures, and this extension and refunctioning became more pronounced as superhero comic book readers slowly marched toward the formation of a collector culture. Variation was preserved by the multiverse concept, and this self-conscious choice to preserve variation suggests a secondary form of the traditionality at work in superhero comic books. After the creation of Earth-1 and Earth-2, DC creators felt free to engage in variation characteristic of traditional cultures without the hesitations that would inhibit a mind shaped by literacy. Whether or not this variation was completely self-conscious will be discussed in this chapter, but, primary or secondary, this approach to storytelling derives from orality in a way that crowds out literacy. In years to come, the unlimited possibilities of the multiverse would be considered unwelcoming to new superhero comic book readers, especially as the industry in the 1980s tried to attract older readers (presumably more fully conditioned by the ideals of literacy). As a consequence, the most concerted attempt to make comic books literate would be mounted by Marv Wolfman's ultimate team-up/crossover comic book series titled *Crisis on Infinite Earths*. Within the series, Wolfman invented a villain that threatened to destroy all the parallel universes, but, because of the intervention of nearly all the DC superheroes, he was halted, and all remaining universes were combined into one. In addition to destroying the multiverse concept and creating narrative unity, this gave DC the opportunity to start over (again) with new and updated "authoritative" origin stories. This chapter will demonstrate how this "clean up" of the DC superhero universe was a miserable failure born of impulses of literacy largely incompatible to the medium. In addition to the persistence of variation and the survival of elements of both the Golden and Silver Ages in the supposedly new Modern Age stories of DC's post–Crisis years, DC would officially reinstate the multiverse concept in short order with series like *Identity Crisis*, *Infinite Crisis*, and *52* (apparently unable to resist the traditional culture of the medium). Likewise, Marvel superheroes would undergo a transition, unable to resist the traditional culture's desire for variation represented by series like *What If?* and more importantly with Alex Ross's epic of Marvel future history, *Earth X*. While literacy does become a marked presence within the dominant superhero multiverses at several points, these points do not lead to a new age of literacy in superhero comic books. Instead, when literacy briefly becomes a marked presence, it serves largely as an indicator of the medium's quick transition from something like primary orality to secondary orality (or what we will be calling *new traditionality*).

As already set forth in my references to Parry, Lord, Ong, and McLuhan, the shift from the practices and technologies of orality to the practices and technologies of literacy indicate a shift in the way thought is structured. However, one aspect of this idea should be described more clearly before proceeding: the biases of the scholars who set forth this idea. Parry and Lord were both scholars of the classical epic, and they approached their work with tools associated with the comparative study of linguists (and thus their scholarship has appealed alternately to classicists and linguists). Within the dominant trends of each of these groups, there are certain leanings that describe the evolution of human thought primarily as an evolution of human consciousness, shying away from more modern and more radical conceptions of the human mind. However, Ong and McLuhan not only have a broad field of study but also utilize a broader base to develop criteria used to evaluate thought and society. Part of that broader base would include the ideas of 20th century psychologists, including prominent psychoanalysts such as Sigmund Freud and cognitive psychologists such as Erik Erikson. Having already noted McLuhan's doubts about the validity of the unconscious,[2] I will be focusing primarily upon Ong's sense of how the unconscious mind relates to this shift from orality and literacy; I want to demonstrate how various superhero comic book creators often unconsciously apprehend the workings of their medium even though they might lack the terms to describe it properly. This has been an implicit part of the ground covered thus far but becomes more important as creators come closer to actually confronting the traditional basis of superhero comic books (despite their unawareness of the formal study of traditional cultures). In chapter 4, I referred to Ong's description of the abilities of the person in a traditional culture to do many things within the context of the human lifeworld that that person is unable to describe clearly with words. One of the things done without much conscious thought is acquiring the spoken word:

> Oral speech is fully natural to human beings in that every human being in every culture who is not physiologically or psychologically impaired learns to talk. Talk implements conscious life but it wells up into consciousness out of unconscious depths, though of course with the conscious as well as unconscious cooperation of society. Grammar rules live in the unconscious in the sense that you can know how to use the rule and even how to set up new rules without being able to state what they are [Ong, *Orality* 81].

Although we might call the composition that occurs in the midst of an oral poet's performance intuitive, we should not be satisfied with that characterization (especially since a literate bias toward objective understanding would view intuition derisively). Instead, what the oral poet does with the epic poem should be considered an extension of the inherent tendencies that all human beings have to acquire language (with the acquisition of language requiring very little conscious thought). At an unconscious level, the oral poet knows well what is happening within the performance of the epic poem but cannot describe it as well as the writer who regards his or her work much more consciously; in his discussion of John Milton as an epic poet shaped by the literate culture in which he lives, Ong states that "Milton's [logic] ... is highly significant in the evolution of consciousness, which is to say in the extension of consciousness into the areas of life formerly preempted by the unconscious and subconscious" (Ong, *Interfaces* 190).[3] (And if we're willing to accept that superhero comic books are traditional art, this is something that should cause us to regard more highly many of the comic book creators unable to clearly articulate the intricacies of their work (such as Siegel, Lee, etc.)) The work in which Ong connects with Freudian theory most explicitly is *The Presence of the Word*, where he uses the psychosexual stages to create a general framework for cultural development (i.e., orality is the oral stage, literacy is the anal stage, and electronics is the phallic and genital stage). Ong would not return to this framework in later writings, and, therefore, this should be understood as an idea from which he retreated (probably rightly so). However, in the other references, the unconscious is not tied so tightly to Freud that it brings along with it all of the psychosexual baggage associated with his theories. Instead, the unconscious, as used by Ong, is the workings of the mind of which one is unaware, a much more general concept that many classicists and linguists could accept. If any connection with Freud should be drawn, Ong's general notion of the unconscious is much less like that in Freud's early work, such as *Three Essays on the Theory of Sexuality* (from which the psychosexual stages are drawn), and much more like that in *Civilization and its Discontents*;[4] although Freud's sense of humankind's primitive instincts would be somewhat different than Ong's, Freud would regard civilization as a force that caused people to fundamentally restructure thought and to be more separate from their unconscious life.[5]

Even if we set aside Freud's social theories, there are other reasons to make connections between the culture of orality and the concept of the unconscious. At the center of psychoanalysis throughout the entirety of Freud's career would be his advocacy of talk therapy and the analysis of dream images that together defy many conventions of literate culture's study of the real world. In addition, while Freud understood himself as a product of the best parts of civilization and was wholly inclined to scientific analysis, his basic theories created a model of the mind at odds with the classical ideas of Plato. Likewise, while Freud identified with the high culture notion of the literate world, the historical connection between the births of psychoanalysis and various forms of new media (such as film and comic books) should not be understood as simply coincidental. As already suggested in chapter 4, the new medium of film awoke some of the same tendencies of orality as comic books, and film theory has been highly indebted to psychoanalysis (from the foundational notions to Freud to the semiotic reinterpretations of Jacques Lacan). With all this stated about Freud and psychoanalysis, I want to work with the idea of the unconscious in a way similar to Ong that avoids many of Freud's still controversial and sometimes unsupportable psychosexual fixations. Nevertheless, the unconscious ideas of superhero comic book creators become more important in the works to be mentioned within this chapter, as they seem to make concessions to literacy. Even as they make those concessions, these creators develop stories that work in basic epic terms and also develop potent subtextual metaphors that describe the workings of orality within superhero comic books (again, even though these creators are completely unaware of the specifics of scholarship of orality and literacy). For instance, this chapter will demonstrate not only that the multiple earths of DC superhero comic books institutionalizes variation but also that the multiple earths concept works as a metaphor to describe the basic workings of primary and secondary orality. Likewise, this chapter will demonstrate not only that *Crisis on Infinite Earths* (and its aftermath) tries unsuccessfully to end variation in the DC multiverse but also that the series and its subsequent revisions (or variation if you will) works metaphorically to indicate the incompatibility of superhero comic books and literacy.

Before directly discussing DC's multiverse and its implication of unlimited variation in superhero comic books, it is necessary to recapitulate the types of variation identified as essential in the telling and retelling of epic poetry. Variation takes place through single tellings of a story due to the episodic structure of an epic poem (a memory-driven story returns to the same event many times and each time supplies different details). This creates a sense of never-ending potential within each story unit, an openness that precludes the strict closure of works in the literate era. As previously mentioned, this can be seen in the formulaic retellings of all superhero stories of the Golden Age (and often, beyond), similar but different stories that involve the same heroes facing a similar conflict with the same type of villains, with that conflict resolved in a similar way (all part of the superhero's epic cycle). Variation also takes place through *re*tellings of such a story (a memory-driven culture preserves the essential story but the unavoidably rearranges phrases and other story elements). This creates variation to different degrees as the change in some phrases are inconsequential but the change in other phrases necessitate the change of still other phrases and so on. As previously mentioned, this can be seen in the retellings of past superhero origins that subsequently become *the* origin story and the telling of imaginary superhero stories that subsequently become part of the "real" or canonical. In both cases (but especially in the second), the variation is not acknowledged as such because the dynamics of memory unconsciously add or correct details from the previous version with the details of the now more important current version. In traditional culture, currency always supersedes primacy as the story is remembered in essence, and the primary version is never truly known. This type of replacement by the current version is still often seen even after the advent of printing press culture because of the relative inaccessibility of original text (and thus Thomas Kyd's *The Spanish Tragedy* is supplanted by William Shakespeare's *Hamlet*). This is especially worth mentioning since superhero comic books were considered disposable by most readers before the concerted collector culture of the 1980s.[6] In addition, even for regular readers who followed superheroes over the course of years, enough variations existed that it was difficult to read them all and, I would argue, impossible to remember them all.[7]

As Albert Lord has indicated, within the context of oral culture, there is no variation as there is no original to be varied (Lord, *The Singer of Tales* 101) but that does not mean that we don't now recognize that variation takes place within oral cultures. This is the fundamental paradox of a literate culture's appreciation of oral cultures: "Without the mental processes implemented by writing and print, it is impossible even to discover that there are such things as oral cultures" (Ong, *Interfaces* 257). Within the context of literate culture, it is nearly impossible to not notice variation as variation because the original exists in a recorded form, usually as a print record. And literate culture tends to privilege that which came first, placing value on primacy and labeling the subsequent variation, as derivative. Therefore, much less variation exists, as the subsequent version is likely to be derided as "unoriginal." When variations of literary works do exist, two things are generally understood as prerequisites for the new text: (1) the original has likely been read before the variation and (2) the variation is so extremely different from the original that it gives a fundamentally different meaning to the original. For instance, Jean Rhys's *Wide Sargasso Sea* tells the story of Antoinette (later known as Bertha), the mad woman in Mr. Rochester's attic in Charlotte Bronte's *Jane Eyre* (who was a flat character that simply served a narrative function in the original). Lin Haire-Sargeant's *H: The Story of Heathcliff's Journey Back to Wuthering Heights* explores unrevealed parts of the life of Heathcliff, the romantic anti-hero of Emily Bronte's *Wuthering Heights*, and rewrites the story by incorporating other Victorian characters and authors (and by giving Heathcliff and Catherine a happy ending). Whether Rhys's and Haire-Sargeant's stories stand on their own terms is debatable but it seems these creators did not set out to create new authoritative versions of either *Jane Eyre* or *Wuthering Heights*, expecting the originals to remain primary and retain their primacy. Thus, working with these two variant texts, we have one, *The Wide Sargasso Sea*, that works within the factual details of the original text and thereby, doesn't disrupt the authority of the original text per se; we have another one, *H*, that works outside the factual details of the original text but acknowledges itself as an alternate take by including almost absurd details (and thereby doesn't disrupt the authority of the original text per se). Nevertheless, by adding a fundamentally different meaning to the story, this impulse toward variation may still have at least something in common with the unrecognized variation of stories within oral culture.

As noted in chapter 5, the popularity of superheroes was waning in the post-war years because of a variety of factors that probably had much to do with creators' inability to update them appropriately.[8] Few superheroes managed to maintain popularity near their original level in the years leading to the congressional hearings dealing with comic books and juvenile delinquency; the exceptions to this rule included DC superheroes such as Superman and Batman, who justified the continued production of new stories about these characters. Therefore, stories of other heroes, such as the Flash and the Green Lantern, were seen only in reprinted form, if seen at all, but, as also noted in chapter 5, Fredric Wertham's campaign against comic books inadvertently reinvigorated the superhero; this new era of superheroes (subsequently known as the Silver Age) would begin with the revival of DC superheroes, and this revival would encourage other publishers to produce superhero stories and kick-start the Marvel revolution. With All-American Publications absorbed by the company to be known as DC, the editors decided to revive some of the All-American heroes in a way that changed the heroes in limited degrees, simultaneously harkening back to the roots of American comic books and updating superheroes to make them relevant to the culture at large. (This simultaneous movement of harkening back and updating is theoretically what is regularly done with the retellings of epic poetry.) As recounted by Dan Dido, Julius Schwartz, then chief editor of DC, would eventually describe this movement in terms generally reflective of traditional culture's need to update: "Julie Schartz said that every ten years or so you needed to give the universe an enema ... clear out all the old stories, and make way for new tales" (Dido 5); but of course, the old in the traditional culture of the superhero comic book industry would never be completely cleared away. The first hero of the Silver Age would be the Flash, who differed from the Golden Age Flash only in terms of minor details (that would eventually be amplified over time make the characters more distinct from one another). While the original Flash was Jay Garrick, a college student who gained his ability to move at superhuman speeds through a lab accident, the new Flash was Barry Allen, a police scientist who gained his ability to move at superhuman speeds through a lab accident. Although their costumes differed moderately, both characters donned costumes and fought crime under the superhero alias of the Flash. With the success of the Flash, DC similarly reworked the Green Lantern, Hawkman, and the Atom, and, with each hero, creators were encouraged by fan response to experiment a bit more with each new reworking. For instance, the Golden Age Green Lantern received abilities from a "magic" lantern that powered a ring of his own making, while the Silver Age Green Lantern gained powers from a lantern that powered a ring, both crafted by aliens who sought to protect the universe. With costumes more significantly different than those of the Golden and Silver Age Flashes, the Green Lanterns were nevertheless connected by a typical superhero trope, usually only thwarted in fighting crime by a fantasy-based weakness: wood for the Golden Age power ring and the color yellow for the Silver Age power ring. These differences gradually increased, but the new incarnation never completely ignored the existence of the original, even when seemingly only linked by a name (such as the Atom, a diminutive physicist, who had no superpowers in the Golden Age but who could reduce his physical size in the Silver Age, thanks to his experiments in physics).[9]

While fitting fairly well into the traditional culture pattern of variations on a basic template, this revision of Golden Age superheroes in the Silver Age would be a footnote in the history of superhero comic books, as a traditional culture phenomenon without multiple earths concepts begun in Gardner Fox's "Flash of Two Worlds." As a long-time veteran within the superhero comic book industry, Fox was well-known as the creator of the Golden Age Flash and of Hawkman, Dr. Fate, and the Justice Society of America, as well; DC editor Julius Schwartz sought Fox to help him bolster DC's superhero offerings in the late 1950s (since many comic book genres specifically targeted by Wertham became clearly untenable in the wake of the Comics Code). Although he did not mastermind the reintroduction of the Flash in 1956, he did helm the design of the new Hawkman and the Atom (originally created by Ben Flinton and Bill O'Connor). While the exact nature of the who-was-handling-whose-superhero issue was somewhat inconsequential in a company that still didn't credit its creators, it is important to mention, as it demonstrates the organic flow of stories from one creator to another (with no one creator being definitively associated with any one hero). Regardless, Fox would eventually return as writer to the new Flash and refine the multiple earths concept in 1961 in issue #123 of *The Flash*. The term *refine* is used very intentionally, as the idea of the parallel universe is not unique to 20th-century literature thanks to time-travel science fiction and the popularization of Einstein's theories of time and space (and not unique to even DC comics, which used the idea several times in Wonder Woman stories in the 1950s). However, "Flash of Two Worlds" would be the first to set up Golden and Silver Age worlds as parallel universes between which travel would be possible, creating a very porous membrane between these two fictive universes. The cover features a man, centrally located, in the foreground, and about to be crushed by a falling I-beam, who yells "Flash! Help me!" Separated by a wall in the exact center of the page is the Silver Age Flash on the left side, running toward the man (and the reader) and answering "I'm coming," with the Golden Age Flash on the right side, doing the same. Although it's not completely clear that they share the same space in a "real" world, the cover itself already demonstrates that the old Flash hasn't been wholly supplanted by the new Flash (implying something more at work than the simple functioning of primary orality).

With a title page that furthers the confusion (Allen and Garrick arguing about who really is the Flash), the story moves back in time to explain how Allen travels to "that 'other' earth" where Garrick lives (Gardner 1). With Allen again late to meet Iris (Allen's tardiness is a repeated joke throughout the series), his girlfriend reveals that the magician she scheduled to entertain an orphan group on this day has failed to show up. Allen volunteers the Flash as entertainment for the orphans and after a change into his costume returns to demonstrate some high-speed tricks (like playing both sides in a game of badminton). For his last trick, the Flash tells the audience that he will make himself disappear (by vibrating so quickly that he seems to fade completely from view); however, after he disappears, he fails to return to the community theater and finds himself not in Central City (Allen's home base) but in Keystone City (Garrick's home base). After finding Garrick's name in a phone book, Allen runs to Garrick's address and explains the preceding events for Garrick and the reader. After recounting the highlights of Garrick's life story to him, Allen explains how his "trick" for the orphans led to his disappearance from his own world and his reappearance on the world of the Golden Age Flash:

> The way I see it, I vibrated so fast — I tore a gap in the vibratory shields separating our worlds! As you know — two objects can occupy the same space and time — if they vibrate at different speeds! My theory is, both earths were created at the same time in two quite similar universes! They vibrate differently — which keeps them apart! Life, customs — even languages — evolved on your earth almost exactly as they did on my earth! Destiny must have decreed there'd be a Flash — on each earth! [Fox 8–9].

With the pseudo-science explanation in place and after retelling his own origin, Allen reveals to an inquisitive Garrick how he knows everything about the Golden Age Flash, from his secret identity to his origin:

> Indeed, reading of your Flash adventures inspired me to assume the secret identity of the Flash!... You were once well-known in my world — as a fictional character appearing in a magazine called *Flash Comics*!... A writer named Gardner Fox wrote about your adventures — which he claimed came to him in dreams! Obviously, when Fox was asleep, his mind was "tuned in" on your vibratory earth! That explains how he "dreamed up" the Flash! The magazine was discontinued in 1949! [Fox 10].

Garrick confirms that he retired in that year (suggesting that his superhero story came to a natural end initiated by the character rather than falling from popular interest). Garrick had been considering an end to his retirement and a return to his life as the Flash, especially in light of a recent series of bank robberies perpetrated in Keystone City. After this point, the story becomes a rather standard superhero team-up, with the two accomplishing what they couldn't separately (in this case, defeating the combined powers of the supervillains known as the Thinker, the Fiddler, and the Shade). With their superheroic mission accomplished, Allen returns with Garrick to the place where he entered Garrick's world, invites Garrick to visit Central City, and vibrates back to his own world. After confirming he has in fact returned to his own world, the Flash visits Iris who, as an intrepid reporter, questions him about his unexpected disappearance. After deflecting the question by saying newspaper readers would deem it so fantastic as to be "pure fiction," the next panel features a contemplative Flash, turning his eyes toward the reader and thinking, "The only ones who'd believe it would be the readers of *Flash Comics*! That's why I'm going to look up Gardner Fox who wrote the original Flash stories and tell it to him! He can write the whole thing up in a comic book!" (Fox 25).

Although tempting to read this story as only a stunt to satisfy the long-time reader (as well as the long-time writer), the explication of it is particularly thorny as a creation at the crossroads where literacy meets the traditionality of superhero comic books. Similar to the creators at Marvel comic books who engaged a traditional form and pushed it toward literacy in a way that was semi-intentional, Fox understands the basic form of the medium well enough to acknowledge its essential nature and similarly begin to see it as something else. Several aspects of "Flash of Two Worlds" conform to the expectations for traditional stories, most notably the portions over which I glossed, such as the type characters and the resolution of basic conflict with heavy villains. However, more interesting is Fox's parallel earth concept that in its basic design seems to indicate a new order in the superhero comic book industry. The return of the Golden Age Flash clearly violates the standard practice in traditional culture where the new variation wholly replaces the old, lost to the malleable recesses of cultural and individual memory. With the same look and life he had, as developed in the original run of his series, the Golden Age Flash returns to active duty as a superhero (with only a few years added to his life to account for his uneventful time away from the attention of comic book readers). This attention to the "real" time of a linear narrative and the science fiction verbiage used to explain the simultaneous existence of the stories (and worlds) of these characters indicates an approach

The Flash breaks the fourth wall, talks to the reader, and complicate conventional divisions between the real and the fictitious (from *The Flash* #123, p. 25).

potentially in line with a literate worldview. However, Fox's parallel earth concept contains within its basic design a metaphorical description of the traditionality of the superhero comic book industry and does something other than simply push the Flash toward literacy. After all, "Flash of Two Worlds" contains not only a science fiction explanation but also something in its pseudo-science that is hard to parse out as definitively literate: a mythic story about the nature of creation much more in line with traditionality. The new story of the Golden Age Flash is contained within the story of the Silver Age Flash and is only really important as it relates to Barry Allen; the fact that the adventure takes place in Keystone City is irrelevant as the story deals more with a revelation about the actual existence of a fictitious character who inspired Allen. Furthermore, Fox would soon after identify these earths in a nonchronological way with the Silver Age earth as Earth-1 and the Golden Age earth as Earth-2 (designations that have mystified generations of readers but make sense if mindful of traditional culture's emphasis on currency). With this almost obvious reference to the conventions of traditionality versus literacy (even though it is unintentional), this story represents something more than the blending of the two as the general evolution in Marvel's early years. What takes place within the creation of the DC multiverse is the advent of secondary orality in superhero comic books (indicating, even with Marvel comic books included, the superhero comic book spends next to no time as an exclusive product of literate culture). Fox's intention to create superheroes that were different but the same reflects an industry becoming aware of its own practices and the multiverse reveals this awareness, a self-consciousness that works to re-create traditional superheroes.

In order to better articulate my particular use of the term secondary orality, it is necessary to return to Ong and explain how my use expands Ong's ideas in some unorthodox ways. Related to the creation of the "global village" (McLuhan's term used to describe a new sort of community formed in the wake of electronic media), the phenomenon of secondary orality grows from the advent of new media and produces a community somewhat similar to that of the tribal organization of traditional culture.

> [E]lectronic technology has brought us into the age of "secondary orality." This new orality has striking resemblances to the old in its participatory mystique, its fostering of a communal sense, its concentration on the present moment, and even its use of formulas. But it is essentially a more deliberate and self-conscious orality, based permanently on the use writing and print which are essential for the operation of the equipment and for its use as well. Secondary orality is both remarkably like and unlike primary orality ... before writing, oral folk were group-minded because no feasible alternative had presented itself. In our age of secondary orality, we are group-minded self-consciously and programmatically.... Unlike members of a primary oral culture, who are turned outward because they have little occasion to turn inward, we are turned outward because we have turned inward. In the like vein, where primary orality promotes spontaneity because the analytic reflectiveness implemented by writing is unavailable, secondary orality promotes spontaneity because through analytic reflection we have decided that spontaneity is a good thing [Ong, *Orality* 134].

Ong's emphasis is squarely on new media forms that include sound recording and the verbal delivery of written text; however, Scott McCloud makes the case for the comic book experience as a sort of synesthesia in which sounds are "heard" (25) and McLuhan claims that comic books synthesize literacy with a new sort of sound experience with its preliterate visuality (*Understanding Media* 151–152). Even without those arguments in play, it's possible to consider comic books within the definition of secondary orality as it seems to develop the same sort of group dynamics as the other media, a new form of older things. With secondary orality, we are in the midst of a culture aware of the differences between exteriority of traditional culture and the interiority of modern culture and that culture makes a self-conscious choice to embrace the practices of traditionality. There is a paradox to moving outward only because we've turned inward and to moving toward spontaneity in a deliberate fashion but this is nevertheless the essence of secondary orality (what we see manifested in increasing ways throughout the "history" of DC's multiverse). If one is willing to push Ong's claims a bit, one can recognize that this move is not only beyond orality and literacy but also toward those things quintessentially postmodern. Especially important to this claim is a self-consciousness that doesn't lead to literacy but to the ideas of postmodernism (revealed as variations of oral culture). I refrain from using the term postmodernism too freely (as it has become so theoretically loaded) and mainly, because I will discuss certain postmodern concepts more thoroughly in chapter 8. Nevertheless, I feel that it must be used here not as an end in itself but rather as a means to better explain the concept of secondary orality that is extremely important to media studies and yet only explicated to a limited degree by Ong (at least in comparison to primary orality and literacy).

Again, Ong understood secondary orality as the result of electronic media that reproduced the human voice and reinstituted immediacy and openness in that way (film, radio, television, etc.). While I agree with this limited association in some respects, I more strongly believe it should be broadened to include other media (especially comic books and media of the digital age like hypertext novels); after all, a self-conscious short circuit of the conventions of literacy takes place even in modern and postmodern literature such as James Joyce's *Finnegan's Wake* and Luigi Pirandello's *Six Characters in Search of an Author*.[10] My justification for including literature is that such literature is produced like psychoanalytic theory, in a timeframe that includes the advent of forms of new media by creators inclined toward the practices of orality inherent within other mediums. Regardless, the concept of secondary orality can be clearly seen as something related to the foundational ideas of postmodernism. In *The Postmodern Condition*, Jean-Francois Lyotard would criticize meta-narratives, suggesting that universal explanations (the objective knowledge sought by Plato) could no longer be supported in recognition of the inherently diverse nature of world culture. While the tribe might be everything in the situation of primary orality, the global village is aware of its fragmentation and moves past literacy by recognizing that there are many tribes, each with a theoretically valid point of view.[11] Similarly, in *Postmodernism*, Fredric Jameson suggests that postmodernism works to destroy the aesthetic conventions that preceded it and that were predicated on the ideals of originality.[12] While the traditional culture might produce episodic and formulaic narratives as a matter of course, postmodern culture chooses to work in something like pastiche or bricolage because it is asserted that nothing can be wholly unique or owned by a creator. These "postmodern" moves are moves toward orality that forsake the unconscious practice of primary orality for something much more self-conscious; this progression from primary orality to secondary orality is exactly what can be seen in the increasingly complicated notion of the DC multiverse. The connections that I've just made are not set forth to suggest that Gardner Fox is any more aware of how his narrative choices relate to postmodernism than of how they relate to some sort of orality. However, as unaware as Fox might be of the powerful metaphor for orality in the demarcation of Earth-1 and Earth-2, this unconscious sense of traditional art is very interestingly part of a story in which Fox does make several self-conscious narrative choices (basically making steps in the direction of greater awareness within the industry). As Freud would suggest about the depths of the unconscious and Ong would imply about the intricacies of orality, one can only begin to see them once one begins thinking in self-conscious terms. The above-mentioned connections are set forth to suggest that ideas of postmodern are very much related to the ideas of secondary orality and this helps us to understand the most interesting parts of "Flash of Two Worlds" (and the subsequent development of the DC multiverse). Before returning to this story, I want to establish one more aspect of this discussion that will help us deal with these superhero comic books as a phenomenon of secondary orality but not constantly recall Ong's more limited definition of the term. Since we're dealing with something that is not oral in the conventional sense of the word, I again recommend using the newer and broader term of *traditionality*. And since we're potentially dealing with many forms of new media as well as comic books, it might make sense to combine *new media* with *traditionality*. However, as already noted, I consider secondary orality to be manifested in literature as well and therefore, the term *new media* isn't inclusive. Therefore, while we could use something as clumsy as *new media traditionality*, it makes more sense to just leave the *media* as implied and call this *new (media) traditionality* or simply *new traditionality*.

As noted in chapter 5, although Lee and Kirby's appearance in *Fantastic Four* #10 is often identified as postmodern, it is much more like an oral poet's playful attitude to a story that is really not the poet's own (something that may be related to the advent of literacy). As also noted, the cover of *Fantastic Four* #10, rather than the story that follows, is much more in line with postmodernism or what we will call new traditionality; the playfulness embodied within Lee and Kirby previewing and critiquing their own comic is much more prevalent in "Flash of Two Worlds." While Fox never makes an appearance in this issue of *The Flash*, his presence is even more notable as a storyteller because of the looping of one fiction upon another and the questions this looping poses about reality (or more accurately our means of knowing reality). As mentioned, Barry Allen, the Silver Age Flash, tracks Jay Garrick, the Golden Age Flash, to his home because he recognizes the significance of his newfound location (Keystone City). Allen had read about Garrick as the Flash in *Flash Comics* and in direct reference to this earlier event in the series (that still clearly separated reality and fiction), Allen was inspired to become the Flash by this comic book character. On one hand, this aspect of the story provides an excuse (if not a rationale) for the cliché of the superpowered hero who immediately dons a costume to fight crime upon discovering his or her superpowers; and beyond the comic book "life" of Allen, this story also acknowledges the original basis for a story that in an oral culture would be lost forever (if "lost" could be appropriate in reference to oral culture). On the other hand, this acknowledgment of the past version that superficially seems in line with the goals of literate culture is neither wholly explanatory in a sense of realistic fiction nor wholly satisfactory in terms of establishing primacy as the most important aspect of literate culture's desire to catalogue. The line between fiction and reality is blurred, a line established much more clearly in literate culture in order to maintain one's ability to distinguish between the subjective and objective, the story and life, the false and true. The story of the Golden Age Flash is a fiction told in a comic book that inspired the Silver Age Flash but the story is also a reality (as much as Silver Age Flash is a reality) in that Allen's power now allows him to interact with Garrick. Even with the explanation that Fox "tuned in on your vibratory earth" (nearly absurd on its surface and sounding more magical than scientific), the story doesn't do what variations must do within a literate culture: establish one story as a fiction and the other as reality. Instead, the story is a self-conscious celebration of variation as it exists within oral culture and within superhero comic books, with the new supplanting the old to some degree, but with variation itself extolled as a virtue by revealing it at work. The awareness of new traditionality (something that could move "beyond" the conventions of orality but chooses to nevertheless embrace them) is best demonstrated in last panel of the issue (something that does anything but bring the story to a close). After breaking the fourth wall convention of comic book panel illustration by looking toward the reader, the Flash suggests that this real world would never be believed by readers of a newspaper, ethically bound to report the objective facts of stories in the real world. Instead, Allen will relay the story to Fox, who will "write the whole thing up in comic book." This decision to tell Fox the story moves away from the idea that Fox unconsciously "tuned in" when writing stories of Golden Age Flash (a metaphor for traditionality) to the way he will now work with material directly given to his conscious self (a metaphor for new traditionality). In addition to playfully recharacterizing which medium is most likely to provide access to the real world and to the truth (newspapers or comic books), this also breaks from conventions by violating the immediacy of the story; that real world moment may have preceded the Fox's writing of the real world story of "Flash of Two Worlds." Regardless, this is a celebration of variation that breaks from Aristotle's insistence that stories fool the audience into thinking they've experienced reality, and, again it does so playfully, as the story currently read might be imaginary, real, and/or a variation on the real. This playfulness ultimately makes variation more important than primacy, authenticity, and even originality (after all, Allen makes a long list of similarities between his world and Garrick's world).

As strong a representation of new traditional art and the practice of new traditionality as Fox's story might be, Fox was still working within the a comic book industry that hadn't changed much in thirty years; as much as he may have been self-consciously playing with this story, he still had the responsibility to produce many stories every month. The sheer volume of his output prevented him from demonstrating too much more self-consciousness in his multiverse stories to come but this comment in itself brings up the interesting question of whether one need be more self-conscious to maintain new traditionality. Regardless, Fox would often talk about providing good entertainment and pleasing the fans, and it quickly became obvious to him and his colleagues that the multiverse stories pleased fans. This is interesting in that only the minority of readers were fully aware of the adventures of the Golden Age superheroes: "That story, 'Flash of Two Worlds,' captivated the comics fans of the day, most of whom were unaware that there'd ever *been* another Scarlet Speedster. Readers demanded a sequel, and then another. They wrote in by the thousands, begging Schwartz to show more of the Golden Age heroes" (Waid, "Introduction" 3–4). This evocation of pastimes for a culture that knew the Golden Age heroes existed in the past but really only experienced them in the present is a description that fits the traditional culture. The self-conscious nod to the readers became the cliché of the multiverse stories, such as in *Flash* #137, "Vengeance of the Immortal Villain," which reintroduces the Justice Society of America (JSA). After disabling the threat of Vandal Savage's "sky-light machines" with Garrick and the JSA, Allen calls Iris for a date only to find out she can't because she's been assigned to uncover the source of the mysterious sky-lights. Allen looks toward the reader and thinks, "If I want to see Iris tonight, I better hustle right over to her office — as the Flash — and tell her the whole story" (Fox 25). While not quite the nuanced and multifaceted idea presented at the end of "Flash of Two Worlds," it demonstrates how the awareness of new traditionality may become part of the system and no longer wholly requires the self-consciousness of the individual creator to perpetuate. Along those lines, the editors at DC Comics saw the multiverse as the opportunity to pair up other Golden Age and Silver Age superheroes, such as the Green Lanterns and especially the Justice League and the Justice Society; with readers thrilled by the interaction of some of their greatest DC superheroes, they were even more excited to see practically all DC superheroes share the same space.

This required some explanation, as some superheroes like Superman and Batman had enjoyed continuous publication and therefore were already part of the world shared by the Silver Age Flash and Green Lantern. However, the Earth-2 Superman and Batman were represented as very similar to but suddenly twenty years older than the Silver Age Superman and Batman. In an impulse that may have squared the differences between Earth-1 and Earth-2 versions of these characters, Earth-2 versions possessed some characteristics that had been changed and forgotten by most (i.e., the Superman of Earth-2 was Kal-L, while the Superman of Earth-1 was the more recent Kal-El). However, there were so many changes over that years, and those changes were made so incrementally and consistently that it was impossible to recognize what traits distinctively belonged to the "old" Superman of Earth-2. In any case, Earth-2 allowed writers to explore certain facets of these characters that, at the time, could never be explored within the regular series of adventures of these two heroes (such as Superman marrying Lois Lane and Batman retiring, thus allowing his sidekick Robin to take center stage). As readers could look back and forth between the end of Superman's story on Earth 2 and the on-going stories of the younger Superman on Earth-1 with no real cognitive dissonance, readers could also experience almost unending variation as the multiverse expanded; the love of variation seemed to feed itself and further encourage variation as an end in itself. For instance, in *Justice League of America* #29, Earth-3 was discovered as a world where most things were dissimilar and the Justice League members were villains, comprising the Crime Syndicate of America. Sometimes, the creation of parallel earths was more practical as DC acquired superheroes from other comic book publishers (with Earth-4 containing the Charlton heroes and Earth-S the Marvel family). Other times, the creation of parallel earths was more creative and self-conscious with the discovery of Earth-Prime in *Flash* #179. Earth-Prime represents the earth in which we live without real superheroes but with DC publishing stories of a multiverse of superheroes. Necessarily, this version of the earth would, from its inception, not be allowed to exist in its own terms (with multiverse stories coming to writers unconsciously tuned into the multiverse). If it had existed on its own terms, this earth could be the real to the fiction of the DC multiverse; regardless, it does not, and, in *Flash* #179, the Flash visits Julius Schwartz and enlists his help in returning to Earth-1. As time passed, superhero visits to Earth-Prime would continue, and, in addition, Earth-Prime would eventually host its own superheroes.[13] Perhaps most interesting of the subsequent visits is a return visit in *Flash* #228; the writer, Cary Bates, travels from Earth-Prime to Earth-1 (and eventually Earth-2), discovering not only the basis of his inspiration but also that he can influence events on parallel earths. And he eventually becomes a supervillain in *Justice League of America* #123. Staying true to superhero cliché, the supervillain would be thwarted by superheroic might but also with the help of another DC writer who rewrites the destruction Bates caused on Earth-2. By producing yet another variation of the story just told and describing the relationship of the artist to the Muses behind the curtain, this story reveals and revels in the traditionality of superhero comic books. Participation is key and the reader plays a role as the person to whom Barry Allen speaks and as the person who participates with a host of others enabling the storytelling in Earth-1.

While not completely dismissing the orientation of hard science fiction (which is more literate than oral), the pseudo-science of the multiverse is largely an excuse for a certain kind of storytelling. The logos of hard science serves as an excuse to return to the mythos of superhero variation, and the either/or paradigm of scientific objectivity is forsaken for a multiverse of possibilities that address the current culture.[14] One of the on-going and important paradoxes of the DC multiverse is that it acknowledges the creator's significance (in a time when creators began to receive credit on title pages) while it also asserts the creator's irrelevance. After all, in conceptual terms set forth by the multiverse stories, the worlds of superheroes exist separately from the creators, and the creators cannot properly be said to have made them (much less to own them). While the public relations machine known as Stan Lee would have interpersonal skills that completely mobilized superhero comic book fans as a community, DC had the narrative explanation of why fans were so important; the multiverse refused to separate creators from the audience because fans were like the creators, "tuned in" to the world of superheroes. As described in Bill Schelly's *The Golden Age of Comic Fandom* (devoted to the studying the new development of the superhero fan community in the 1960s), Jerry Bails is the one fan most singly responsible for the formation of superhero comic book fandom with the fanzine *Alter Ego*.[15] However, Bails's was not part of the Marvel generation of readers, and his interest stretched back to the Golden Age, particularly to *All-Star Comics* (which featured the stories of the Justice Society of America). With an interest in collecting back issues in order to read more stories of past heroes, he began his life as a fan by writing DC in 1960 and starting a long correspondence with Gardner Fox — in the hope of bringing back Golden Age superheroes. Although Bails considered his efforts a success with the debut of the Justice League of America, his correspondence undoubtedly has some bearing on Fox's later decision to develop Earth-2 and the multiverse. Through their relationship, we recognize something much different from the distance between the writer and the audience in literate culture, where the audience is always a fiction. In this case, Bails became part of an interactive community based on the ideals of traditionality and contributed to the development of a concept that further validated his participation. Moreover, as an adult who self-consciously turns back to the comics of his youth and advocates for them, he serves as an exemplar of new traditionality in that he turns outward after turning inward: organizing the first comic book conventions (Pustz 158). Furthering the continuous circle of influence within this dynamic community, Fox would put Bails in contact with another letter-writing Golden Age fan named Roy Thomas; initially a contributor to Bails's *Alter Ego*, Thomas would take over as editor and become more well-known in years to come as a writer and editor of Marvel comic books.

Literacy Rears Its Head in the Form of Marv Wolfman's Most Terrifying Creation: The Librarian

However, the traditional community of comic book fandom would eventually be challenged by the formalization of comic books as collectibles, often worth significant amounts of money (due to the publication of the first *Overstreet Comic Book Price Guide* in 1970) and by the transition from fanzines to professional magazines devoted to comic books (such as the publication of *The Comics Journal* in 1976).[16] As the comic book lost its identity as disposable pamphlet, it would come to be regarded more as an artifact of a commercial economy and less as a vessel for story. In the wake of Jack Kirby fighting to retrieve his original artwork from Marvel (physical, permanent, and saleable artifacts of his artistic life), DC would officially adopt a policy of returning artwork to their creators (thus making their work seem more material and less ephemeral). Guides encouraged continuity obsession and literate-minded fans-turned-critics took fans further from the love of traditional superhero comic books by questioning the artistic value of such stories;[17] by the standards of literacy, the multiverse stories would be considered kitschy at best. Into this scene came Marv Wolfman, publisher of a fanzine in the late 1960s and staff writer at Marvel comic books (under Roy Thomas) in the early 1970s.[18] In many ways, Wolfman was an active part of multiverse experience of DC comic books, initially thrilled by the Justice League/Justice Society team-ups, but, over time, whatever pleasure he had for stories of parallel universes was lost. This sense of loss grew with letters from DC readers in the early 1980s with questions about the contradictions of continuity within the various DC universes (Wolfman 5). Working with the idea that the multiverse was off-putting to new readers and that "DC could simplify its continuity and lure new readers into the fold," Wolfman returned to a story idea he had as a fan: a limited series featuring all of his favorite heroes from various parallel universes (Wolfman 6). If the dynamics of literate culture were not clear enough in his words expressing his desire to simplify *continuity* (eliminating variation), the story from which Wolfman drew inspiration originally featured a character named "the Librarian." Originally the Librarian was a villain who catalogued information about superheroes to be sold to the highest bidder, but Wolfman's new variation on that story would understand the librarian character's simplification and consolidation of information as a noble effort.[19] Regardless, Wolfman's noble effort to destroy the multiverse and create one single universe (an attempt to reassert a literate worldview after DC's transition to secondary orality) had problems that would cause it to fail in significant ways.

This concession to literate thought may have seemed necessary to the editors at DC as superhero comic books were losing their adolescent and teen readership in the 1980s due to the lure of video games; rather than recapture the youth interest, DC (and Marvel) were making changes to cement the interest of older readers (most notably with more mature story lines — my focus in chapter 7). When it came to the multiverse, Wolfman was probably right about excessive backstory knowledge being off-putting to new readers, but, once again, comic book creators identified traditionality with youth psychology and literacy with adult psychology.[20] In any case, his proposal for *Crisis on Infinite Earths* was accepted at the beginning of the 1980s and Wolfman began the long process of research to square his story with past stories of the various worlds in the DC multiverse. The very notion of research on the part of a creator sets this story at odds with traditionality in its most basic sense, but Wolfman believed respecting past continuity was essential to retaining old readers as he created a foundation for the new.[21] (This simultaneously hints at the Wolfman's misunderstanding of Fox's playful multiverse concept but also describes the turn taken by readers of DC's multiverse stories in a comic book culture losing its love of new traditionality because of various above-mentioned external factors.) The plans for the series were announced at a comics convention in New York City in 1981, but Wolfman's extensive research meant the series would not be released until 1985 (the year of DC's 50th anniversary).[22] Wolfman's story, illustrated by George Perez in his highly detailed and realistic style, begins in medias res with a mysterious force destroying entire universes within the multiverse. An incredibly powerful character named the Monitor collects superheroes and supervillains from various times and places in DC's multiverse to fight against this force and to preserve existence itself. In the course of the story, it is revealed that an ancient experiment by an otherworldly scientist named Krona inadvertently created the multiverse; the experiment also created the Monitor and the anti-matter being destroying the multiverse (simply known as the Anti-Monitor). Initially, the superheroes and supervillains fought to protect devices that would combine the surviving earths of the multiverse into one earth and protect it from the Anti-Monitor. As the battle between those fighting for the Monitor and Anti-Monitor continued, more and more characters were drawn into the battle from many parts of the DC multiverse in an exaggerated variation on the annual Justice League/Justice Society team-ups. After a temporary defeat of the Anti-Monitor, supervillains band together to take advantage of the newly formed single earth. However, the battle royale between superheroes and supervillains is interrupted by news that the Anti-Monitor has traveled to the dawn of the multiverse to stop Krona's experiment and thereby foil their recent efforts to preserve the earth. The heroic work of the superheroes ultimately destroy the Anti-Monitor, but, while Krona's experiment proceeds, the energy released from the Anti-Monitor's destruction merges the characteristics from the five earths surviving in 1985 within a single universe.

Wolfman's story is a product of a literate impulse in that the story is told with the ulterior motive of simplifying the DC multiverse; the variation that is extolled within the new traditionality of the multiverse stories of the 1960s is decried by the positions taken by the narrator and various characters. At the very beginning of the story, accompanied by images of a big bang and the multiplication of a single earth, the narration reads:

> In the beginning, there was only one, a single black infinitude ... so cold and dark for so very long ... that even the burning light was imperceptible. But the light grew, and the infinitude shuddered ... and the darkness finally ... screamed, as much in pain as relief. For in that instance, a multiverse was born. A multiverse of worlds vibrating and replicating ... and a multiverse that should have been one, become many [Wolfman 11].

I could quibble with Wolfman's choice of phrase such as "a multiverse that should have been one," problematic as anything prefixed with "multi-" is necessarily more than one (and I could perhaps even suggest that this unconsciously reveals the confusion at the heart of this work). However, the overall intention of this introduction is fairly clear: to identify the multiverse as something unintended and unnatural (the darkness screams upon its creation). This is later elaborated upon by the Monitor who states, "The universe was split apart at the dawn of time ... each one weaker than the whole it was meant to be..." (Wolfman 114). Moreover, this is furthered by rewriting the story of the mad scientist, Krona, whose experiments were said to unleash evil upon the universe in the team-up story of Golden and Silver Age Green Lanterns in *Green Lantern* #40. In *Crisis on Infinite Earths*, that evil is the creation of the anti-matter universe and the endless replication of universe, making the variation practiced by new traditionality not only unnatural and weak but also evil. At the end of the story, we visit Arkham Asylum where most of the final words are given to the Psycho-Pirate, a supervillain who aided the Anti-Monitor and unlike most DC characters, still remembers the multiverse:

> I remember all that happened, and I'm not going to forget.... You see, I like to remember the past because those were better times than now. I mean, I'd rather live in the past than today, wouldn't you? I mean, nothing's ever certain anymore. Nothing's ever predictable like it used to be. These days ... y-you just never know who's going to die ... and who's going to live [Wolfman 364].

By putting these words into the mouth of one of the most vile supervillains within the story, his statement works as an antithesis of what one would traditionally expect from a superhero story. The Psycho-Pirate prefers the pre–Crisis multiverse days of the DC universe where things were better, certain, predictable, and governed by the standard conventions of superhero stories. Thereafter, he is welcoming readers to what he considers worse and therefore, what readers should consider better: a darker more uncertain world where stories are not governed by the clichés of traditionality. The last words of the narrator state, "Not the end; the beginning of the future" (Wolfman 364), signifying a future orientation more characteristic of literacy than traditionality. In addition the successive panels that feature the above-quoted text move further and further from him, making the reader increasingly less likely to identify with his perspective.

Despite the stated goal of *Crisis on Infinite Earths*, the work is divided between the impulse toward literacy and a welcoming of new readers on one hand and the practice of new traditionality and an insider's love of the multiverse on the other. After the series was published, regular DC titles were restarted with new origin stories based in the mid–1980s that jump-started the careers of superheroes who did not remember the Crisis. Therefore, in theory, new readers would not read the series, and the series merely provides a means for old readers to make the transition to DC's new vision of their universe (but in that way, the series itself works in a paradoxical way by eschewing the multiverse and paying homage to it). Wolfman's style is inspired by that of Stan Lee, who sought to give depth to his superheroes but relied heavily upon type to further the plot (in this case seeing Superman as a soaring symbol of new hope who interacts with Batman as a brooding emblem of dark justice). The complexity of character and plot seems present only for the same reason that it was present in other multiverse stories; heavy heroes interact not only with each other but also with other variations of themselves. As indicated by Wolfman himself, the story is the ultimate fanboy team-up fantasy, something that provided some of the impetus for the multiverse in the first place: "I always wanted to see a single story featuring *all* the DC superheroes from the past, present, and future" (Wolfman 5). Thus, we see the Golden Age Superman fighting alongside Silver Age Superman and Jonah Hex from the wild West of DC's superhero past fighting alongside the Legion of Superheroes from the 30th Century of DC's superhero future. If anything, with the series as the grandest team-up/crossover event ever, the story expands the desire to see together more heroes unlikely to be seen together (Perez's panoramic, richly detailed double page spreads set the crossover event series standard of depicting dozens of superheroes and supervillains in battle). Despite the express purpose of establishing a fixed, consistent, and most important, authoritative reality for the new DC universe, the series works like previous team-ups of earlier multiverse stories, blurring the line between fiction and reality in yet another way. The greatest triumph of the combined efforts of all DC superhero characters is the saving of the universe and also, the subsequent erasure of what has come before in the multiverse, to be replaced by a new history of the DC universe. Therefore, since plot dynamics make it unclear whether the old history of the DC multiverse or the new history of the DC universe has greater claim as reality, neither seems to deserve the term *fiction*.

Long-time comic book fans barely mourn the passing of a favorite comic book character because they live with the assurance that that character will return via one convoluted explanation or another; this is a result of the traditional tendencies of the superhero story that work against the permanence of linear history and promise that the story will be retold. Yet, those fans still do mourn every time that Superman dies, apparently moved more by the pervasive impact of the current story than the impermanence of the event. This certainly would have to be the case in *Crisis on Infinite Earths*, which featured the deaths of many superheroes, most notably Supergirl and the Barry Allen Flash. Readers reacted (and still react) emotionally to these deaths even though these deaths, could be regarded as even less significant than a typical superhero death; by the time they died during the original run of the series, it had already become common knowledge that the entire history of the DC universe was to be rewritten and many of these characters would return in one way or another. However, they would never return in that exact same *variation* and for a reader working within the self-conscious experience of new traditionality, this would be something to mourn. Moreover, before we "hear" the final words of the Psycho-Pirate in his padded cell, we are privy to the diagnosis of a psychiatrist who describes the Psycho-Pirate's delusion about the "multiple earths" and remarks that he's never before seen this type of psychosis. But readers of the series also remember the "reality" of the multiverse and are unlikely to forget it as a precedent for the new DC universe. Thereby, this brings forth the greatest paradox of a work that could only achieve its literate "clean-up" goal by making itself obsolete, unread by future generations of DC superhero fans. If this had been the case (and it has not been the case with bound collections of the series in continuous print since their debut), the supposedly literate shape of the DC universe would merely have proved the traditionality of superhero comic book culture (only interested in the most current version). Ironically, the series is now often referred to as an "epic" part of the history of DC superheroes, a claim that can only be made by directly acknowledging the "mess" of multiverse stories that made it possible. While the series may have been motivated by a desire to return to some logically consistent literary Eden with no variations or contradictions, *Crisis on Infinite Earths* reveals that that particular Eden never existed. Even in its own terms, the series is largely a work of secondary orality that cannot help but love the variations of the DC multiverse (best represented by Wolfman's unwillingness to kill or combine into the whole certain superheroes like the Golden Age Superman and Superboy — both transported to a paradise dimension at the end of the series). Also, Wolfman seems unwilling to forget the Crisis story line itself, adding to it in years to come in *Legends of the DC Universe*, featuring a Crisis timeline story of the Flash of Earth-D. Wolfman would also novelize the story (published in 2005) in another variation told from the perspective of Barry Allen; with yet another aspect of the Crisis story line centering on the Flash (the starting point for DC's multiverse), Wolfman's understanding of the story over time seems to be one increasingly in line with the self-consciousness of new traditionality.

Regardless of Wolfman's original or eventual sense of his own work, the DC universe would be structured around this event from the 1980s onward. However, the changes made in order to give the DC universe a shape clearly based on the tenets of literacy would not survive. In fact, a quick survey of the changes reveals that they can probably only be called changes at the most superficial level and were in fact part of the new shape of traditionality in superhero comic books. In the months immediately before the release of *Crisis on Infinite Earths*, final stories of various DC superheroes were told, such as one where Superman relinquished his powers and made a life with Lois Lane ("Whatever Happened to the Man of Tomorrow") and another where Wonder Woman married Steve Trevor on Paradise Island ("Of Gods and Men").[23] In *DC Comics Presents* #87, Earth-Prime became less like our world with the advent of Superboy in that superhero-less world. These "final" stories were told only because of the promise of new retellings — yet another variation of the stories was due on the newsstands the very next month. (In fact, Superboy-Prime would become part of the Crisis story line, later resurface in the DC universe, and have his story retold without this tie to the DC universe in *Superman: Secret Identity*.)[24] In *How to Read Superhero Comics and Why*, Geoff Klock states, "The irony of the *Crisis* was that its methodology, in simplifying continuity, was used to make superhero comics more rich: any attempt to make superhero comics into something streamlined, clear, and direct ... only results in another layer of continuity" (21). The subsequent retcons of DC superheroes are meant to clean up continuity but largely retell the stories with many of the same convolutions. Beyond the mandate that the multiverse did not exist, superheroes were to be less fanciful and more realistic, and all these mandates (primary and secondary) seemed to be driving John Byrne's *The Man of Steel*, a limited series that retold Superman's origin and set up the various Superman series to restart. Superman's powers were lessened and thus, there would be no flying in space without oxygen, moving entire planets with his strength alone, or embarking on time travel on a regular basis. However, his powers were not lessened to the point of his original depiction (he still flew and possessed x-ray and heat vision) and the later of two pseudo-science explanations of his powers was employed (the yellow sun and not earth's lighter gravity). Moreover, Superman's origin was retold with relatively little variation excepting another costume change for Jor-El and Lara, combining elements drawn from various origin stories over the years including the Superman movies. With *The Man of Steel* and three Superman series soon to follow, almost the entire cast of Superman would return with friends like Jimmy Olsen, love interests like Lana Lang and Lois Lane, and enemies like Lex Luthor and Bizarro. Certain changes were made (in that Lex Luthor was less mad scientist and more power-hungry billionaire, and Superman's alter ego, Clark Kent, was less mild-mannered and incompetent and more intrepid reporter) but on the whole, Byrne simply negotiates and creates past variations on the cliché with minor updates. For instance, the series ends with Byrne drawing Superman in a majestic pose with the sky in the background (a standard depiction popularized by artists like Curt Swan) thinking thoughts he thought long before the Crisis: "I may have been conceived in the endless depths of space ... but I was born when the rocket opened, on earth, in America ... Krypton bred me, but it was Earth that gave me all I am" (Byrne 22). In addition to continuing the assimilation story of Superman as the ultimate immigrant, Byrne demonstrates that his return to many Superman clichés is self-conscious with certain nods to the past; issue #5 begins with Superman holding a man in a purple and green battlesuit (typical of Luthor's past costumes) and saying "You're getting sloppy, Luthor" with the next panel revealing that the Luthor he addresses is sitting behind his desk in a business suit (1–2). However, this move hardly negates the clichés that are redeployed in this Superman origin and simply demonstrates that DC's new order is not the cliché-breaking of literacy but the self-conscious cliché-deployment of new traditionality.

From Zero Inconsistencies to Many Happy Inconsistencies: What If Earth X Never Ended?

While the editorial mandate at DC may have been to preserve the cleanliness of a newly remade universe as consistent and self-contained, it seemed that such a mandate was both impossible to maintain and perhaps not even desirable. In *Batman: Year One* (a retelling of Batman's origin released at roughly the same time as Byrne's *The Man of Steel*), Frank Miller and David Mazzucchelli presented a gritty and violent story of the Dark Knight as a vigilante set against a corrupt police force. Although this is my seem more cliché-breaking than Byrne's Superman with complex depictions of Bruce Wayne and Jim Gordan, it recalled the dark paranoia of the Finger and Kane years and the Thomas and O'Neil years; and Mazzucchelli's realistic but moody art drew heavily on the film noir conventions that inspired

Kane, colored with a variety of shades in the grayscale. These points aside, this series would be followed by Mike Barr's *Batman: Year Two* that created a different sense of Gotham than *Year One*; it was less violent and more simplistic, drawn by Todd McFarlane in a less realistic and stylized way and colored more in line with traditional four color comic books. Thus, one of the ways the industry would find it nearly impossible to maintain a consistent and self-contained universe is that creators are regularly changed, and, even with a literate culture's mandate in place, creators have their own sense of the authentic version of a superhero and unconsciously bring their own variations to the story. Such variations would seem to be inevitable, but the self-conscious choices to refer back to the multiverse are not. In 1988, Alan Moore's *Batman: The Killing Joke* revealed the forever obscure origin story of the Joker; yet, even though that origin was very much in line with the darker tone of the Modern Age, it made specific references back to pre–Crisis (and somewhat silly) aspects of previous Batman stories: the giant penny and T-Rex in the Batcave and a picture of the Batfamily including Batmite. During Grant Morrison's run on *Animal Man* (1989–91), Animal Man encounters Psycho-Pirate and is exposed to his memories of the multiverse and also the idea that he exists as a comic book character; this eventually leads to a heavy-handed postmodern moment where Animal Man interacts with Morrison himself. Obviously, these things didn't slip by continuity editors; the industry professionals in charge of DC's continuity didn't prevent such stories but often fell back on the explanation that they were non-continuity stories. Regardless of the explanation, this allowance by editors implies that they understand the variation inherent within new traditionality to be part of the natural order of superhero comic books (and incidentally, both *Batman: The Killing Joke* and Morrison's run on *Animal Man* have been largely absorbed by DC continuity).

The literate goal of *Crisis on Infinite Earths* would be nearly impossible to achieve, because the culture would reject stories of classic superheroes without their clichés (self-conscious use of clichés included) and because the culture couldn't stop referring to pre–Crisis events (and editors couldn't stop them from doing so). In addition, superheroes still lived according to a standard conceit and continued to not age as time passed around them (i.e., ten years after the Crisis, Superman looked just as young as he did when Byrne re-created him). Therefore, in order to maintain the facade of literacy, another Crisis would be in order. In ten short years after *Crisis in Infinite Earths*, the continuity problems had become too numerous to mention, with superheroes existing in the universe before their official reintroductions and with creators borrowing from past stories in the post–Crisis timeline before "official" reintroductions made those borrowings obsolete. For instance, DC often featured pre–Crisis versions of superheroes on teams like the Justice League in the post–Crisis timeline until the company finally produced new versions. In this case, *Zero Hour: Crisis in Time* was a crossover event series that worked similarly to Crisis to address such continuity problems with a power-mad Green Lantern trying to remake time in order to undo the destruction of Coast City. Similar to the original Crisis story line, it was born of conflicted goals, in the end also erasing previously mentioned post–Crisis aesthetic conflicts (keeping *Batman: Year One* and eliminating *Batman: Year Two*). Of course, this could be interpreted simply as an attempt to build a better cliché. Regardless, the crossover events with ulterior motives clearly drawn from the original Crisis would cease thereafter and in tentative ways, the new traditionalism suggested by the multiverse was incrementally restored. For instance, the future history of DC universe would be told in 2000 in Mark Waid's *The Kingdom*, which features the son of Superman and Wonder Woman on a quest to restore the multiple earths (or what in this series is called Hypertime)[25]; the most notable scene is the one in which their son reveals his motives and displays a plethora of scenes representing scenes from the multiple earths in their original rendering, a pastiche/bricolage at odds with the more consistent artistic style of the series itself.

Even more important would be Peter David's 2002 "Many Happy Returns" arc of the new *Supergirl* series (more important because DC didn't feel the need to distance the story from their regular continuity as they had with *The Kingdom*, an "Elseworlds" story).[26] Despite the original intention to limit the Superfamily, Supergirl and Superdog would return, but Supergirl would not be another survivor of Krypton. Instead, she would be an artificial lifeform created by Lex Luthor and merged with a woman named Linda Danvers. However, in "Many Happy Returns," Kara Zor-El, the Silver Age Supergirl, would arrive in the post–Crisis reality of the DC universe (for a complicated reason unnecessary to explain). After building a life in the post–Crisis world with the help of the post–Crisis Supergirl, they discover that she must return to her original reality or the battle against the Anti-Monitor will be lost. In an effort to save her new friend, Linda Danvers takes the place of Kara. Eventually, it is discovered that this ruse can't work, but, before that point, David and Benes have the kind of self-conscious fun possible only if engaging in the practices of new traditionality. For instance, in a splashpage, Superman introduces the Linda Danvers Supergirl to the world by flying down the street in a ticker tape parade modeled closely on the cover of *Action* #285 in 1962 (in which Supergirl was first introduced to the world). Superman and this Supergirl fall in love and at their wedding, Lois Lane and Lana Lang stand in the background and share this funny and clever conversation that exists inside and outside the new reality of this issue: LOIS: "Please — oh please — let it be a hoax!" LANA: "Or a dream!" BOTH: "Or an imaginary tale!" (David 114). The issue in which Linda lives an alternative life but discovers that Kara is the one who must return to her original destination features a cover modeled on the issue of *Crisis on Infinite Earths* in which Supergirl dies; on the original cover, Superman holds a limp Supergirl (Kara Zor-El) in his arms, and, on the new cover, the Linda Danvers Supergirl holds a limp Kara Zor-El Supergirl in her arms.[27] In addition to clearly reinstating the "real" existence of the pre–Crisis timeline, this image shows that *Crisis on Infinite Earths* was absorbed by the new traditionality of the multiverse stories and therefore, became just another cliché.

The inevitable reappearance of the multiverse was made official by DC in 2004 with another crossover series titled *Infinite Crisis* written by Geoff Johns and illustrated by Phil Jimenez with George Perez (the artist on *Crisis on Infinite Earths*).[28] After Wonder Woman kills in an act she considers necessary to save the world, Superman, Batman, and Wonder Woman are at odds, and Superman begins to reject his role as a god-like hope for the world; the public doubts the heroism of superheroes in general, and they're not alone. The Superman of Earth-2, Superboy of Earth-Prime, and Alexander Luthor (the son of the heroic Lex Luthor of Earth-3) observe the earth from their pocket universe in dismay. Highlighting the darkness characterizing superhero stories in the Modern Age, *Infinite Crisis* features the return of these three characters, intent on remaking the earth into a better place by replacing the post–Crisis earth with something better, purer, and more innocent like Earth-2. (Alexander Luthor would keep the true nature of his plan from the Superman of Earth-2 with his intention to form a new earth by accessing the multiverse and selecting the best parts of the parallel worlds.) As a sequel, this series could never exist in its own terms, but it does even more than reopen a chapter of DC history supposedly closed off forever by the authority of a DC editorial decision. It serves as a commentary on the criticisms of Modern Age superheroes with their complex psychology, consequential violence, and dealings with a global society forever at conflict that may not want them anymore. Rather than uphold values, they seem to be at odds with the dark world around them — in the words of the Earth-2 Superman, before he breaks the barrier between his pocket dimension and Earth: "I'm beginning to see it. This is what the world does to legends. It corrupts them ... or it destroys them" (Johns, *Infinite* 23–24). In this Superman's summary of *Crisis on Infinite Earths*, he further articulates the transition from the heavy heroes and moral standards of the Golden and Silver Ages to self-questioning heroes and nihilism of the Modern Age, approximating a reader's reaction:

> From our place, we watched this new earth grow. The potential was there. And it started off so well. So full of hope. I felt confident the earth was in good hands. But soon after, we learned there was something inherently wrong. This new earth was anything but better. A darkness seemed to spread. Warping the heroes lives. Some died. Other lost their way. We watched for years, hoping everyone would find inspirations again. But as we continued to look on ... things got worse [59–60].

As if to drive home the points about the darkness of the post–Crisis universe, acts of violence are graphically depicted (such as Superboy-Prime decapitating Pantha, and Black Adam poking the eyes of Psycho-Pirate through the back of his head). As the plot moves forward, a conflict created between those swayed by the rhetoric of the Earth-2 Superman and those who want to fight for the world that now exists. Eventually the Superman from Earth-2 dissociates himself from the increasingly zealous and merciless Superboy-Prime and Alexander Luthor; he is convinced by an argument made by the Superman from post–Crisis history that the Earth-2 he wants to restore is far from a perfect earth: "If you're from this earth it can't be perfect. Because a perfect earth doesn't need a Superman" (160). Without completely restoring the multiverse, the series acknowledges the multiverse and the variations of past that may not exactly be in the present but profoundly influences it nonetheless.[29] For instance, after Batman rejects the idea of remaking the world, Batman's life becomes a metaphor for the history of comics as he speaks to Nightwing (the first Robin): BATMAN: "The early years. I've forgotten if ... they were good for you, weren't they?" NIGHTWING: "The best" (120). Perhaps even more to the point is the inspiration that Superman and Wonder Woman receive from the idealism of the Golden Age versions of Superman and Wonder Woman, surrendering the worries of a rounder character for the moral imperatives of a heavy character:

> WONDER WOMAN: We've all made mistakes, Superman [Earth-2]. But it's not too late to learn from them...
> SUPERMAN (EARTH-2): How can you still have faith in your earth?
> SUPERMAN (EARTH-1): Because they still have faith in us.
> SUPERMAN (EARTH-2): We have a job to do [178–179].

Through this series, the post–Crisis DC universe becomes happily reconciled with the not only the multiverse but with all of the DC superhero stories that preceded it; this is not to say that literacy is reconciled with traditionality, as literacy is set aside in this series that acknowledges the new traditionality of current superhero comic books and the traditionality that preceded it. The clichés well known within superhero comic books are used from simple references (such as "This is a job for Superman" yelled by Superman as he breaks out of the pocket universe) (40) to more complex and clearly self-conscious references. When the Lex Luthor of Earth-1 is overcome by Alexander Luthor, he is wearing his purple and green jumpsuit, and, when the Superman of Earth-2 attacks the post–Crisis Superman, he lifts a car above his head in exactly the same pose assumed on the 1938 cover of *Action* #1. When Alexander Luthor brings back the multiverse, we see the innumerable variations of Superman (as a pastiche/bricolage), and, when the Wonder Woman relives her origin through the Wonder Woman of Earth-2, her story is rendered in the various styles of artists throughout the history of Wonder Woman comic books. Especially notable is the portion in which Alexander Luthor is trying to find all earths that might help him make the perfect earth, saying "Earth-Prime... Where are ... You" (203). In the panel in which he utters the word *You*, Alexander Luthor has turned toward the reader, and, in the panel-less space that follows, he reaches both hands out toward the reader. In a move reminiscent of the Flash's turn toward the reader in "Flash of Two Worlds," Johns furthers the interaction of the comic book world and the reader's own as much as the conventions will allow. Furthermore, the threat posed by the other conspirators doesn't end with the change of heart for the Superman from Earth-2, as both Alexander Luthor and Superboy-Prime continue their campaign, with Superboy-Prime becoming the largest threat. Although I don't want to push this too far (as Johns had a limited number of characters placed in Wolfman's other dimension), it is notable that the greatest threat to the superhero comic books' universe becomes someone from our world, disappointed that the post–Crisis universe didn't shape up as "intended."

In a break from the mandate against multiple earths, *Crisis on Infinite Earths* (*left*) is recalled in a *Supergirl* story (*right*) that provides a variation on one of its most famous moments (from *Crisis on Infinite Earths* #7, cover detail and *Supergirl* #79 (vol.4), cover detail).

At the end of *Infinite Crisis*, the superheroes triumph (of course) and idealism is restored, but the story doesn't end, promising more as a traditional story might. The last words belong to Superboy-Prime plotting his escape from a Green Lantern containment field, and the series itself leads directly into the series *52* in which the DC multiverse is not only acknowledged but also fully reinstated.[30] In this way, *Infinite Crisis* is probably the most intentional post–Crisis recommendation of the new traditionality of superhero comic books, at least in a metaphorical form.[31]

Although this chapter is primarily and very intentionally devoted to the DC multiverse stories as an example of secondary orality in superhero comic books, mention must also be made of the Marvel superhero universe that began to take steps in this same direction (becoming less in line with literacy and more in line with new traditionality in the 1970s). Marvel would have less of an obvious need for the sort of parallel universes seen in DC comic books, as the Marvel history was much shorter and continuity editors became fixtures by the end of the first decade of Marvel superhero publishing. There would be no significant interruption in the publication of Marvel superhero titles, and, even when a title was canceled, creators maintained the illusion that particular characters continued to live and interact with rest of the Marvel universe. However, Marvel did share two things in common with DC in that (1) they also maintained the conceit that their superheroes never aged as the world changed around them and (2) they had fans who loved to ask questions about how stories would change if a certain pivotal events occurred differently. The first of these two things would require some retcons of the stories such as updating the discovery date of a frozen Captain America from the 1960s to the 1990s; this would often lead to a collective uproar from Marvel fans devoted to the notion of continuity and who ironically considered strict adherence to Captain America's sixty years of life essential to Marvel realism (not put off by the fact that he and his friends didn't age).[32] The second of these two things resulted in a series first published in 1977 and simply titled *What If?* that explored the what if questions of fans, such as "What If Spider-Man Had Joined the Fantastic Four?" (in *What If?* #1). While the series was an anthology comprised of various one-shot other possibility stories about the Marvel universe by various creators, the most interesting aspect of this series was that it was introduced by Uatu, the Watcher. Apparently, he had been charged with not only watching the superhero earth with which Marvel readers had become familiar but also earths that exist in parallel universes. In the first issue, Uatu explains:

> I know all that is — most of what had been — and much of what will be. I have also many windows into the strange parallel worlds of what might have been... I know, as well as do you privileged ones now receiving my telepathic message, that this has never happened — at least not in your time continuum. But there are worlds within worlds — and worlds which exist side by side with your own, separated from it only by the thinnest of cosmic gossamer. There is, for example [and Uatu lists previous parallel world stories in Marvel comic books] [Thomas 1–2].

Although it provided an obvious excuse for the series, this framing device ("worlds within worlds — and worlds which exist side by side with your own") was unnecessary and created a multiverse structure much like that of the DC universe. The inventor of the series and author of that first issue is Roy Thomas, former correspondent with Gardner Fox, friend with Jerry Bails, and contributor to and editor of a prominent fanzine.[33] Later, in a way that realized the potential seen on the cover of *Fantastic Four* #10, *What If?* #11 asked what would happen if members of the Marvel "bullpen" like Stan Lee and Jack Kirby had been given the powers of the Fantastic Four. In another self-conscious nod to not just endless variation but to the permeable barrier between superhero worlds and our own, the letters page was titled "What Now?" and was supposedly Uatu's reaction to another pile of letters. The second *What If?* series eventually dropped the specific "what if" questions, stressed the alternate universe idea, and often dealt with alternate universes extensively with multi-issue arcs.[34] At the end of the run for the second series, Spidergirl was introduced, subsequently becoming the flagship title in MC2 in the late 1990s, a line of comic books that told stories of the future history of an alternative Marvel universe. Aside from merely identifying that Marvel was moving away from a strict sense of continuity and toward new traditionality's embrace of variation, it is worth noting that this future history somewhat ironically set out to evoke the ethos and style of the Silver Age (much as Earth-2 had done much earlier for DC by returning to the Golden Age).

Since the 1980s, some of the most popular stories had been stories of alternative universes such as the X-Men's "Days of Future Past" and "Age of Apocalypse" that became known largely because of the crossovers of characters from one universe to the other. Alan Moore would randomly pick the designation Earth-616 for the primary Marvel universe as a homage to the DC tendency to number alternate earths (Rhoades 69).[35] In addition to the natural trend toward new traditionality in the closely related ideas of the big two superhero comic book publishers, the fact that creators often worked for one and then the other doubtless accelerated this trend. (In fact, this creator exchange would be intensified in 1996 when Marvel created a story line in which Franklin Richards (son of Mr. Fantastic and the Invisible Woman) created an alternate reality; the major superhero titles would be farmed out and retooned by Image and Wildstorm creators in the various "Heroes Reborn" series.) Regardless, the idea of a multiverse (or omniverse as it was sometimes called at Marvel) was becoming increasingly important to Marvel even though there wasn't the same practical imperative that existed at DC with two Flashes, two Green Lanterns, etc (i.e., the crossovers were more varied not focused as centrally on two earths). Perhaps most interesting in light of the anxiety that propelled *Crisis on Infinite Earths* is that Marvel has never demonstrated a desire to clean up their omniverse and have in fact taken steps that are quite contrary.[36] In order to attract new readers in the 2000s, Marvel decided to create another universe, not subject to 40 years of continuity issues and less inclined to use stories of magic and alternate universes. With *Ultimate Spider-Man*, *Ultimate X-Men*, and many other Marvel Ultimate titles telling the stories of familiar heroes from the beginning, the irony of Marvel's new cleanly Ultimate universe (with less alternate universes and therefore less continuity issues) is that it is yet another universe. Often written with ideas that only make complete sense to a reader familiar with previous stories, the Ultimate line has at least as much crossover reading by old readers of Marvel comic books as first-time reading by new readers. In sales, the Ultimate line has not yet eclipsed the original Marvel titles, but the neck-in-neck competition between *The Amazing Spider-Man* and *Ultimate Spider-Man* demonstrates that the self-consciousness of the Ultimate line is appealing and that someday the Ultimate line could supplant the original — this seems to be promised by the "Ultimate" title itself (although such a phenomenon is more likely to happen in a culture shaped by traditionality than new traditionality). While Marvel editor Joe Quesada stated that there would be no crossovers between Earth-616 and the earth portrayed in the Ultimate line, he also stated that the earth portrayed in the Ultimate line is part of the Marvel omniverse (Rhoades 69). Last but not least, the Ultimate universe seems as inclined to alternate universes as the original Marvel line with the superhero zombie universe of *Ultimate Fantastic Four* #21–23 spinning off into its own incredibly popular series.[37]

In the Marvel omniverse, the most sprawling and self-conscious embrace of new traditionality in terms of technique and content would have to Alex Ross and Jim Krueger's *Earth X* series. In a future history of Marvel superheroes, everyone on earth has mutated and has some sort of superpower, but, in the course of the series, the original superheroes of the Marvel omniverse become involved in increasingly metaphysical conflicts, leading to a battle for paradise itself. In some ways, the story initially seems to take a literate culture's explanatory approach by offering a reason for the plethora of superheroes on the earth (with the planet Earth being a womb for the next god-like Celestial to be born and therefore, giving off an emanation that produces superheroic powers). However, this only works via some rather significant retcons (probably the most controversial being that of Wolverine, no longer a mutant but a descendent of one of Jack Kirby's lightest creations: Moon Boy). This sort of reweaving is characteristic of epic poetry, and epic scope is given to the entirety of the Marvel omniverse, something often done in the retellings of oral cultures (including the most artistically bereft parts of that omniverse: like Moon Boy but also old toy tie-ins like the Micronauts and Rom). Further along these lines, the self-conscious approach of the series seeks not so much to elevate superhero stories as to reveal the integrity that has always been there. References to high-culture concepts rarely associated with comic books abound and include complete discussions of Nietzsche's overman and the Einsteinian physics behind the notion of the multiverse. In addition to the new Watcher (Machine Man) calling upon heroes from alternate worlds for aid, superheroes are also seen in their afterlife incarnations. In a love of variation (including its own retcons) that becomes a sort of logic beyond logic, the series works in a way that is post–Enlightenment, postmodern, and postliteracy. For instance, when the character of Belasco was first introduced to Marvel comic books, his kingdom set forth as the model for Dante's "Inferno," a literal place that Dante had visited. However, in that introduction in *Kazar* #11, the warning over the gates is a misquoted version of the warning over the gates to hell in Dante's "Inferno"; rather than avoid the misquotation entirely, the narration makes a reference that indirectly engages the debate about primacy versus currency: "[He] leads them into the heart of sentinel city ... to a place once considered an Atlantean amusement park fashioned after Dante's "Inferno." Still others suggest it inspired Dante. But since it is a doorway into the realm of limbo, who can say which came first?" (Kreuger, *Universe X* 164). Of course, a literate mind would always be able to determine which came first, but Ross and Krueger exploit the conventions of their own story to make that unclear. What is most relevant throughout the story is current history and the way it causes past things to be reinterpreted. Thor and Loki who discover not only that their rivalry was invented by their father but also that their father was invented by man's need for him and thus, a new order of belief takes the place of the old.

Like *Crisis on Infinite Earths*, the multiplicity of earths becomes the central focus of the work[38] but with a slightly different conclusion, something more in line with *Infinite Crisis*. Machine Man explains the omniverse to Vance Astro and identifies the way the Marvel superheroes are endlessly updated:

> [Alternate realities] exist because Mephisto believed he was the devil of the dominant religion. So much so, that to flee the coming spoken-of prophecy, he created alternate worlds to escape into... The further from the original source a present gets, the more skewed it becomes. In this era, for example, Reed Richards no longer fought in World War II, he fought in Vietnam. And I would expect there are some eras that exist now where he never fought at all. Tony Stark never created weapons that were used for the Korean War in this era, he did it for desert storm... [Astro asks how far this reality lies away from the source.]

Reed Richards sets out to rescue his son and the *Earth X* series provides an open ending with a C.S. Lewis quotation: "they were beginning Chapter One of the great story ... which goes on forever; in which every chapter is better than the one before" (from *Paradise X*, Vol. 2, p. 340).

> As to the version we are, we're the ones who aren't going to accept recreation for the sake of a devil we give too much credit to [Krueger, *Paradise X* 236–238].

Again, multiple realities are the consequence of an act committed an evil act (Mephisto trying to avoid his destruction at the end of time).[39] However, in this case, the end result won't be merging earths but merely ending the further multiplication of realties. For better or worse, primacy is not only a secondary issue but also an irrelevant issue because the original can neither be found nor preserved. Instead, it is the version that is now known that must be embraced and for which the superheroes must fight (always true in every generation and in every variation of superhero story). The further multiplication of realities is only ended within the confines of this series and the multiplication is bound to continue even beyond this epic future history. Even before *The Official Handbook to the Marvel Universe* declared that the *Earth X* took place in the future of an alternative earth (9997 not 616), Ross and Krueger acknowledge within the confines of their series that the story never ends. After saving all that is known including Paradise, the penultimate panel features Mr. Fantastic giving a message to be relayed to his wife, the Invisible Woman; he is off to "rescue" their son who became the new Galactus and destroyed the Celestial gestating in the earth. Even when the story ends, it remains open and doesn't end.

Occasionally, DC and Marvel will provide fans with answers to their ultimate team-up questions by bringing together Superman and Spider-Man or Justice League of America and the Avengers (more on intercompany team-ups in chapter 8). Therefore, even the DC universe is listed as one of the universes within the Marvel omniverse,[40] that (if they wanted to be true completists) would require the editors to list all the universes in the DC multiverse. But would they list all the universes identified before the Crisis, after the Crisis, or both? While the question is facetious, it also meant to highlight the strange literate-minded attempt to catalogue information in an industry that knowingly and willfully varies past "worlds" in an ever-increasing ways. However, this may also be an essential element of new traditionality: wanting to see the original stand alongside the current and believing that there is a richness that results from the interaction of historically disparate incarnations of heavy heroes. In Mark Millar's 2003 Elseworlds comic book *Red Son*, the question "what if Superman's rocket had landed in the Soviet Union" is given full play with the supporting cast of Lex Luthor, Lois Lane, Batman, and Wonder Woman present for a story that seems to violate all clichés of the superhero genre. However, after America's champion, Lex Luthor, manages to defeat the great Soviet threat of Superman, Superman, thought dead, actually becomes a mild-mannered reporter in order to avoid the attention of others. Because of his alien physiology, Superman lives for centuries watching the continuing ascendency of the Luthor family, eventually known as the house of "L." When the planet is threatened with disaster from its red giant sun, no one believes the predictions of calamity from Jor-L, who is forced to send his only son away from the planet and to a past time in a rocket of his own design. The promise of a new Superman works together with the inability to escape cliché in this incredibly self-conscious work. With the way that the original story becomes seemingly irrelevant in the face of the present story (the new Superman depicted at the end will likely be the Soviet Superman of *Red Son*), we can recognize how new traditionality turns outward because it has turned inward. Millar suggests the story is unable to escape its own variation, conditioned by a postmodern culture based on new traditionality (where a story of a Soviet Superman is only meaningful because it varies the cliché of an American Superman). Variation on the cliché is what shapes the thought of Modern Age comic book creators (and Modern Age comic book readers) and the idea of originality promised by *Crisis on Infinite Earths* is impossible to maintain. In Ong's discussion in *Interfaces of the Word* concerning John Milton's *Paradise Lost*, he identifies the literate goals behind Milton's desire to craft an epic poem as bound to make the work problematic. Seeking to justify the ways of God to man, Milton does the opposite of what oral poets would do: accept that the ways of God simply are, and provide an alibi for the current state of humankind. Thanks to the traditional nature of the medium and industry, the multiple worlds of superheroes simply are and another one will always be added to the mix. Literate culture often understands postmodern culture as something profoundly threatening in that it seems to lack the depth of thought that leads to certainty. However, new traditionality doesn't signify the loss of depth but rather deep thought that encourages a return to the most recent representation of a cliché because there is nothing better, more certain, or more fulfilling. The new traditionality of superhero comic books celebrates the new because it is a variation on the old and there is nothing to move beyond. Therefore, some of the greatest comic book creators, such as Frank Miller and Alan Moore, produce nearly universally acclaimed work in the Modern Age because they vary and redeploy superhero clichés (but that's a story for the next chapter).

CHAPTER 7

More Than Service to the Publishers

Artists Aware of Technology (and the Audience)

This chapter will be devoted to an analysis of the great works of the two authors who cemented the characteristics of the Modern Age (and the new traditionality) in superhero comic books: Frank Miller and Alan Moore. In the works they have produced (particularly in Miller's *The Dark Knight Returns* and Moore's *Watchmen*), these creators have enacted even more fully the new traditionality described in the last chapter. Moreover, both demonstrate a deep awareness of what the medium was before the advent of the Modern Age and how they participate in a new era more fully in dialogue with media technology surrounding comic books. Similar to the case I made about Gardener Fox, my argument is not that Miller and Moore thought about superhero comic books in the terms that I suggest are the most accurate way to describe them (terms like traditionality and new traditionality). Even when artists have a deeper awareness of their medium and their material, they are not always the best representatives of how their works fit into larger academic paradigms running parallel to their own era. Regardless, if one has low expectations and doesn't anticipate creators will be any more aware of culture than a fish is aware of the rushing water, one would have to be extremely impressed by Miller and Moore, both enacting not only a self-conscious approach to but also incisive criticism of their medium. The early parts of their careers in superhero comic books demonstrates a clear awareness of the tropes of superhero via their selective use and reworking of the clichés of superhero stories. However, *The Dark Knight Returns* and *Watchmen* demonstrate that they are interested in making superhero comic books into something that confronts the reader's expectations and makes the reader more fully aware of those expectations. In addition to forming the basis of these works by critically deploying superhero clichés, Miller and Moore use each of these works to bring the reader closer to a realization of what superhero comic book readers have long experienced. Miller and Moore's great works seem to proceed in a way somewhat against general mechanics of comic book reading in that *The Dark Knight Returns* and *Watchmen* serve as a new *authoritative* source for superhero stories. However, through their careful intellectual revisioning of the comic book and the superhero, they actualize and realize the natural dream of every comic book reader: to create a tapestry based on the favorite parts of the superhero stories, shaped to serve cultural (and therefore, personal) needs. These works are profoundly open-ended, a fact that sets them squarely in line with traditionality, new traditionality, and postmodernism. Moreover, *The Dark Knight Returns* and *Watchmen* foreground issues central to many self-conscious comparisons of traditionalism and literacy: tribalism versus civilization, bricolage versus logic, and abstraction versus realism. Although the comparison may seem grandiose, I want to think of Frank Miller and Alan Moore as the Homers or Beowulf poets who are completely aware of the new media age, working with a medium quickly being changed by the proliferation of other media forms. Before describing the various social forces at work that developed the characteristics of the Modern Age and embarking on an extended analysis of *The Dark Knight Returns* and *Watchmen*, I want to acknowledge that these two works are considered by most scholars to be the defining works of the Modern Age. I mention this to explain choosing these works but also to acknowledge that my choice of these works is not original. I feel that too much scholarship is misguided by the desire to be "original" and to move in unorthodox directions and I believe there is a good reason these works are at the forefront of most people's understanding of the Modern Age.[1]

Distribution Changes the Perception of the Comic Book: The Direct Market as Purveyor of High Art and Haven for Superhero Comic Books?

As had been the case with the dawn of the Silver Age, many forces worked together to ensure the continued dominance of the superhero within the American comic book industry, one of the foremost undoubtedly being the continuation of a securely established product within a large industry. Nevertheless, the way that the industry understood itself changed in the 1980s due to the creators' rights movement, direct distribution, the improvement in print technology, and most importantly, the shift in the consumer market. The traditional anonymity of the superhero comic book creators was being lost because of much more than the crediting of writers and artists in the superhero comic books of the 1960s. During the 1960s, most writers and artists still considered themselves to be skilled workers with very few thinking of themselves as artists. Any industry workers who sought to form associations were doomed to failure because "creators felt too vulnerable and anxious about antagonizing their employers. [The movement] also suffered from a Cold War political culture that tended to equate unionism with Communism and organized crime" (Wright 255–256). Stan Lee is often identified as emblematic of this mindset in his move from (what others perceived as) a highly creative writer to a figurehead "more interested in marketing established formulas" (256). As such anxious ideas lost their momentum in the 1960s, the fan culture grew in the 1970s and creators became more well known to consumers through the dialogue on letters pages and their presence at conventions. Consequently, the first large step toward creators' rights (encouraging creators to have individual identities that were more important than their corporate identities) came through complaints made about low wages and job insecurity through the fan press. With a new generation of creators aided by more specific copyright law and led by the likes of Neal Adams, the formation of guilds to bargain for more rights took place.

Among the people within the industry who looked at the financial bottom line, the assertion was widely made that superhero comic book creators were becoming too pretentious and therefore, would no longer appeal to the widest consumer base (Wright 258). While this may or may not have been true, the creators who lobbied for more rights found they had little leverage as the revenue for comic book sales was falling again: "the Marvel-led resurgence of the 1960s had foundered by the 1970s to the point where extinction seemed like a real possibility.... With their low cover price and tiny profit margin, comics had become more of nuisance than a moneymaker for distributors" (Dean 49). Those distributors dealt with newsstands and drugstores who no longer sold dime novels and instead would rather devote shelf space to glossy magazines that sold for a dollar or more. With most of the revenue coming into DC and Marvel comics through the licensing of their characters, the importance of continuing to produce new stories of superheroes in comic book form was called into question. However, "as traditional comic book retail outlets disappeared throughout the 1970s, new ones opened up" (Wright 260). Direct-market comic book stores were established to cater to the increasingly more opinionated comic book audience, and these stores were financially encouraged to expand by the burgeoning collector's market for past issues of comic books and collectibles. As this direct marketing model became successful, advances in print technology allowed the established companies to use higher-quality paper and therefore, produce higher-resolution artwork to justify higher prices increasing their profit margin. In addition, since printing was much more affordable this led to the establishment of many upstart companies (such as Eclipse, Pacific, First, and Comico) and a boom in independent black and white publications.

At this time, video games did what television had failed to do: steal the youth and teen audience from superhero comic book publishers. However, publishers worked feverishly to maintain their current audience as they grew older with superhero stories that were darker and more complex; "surveys of the direct market indicated that fans still wanted comic books about superheroes, albeit with more 'realism'" (Wright 262). Comic book companies found that the lure for readers was no longer just a well-known superhero character but now a well-known writer or artist. This meant greater benefits for workers in the industry, especially those that were identified as star creators:

> [The] new publishers, needing incentives to draw popular comics creators from the majors [DC and Marvel], offered deals that creators had only dreamt of before. The bulk of titles published under Pacific, Eclipse, and First were creator owned or co-owned with the creators.... In 1982, a year after Pacific started publishing, DC began offering royalties and Marvel followed suit shortly thereafter [Dean 57].

Suddenly, the issue of creators' rights was back on the table with the help of political agitations from independently published creators such as Dave Sim and Scott McCloud.[2] After the remarkable survival of the traditional culture of the superhero comic book industry in the wake of Fredric Wertham, these changes to the industry could be read as threats to that traditional culture.

> [They] essentially redefined the comic book audience.... The result was a loss of entry point for new readers, and the comics industry found itself serving an aging-fan customer base with stories that were impenetrable to anyone outside that base.... The greatest flaw of the Direct Market may have been that it was too successful ... so successful that it became a kind of closed circuit [Dean 57, 59].

Such changes include things that seem to be antithetical to traditional culture: recognition of the creator, appeal to only selective parts of the population, and a search for and resale of artifacts from the past. However, this state of affairs lasts only for roughly a decade, revealing itself to be a transitional phase (the end result will be discussed at the end of this chapter with each of the above mentioned things revealed as something quite different than they first appear). At this point, I'll merely mention that these changes give superhero comic books that adult audience that Walter Ong said the art of oral culture must have.³ More importantly, the actual existence of a real traditional culture becomes less relevant to the existence of new traditionality (rather than emulate and reinforce an existing culture, new traditionality self-consciously seeks ideas that produce virtual cultures). In other words, the "poet" of new traditionality may live in circumstances that are profoundly literary but choose to seek out the traditional culture evoked by the medium in which the creator works; at the very least, this creator will choose to negotiate between traditionality and literacy. With this notion in mind, the proof is in the continued existence of new traditionality in the work of this Modern Age of comic books, regularly dated to the early 1980s but seen most clearly in the germinal works of 1986: *The Dark Knight Returns* and *Watchmen*.

The clearest comic book antecedent to Modern Age ideas would be the Chris Claremont/John Byrne era of *The Uncanny X-Men*, a title originally created by Stan Lee and Jack Kirby. Revolving around Professor Xavier's School for Gifted Youngsters in its Silver Age beginnings with Lee and Kirby, the story deals with the education of super-powered students in Professor Xavier's desire for them not only to learn how to master their powers but also to serve all of humanity. Like Professor Xavier, the students are mutants, endowed with superpowers by their genetic makeup and seen as both freakish outsiders and profound threats to basic human existence. Most often, they were placed in contest with other mutants who fought to establish mutant supremacy, believing their actions to be justified as mutants, they were the next step in human evolution. Unlike so much of Lee and Kirby's work from the 1960s, the X-Men didn't manage to create popular interest and after struggling to find an audience for 66 issues, the title became a reprint-only series. After much speculation by scholars and fans, no definitive explanation has been reached to explain the initial failure of the title (although the nearly critically useless label of "ahead of its time" has often been used). While they certainly departed from the status quo superheroes loved by the authorities at DC Comics, the X-Men shared many of the characteristics held by other Marvel superheroes that appealed to teenage and college readers in search of more realistic stories of outsiders. However, it could be the Lee pushed the subtextual outsider status of the vigilante superhero too far to the forefront in an era that still feared the Communist outsider and worried about violent revolution threatened by some black activists. As noted above, these ideas managed to keep Lee and other comic book creators in check (outside the fictional worlds of the superhero stories) as would-be agitators for creators' rights. In any case, it wasn't until 1974 with an almost completely new line of X-Men students/superheroes that the general concept and the series managed to develop a loyal and enthusiastic fan base.⁴

The stylized, detailed, and cinematic renderings of Byrne took reader expectations to a new place, much like Kirby and Ditko before him. However, more important would be that Claremont amplified the dysfunction within the team seen previously and most notably in Marvel series like *The Fantastic Four*; "the continuing use of unresolved conflicts between the individual characters ... outlasted any individual plot-line and were the main driving force of the comic's development" (Reynolds 86). These conflicts became significant parts of the formulae of the comic book and served as mechanisms by which the idea of the superhero was analyzed in a way that was subtly self-conscious. One of the primary sources of conflict within the team was found between its leader, Cyclops (a carry-over from the earliest incarnation of the team), and Wolverine, a coldly determined avenger who fought with indestructible claws. "Wolverine ... is violent without a clear moral center, unconcerned with hiding his identity from the world, and unaware of his origin ... [and thereby] Wolverine works primarily as a foil by which the traditional superheroism of a character like Cyclops might be reevaluated" (Wandtke 18–19). Through Cyclops and Wolverine, Claremont sets up a dialogue between Silver Age sensibilities and what would become the superhero of the Modern Age: more violent and more appealing to adult disaffection with the world in the wake of Vietnam War and Watergate.[5] The conflict within the team would be taken to an even greater level as the mutant known as the Phoenix (the object of both Cyclops and Wolverine's affections) found she could not control her massive telekinetic and telepathic powers. Driven insane, she embraced her more primal desire to destroy and became what most readers would consider evil (and therefore, someone to be fought by the X-Men). As Claremont explored the darker side of someone with nearly limitless powers like those of Superman, the self-consciousness storytelling of what would be the Modern Age took shape. With this in mind (together with the notion that Miller and Moore most fully represent the new traditionality of the Modern Age), it should come as no surprise that Miller illustrated Claremont's well-known *Wolverine* limited series, a self-aware overall treatment of the character.

This era would be the one in which Miller and Moore enter the superhero comic book culture and become the most articulate arbiters of the tensions between comic book traditionality and the larger forces of literacy: an era of creator renown, limited audience, collector appeal, and increasing self-referentiality. I have already made the case that the infiltration of orthodox literacy into superhero comic book ethos was sporadic and short-lived, unable to infiltrate the orthodox traditionality of the medium and merely a brief point of transition to new traditionality. But at some level, the trajectory of Miller and Moore's careers leading to *The Dark Knight Returns* and *Watchmen* do not obviously identify them as standard-bearers for the traditionality or even new traditionality of superhero comic books. While they are very clearly self-conscious practitioners within their medium who invite readers to be self-conscious consumers, their self-consciousness (and careful study) seems not part of traditionality but part of a literate sensibility that gives way to new traditionality. In his introduction to differences between orality and literacy, Walter Ong makes this point about literacy: "[A]bstractly sequential, classificatory, explanatory examination of phenomena or of stated truths is impossible without writing and reading. Human beings in primary oral cultures, those untouched by writing in any form, learn a great deal and practice wisdom but they do not 'study'" (*Orality* 8–9). We should not ignore that Miller and Moore's rise to prominence coincided neatly with the development and publication of *Crisis on the Infinite Earths*, the prime example of the attempt to make superhero comic books literate. With this acknowledgment made, *The Dark Knight Returns* and *Watchmen* serve as narrative studies of the cultures of traditionality and literacy and are followed by works in Miller and Moore's careers that forcefully embrace new traditionality. Thus, the full trajectory of their artistic output from these self-conscious and influential practitioners suggests an intellectual embrace of Modern Age superhero comic books as new traditionalism. Regardless, both had rather humble beginnings, as great artists often do.

Frank Miller was born in Vermont, far from the mean streets of big cities he became famous for depicting in his comic books; he dreamed of breaking into the monolithic comic book industry as an artist but his realistic and moody illustrations (inspired by Neal Adams and film noir) were rejected by the large companies that controlled the industry. Eventually, his persistence led to a series of freelance jobs for Gold Key, DC, and then Marvel, the publisher that gave him his first big break. After illustrating several issues of *The Spectacular Spider-Man*, Miller was moved to the underperforming *Daredevil* as a regular artist where he began co-plotting with the writer, Roger MacKenzie. Although his illustration was not a radical departure from the realistic and detailed style popularized by Neil Adams and John Byrne, he utilized a remarkable sense of pacing, an ability to manipulate time through page layout (similar to the work of Will Eisner).[6] Once Miller took over writing as well as illustrating the title, he did this even more effectively as noted by Robert Harvey by referring to *Daredevil* #164 in which reporter Ben Urich learns that Daredevil is really the blind lawyer named Matt Murdock.

> Miller manipulates time with his breakdowns.... The action depicted Urich putting a cigarette in his mouth and lighting it — suggests just how long it takes him to decide. Not long, really. But by focusing on each facet of Urich's action in narrow, precisely parallel panels, Miller stops time with each panel.... the tiers of narrow panels that embrace almost unvarying compositions draw attention to themselves by their uniformity. Our eye is thus directed to the panels that carry the key scenes in the story; the visual emphasis underscores narrative importance [Harvey 168–169].

In addition to mastering the formulae that constitutes the traditional language of comic books, Miller incorporates into the series aesthetic more heavy shadows and a play between black and white (making the realistic figures more stylized and more iconographic). As a blind superhero with his other senses heightened, Daredevil is regularly depicted with his head tilted in a way the causes his eyes to be lost in the shadows.

After Miller became a regular writer for the series, an extended arc demonstrated his interest in a self-conscious exploration of the superhero mythos. Miller created Elektra, a woman who was once Murdock's college love but had become an assassin working for Daredevil's greatest enemy: the crime boss known as Kingpin. Despite her fairly clear status as a femme fatale and villain, Daredevil continued to see her as noble and merely a victim of circumstance (demonstrating his metaphorical blindness). Much more so than Stan Lee before him, Miller blended the superhero story with another genre (in this case, the crime story) as a means to reveal and examine the underpinnings of the superhero story.[7] This is most clearly presented in "Roulette," the last issue of Miller's first run on the series, in which Daredevil takes turns playing Russian roulette with his then-paralyzed arch-enemy, Bullseye. Daredevil is brought to this point of crisis by a child who shoots another child, a child who is inspired by his criminal father but also by a videotaped fight in which Daredevil defeats Bullseye. Revisiting a tension in the character often accentuated by Miller, Daredevil reflects on his father, a boxer who asked his son to find a way to live without fighting with his fists. Daredevil is unable to fully see the irony in his father's request just as he fails to fully acknowledge the contradiction of his life as lawyer by day and vigilante by night; however, this contradiction becomes clear to the reader. In addition to the above story elements that work to indict Daredevil as a bad influence mostly unaware of himself as a negative role model, he is involved in that game of Russian roulette with Bullseye; the paralyzed Bullseye has no say in playing the game and Daredevil only reveals at the end that the gun has no bullets. At the start, the superhero is portrayed as more culpable than the supervillain and at the end, as patently unfair and selfish, playing the game for his own satisfaction. Miller's initial send-off to his first extended superhero story exposes the violent fantasy that propels almost all conflict in superhero stories and encourages the reader to question it.

The technical virtuosity praised by Robert Harvey is demonstrated in this issue as Miller develops a connection between the concrete and abstract through panel arrangement and artistic renderings beyond the confines of realism. When the narrative frame for the story (the game of Russian roulette) is established, Miller returns to the most recent morally questionable decision made by Daredevil. After recounting that he is responsible for Bullseye's paralysis, Daredevil states (within the confines of four narrative boxes), "Of course, in a way, you did worse to me ... / Yes ... much worse ... / You murdered Elektra ... / ... The woman I loved" ("Roulette" 208). Each box is contained within a separate panel, and those panels break up a single image of Daredevil's face, working outside the standard expectation that each panel takes the reader to another point in time. Instead, the panels fracture a unified visual representation of our superhero. In a variation on this technique taking us outside the movement of time as typically created by the layout of the comic book page, Miller repeats the same image of Daredevil pointing the gun at a wide-eyed Bullseye on pages 11, 12, 14, 15, 16, and 21 (original pagination). While the narration seems to move Daredevil's story and/or Daredevil's argument forward, the subsequent panels return to an image frozen in time, an image that undermines the assumed nobility of typical superheroism. The repetition heightens general characteristics of the act, ranging from its cowardliness (Daredevil pointing the gun at Bullseye) to its random outcome (Russian roulette seeming to be the determiner of Bullseye's fate). Page 21 is a series of five horizontal panels, the middle three bringing the reader closer to Bullseye's bandaged face by magnifying the image, forcing identification, and intensifying the drama of his helplessness; the final panel is a close-up depiction of Daredevil's gun as he pulls the trigger in an image that looks deceptively like Bullseye's eye. The entire story (and especially the frame story) utilizes symbolic images and plays with the potential abstraction and interchangeability of real world images in a way that accentuates the themes (and more fully realizes comic book tendencies outside the realistic style that Miller had long emulated). Bullseye's bed seems to float in space rather than exist in an actual room, and Daredevil seems to be the only thing really connected to him, the two isolated together in a final, large panel that makes their space an island in the midst of darkness. Miller's self-conscious experimentation with the superhero motif coincides very much with his experimentation with and fuller realization of the comic book as a traditional art form.

Alan Moore was born in Northampton, England, far from what seemed to be the center of the superhero comic book world in the 1950s. However, Moore would seek out both English and American comic books, and he became well versed in the adventures of superpowered heroes. After working for a short while in the 1970s as a freelance comic strip artist, Moore was offered the opportunity to work on the anthology magazine *2000 A.D.*, and his subsequent work on *Doctor Who Magazine* gained the attention of executives with Marvel UK. In short order, Moore developed a reputation as an edgy, inventive writer who provided his illustrators with detailed scripts and who revised the superhero in radical ways. His early breakthrough would be the reworking of Marvelman, created in 1954 as an English imitation of America's Captain Marvel. Debuting in the short-lived anthology *Warrior* (also featuring Moore's *V for Vendetta*), *Marvelman* placed the rather innocent boy-as-grown-man superhero into a much more realistic and disturbing context. A flabby, middle-aged Mike Moran recovers his lost memory of his life as the superhero Marvelman. The idyllic story of Marvelman recounted in the 1950s comic book was merely a cover story to disguise the government's sinister use of him as a weapon:

> Through this narrative turn, Moore questions the character's positive, stabilizing function ... awareness of his powers bring him to meditate on his nature and to acquire mixed feelings of compassion and contempt toward the human race. In short, is character represents Moore's first attempt to deconstruct the superhero and to turn him into a melancholy, disillusioned figure who is far removed from the peace of mind of earlier times [Di Liddo 49].

Far from being an agent of the state meant to gently extol the status quo, Marvelman engages in extremely violent actions with dire, anti-institutional consequences and becomes a messiah-like figure that reshapes the world. However, the artistic renderings of Gary Leach and Alan Davis walk a line between a more realistic superhero and an iconographic, boldly colored superhero that intentionally recalls Marvelman's child-friendly past.[8] Moore was brought as a creator to American comic books by DC and like Miller, was offered, in a typical test of the new talent, an underperforming title: *Swamp Thing*. Created for DC's *House of Secrets* by Len Wein in the 1970s horror revival seen in mainstream American comics, *Swamp Thing* crossed the tropes of the horror story with that of the superhero story. In a way that seemed to intentionally recall the horror stories that troubled Fredric Wertham, Moore would open his first issue of *Swamp Thing* with this text complimented by Stephen Bisette's bloody and distorted images:

> My name is Jason Woodrue. Doctor Jason Woodrue. I'm here in my apartment. I'm watching the rain ... and I'm thinking about the old man. He'll be pounding on the glass right about now ... or maybe not now. Maybe in a while. But he'll be pounding and ... and will there be blood? I like to imagine so. Yes, I rather think there will be blood. Lots of blood. Blood in extraordinary quantities [Moore, *Saga* 13].

With a macabre first-person narration like that of E.A. Poe, Moore creates suspense through a sort of nether-space in time ("right about now ... or maybe not now") in which a threat may appear at any moment.[9] In addition to throwing off the limitations placed on Silver Age comic books by the Comics Code, Moore rewrites the history of the Swamp Thing. In Len Wein's original version, Alec Holland was the scientist turned into a humanoid swamp creature by a lab accident, a superheroic monster trapped in his swampy form. In Alan Moore's first story, he is revealed as a portion of the swamp made sentient by the accident, and that portion of the swamp inadvertently believed itself to be human because it consumed the decaying body of Alec Holland. Throughout the course of his run on the series, Moore explored what it might mean to be a being capable of thought but essentially vegetable in nature. Although Moore called it hard science fiction, he kept the Swamp Thing connected to the DC superhero universe. In one notable story, he confronted Batman and Gotham City as an embodiment of the decay of the industrial world that threatened the natural order that the Swamp Thing represented. Moreover, as the Swamp Thing recognized that his god-like sentience allowed him to manipulate all plant life on earth, he grappled with why he should or should not end thirst, hunger, and human suffering in general. The Swamp Thing asked questions that Superman never asked but perhaps should have.[10] Moore continued to maintain the Swamp Thing's connection to a superheroic world, seemingly to offer the Swamp Thing as a commentary on superheroic tropes.

As the popularity of the Swamp Thing grew, so did Moore's reputation, and he was used extensively by DC as a writer of fill-in stories for their superhero titles. Eventually, he was given the opportunity to work with their flagship characters, Superman and Batman. Particularly notable are the Superman stories, one being a Superman annual (that showcased his first work with Dave Gibbons, his artistic partner for *Watchmen*) and the "last" Superman story (a false ending of the Superman series before the revisions of *Crisis on Infinite Earths*).[11] The annual ("For the Man Who Has Everything ...") depicts a Superman immobilized by an intergalactic plant that feeds off the being to which it attaches itself (but grants the being its heart's desire). The intergalactic villain, Mongul, sent the plant to Superman so that he might conquer the earth. Dave Gibbons uses clever panel construction to move the reader back and forth between the real world and Superman's fantasy of a Krypton that was never destroyed. However, Superman's fantasy is marred by visions of civil unrest on Krypton, and it becomes clear that Superman has been living out his heart's desire in the real world of Earth (despite the trauma of losing his parents and home planet). Superman realizes his life is everyone's fantasy and eventually reacts angrily to Mongul because he loses his justification for a basic human desire: for things to be better for himself. In addition to blurring the lines between fantasy and reality in this way, the story ends with the plant immobilizing Mongul who then experiences his heart's desire of conquering the earth. The "last" Superman story ("Whatever Happened to the Man of Tomorrow?") was what Julius Schwartz would identify as "an imaginary story" (Moore 166), harkening back to the alternate Superman stories of the 1960s discussed in chapter 3. The poem that introduces the story states, "This is an imaginary story... Aren't they all?" immediately calling into question the line between canonical and noncanonical that is essential in literate culture. In the course of the story, Superman's friends (and enemies) are systematically killed in a design created by Mr. Mxyzptlk, a villain usually used for comic effect but here made into something more sinister. While utilizing the darker tone characteristic of the Modern Age, the story is highly sentimental and recalls previous ages in notable ways, drawn by Curt Swan, the Superman artist famously associated with the hero's Silver Age adventures. The story includes many of the plot elements of past ages, such as the future history Legion of Superheroes and Superman's fortress of solitude (a memorabilia-filled arctic getaway for Superman that is opened with a giant key that only Superman can lift). However, through the weight of this tragic story, Moore brings great pathos and meaning to these stereotypical, nearly comical trappings of the Superman mythology; one of the most striking scenes is a splash page that features Superman (normally indefatigable in Swan's renderings) crying in the presence of Superdog and surrounded by full-scale models of monsters that he has battled.

As we survey the work by Miller and Moore that lead to *The Dark Knight Returns* and *Watchmen*, we should consider how such work might fit into the paradigm of new traditionalism. As the youth market was increasingly drawn from comic books to video games, the major comic book companies realized that they were no longer developing product primarily for that demographic. If we think about this from the perspective of company executives and their idea of income, this takes us far from a strict notion of stories as they exist within traditional culture. However, as I've tried to suggest, storytelling and the popularity of certain stories always involves a sort of commerce (even though it might not quite be the crass commercialization of companies driven by capital in the postindustrial world). Also, in the 1980s, these companies would use direct sales to comic book stores to increase their profit margin: "Direct marketing ... promised to offset much of the cost and waste associated with traditional distribution.... Manager of DC's business affairs, [Paul] Levitz explained ... the major publishers were 'conspicuously aiming their efforts directly at the fan market as their chief area of growth'" (Wright 261). For creators like Frank Miller and Alan Moore, this provided an opportunity to reach an engaged (and engaging) adult audience with their stories of iconic superheroes who interacted with culture at a fundamental (and literal) level. Miller and Moore would eventually develop an adversarial relationship with the major superhero companies (Miller with both Marvel and DC, and Moore with DC); they were involved in the creator's rights movement spearheaded and eventually left the major companies to find more creative freedom. This fact distances them from the centralized power of DC and Marvel but brings up a philosophy that seems to run counter to basic ideas related to anonymity of traditional art. Central to the creator's rights movement was the ideas of ownership and control (and securing legal counsel to insure that ownership and control were maintained).[12] In addition, both Miller and Moore ushered in an era in which creators seemed to become more important the superhero whose stories they produced. For instance, when Frank Miller moved from Marvel to DC, his first title was a limited-run science fiction series called *Ronin*, an original creation that fans bought because it was a work by Frank Miller.

While their work clearly is written for adults, as Walter Ong insists traditional epics must be, Miller and Moore's "great works" of the Modern Age of superhero comic books seem to have been understood as high art. In an article from 1986 in *The Atlantic Monthly* and another two articles from 1988 in *Time* and *Newsweek*, writers struggle to justify these works as high art and thereby reconfigure the status of these graphic novels as popular and clichéd superhero stories.[13] As Sara J. Van Ness argues, the question of whether or not *Watchmen* might be considered literature obsessed early critics of the work (5). Perhaps the most interesting of the three articles is Lloyd Rose's "Comic Books for Grow-Ups" as it is the most critically sophisticated but it ends with a position similar to that of Jules Feiffer in *The Great Comic Book Heroes* (profiled in chapter 1):

> What they have created may not exactly be art, but in America the self-conscious and self-defined avant-garde always has always had unruly twin the low-culture entertainment that turns out to be a junk parable.... We're in a subaesthetic area, with no redeeming intellectual or social qualities, only instinct and rude energy. In this despised and largely unexplored terrain Miller, Sim, and Chaykin have staked their claims. Their success is an apotheosis of the uncritical fannish attitude, the triumph and redemption of the shameless love of trash [80].

Like Feiffer, it seems what we have is junk that is important, almost necessary trash with the added component of self-consciousness. Clearly Rose operates with a distinction between what is high and low art, identifying certain comic book work as potentially avant-garde but ultimately associated with elevated trash. In short order, he seems to describe traditionalism, literacy, and new traditionalism from a perspective biased by literacy. With all of these things in mind, I would like to turn to John Miles Foley, not only as a significant scholar in the field of oral tradition studies but also as a notable shaper of the new direction of that field. In both *Immanent Art* and *The Singer of Tales in Performance*, Foley makes the argument that oral tradition cannot be defined universally (as every oral tradition differs based on its unique context) and moreover, orality should not be monolithically defined against literacy (as oral traditions often exist within literate cultures). At his *Pathways Project* website, he states:

> In fact, [this affords us] the opportunity to emphasize how the worlds of orality and literacy, once thought to occupy mutually exclusive orbits, can and do coexist and interact in myriad fascinating combinations, within the same culture or region and even within the same person. Not only do OT features persist alongside and into texts, that is, but a single individual may be fluent in both expressive media [Foley].

Although Foley would probably not stretch his argument so far as to accommodate image-based texts produced in a commercial environment, I think it can and should be stretched in this way; if it is, we can begin to regard Miller and Moore as self-conscious practitioners in a secondary orality (or new traditionalism).[14] With so much of their work drawn from the clichés of superhero comic books, their supposed radical changes need to be understood as mediated by other factors and should still be understood as new traditional. Bradford W. Wright makes this observation about the state of comic books in the wave of the creator's rights movement:

> Yet if creators' rights advocates expected incentives to unleash a great flowering of literary and artistic advancement in comic books, they were mistaken.... If anything, in fact, the

superhero genre became more entrenched than ever because the much-trumpeted creative incentives actually rewarded commercial success, not necessarily innovation [262].

In reference to this quotation, it is important to note that Wright's focus in his study of American comic books is largely fixed on superhero comics, and he chooses not to mention the growing presence of alternative genres in the 1980s with Harvey Pekar's *American Splendor*, the Hernandez brothers' *Love and Rockets*, and Art Speigelman's *Raw* (works mentioned in the important popular articles referenced in this paragraph).[15] With that acknowledgment made, Wright's statement is a generally accurate assessment, and the American comic book audience serves as a corrective to writers that might want to stray too far from the fold (just as traditional audiences always have).

Much was made of the reinvention of the superhero during the Modern Age but neither Miller nor Moore rejected the past of superheroes. Both reinterpreted characters, such as Daredevil and Superman, but each told stories that intentionally harkened to tropes used throughout the long history of each character (from the superheroes' sidekicks and rogues galleries to the idealism of character and the standard contrivances of plot). The self-conscious treatment that simultaneously reveals and maintains the cliché can be seen perhaps most clearly in Moore's "Whatever Happened to the Man of Tomorrow?" The narrative frame of the story is situated in the future in which Lois Lane, happily married with a child, is interviewed by an intrepid reporter looking to discover the answer to the title question. She reveals that Superman ended his career by intentionally exposing himself to gold Kryptonite and taking away his own powers. With a return to the frame at the end, Lois has a conversation with her husband, brown haired and mustached, but clearly a retired Superman. With their son crushing a piece of coal into a diamond in the foreground, Lois's husband says "Superman? He was overrated, and too wrapped up in himself— he thought the world couldn't get along without him." When Lois suggests that they might live happily ever after, she coyly asks, "Sound good to you?" He replies, "Lois, my love ... what do you think?" (Moore, "Whatever" 214). In addition to using something so specific as gold Kryptonite to end the story, Moore playfully develops the "imaginary" story with familiar conventions: the happily ever after with Lois and the promise of a Superman for another generation. Most significantly in the regard to new traditionalism is the last panel; with "what do you think?" Superman has turned away from Lois and toward the reader as he closes the door to their room. Breaking the fourth wall and speaking to the reader is reminiscent of the end of "Flash of Two Worlds," our quintessential example of new traditionalism in superhero comic books (see chapter 6). It is a playful response to Lois but also a question to the reader who Superman thus involves in the shape of the story.[16]

The New and Improved Rorschach Test (or, How Miller and Moore Analyze the Superhero)

While this is only one example in the midst of many other superhero stories written by both, it is not unique to either (despite the growing differences between these two writers hereafter discussed); it is simply distinctive. In order to further this claim, I will begin my examination of *The Dark Knight Returns* and *Watchmen* by highlighting several aspects of their plots. Miller's *The Dark Knight Returns* is a Batman story and begins with Batman in his 50s. By beginning in the middle of things (or at the end of things), Miller necessarily has to work with clichés already in place for the character, the collective knowledge of the community. As a boy, Bruce Wayne witnessed his parents killed in Crime Alley and commits his life to fighting crime; Wayne chooses the bat as a costume and symbol to frighten criminals and thereafter, uses his intellect and the family fortune to develop the means to realize his fanatic fight against crime; the police commissioner, Jim Gordon, and Wayne's butler, Alfred Pennyworth, enable Wayne to do what he does in Gotham City as the Batman; he operates as a vigilante, fighting against colorful, questionably sane criminals that serve as a counterpoint to his law and order. In *The Dark Knight Returns*, Batman has retired and Gotham has endured a crime-ridden spiral into despair as the gang that calls themselves the Mutants now control the city. Wayne is a shell of his former self, suicidal and thinking of Batman in the third person. When Wayne returns to fighting crime as Batman, Miller extends Batman's vigilante status by revealing that he lives in a world that has forced superheroes out of existence. With Cold War paranoia as a motivating factor, all superheroes were viewed as suspicious threats and all were forced into retirement with the exception of Superman (who works at the behest of the national government). When Bruce Wayne brings Batman out of retirement to fight the mutants, he is viewed as a public enemy, particularly by the national government. The need for Batman and his effective action demonstrates the ineffectiveness of the national government and this leads to the series' ultimate conflict between Batman and Superman.

Miller's expensive ($2.95), square bound, and glossy papered four-issue series (eventually to be collected and kept in continuous print as a graphic novel) would seem to depart from traditional aesthetics by providing a close to the story of Batman and by fixing a certain extreme interpretation of Batman with a permanently available version of that story.[17] Miller himself suggested that he had a diffident relationship with the source material with statements such as "We've got 50 years of crap, and people talk as if we have a heritage behind us. We've got lots of bad stories, just one after another. There is good work back there, but there isn't a lot of it. And there isn't enough to have made an impression on the world at large" (George, *Frank Miller* 39). By distancing himself from his source material, this places Miller in a somewhat disingenuous position characteristic of creators in the literate world supposedly creating something cut from new cloth. However, Miller balances this perspective with other statements such as "In the early adventures of Superman and Batman, the superhero was an unusual, often mystical element that focused and defined real-world situations and issues in a way that was clearer and more direct than a simple recitation of the facts could" (34). As someone who consciously distances himself from the traditions of superhero stories and yet harkens back to them as mystical, real-world influences, Miller seems more likely than most to operate in a fashion out of step with the conventions of literacy. With that stated, Miller works in the self-conscious vein of new traditionalism that allows him to develop a variation on the existing story that evokes Batman stories of old.[18] While Miller and Moore would be credited with fashioning the mentality of the nihilistic and violent superhero of the 1990s, both have stated that that was far from their intention. Miller may seem to extend the clichés of Batman's superheroism to a breaking point, but he largely redeploys and accentuates standard tropes associated with the genre and medium from the split identity of the superhero to the tension between the superhero as vigilante and agent of the state. The paranoia builds on the film noir inspiration of Batman but also comments on contemporary U.S. politics; like Umberto Eco suggests to a degree in "The Myth of Superman" and as has been seen with epic heroes, the superhero is both timeless and relevant.

Alan Moore and Dave Gibbon's *Watchmen* is superficially a thornier example of a work of new traditionalism in that it reads as a work that more clearly wants to set superhero tropes aside with a story highly critical of the genre. Even Miller states, "It was funny how *Dark Knight* and *Watchmen* were grouped together, because even though both of them represented kinds of end points, they were approached from completely opposing points of view. Alan was eviscerating the entire notion. I was very sentimentally celebrating it" (George, *Frank Miller* 105). While I might take issue with Miller's characterization of the two works as "end points" made with "completely opposing points of view," I think he accurately sums up the popular understanding of the two works in comparison. However, every story has a life beyond the author's own sense of it (both in traditional and literate contexts). Moore states that he intended to do something different with a self-contained superhero universe that he could creatively control (John B. Cooke, *Q9*). While Moore superficially works with an original cast of characters and crafts a story with a discrete beginning and ending, there are many aspects of the story that defy the understanding of the story as literary. To begin, the characters were based on the Charlton superhero universe and Moore's original proposal dealt with "Who Killed the Peacemaker?" When DC editor Dick Giordano rejected Moore's original proposal in order to preserve the recently acquired Charlton superheroes as they were, he still encouraged Moore to work with the story idea. Moore states:

> I forget how much of the idea was in place then, but I think that it would start with a murder, and I pretty well knew who would be guilty of the murder, and I've got an idea of the motive, and the basic bare-bones of the plot — all of which actually ended up being about the least important thing about Watchmen.... Eventually, I realized that if I wrote the substitute characters well enough, so that they seemed familiar in certain ways, certain aspects of them brought back a kind of generic super-hero resonance or familiarity to the reader, then it might work [John B. Cooke].

Curiously, the story that would become *Watchmen* began as what Walter Ong characterizes as the ultimate product of literate storytelling: the mystery with its closed ending. As Moore states, the resolution (the closed ending) of the murder mystery eventually became unimportant, and resonance between source characters and newly created characters became important. Charlton superheroes, including the Peacemaker, the Question, Captain Atom, Blue Beetle, Thunderbolt, and Phantom Lady all have a correspondence to characters in *Watchmen*, but *Watchmen*'s characters are more widely connected to superheroes in general as a consequence of the change. Working the clichés shared by superheroes in general, the Comedian not only resembles the Peacemaker but Captain American and Nick Fury; Rorschach not only resembles the Question but Batman and Wolverine, and so on. As a consequence, Moore's practice resembles something like a self-conscious version of the referentiality that Foley describes in *Immanent Art*, with a specific element evoking the larger context of the tradition itself (7).

Watchmen does begin with the murder of Edward Blake, the Comedian, and Rorschach investigating the crime. In the wake of the Keene Act, a nearly decade-old piece of legislation that outlaws superheroes, the Comedian and Rorschach represent the two extremes among the superheroes who did not retire. The Comedian works for the U.S. government and his amoral love of violence serves him well in that capacity both in domestic and international conflicts; Rorschach continues to work outside the law and his paranoid, obsessive perspective convinces him that only his morally motivated violence outside the system can realize true justice. Other retirees include Rorschach's ex-partner, the rumpled Dan Dreiberg (formerly Nite Owl) who seems a weak reflection of his former self, the super-intelligent Adrian Veidt (formerly Ozymandias) who uses his superhero image to amass great wealth, and the lonely Laurie Juspeczyk (formerly Silk Spectre) who lives at a government facility mainly to keep her boyfriend Dr. Manhattan happy. None of them believe Rorschach's anxious ravings about a masked-killer until certain elements begin to validate this theory, like the exile from earth of Dr. Manhattan (the only truly super-powered costumed crime fighter). Like *The Dark Knight Returns*, the outsider status of the superheroes is accentuated through not only the Cold War legislation of the Keene Act but also the disturbingly sociopathic Rorschach (lost in his mask) and perversely dispassionate Dr. Manhattan (lost in his powers). With the costumed crime fighter phenomenon beginning roughly at the same time superhero comic books first appeared (both Nite Owl and Silk Spectre are second generation superheroes), history has departed from one we know. Alan Moore states:

> Our intention was to show how superheroes could deform the world just by being there, not that they'd have to take it over, just their presence would make the difference... On another level, if you equate [an incredibly powerful superhero] with the atom bomb, the atom bomb doesn't have to take over the world, but by being there it changes everything [Groth and Fiore 100].

Richard Nixon is still the president in 1985, and the nuclear clock is perilously close to midnight (and nuclear armageddon). Convinced of Rorschach's masked-killer theory, Nite Owl and Silk Spectre team with Rorschach and discover too late that Ozymandias has planned a hoax alien invasion of New York, killing millions of people to substantiate the hoax. As a consequence, the USA and USSR end their nuclear stand-off and pledge to work together to protect the earth against their new common enemy. Again, the work seems to stretch conventions to a breaking point but the stretching more clearly identifies the tropes at work. In addition to those already mentioned in relation to *The Dark Knight Returns* is one also used by Miller but which is so much more obvious in *Watchmen*: the self-conscious presentation of the power fantasy. Rather than featuring Spider-Man clobbering the Green Goblin in order to save a busload of children, *Watchmen* exposes the tenets of that moral paradigm by showing Ozymandias kill millions of people in order to save billions.

The Dark Knight Returns and *Watchmen* address concerns central to the study of traditional and literate cultures, most notably the tension between the tribalism of the traditional world and the civilization of the literate world; in the process of exploring this tension, these works transition to their treatment of new traditionality through critiques of new media and examinations of the way time is perceived. In other words, Miller and (perhaps more so) Moore have the instincts of scholars who put their ideas in a narrative form (self-conscious practitioners of traditional art). Again, as I stated in reference to Gardner Fox, I do not mean to suggest that either creator has a first-hand familiarity with studies of orality and literacy (or even media studies in general) and thereby implements ideas specifically drawn from such fields. However, I do mean to suggest that an intimate awareness of comic books and graphic novels necessarily leads to a consideration of the medium and the culture in the terms outlined in this study. To continue, it is important to consider a tension between tribalism and civilization that is central to both works and that drives the narrative development of each. The traditional culture is the tribal culture, one that thinks very little of the individual or the world outside the tribal unit; the literate culture is the civilized culture, one that validates the individual and various cultural units as equally valuable within the wider global culture. The long acknowledged starting point for such studies is Claude Levi-Strauss's *The Savage Mind*, a book whose title in French begins with a bit of wordplay; "savage mind" also implies wild or undomesticated thought. Therefore, central to Levi-

Strauss's work is the idea that the mind of the "savage" is not uniformly different from the mind of civilization, but, rather, it is the content and conditions that affect the mind that has changed (Fox 19). According to Levi-Strauss, the tribal mind works in ways that knit together people and thoughts that would be regarded as individual within the context of civilization. After establishing that the mythic, totemic thought of tribes as a means of problem-solving and confronting reality in a way not clearly recognized in the scientific thought of the civilized world (17), Levi-Strauss describes such thought as bricolage:

> Mythical thought appears to be an intellectual form of "bricolage."... Science as a whole is based on the distinction between the contingent and the necessary, this also being what distinguishes event and structure.... Now, the characteristic feature of mythical thought, as of "bricolage" on the practical plane, is that it builds up structured set, not directly with other structured sets but by using the remains and debris of events.... Mythical thought for its part remains imprisoned in the events and experiences which it never tires of ordering and re-ordering in its search to find them a meaning. But it also acts as a liberator by its protest against the idea that anything can be meaningless with which science at first resigned itself to compromise [21–22].

This is an important facet of the current discussion because it not only describes the practice of traditional storytelling but also describes the supposedly paranoid psychology of Miller's Batman and Moore's Rorschach. Individual elements are given meaning not in their own terms but by their relationship to other variables within the system (whether that be an epic poem, a comic book, or a worldview).

Although not as extreme in his opinion as Sigmund Freud in *Civilization and Its Discontents*, Levi-Strauss does suggest that the attempts of Rene Descartes and Jean Paul Sartre to separate the individual from the group diminishes certain basic human tendencies to think (249). While subsequent scholars (such as Jack Goody) have suggested that Levi-Strauss drew too discrete a line between the savage and the civilized, Levi-Strauss remains the standard for such cultural studies. Referring to Levi-Strauss's sense of the savage mind, Robin Fox demonstrates the problems with understanding the move from tribal to civilized as an evolutionary move in *The Tribal Imagination*. After teasing out the problem of universal human rights by suggesting revenge was a human right in tribes, Fox examines how the civilized world's notion of human rights differs from that of the tribe. Laws against drug abuse, infanticide, and abortion show how:

> non-kin collectives are taking over the function that originated and have their logic, in the kin group.... It is in the interest of a nation, for example, to reproduce itself. Thus it tends, in its delusional-ideological system, to pass itself off as a super kin group. At a primitive level of evolving humanity ... there was no need for such pretense. The kin group was the social collectivity. This is why I have argued ... that at the most basic, and hence most "human," level, there is no "rights" issue [48].

This growth of civilization in the Western world pushes people beyond reliance on kin groups and toward laws that require faith in strangers to enforce what is now referred to as human rights within the democratic order of modern civilization (69). The tribe or kin group was the basis for all understanding and valuation in the world (as limited as the geography of that world might be) and the individual had no identity outside that group. Although I don't want to fall into the trap of romanticizing traditional culture, these types of studies are important correctives for a civilized world that tends to privilege the society and art of literate culture. In addition, Levi-Strauss and Fox are quick to point out that the tribal (or as we have stated, the traditional) mind hasn't been replaced; it coexists within the civilized world in ways domesticated to relative degrees. As a consequence, civilization has not replaced the tribal, and, as a consequence, the savage mind competes with and also informs the basic tenets civilization.

In *The Dark Knight Returns*, we begin with Bruce Wayne in Gotham City, and, in short order, it becomes clear that he has a symbiotic relationship with the city. Through a newscast, it is revealed that the gang calling themselves the mutants commit horrific crimes despite Commissioner Gordon's best efforts to stop them. Batman has been in "retirement" for ten years and the city and Bruce Wayne have become more socially and psychologically troubled in the meantime. The color palate has expanded in Modern Age comic books and Miller (and colorist Lynn Varley) uses a variety of grey tones to evoke the bleak despair of Wayne in Gotham.[19] In the city's first street level depiction, Wayne walks through an urban landscape filled with trash and street people carrying signs with phrases such as "We are damned" (Miller, *The Dark Knight* 12). Wayne walks to Crime Alley and muses, "But Batman was a young man. If it was revenge he was after, he's taken it. It's been forty years since he was born ... born here. Once again, he's brought me back—to show me how little it has changed" (13). Mutants then approach Wayne seemingly to torture and kill him, but they leave him, saying, "Look at him. He's into it—Can't do murders when they're into it" (13–14). Like the city, Wayne has a schizoid personality, torn between decay and corruption and a nostalgic sense of what might have been. Suicidal with an end times sensibility, the nostalgia is probably baseless, as divorced from reality as Wayne's sense of self (with Batman as another person). With his reference to Batman (and with Batman's eventual return), there is a question of how Batman fits into the scheme: as the noble knight who will save the holy city or as something else, not wholly good but necessary to save the world Wayne knows.

> The enemy of the Dark Knight texts is also Gotham City. Its very structures and history engender crime.... This postmodern Batman quickly discovers that crime is a structural feature of the city as a whole and not simply the willful actions of the have-nots, who isolate themselves from the wealthy and proper citizens of Gotham ... the bat is no longer a model; it is now a totem.... [W]hat is required is that one become an animal, a human-becoming-animal, a human-becoming intense. Miller's Dark Knight is such a "becoming," a creature no longer under rational control, because rationality as a convention only protects the powerful and refuses to address the issues at hand—a city of human beings threatened by various criminal elements [Nash 40, 41–42].

While Jesse Nash includes Miller's *Batman: Year One* in his discussion of *The Dark Knight Returns*, his points have the greatest relevance to *The Dark Knight Returns*. Essential to this discussion is the way that Wayne represents his city like an epic hero would with the city as the highest value (and not abstract morality represented by the law). However, the city is besieged by crime because of its participation in larger social structures of the civilized world; civilization is represented by television correspondents who entertain for that sake of ratings (rather than inform), a mayor who placates with politically correct appointments (rather than leads), and an army general who profits from illicit arms sales (rather than protects). Batman's sensibility is far less civilized and far more tribal, a sensibility that by the standards of a modern literate perspective would be considered to be less than human.

Once Batman returns, he maintains a clear code of conduct (refusing to kill the Joker and even keeping children from swearing unnecessarily) but he revels in his outsider position. This ranges from the memory of his congressional testimony that superheroes "have to be criminals" (Miller, *The Dark Knight* 135) to his scare tactics around contemporary outlaws such as growling ("He never used to make sounds") (38). Wayne defeats the mutant leader and reorganizes the tribe formerly known as the mutants as the sons of Batman in the service of the city that has lost its way through domestication. Since his concerns do not extend beyond the confines of Gotham City, he is politically, though not tactically, oblivious to the larger significance of his actions in a democratic country in a global context. In what Robin Fox might call "a delusional-ideological system," a Ronald Reagan-like president struggles with his potential loss of power. In a system based not on kin connection but on

Superman is given the Disney treatment with his idyllic surrounding, representing the way he has been co-opted by American culture (from *The Dark Knight Returns*, p. 118).

the abstraction of law, he recognizes that it is better to have a problem than fix a problem outside the law. In a now famous series of panels in which the American flag becomes the symbol on Superman's chest, the president says:

> Just between you and me and the fence post, I'm worried about a friend of yours.... Son, I like to think I learned everything I know about running this country on my ranch.... It's all well and good ... on a ranch, I mean ... for all the horses to be all different colors and sizes.... It's even okay to have a crazy bronco now and then.... Does the hands good to break him in ... but if that bronco up and kicks the fence out and gets the other horses crazy ... well it's bad for business. World's changed son. It's not like the old days [84].

Of course, Batman is the "crazy bronco" who reminds us of the "the old days," and Superman is the arm of the U.S. government, the new world order. At Superman's request, Clark Kent and Bruce Wayne meet out of costume in a field, and Miller renders each within the panels that depict their relationship in particular ways. Kent is regularly in the foreground, huge as the agent of the state, and surrounded by butterflies and flowers, as in a Disney cartoon, an association with the commercial style of a monolithic corporate entity. With Wayne in the background with a wolf-like dog, Kent does his best to communicate the rhetoric of the U.S. government: "Times have changed and you — well, it's just not healthy. You'll burn yourself up. I know, you look better than you have in years but... These aren't the old days, Bruce... World's got no room for... Sooner of later, somebody's going to order me to bring you in. Someone with authority" (118–119). He consistently uses the excuse that the world is different and uses the idea of authority, like the President, as a means to control Wayne. However, for Wayne, authority is not separate from the self (or Gotham City) but is a part of the bricolage that relates all things to the self and the story that is told within the culture; since he is thoroughly implicated in a tribe (an association considered to be morally ambiguous by modern standards), he is not threatened by the implication of his rebuke of Kent: "Nobody can make you do anything you don't want to do, Clark" (119).[20]

While Miller himself declares he has a romantic sense of Batman and many have understood his treatment of Superman to be a straightforward criticism of the government stooge, Miller's study of this conflict is more nuanced, not clearly favoring tribalism over civilization. Miller creates a parody of "basic" human rights by putting the argument for them within the mouth of a criminal: "No! Stay back — I've got rights." After kicking him out the window, Batman responds with "You've got rights. Lots of rights. Sometimes I count them just to make myself feel crazy" (Miller, *The Dark Knight* 44–45). This violence seems justified in narrative momentum that is typical of a superhero adventure story, especially when Batman's media coverage seems to call the new Robin to action on the very same page. However, corresponding to the call to a new hero on the next page is the call to an old villain (as Batman's media coverage calls the Joker, currently in Arkham Asylum, out of his catatonic state). The return of Batman as a powerful and violent counterpoint to the Joker has positive and negative consequences, as later represented in other media coverage; after reading about "a man who dresses up as a monster and makes things right," a mentally unstable boxer and criminal dresses up like Batman and attacks someone with a gun. The violence and weapons that Batman uses escalates in effect and size in an effort to restore law and order, and the criminals learn from his example. Moreover, the basis of Batman's new tribal sensibility begins to fracture as some of the ex-mutants become sons of the Joker (representing Batman's most significant rival), and others become the Nixons (representing cynicism and general disillusionment with democratic civilization). And Batman is, from the start, enabled by a fortune that is based on capital wealth established and maintained far outside the confines of a tribal mentality. On the other hand, Superman is portrayed as anything but a hapless accomplice to the new order of civilization in which corruption seem to be a surety — thanks to the desire of individuals within a large system to pursue their own selfish agendas. Superman necessarily has a global perspective thanks to his powers, portrayed by Miller by putting the reader in Superman's vantage point as he descends from his flight above Gotham city. Through Superman's thoughts, we learn that superheroes were forced into retirement by a paranoid populace and Superman's fealty to the U.S. government allows him to simultaneously protect less powerful superheroes and do some good. In an ironic interplay of image and word, Superman lifts a Soviet tank over his head and thinks, "They'll kill us if they can, Bruce. Every year they grow smaller. Every year they hate us more. We must not remind them that giants walk the earth" (129–130). Superman continues to embody the rhetoric of civilization with rules that protect the weak and deny the tribal notion that might makes right.

Miller extrapolates in part from the origins of Batman and Superman. With Batman's parents murdered in front of him in Crime Alley, his origin seems to have everything to do with the failure of both civilization and the rights of man. In contrast, with Superman as an alien adopted by and integrated within the farm country (Kansas) and urban center (Metropolis) of the United States, his origin seems to have everything to do with the success of both civilization and the rights of man. However, another irony of Superman's actions as related to his words is that the rights of man extend only so far as the U.S. border; he attacks the Soviet Union, a country that could only be made an enemy by oversimplifying it and establishing it as a backward anti-democracy.[21] The limitations of civilization are represented in the president's public address concerning the localized conflict that calls Superman to action against the Soviet Union:

> Let me tell you nobody's running off half-cocked, no sir ... but we sure as shooting aren't running away, either. We've got to secure our — ahem — stand up for the cause of freedom ... and those cute little Corto Maltese people, they want us there, just you ask them ... meanwhile, don't you fret ... we've got God on our side ... or the next best thing, anyway [Miller, *The Dark Knight* 119].

From the conflict itself to the President's near misspeak about securing something for ourselves (rather than fighting for the general abstraction of freedom), the limitations of global civilization are exposed by portraying Superman's power as a means to control another culture; since people of the United States are so far removed from the Corto Maltese, asking them their opinion is out-of-the-question. As will be seen in an even more pronounced way with *Watchmen*, *The Dark Knight Returns* has an apocalyptic mood, and this is most fully realized when the Soviets launch a missile at the United States, a "coldbringer" that disrupts the use of electrical and mechanical systems. As a consequence, Gotham City is robbed of all trappings of civilization, and the authority of a horse-riding Batman is all that enables people to band together and fight the chaos that ensues. With Batman a more clear-and-present danger to the administration's power, Superman is sent to stop him. With robotic armor, Batman almost wins the battle that he fights with Superman, because he always saw civilization and Superman as a threat; concerning the Kryptonite that weakens Superman, Batman says, "It wasn't easy to synthesize, Clark ... took years and cost a fortune" (194). In the end, Batman seems to die from heart failure caused by the strain of the battle; however, it was his plan for it to appear so, inducing the heart attack with drugs. Initially, assuming Batman's death to be real, Superman cradles Batman in his arms and barks at approaching soldiers, "Don't touch him" (196). When Batman revives from this self-imposed "death," Superman discovers his ruse but allows Batman to work underground with his militia-like tribe consisting of the new Robin and the sons of the Batman. Some might suggest that Miller stacks the cards in favor of Batman's tribal leadership with the coldbringer missile that temporarily disrupts civilization's technology and they might be right; however, the unspoken alliance between Batman and Superman at the end suggests something about the way Miller sees the uneasy coexistence of the two in the modern world.

If Miller builds to an end with an uneasy alliance between tribalism and civilization that favors the tribal hero, Moore builds to an end with much more tragic consequences because of the coexistence of these two mentalities and their unacknowledged tensions. In *Watchmen*, we begin with Rorschach at the scene of a crime, the murder of the Comedian. Over the series of seven panels, the perspective pulls away from the Comedian's blood-splattered smiley face pin on the street where he fell, far below his apartment. Through text that represents Rorschach's journal, we are exposed to a psychology that seems to depart from what we would expect to encounter in a superhero story; however, as the story progresses it seems more like the psychology of Batman in *The Dark Knight Returns* (superhero psychology pushed to its extremes and laid bare).

> This city is afraid of me. I have seen its true face. The streets are extended gutters and the gutters are full of blood and when the drains finally scab over, all the vermin will drown. The accumulated filth of all their sex and murder will foam up about their waists and all the whores and politicians will look up and shout, "Save us!"... And I'll look down and whisper, "No." They has a choice, all of them. They could have followed in the footsteps of good men like my father or President Truman. Decent men, who believed in a day's work for a day's pay. Instead they followed the droppings of lechers and communists and didn't realize that trail led over a precipice until it was too late. Don't tell me they didn't have a choice [Moore, *Watchmen* I. 1].[22]

Like Batman, Rorschach is not understood as a hero by a civilized world that seeks to pathologize evil as sickness that might be cured. Instead, Rorschach is an extremist with a black and white sense of the world and a nostalgic love for a perfect tribal culture that never existed as he thinks it did. Moreover, his defining moment as masked crime fighter is discovering a child's murder, and this not only causes him to leave behind civilized ways of dealing with criminals but also teaches him that there is no transcendent basis for his separation of the sheep and goats: only the abyss and what is required by the current situation. The shifting of perspective according to circumstance is something that is accentuated by the subjective (and literally, ever-changing) nature of the Rorschach ink blot that is Rorschach's mask. Moore and Gibbons seemingly understand Rorschach as the violent and disturbing end result of the comic book hero (much in the vein of the hero described by Jewett and Lawrence in *The Myth of the American Superhero*); he is made even more threatening as a cultural product in his early presentation scaling the wall to the Comedian's apartment (as Adam West did so comically in the Batman television series) but then emerging through the apartment window (as if he were stepping through the panel).

While Miller's Batman and Moore's Rorschach would have a tidal wave influence on the industry for the following decade,[23] Rorschach is not the center of the text. Moore states: "I don't think there is a center of the book. Part of what *Watchmen* was about is that all the characters have very, very distinctive views of the world" (Khoury 113). As opposed to *The Dark Knight Returns* that centralizes a character with a more clearly tribal sensibility, *Watchmen* offers several other perspectives (but all of them seem to be formed relative to the tension between tribalism and civilization). The primary threat seems to not be the masked-killer that Rorschach is tracking but the brinksmanship of the United States and the Soviet Union. Since all superheroes with the exception of Dr. Manhattan lack superpowers, they sit on the sidelines of the world-threatening conflict, no more potent than any other human being—or so it seems. Dan Dreiberg and Laurie Juspeczyk, retired from their respective roles as Nite Owl and Silk Spectre, are second-generation superheroes, not entirely fulfilled as superheroes and even less fulfilled in their "retired" lives. As Geoffrey Klock suggests, Dreiberg "visually suggests an impotent, middle-aged Clark Kent" (66). Adrian Veidt (Ozymandias) has achieved a great level of financial success in his retirement but seems strangely unfulfilled by his prominent role within a capitalist culture (represented well by a panel that features his lonely self standing in the background and his desk littered with Ozymandias figures sitting in the foreground). Part of whom Adrian Veidt is revealed to be is carefully concealed from both the omniscient perspective of Dr. Manhattan and the reader. Amassing a fortune for clandestine purposes, Ozymandias is the architect of a scheme to save the earth from its own worst impulses, manifested in nearness to nuclear armageddon. Ozymandias realized that the two great civilizations of the East and West were no longer bound together by kinship, and, as civilized nations still sought to exert their will upon the other, he recognized:

> I fought only the symptoms, leaving the disease unchecked.... Brutally, I'd been brought nose to nose with mankind's mortality; the dreadful irrefutable fact of it. For the first time, I genuinely understood that earth might die.... I saw East and West locked in an escalating arms spiral, their mutual terror and suspicion mounting with the missiles.... The plan Blake had uncovered was this: to frighten governments into cooperation, I would convince them that the earth faced imminent attack by beings from another world.... My new world demands less obvious heroism, making your schoolboy heroics redundant [Moore, *Watchmen* XI 19, 21, 25, and XII 17].

Unlike Rorschach who insisted upon still trying to operate as a tribal leader, Ozymandias sought to operate as a supposedly civilized leader who nevertheless relied upon the basic human desire to destroy the other. In Rorschach's (and Batman's) estimation, this desire is the human condition for better or worse, but, in Ozymandias's estimation, a new world can be created. Yet, Ozymandias's methods require much consideration as his destruction of New York in a staged alien attack is simply an elevation of the power fantasy associated with superhero stories: "schoolboy heroics" taken to their logical end. If he's frightening governments into cooperation, he does not cause the world to "evolve" beyond its tribal tendencies to a more fully civilized world; he reinforces the basic ideas of tribalism that pit one nation against another. His reason works not as pure reason is said to work but rather as a bricolage that fits pieces together to make a coherent whole.

While Rorschach embraces the tribal and Ozymandias cannot escape it, John Osterman (Dr. Manhattan) should be able to rise above the tension in human consciousness between the tribal and civilized. With fantastic abilities that involve matter manipulation and perception that extends beyond linear time, Osterman works for the government in various capacities over the years but currently develops scientific research. Since an accident at a quantum research facility gave him his powers, Osterman has drifted away from his human feelings as his consciousness expanded; he has become less Osterman and more Dr. Manhattan, the name given to him by the U.S. government to associate "their" superman with the atom bomb.[24] Ozymandias hides his activities from Dr. Manhattan by using tachyons to create a sort of static interference with Dr. Manhattan's ability to see the future; as a consequence, Dr. Manhattan is tricked into exile. After being informed by a reporter that his presence has caused cancer in those near him, a horrified Dr. Manhattan leaves earth to create a space for himself in isolation on Mars. Once he is on the moon, the reader is exposed to the way in which Dr. Manhattan experiences time, in a nonlinear, flat sense of time in which all moments are grouped together (much like a comic book page and in particular, a comic book page in *Watchmen*, often disregarding linear development):

> The photograph is in my hand. It is a photograph of a man and a woman. They are at an amusement park. In twelve seconds time, I drop the photograph to the sand at my feet, walking away. It's already lying there, twelve seconds into the future... The photograph is still in my hand. I found it in a derelict bar at the Gila Flats test base twenty-seven hours ago. It's still there... I'm still looking at it.... It's October, 1985. I'm on Mars. It's July, 1959. I'm in New Jersey, at the Palisades Amusement Park [Moore, *Watchmen* IV 1–2].

After he drops the photograph, we return to images of him holding it in a way that enacts the experience Dr. Manhattan has of time. Sara J. Van Ness suggests that Watchmen effectively uses this technique throughout to further create a sense of participation in the medium (that I would suggest defies the conventions of literacy): "Watchmen's cyclical and layered narrative structure invites the readers to participate in the meaning-making narrative ... to create a narrative that extends beyond the end" (Van Ness 77). In his survey of Dr. Manhattan and time, David Barnes extends this to cover the medium itself: "In comics both the past and the future are real and visible. Unlike in other media, in comics the past is more than just memories of what occurred on the screen moments before and the future is more than just possibilities. No panel is less important than another; all exist between the singular covers of the comic boo object" (58). While he stresses the physicality of the comic book, the point about the relative value of parts of the narrative enacts the ethos of traditional art.

Eventually, Dr. Manhattan returns to earth and brings Juspeczyk, his former girlfriend, to Mars, because his sense of time determines that "Now, I believe we have a conversation scheduled; you want to talk to me" (Moore, *Watchmen* VIII 23). The problem of his action in relation to what seems to be immutably determined events is further complicated when he is hurt to hear that she is now with Dreiberg. While he indicates his emotional reactions have been predetermined, his perspective on time doesn't completely justify anything other than a dispassionate sense of things from the time of his accident onward. However, this sense of Dr. Manhattan works only within the logical notion within the literate mindset that makes free will and destiny mutually exclusive. Like the heroes in ancient epics, Dr. Manhattan seems to have a sense that the two are mutually dependent on one another. Moore describes it this way: "Whereas once there was this great eternal present [for earlier or more primitive cultures], we ... as a species, adopted this different notion of time, [a] rather simplistic and fatalistic idea of past, present, and future" (Vylenz, qtd. In Van Ness 79). The apocalyptic feel of Watchmen is thereby modified by an alternative view of things much more in line with "the primitive cyclical state, [the] 'ring composition' ... of the epics that seem so disorganized and episodic to us" (Fox 27). We should return to Moore's claim that no one character's viewpoint is more authoritative than any others' (even if Dr. Manhattan has some sort of enhanced conscious awareness). However, with that acknowledgment made, the conversation between Dr. Manhattan and Juspeczyk leads to her experiencing time as he does and realizing that her father was the Comedian; her father attempted to rape her mother before the two consummated their relationship with the coupling that led to Laurie's conception. In frustration, Juspeczyk throws a bottle of Nostalgia perfume (made by Ozymandias's corporation) at the intricate glass structure built by Dr. Manhattan on Mars; symbolically, Nostalgia, a product of the literate world and a metonym representing the corporate empire central to Ozymandias's scheme, is destroyed together with the new world of a "greater" mind. Before Dr. Manhattan's return to earth and confrontation with Ozymandias, a commentary is thus made on the constructed nature of the "new," modern world.

When it comes to the difference between what is tribal and civilized,[25] characters do not line up in ways that are quite as neat as *The Dark Knight Returns*. However, while Miller seems to be more interested in exploring the tension between these two pure categories, Moore seems to be more interested in exploring the nuances of tribalism and civilization in a world where traditionalism and literacy coexist. With his positive feeling to past eras of civilization within the United States, Rorschach is an imperfect representation of tribalism and moreover, with his exploitation of a human weakness associated with tribal behavior, Ozymandias is an imperfect representation of civilization. While Miller works with territory much more discretely covered by Claude Levi-Strauss, Moore works with that territory as modified by Foley's argument for the specificity of individual context. Both Miller and Moore develop positions that question the superiority of a literate worldview and an enlightenment sense of technology, but Moore does this even more so with Dr. Manhattan. If civilization were the evolutionary end of tribalism, Dr. Manhattan should be an even better representation of civilization than Ozymandias (a character flawed by his more human limitations). After learning of their inability to stop Ozymandias (and questioning whether they should), Dreiberg and Juspeczyk sleep together; when she asks of what he smells, he responds, "Nostalgia" (Moore, *Watchmen* XII 22). They are humans defined by both human desire and their limitations for better or worse, and it makes Dr.

When Juspeczyk throws a Veidt perfume bottle, "Nostalgia" breaks apart and destroys Dr. Manhattan's new world, only perfect without other people (from *Watchmen* #9, p. 25).

Manhattan smile. Freeing himself of the emotions that bound him to Juspeczyk is something that takes place just moments after killing Rorschach. Despite the consequences, Rorschach insisted, "Evil must be punished. People must be told." (XII 24); as he realized Dr. Manhattan's intentions to kill him, he said, "Of course. Must protect Veidt's new utopia. One more body amongst the foundations makes little difference" (XII 25). Despite the dispassionate (and literate) nature of logic that seems to allow Dr. Manhattan to rise above himself for the sake of civilization, he gives Ozymandias a hint that his "new utopia" may simply be a delay to inevitable human conflict. When Ozymandias states that it all worked out in the end, Dr. Manhattan replies, "'In the end'? Nothing ends, Adrian. Nothing ever ends" (XII 27). This final statement is ambiguous, but it suggests that he was knitting together moments at this point in time (Dreiberg and Juspeczyk's happiness and Ozymandias's utopia) as a sort of bricolage even though he was aware, via his perspective of time, that they wouldn't last. Although these words from Dr. Manhattan's are his last, they are not the last in the text. Regardless, Moore seems to share this sentiment: "There is not an outcome. The fat lady hasn't sung yet, she perhaps never will. In the real world, everything is not parceled into stories ... there aren't any endings except for in fiction" (Khoury 114). The last sequence in the series features an assistant at *The New Frontiersman*, a conspiracy newspaper to which Rorschach sent his journal immediately before confronting Ozymandias. As he reaches toward the journal, the editor tells him, "Go on just run whichever you want ... I leave it entirely in your hands" (XII 32). The ending of both *The Dark Knight Returns* (with Batman about to start a new crusade) and *Watchmen* (with Ozymandias's secret potentially to be revealed) are notably open-ended.[26]

The Comic Book's Secret Identity as Comic Book Critic (and Its Respectability within a New Paradigm)

To further identify the self-conscious intentionality of the cultural criticism of these two works, both Miller and Moore enact an analysis of the medium as it relates to other mediums and itself. In *The Dark Knight Returns*, Miller transforms comic book panels into television screens to represent media coverage of events in the series. Identified by McLuhan as a cool medium like comic books (a medium requiring participation), television news, with its talking heads directly facing the reader, doesn't fare too well. Television personalities rapidly transition from stories of horrific violence to stories of uplifting human interest with affect to match each.[27] The civilized notion of equal time opens up the possibility that everyone has a valid opinion; evil is pathologized as the result of mental illness that can be cured, and Batman's notions of law and order are ridiculed.[28] Ultimately, the panel as screen is still a panel, and Miller, therefore, potentially levels similar criticism at comic books (now with no real morally centered heroes and a love of excessive violence). Much of the negativity has to do with the particulars of news coverage on television, but the series still forces the reader to contemplate the way that comic books works like television and participate with culture. Tim Blackmore states, "Miller's unprecedented 16-panel grid works cinematically to produce a dark, claustrophobic world. The use of the confining screen also reveals Miller's view of the TV generation: they can be convinced of anything with ease. The regular, unbreakable grid, is a symbol of how ordered and small the lives of people are" (43). The reference to the comic book medium is much more direct in Watchmen. Moore uses elements that run along with the superhero story that are: parallel (such as Hollis Mason, the first

Nite Owl, killed as an old man), meta-textual (such *Tales of the Black Freighter* comic book reader at a newsstand), and para-textual (such as excepts from the book *Under the Hood* or the newspaper *The New Frontiersman*, included at the end of each issue). In the world of Watchmen where superheroes are part of history, there are no superhero comic books and pirate comic books are the rage. With a youth reading the comic at a newsstand, panels of Watchmen represent the panels of his comic book, and text from the comic book overlaps scenes from the main Watchmen story line. *Tales of the Black Freighter* features a mariner who survives the destruction of his own ship by the Black Freighter and builds a raft of human bodies to travel home and warn his hometown about the Black Freighter. When he arrives home, he kills three people, including his wife, who he mistakenly identifies as the crew of the Black Freighter. At the end, the mysterious ship arrives to claim the mariner. While the story resonates with certain other stories in Watchmen, the most salient features are the traditional newsstand context for comic book reading and porous membrane between the "reality" of the Watchmen world and the content of period horror comic books. The sense of comic books in each is potentially dark but also speaks to the power of a medium that encourages participation and a postmodern sense of constructed reality in line with new traditionality.[29]

Although both *The Dark Knight Returns* and *Watchmen* are regularly credited with bringing realism to superhero comic books, *realism* is a slippery term, referring to artistic conventions that create a reality effect. Certainly, these stories lack most of the fantasy-driven plot situations of the Comics Code era (such as Catwoman threatening Robin's life so that Batman will marry her). However, as already mentioned, both creators work with existing characters and explore a thematic landscape created by the conventional superhero story. In each case, the illustration recalls more abstract (or as Scott McCloud would identify it, iconographic) art typically identified with the traditional work of illustrators such as Joe Shuster and Jack Kirby. While the color palate is more sophisticated, with both the use of secondary colors and monochromatic blends,[30] images are drawn to straddle a fence between a real world context and the abstraction (like traditional art does). Through his tenure on *Daredevil*, Miller seemed to be part of an industry-wide march toward greater realism initiated by Neal Adams and John Byrne and later continued by Arthur Adams and Jim Lee. However, with *Ronin* and then especially with *The Dark Knight Returns*, Miller incorporates the influences of Moebius and certain manga artists (Groth and Fiore 59) known for their more abstract and symbolic styles. Batman and Superman are block-like, often accentuating their size and creating striking shadow effects, and other characters like the president are near caricatures; as inker, Klaus Janson accentuates the rough edges of Miller's pencils with jagged edges to lines and in some cases, lines on figures are barely closed. Dave Gibbons's style is abstract as well, in a way that even better recalls the iconographic line drawings of superhero comic book pasts. While he develops exhaustively mapped cityscapes and heavily detailed backgrounds, his figures are rendered simply and iconographically in the tradition of Curt Swan's illustration. While complex shadow-effects are sometimes used, all characters, especially in costume, resemble Silver Age superheroes in their design from coloring to costume. Details are important as indicated by covers of the individual issues, close-up renderings of images contained at the beginning of the issues.[31] The page layout of *The Dark Knight* has already been mentioned, but *Watchmen* calls attention to its own construction with the "Fearful Symmetry" chapter, symmetrical in a methodical way (that recalls the construction similarities between oral poetry and comic book page layout). A more symbolic sense of the superhero world is developed with each superhero serving as a visual allusion to other superheroes in the history of superhero comic books. Likewise, it reinforces the circular reading experience by layering certain images with subsequent new meanings. The blood spatter on the Comedian's smiley face pin (a significant combination of symbols right there) recurs many times throughout the text; for instance, the embrace of the newsstand owner and comic books reader (as illuminated by the detonation of Ozymandias's doomsday device) resembles the blood spatter and adds to its meaning. The smiley face itself is replicated with varying degrees of specificity, from the doomsday clock to the Galle crater on Mars to the smiley face on the sweatshirt of the assistant at *The New Frontiersman*. (The assistant drops ketchup on his sweatshirt in the exact same spatter configuration as on the Comedian's pin.) For Moore (even more than Miller), superhero comic books are something other than other mediums that enable the creation and interplay of meaning in a way that extends beyond the literate world to encompass new traditionality.

In my estimation, Richard Reynolds description of *Watchmen* as a work that "transcends the accumulated myths through which superhero texts are read" (117) doesn't work completely. As noted, these two works seem to follow the pattern established in the early work of Miller and Moore and radically revise the superhero. However, as indicated by Moore in his estimation of *The Dark Knight Returns*, there is a double-play at work: "Everything *is exactly the same*, except for the fact that it's all totally different" (italics are mine to balance Moore's end of sentence emphasis, qtd. In Pearson vii). Like superhero comic book creators before them, their work is much more evolutionary than revolutionary. In addition to building on the variation ethic firmly established within the industry (see chapter 6), they make more formal the narrative analysis of conventions particular to the medium and new traditionality. While the resolutions of these series do not make definitive claims about the place of tribalism or bricolage in the Modern Age, they advance the sophistication of their craft and the self-conscious approach to the medium for an adult audience. As comic book historian Roger Sabin notes, "The effect of *Dark Knight* and *Watchmen* was ... not to revolutionize comics, as has often been supposed, but to introduce a new readership to these 'graphic novelistic' possibilities" (165). In addition to the newly developed direct market for these series mentioned at the beginning of the chapter, the expensive issues in each series, printed on high-quality paper, were soon after bound and marketed as graphic novels; as Sabin points out, the industry solicited reviews from mainstream critics and created advertising campaigns that extended beyond the direct market (165). As far as DC was concerned, the ultimate end for these works was general respectability, and the elusive marker of mainstream popularity and high culture: the bookstore. Certainly, the industry itself was impressed with *The Dark Knight Returns* and *Watchmen* winning multiple Eisner, Kirby, Eagle, and Harvey Awards but this was extended in several notable ways. Together with Art Speigelman's *Maus*, these two works led to the major articles in *The Atlantic Monthly*, *Time*, and *Newsweek* previously mentioned in this chapter (and arguably, eventually led to the continuing coverage of graphic novels in *The Atlantic Monthly*, *Rolling Stone*, and *Entertainment Weekly*). *The Dark Knight Returns* and Miller's subsequent *Batman: Year One* became the new standard by which all Batman projects were judged not only for comic books but also for tentpole film projects (consider both Burton's and Nolan's Batman films as well as other similarly themed superhero films).[32] A special category was created so that *Watchmen* might receive the Hugo award (for science fiction literature). More significantly in terms of mainstream recognition, *The Dark Knight Returns* was identified by *Time* as one of the ten best graphic novels of all time, and *Watchmen* one of the one hundred best novels (not graphic novels) since 1923. Since so much of its traditional elements came from its position on the margin of cultural respectability, this seems to suggest the end of superhero comic books' connection to the traditional.

While it does do this in some ways, it is important to remember we have been working with self-conscious traditionality (or new traditionality) that technically does not require a marginal status to be traditional. However, there are several factors that cause superhero comics to remain central to at least the American experience of graphic novels and yet still outside the high culture of literacy. As previously mentioned, the direct market was a boon to DC and Marvel, struggling to maintain their hold in their long-standing markets such as newsstands and drug stores. They found success with releases intended as comic book store exclusives such as Marvel's *Dazzler* #1. Eventually, this would lead to paradigm-shifting market experiments like *The Dark Knight Returns* and *Watchmen*. However, the direct market also had the potential to limit rather than expand the adult readership: "if the Direct Market can be said to have rescued the comic book from almost certain death, there are those who would say that the comics-shop distribution network ultimately isolated comics and their readers from the rest of the world" (Dean 49). With print technology much more accessible, black and white publications grew in number at the comic book stores, especially after the unexpected monetary success of the superhero/ninja Eastman and Laird's parody *Teenage Mutant Ninja Turtles*. This created a string of variations that were artistically protected as parodies but really were just variations on the same story: *Adolescent Radioactive Black Belt Hamsters*, *Pre-Teen Dirty-Gene Kung-Fu Kangaroos*, and so on. As Gary Groth mentions, the creators' rights movement may have intended to recognize creators and encourage creativity, but it reinforced many of the business practices of the traditional comic book industry:

> Eastman and Laird fulfilled the failed promise of Siegel and Shuster, resulting in a whole generation of "independent" creators with more righteousness than talent.... This sense of entitlement was further exacerbated in 1988 when the Creator Bill of Rights (authored by Scott McCloud, et al.) debuted.... Careerist motivations took precedence over the love of art in the alternative realism, so in 1987 you had the twin disasters of a declining market for alternative comics — due to the B&W bust — and a proliferation of untalented entrepreneurial artistes enter into the market in droves [61].

Although they now identified themselves as artists, the creators that came to the fore in the direct market boom of the 1980s were thinking more like publishers (as they were workers who wanted to be rich). As Dick Deppey describes, this means responding to what is currently popular and producing more of the same: teenage, mutant, ninja superheroes (69).

Since no one was certain what black and white title might be the next big thing, comic book stores bought excessive amounts of new titles, as did comic book collectors. Of course, a collector's market is a financial situation that works against principles of traditionality (where the first hand encounter is with the story rather than with issues), with variant foil covers immediately put into plastic slipcases to protect the quality of the collectible.[33] However, as suggested by the Groth quotation, the black and white publishers (and several other independent publishers) would ultimately fail as comic book stores and comic book collectors soon realized that they didn't have enough money to buy everything. Since the rapid growth of these overcommitted publishers could not be sustained, they went bankrupt (often with their superhero line-ups purchased by other companies). The failure of these publishers (and the unintended success of an older corporate design to the industry) didn't stop others in the 1990s from declaring their independence from Marvel. Although benefits were now much better than in the day of Stan Lee and Jack Kirby, Marvel still didn't allow full creative control or ownership of creations. A group of Marvels' top creators, including Jim Lee and Todd McFarlane, left to form their own comic groups: Wildstorm and Image, respectively.[34] Both comic groups enjoyed initial success (with Frank Miller and Alan Moore writing for both) but produced largely derivative superhero material. McFarlane would eventually run Image much like the big two, denying creators creative ownership that he had previously promised. Both new groups had financial hard times, and Wildstorm was eventually sold to DC. Ultimately, the problem was a reliance on the old style of comic book delivery: in monthly, pamphlet-style books to sellers who relied largely in monthly sales. The new level of artistic realism was impossible to produce in that time frame, and executives were former creators inexperienced at managing; comic book consumers hoping to buy monthly were frustrated with late deliveries of their titles. DC and Marvel still worked through the severely limited direct market of the 1990s but recognized that the new important destination for their superhero stories was as collected volumes in the bookstores and as always, licensed properties for other media. While many of the elements that would seem to lead superhero comic books away from traditionalism collapse upon themselves, there were many factors in play. Nevertheless, conditioned by the culture, superhero comic book creators tend to replicate the same stories and practices in situations that might seem likely to free them from those conventions. While the introduction of the comic book as graphic novel gives the medium a literate-culture level of respectability, we need to recognize that the audience that now seeks them out in Barnes and Noble has changed. As will be discussed in chapter 8, the ideas of digital culture first began to filter into the mainstream in the 1980s, and, as Foley suggests, the modes of thinking in traditional and digital cultures are remarkably similar. The growth of the direct market and bookstore market for superhero comic books coincided with the growth of: personal computing (DOS in 1981, the Macintosh in 1984, Windows in 1985, and tablet computing in 1993); the internet and related applications (Yahoo in 1994, Google in 1996, Wikipedia in 2001, and Facebook in 2005); and video gaming (*Zork* in 1980, *Pole Position* in 1983, *Doom* and *Myst* in 1993, and *Grand Theft Auto* in 1997). While the particular significances of some of these events will be discussed in the next chapter, here it is sufficient to state that graphic novels did not necessarily become more literate but that mainstream culture became more new traditional. The direct market wasn't something that "isolated comics and their readers from the rest of the world," because the world became more like comic book readers and would approve of the aesthetics of superhero comic books more than ever.

To conclude this chapter, I will briefly mention the subsequent trajectories of Miller's and Moore's careers in order to comment on how their examinations of traditional culture has continued to influence their work; in short, each has stressed different aspects of traditionality in their work. Both Miller and Moore developed a contentious relationship with DC; Miller primarily over DC's then new rating system, and Moore over the rating system and the use of the properties he created for DC. Both left the publisher to work elsewhere; Miller with Dark Horse, and Moore with his own publishing house. In the interview collection *The New Comics*, Groth and Fiore were quick to suggest that both creators had intentions to move beyond superheroes but this seems to expose Groth's bias against superheroes more than actual facts. While Miller developed a hyper-violent, "comic noir" style with his well-known *Sin City* series and Moore developed several alternative projects, such as the erotica *Lost Girls*, both found themselves again working with superheroes in the 1990s, thanks to Marvel, Image, and Wildstorm. Miller worked with characters who made him

In the world depicted in *Top 10*, a typical street scene looks like a comic book convention (from *Top 10* #1, p. 2).

famous at Marvel, with *Elektra Lives Again* and *Daredevil: Man without Fear*, both of which accentuated the crime story aspect of his writing, with the superhero mostly in street clothes. Together with guest work on Todd McFarlane's *Spawn* and his own *Sin City* collections, Miller developed a notable attachment to the tribal "savage" out of place in overgrown civilization. This sentiment reached a height in 1998 with *300* (the tragic and noble battle of Spartans unsupported by Athenian democracy) and in 2001 with *The Dark Knight Strikes Again* (a story of Batman's defeat of a corrupt U.S. government and a parody of what the comic book industry did with ideas from *The Dark Knight Returns*). More self-referential and obviously militant, Miller's work has become less palatable to his fans as have his post–9/11 sentiments against Arab nations (in an National Public Radio interview comparing U.S. citizens whiny about the war on terror to whiny Athenians).[35] In many ways, Miller seems to be less self-conscious about the type of analysis that he enacted in *The Dark Knight Returns* and more emotionally invested in works that extol the group to which he feels he belongs.[36] Moore worked with "new" superhero characters who were really variations on old DC and Marvel characters at Image and Wildstorm, like Jim Lee's *WildC.A.T.S*. Realizing that the market had changed drastically since his departure, Moore decided to write more specifically for a teen audience and to evoke the wonder of superheroic myth (Khoury 174). When he took over Rob Lilifield's *Supreme*, he made the Superman-like character more obviously Superman-like, with variations on Supergirl, Superdog, and Kryptonite and without a sense of *Watchmen*-like tragic realism. Under the Wildstorm umbrella, Jim Lee created an imprint for Moore called America's Best Comics, in 1999, and Moore's titles therein were *Tom Strong, Promethea, The League of Extraordinary Gentlemen*, and *Top 10* (among others). With Tom Strong as a variation on Doc Savage and Promethea as a variation on Wonder Woman in ways not so darkly revisionist,[37] *The League of Extraordinary Gentlemen* and especially, *Top 10* explore variation as a topic that seems to be interesting in itself to Moore. The League is a band of heroes drawn from Victorian fiction (such as Allan Quatermain, Captain Nemo, and Dr. Jekyll), a fictional predecessor of superhero teams that examines the possibilities of creating porous membranes between fictional universes. *Top 10* follows the exploits of a police squad on an all superhero planet where every aspect of the world is related to the collective history of superheroes in our world (from the new album, *Boy Wondering*, by the band Sidekix to a conditioner that promises to hold your hair like Wolverine's). There are more specific inside jokes but the point isn't the jokes so much as it is this world where everything and everyone is related by superhero mythos. While Miller became more aggressive to outsider political enemies, Moore expanded his notion of what should be inside with his ever-widening embrace of variation.

While Miller read *Watchmen* as a much more determined rejection of superheroes than *The Dark Knight Returns*, Moore submitted a proposal to DC called "Twilight of the Superheroes" in the year immediately following the publication of *Watchmen*. Although it had a dark tone comparable to *Watchmen*, a set goal of the series was to restore the multiple earth concept eliminated by *Crisis on Infinite Earths*. The possibilities of multiple earths excited Moore even then, and *Watchmen* could no more be said to the end of superhero comic books than T.S. Eliot's *The Waste Land* is the end of poetry; instead, it simply lays the content and medium-driven conventions more clearly open and thereby, invites further and more varied thought. *The Dark Knight* and *Watchmen* are important tipping points in superhero comic book history that necessarily coincide with the emergence of certain art and technology that form the foundation of digital culture; they firmly establish the self-consciousness of new traditionality as a mode in which superhero comic books might be written and by which they might be analyzed. As chapter 8 will demonstrate, this dawning digital age justifies the new traditional aesthetic and the postmodern sensibility of works such as *The Dark Knight Returns* and *Watchmen*, making them the germinal classics of the Modern Age.[38]

CHAPTER 8

Eternal, Self-Conscious Recurrence (or More Revision)

The Aesthetes of New Traditionality

With the widespread presence of personal computing in the 1980s, the internet in the 1990s, social networking in the 2000s, and video gaming throughout these three decades, the mental habits that accompany the digital age have become a "natural" part of postindustrial culture in the western world. Those mental habits bring to the fore the intimately related mental habits of new traditionalism, theories of postmodernism, and conventions of new media (especially seen in superhero comic books). I use the term *natural* very intentionally because the ideas associated with digital culture are in the process of quickly becoming the new norm. Walter Ong states, "some are inclined to blame our present woes on technology. Yet there are paradoxes here. Technology is artificial, but for a human being there is nothing more natural than to be artificial" (*Faith* 7). Neil Postman would be well known for his pessimistic critique of new media and digital culture; however, such a critique can fall into the trap of failing to see how technology grows out of related cultural fields indicative of human experience. Ong uses the words *artificial* and *natural* with his tongue-in-cheek (as they are not the antonyms most people assume them to be). Following Ong's long-standing recommendation that we do not want to favor one mode of thought over another, we don't want to become infatuated by the promise of new media and digital culture.[1] Therefore, the technological future is not qualitatively better than the past (and the connections I will draw between digital culture and the past before literacy will reinforce this claim). In this chapter, I will argue that the new traditional mindset is reflected in the digital age and will look at how this increasingly dominant paradigm is represented through the following Modern Age superhero comic books (among many others): Geoff Johns's *Green Lantern: Rebirth* (representing the mechanisms of the Modern Age retcon) and Brian Michael Bendis's *Alias*, with Warren Ellis's *Planetary* (representing the self-conscious expansion of the crossover and multiverse motif).

Traditional or Digital? You Say Potato and I Say It's Too Close to Call

As mentioned in chapter 7, in the 1990s, most mainstream superhero comics increased the levels of sex and violence in order to approximate (in rather simplistic ways) what was done in *The Dark Knight Returns* and *Watchmen*. This "grim and gritty" period (represented by titles such as *Spawn* and *Witchblade*) was subsequently followed by a nostalgic period in the 2000s that harkened to the Golden Age, with less nihilistic but more complex stories (represented by *Tom Strong* and *Astro City*). The most interesting aspect of these two decades is that creators have done more than fall into the old habits of multiverse motif (as might be expected with the shrinking of the market after the collector's market bust). Instead, creators have self-consciously chosen and expanded those habits. As described in chapters 2 and 3, the superhero was a multi-media enterprise from its inception, and superhero hero origins were updated roughly every decade to ensure that the superheroes would continue to remain relevant, but never to the degree now seen. The retcon (retroactive configuration of meaning) is a rewriting of superhero origins that has the intended ripple effect of changing everything that went before. For instance, in a Modern Age retelling of Captain America's origin, Captain America would be woken from his state of suspended animation in ice in the 1990s rather than the 1960s; consequently, the Captain America and Falcon stories that originally took place in the 1970s now took place in a few years of the 1990s.[2] However, the market-driven imperative of synergy between different media representations of the superheroes (that never worked seamlessly from the start) has been almost completely and intentionally forsaken.

With Superman as an example (again alive and vibrant in the Modern Age), variations of Superman exist with other creators with other comic book publishers: Wildstorm's *Supreme* (Superman as genetic experiment), Wildstorm's Apollo in *The Authority* (Superman as gay man), and King Hell's *Maximortal* (Superman as a secret in a world also inhabited by Jerry Siegel and Joe Shuster) (among others). As copyright decisions have become less likely to favor conglomerates, this type of variation might not be surprising. However, the new format for comic books (series collected as graphic novels in book stores) means that different versions of Superman from different time periods exist side-by-side on the bookshelf. DC had encouraged variations of Superman's story with the Elseworlds imprint: *Son of Superman* (Superman in the next generation), *Superman: Red Son* (Superman in Russia), and *Superman: Secret Identity* (Superman in a world without other superheroes) (among others). Most notable is the number of rewritings of the Superman origin story in little over a decade in what has almost always resulted in some changes to the Superman canon (a retcon): *Superman for All Seasons* (1998), *Superman: Birthright* (2003–2004), *Superman: Secret Origin* (2009–2010), and *Superman: Earth One* (2010). Again, some critics attached to the literate culture would suggest that this replication is the result of a fundamental lack of ideas among comic book creators allowed to rework material for an unsophisticated (and increasingly insular) comic book reading audience. Yet, this trend can also be noted in other media from the same time period that feature Superman: (1) animated series such as *Superman: The Animated Series* (1996–2000, depicting Superman as classic and modern) and *Justice League* (2001–2006, featuring a darker Superman); (2) television series such as *Smallville* (2001–2011, rewriting Superman's origin and never showing him in costume);[3] (3) films such as *Superman Returns* (2006, featuring another actor and another origin for Superman) and plans for *Justice League* (2007 and 2011, possible working with another actor and another superhero-filled universe for Superman); (4) and video games such as *Superman: Shadow of Apokalips* (2002), *Superman: Man of Steel* (2002), *Superman Returns* (2006), *Justice League Heroes* (2006), and more (running the gamut of Superman variations). Like the discussion that kicked off this book in chapter 1, this list demonstrates that the variation to superhero stories has also become a regular feature of superhero stories outside the world of superhero comic books (although it is still more pronounced in comic books). Rather than the accumulative variation of traditionality over time noted in chapter 3, we can see a radically increased number of variations that are presented simultaneously, the result of self-conscious choices made within new traditional culture. The superhero comic book universe is still dominated by DC and Marvel, and those two publishers are part of other media conglomerates that would correct their aesthetic approach if it didn't work for the public at large—but no correction is needed.[4] The retcon is not the exception to the regular flow of superhero stories but rather the new norm.[5]

As the sales have decreased for monthly issues and the profit margin has increased for superheroes in other media (particular as tentpole films in the summer blockbuster season), the big two are still committed to serial publication of the pamphlet-style books. Comic books are a testing ground for ideas that might or might not make it to other media and thus, superhero comic books have maintained their identity as a sort of ephemeral space; the intentional variation within monthly (and other occasional) publications makes superhero comic books and graphic novels decidedly new traditional. With this general understanding of superhero comic books and the loss of the canonical in play, superhero comic books have become far more obviously at odds with literate culture. Curiously, rather than become less attractive to "serious artists," superhero comic books have become more likely to retain creators and draw new talent from other fields. Superstar superhero comic book creators, Mark Millar and Warren Ellis, often develop non-superhero comic books regularly adapted to film and television (*Wanted*, *Kick-Ass*, *Red*, and *Global Frequency*),[6] but they still return to work on superhero comic books. Likewise, Neil Gaiman has found success both in literature and film (*Stardust*, *Coraline*, and *American Gods*) but returns to work on superhero comic books both inside and outside mainstream superhero universes. Creators who have found their start in other mediums have had long and critically acclaimed runs on superhero comic books, including Brad Meltzer and Jodi Picoult (literature), Joss Whedon and J. Michael Straczynski (television), and Kevin Smith (film). (It's worth noting that Joss Whedon and Michael J. Straczynski have had creative careers closely tied to the digital culture; they both have had strong fan followings on the internet, incorporated fanficiton into their shows, and long before Facebook, Straczynski was well known for directly responding to fan postings.) Among other things, the increasing openness afforded by superhero comic books is appealing to writers more connected to new traditional and postmodern aesthetics.

Bearing the standard formerly carried by Lord and Ong, John Miles Foley is largely responsible for shape of oral culture studies in the 21st century. After producing many books that insisted on the unique nature of oral cultures in different places and times, Foley began to more fully examine the connections between traditional and digital modes of thought. In the essay, "The Impossibility of Canon," Foley questioned the position taken by defenders of the western canon, like Harold Bloom; beginning with a connection between the museum and canon, Foley argues that the concept of the canon is produced by literate culture. With his description of a person at work, he shows the dilemma of having a fixed sense of certain texts by creating the "Museum for Verbal Art":

> The curator of antiquities has no doubt had the worst of it so far: with the scholarship mounting daily about the influence of oral tradition on Homer, Hesiod, and other ancient Greek authors, recycling the same tired portraits of eminent literati has become measurably more difficult. Nor has the curator of medievalia rested untroubled as the rediscovery of oral tradition has spread from era to era and item to item. The exhibit on the Anglo-Saxon

Beowulf has demanded refurbishing, as has those on the *Old French Song of Roland*, the medieval Spanish *Poem of the Cid*, and the Old Norse sagas, all of whose identity as uncompromising literary documents once seemed secure ["The Impossibility"15].

According to Foley, museum and canon share similar misconceptions produced by the ideas of work-as-object and the illusion of stasis. Ultimately, the problem with trying to place oral texts within the canon is that it doesn't account for variation; the subsequently unfair treatment of traditional literature as something that it is not is not intended or born of a sinister impulse: "Oral traditions were not so much unwelcome as unshelvable in the library canon" (18). With the library (and canon) as a repository of information, traditional epics found no comfortable conceptual space for themselves in literate culture before the advent of the so-called "information age" (an age characterized not by the museum but by the internet). The internet is unlike the museum in that it is foremost not a repository of information but a series of "pathways that lead to information" (16).

With the user's ability to interact and link, hypertext already resembles a place that puts the audience in a more authentic relationship with the "text" of oral performance. Unlike the problematic "analog" procedure by which scholars have traditionally compared variation in texts, links enable the audience to encounter not only multiple versions of the text almost immediately but potentially also multiple performances (19). With a reference to the *Odyssey* where the Muse is said to teach pathways because she loves the singer's tribe, Foley pursues even further the analogous relationship between the working of traditional culture and digital culture (or more particularly, oral epics and the internet) (20–21).

> [T]he song exists in ... its movement from here to there, partially predictable and partially unpredictable... The song lives outside any single performance — never mind outside the reduced medium of any one recording or transcription — a series of potentials, a network of pathways that offers innumerable options at the same time that it connects with innumerable unspoken assumptions and implicit references.... Oral tradition can no more be canonize than the Internet can be forced between two covers [21].

Returning to the idea of the internet as a new home for the traditional narrative with the internet's ephemeral space (no physical copy of the narrative exists), he further describes the new attitude required for visitor to this Museum of Verbal Art. The attitude must be interactive as the "museum" goers will become involved in the exhibits, fundamentally shaping their own experience; however, their involvement presupposes that the visitor has become familiar with the basic language that allows them to navigate and also allows them to interpret their own experience. He relates the multiform nature of the referentiality in the epithets of traditional epics to the addresses of Internet webpages as both the epithets and addresses open an incredible number of possibilities for the savvy visitor (26–29). Ultimately, these ideas led to Foley's *Pathways Project*, an online resource that does more than provide information on oral tradition and the internet: "the online version of the *Pathways Project* consists of a network of linked nodes that presents the contents of the book [*Oral Tradition and the Internet*] but also adds many connections and opportunities that books just can't support ... your text will differ from the usual text-consuming scenario" (*Pathways*).

Digital culture consists of various technologies that only in part are represented by the internet. Related technologies include: the advancement of the computer interface through the recognition of icons and manipulation of blocks of information with the Macintosh (1984), Windows (1985) and tablet computing (1993 and more common with the Ipad in 2009); the improvement of the navigation of pathways to information with Yahoo (1994), Google (1996), and Wikipedia (2000, also representing widespread favor of consensus over authority); the creation of new communities and specialized "tribes" with Myspace (2003), Facebook (2004), and You Tube (2005, with linked videos created by "nonprofessional" groups)[7]; and gaming that ranges from narrative driven participation to open-world designs with *Zork* (1980), *Doom* and *Myst* (1993), and *Grand Theft Auto* (1997).[8] While several of these technologies expand Foley's focus (which is clearly hypertextual), the general points about the connections between traditional and digital culture remain the same, ranging from the importance of interactivity to prevalence of pathways to information. The additions that we might want to make that accentuate the case would be the turn toward consensus, the creations of new tribes, and the open-ended nature of narrative in the digital age. Foley's claims seem to be in line with Claude Levi-Strauss's description of tribal psychology: "systems of naming and classifying commonly called totemic drives ... are codes suitable for conveying messages that can be transposed into other codes, and for expressing messages received by means of different codes in terms of their own system" (75–76).[9] Marshall McLuhan referred to the new media age as mythic, because he believed that it worked at a basic level to activate "fundamental truths" (Levinson 160). Of course, oral poetry is no more "natural" than hypertext (Bolter 17), and media is always part of a larger cultural backdrop (148). With something like this in mind, Paul Levinson suggests that McLuhan argued against media determinism by suggesting that new media culture was a conscious choice that reactivates traditional thought: "Remedial media demonstrate the reversal of determinism for specific technologies ... rather than labor under the burden of all written words fixed inextricably to paper from the moment of their conception, we invented the word processor" (202).[10] The consequences of the self-conscious choices of new traditionality is a loss of conventional origin and is centered in many different contexts, from business to social structure to media theory (8). As a starting point for *Hypertext 3.0*, George Landow argues "we must abandon conceptual systems founded on center, margin, hierarchy, and linearity and replace them by ones of multilinearity, nodes, linkes, and networks" (1). Without making an obvious reference to traditional culture, Jay David Bolter makes a critique of the Alexandrian library similar to that of Foley and states, "[i]f in print the subjectivity of the author was expressed at the expense of that of the reader, in electronic hypertext two subjectivities, the author's and the reader's, encounter one another on more nearly equal terms" (168).[11] Yet, while the experience may change for each reader, this fragmentation is not disintegration (10–11), and new media's adventurous treatment of the image contributes to this type of reader experience (49).[12]

Moving onto the innovations of the American superhero comic book, the early 21st century finds the superhero comic book working somewhat beyond the business models that made it a traditional artform in the early 20th century. The choices that made and continue to make the superhero comic book traditional are exposed regularly in Modern Age superhero comic books (as described in chapter 7 with *The Dark Knight Returns* and *Watchmen*). With this in mind, I'd love to make an article by Mark Oehlert more relevant to my study than it actually is; in "From Captain American to Wolverine, Cyborgs in Comic Books," Oehlert charts figures throughout the history of superhero comic books that fit the definition of cybernetic organism (and there are many). This works well as a metaphor and demonstrates a basic (if unconscious) awareness of how the superhero stories anticipate the superhero as an icon of the digital age. However, Oehlert doesn't move in this direction, and it is still within the mechanics of revisionism that we most clearly see traditional and new traditional tendencies at work. In order to represent the Modern Age retcon, I'll be examining the retcon of Green Lantern by Geoff Johns (which not only catapulted Green

Lantern to the DC A-list of superheroes but also led to various other revisions of major DC superheroes by Geoff Johns). I mentioned Johns previously in chapter 6 as the creator entrusted with developing a sequel to *Crisis on Infinite Earths*, a sequel that restored multiple earths in the DC universe and broke the fourth wall in a way just as clever as Gardener Fox with "Flash of Two Worlds." Like certain other creators (Marv Wolfman and Grant Morrison at DC and Chris Claremont and Mark Millar at Marvel), his work with one particular title has had a ripple effect on a superhero universe and like these other creators, he has become a major influence on that universe.[13] The case of Green Lantern is particularly interesting as it fits well with some past discussions of new traditionality in this study. Originally launched in the Golden Age, the Green Lantern was the second of several DC superheroes reworked at the dawn of the Silver Age (the first being the Flash, the source of DC's multiple earths trope). The Green Lantern would "die" in *Zero Hour*, the second of DC's continuity-cleaning, crossover miniseries (like the Flash who died in *Crisis on Infinite Earths*, a miniseries unable to completely clean up continuity as intended). The Green Lantern was brought back to life in various ways but it was Geoff Johns who seamlessly connected all parts of his convoluted story (like a good poet of traditionalism) and yet called attention to the convolutions in all their variety (like a giddy practitioner of new traditionality).

To appreciate what Johns does with the Green Lantern mythology, an overview of the character's history is necessary. Alan Scott, an ordinary railway engineer, is the Golden Age Green Lantern who came into the possession of a magic green lantern from which he made a ring with a variety of powers. Charging it every day with the lantern, he became the caped superhero the Green Lantern. Hal Jordan, a fearless test pilot, is the Silver Age Green Lantern who came into the possession of a green lantern-like device that powered a ring capable of creating anything as long as he had sufficient willpower. Given by the dying alien Abin Sur, he became part of an intergalactic police force governed by the Guardians of the Universe. Like Superman's Kryptonite, the Green Lantern had a fantasy-based weakness in that his ring couldn't work against anything yellow due to an "impurity" in the lantern's power source. After the crossover stories with Earth-2 became popular, the Green Lanterns of the Golden and Silver Ages worked together on a semi-regular basis to fight the enemies of truth and goodness. In addition to the Guardians, major figures in the Silver Age Green Lantern series included Sinestro, a rogue Green Lantern who instilled fear to create order, eventually forging a ring powered by yellow light. Like most superheroes, Green Lantern had a love interest, in this case Carol Ferris, the owner of Ferris Aircraft (and sometimes his superpowered rival, Star Sapphire). As the Green Lantern title struggled in popularity in the 1970s, several other characters temporarily wore the ring as the back-ups for Hal Jordan as members of the Green Lantern corps, such as Guy Gardner and John Stewart. Immediately before *Crisis on Infinite Earths*, Jordan resigned his role as the Green Lantern in order to maintain a relationship with Ferris, and he was replaced by John Stewart. After *Crisis on Infinite Earths*, Jordan returned to his role as the Green Lantern but so did the violent and unstable Guy Gardner (chosen again, this time by a break-away faction of the Guardians of the Universe to be a replacement). In line with the literate goals of Wolfman's crossover series, the general mandate for creators was to create darker, more realistic characters. Consequently, in *Emerald Dawn*, Jordan went from being a broadly drawn, fearless do-gooder, like many other epic heroes, to being a self-destructive man, haunted by very specific past tragedies but potentially capable of realizing great acts of heroism.[14] In a few years, as the new Jordan failed to create new interest at the level of Frank Miller's Batman or John Byrne's Superman, another plot led to the destruction of his home city and further darkened Jordan's character. In *Emerald Twilight*, Jordan uses his power ring to re-create Coast City, but, when stopped in his efforts by the Guardians of the Universe, he goes insane. Attacking the Guardians' home planet, he kills Sinestro, destroys the Green Lantern Corps, and absorbs the power of the main battery for the rings, leaving only one Guardian alive. Eventually, this Guardian, Ganthet, would give the last power ring in existence to another earthling, Kyle Rayner, the latest in the long line of Green Lantern superheroes, and the Rayner would restore the Guardians and the Corps to life.

Already the Green Lantern mythology seems quite convoluted, with Jordan "living" in the popular culture of the superhero comic book for over 30 years at this point, subject to a major shift from the Silver Age to the Modern Age. More importantly, his character is also subject to the short-lived attempt to impose the standards of literate culture on superheroes in the Modern Age with DC's *Crisis on Infinite Earths*. As mentioned in chapter 6, the clean up of the DC multiverse became messy again in short order, not only because creators almost immediately began again to incorporate aspects from multiple earths stories of the past. In addition, inconsistencies crept into the new single universe of the DC universe as a superhero would appear in the Justice League series before his official relaunch, and, subsequently, the relaunch developed the character in contrast with many elements of his post–Crisis Justice League appearances. This meant more clean up, and the answer to this problem was another crossover series, *Zero Hour: Crisis in Time* (1994), featuring Jordan as a villain then known as Parallax. Like *Crisis on Infinite Earths*, the premise of the series is a fascinating study of the literate mind at work in a overwhelmingly traditional environment; it begins with a team of superheroes called the Linear Men, devoted to eliminating time paradoxes and preserving the single time line of one DC universe. With a headquarters located in time at the Vanishing Point (the last moment before the end of creation), they not only preserve a sense of linear time drawn from a literate worldview but also a logical world without contradiction, where other possibilities are the evils that must destroyed.[15] Despite uniting all DC superheroes to combat this evil, the series still works within a comic book world of variation with intentionally comic lines like, "Donna Troy ... You're a Darkstar? But is this really you or a Donna from another reality?" or "Is it just my clothing or am I alternating with variants of myself as well?" (Jurgens 58).[16] Most significant are the characters' references back to *Crisis on Infinite Earths*, a series of events meant to be invisible to all but a handful who experienced them. Consequently, its reason for being resides with the existence of variation against which the superheroes are fighting. Parallax's plan is to destroy all of time, from the end to the beginning, and then to remake the universe as better than it was. Of course, the superheroes triumph against this "villain" driven deeper into insanity by his god-like power, but, ironically, the ultimate goal of series is its attempt to erase the evil of discontinuities. In the trade paperback version, K.C. Carlson, the editor of *Zero Hour*, provides an essay to describe the consequences of the series; it promises that Superman and Batman won't change that much but also repeats the mantra: "This is just the beginning!" Carlson further states, "Virtually anything can happen. It's a brand new universe and you're here to celebrate its birth" (Jurgens 158).

In addition to again preferring the most recent version, *Zero Hour* contains many of the contradictions of *Crisis on Infinite Earths* but adds to it that revision and originality are combined as *Zero Hour* revises *Crisis on Infinite Earths* in order to provide an original starting point. The multiverse eventually returns as a central part of the DC mythology, and when it does, these two clean-up stories (supposedly lost to the memories of most characters) become a central part of the multiverse mythology. This is what Geoff Johns inherits as he develops a story that brings back, as the Green Lantern, Hal Jordan (who, incidentally, was killed by Green Arrow in *Zero Hour* and subsequently became the human side of the Spectre, a superheroic spirit of God's vengeance). When it comes to dealing with the problems that other, more literate-minded creators might have with convolutions on convolutions, Johns states:

> When I get on a book, that's the two things I always want to do. I like the option of having all these toys on the shelf to play with in a story, but you have to add new to it.... And new isn't simply plugging in a new character, like a new villain, to throw in a new villain. New is you need to either reinterpret a character and introduce a new take, a new scope on it, something new to it. The most successful runs in comic-book history, you see that. Look at Frank Miller's *Daredevil*. A defining run for that character. Same with Alan Moore's *Swamp Thing*. People came onto books with characters that were established already but they added something brand new. They looked at them through a completely different lens. I think the danger of throwing everything out is you start to split your audience up. I'm all about being inclusive and new [Wilson, *Q10*].

Although his discourse isn't quite as academic as that of Alan Moore, Johns clearly understands where he is in the history of superhero comic books with reference to both Moore and Frank Miller. He also recognizes that their distinctive runs on various series are not new creations; in fact, adding new elements (like a new villain) is a relatively insignificant act in comparison to the new lens by which the original hero is seen. As Foley suggests about pathways, information means very little but seeing that information in unique ways is central to both traditional and digital cultures. Like the artist of traditionalism, Johns demonstrates an intense awareness of audience, and, like the artist of new traditionalism, he acts self-consciously with "toys on the shelf to play with."[17]

Retcon, Rebirth, and the Long and Exciting Afterlife of Superheroes

Also working with the concept of pathways, Johns finds ways to link jettisoned pasts into a whole that still gives the audience divergent paths from which to choose to understand the story in *Green Lantern: Rebirth* (and the subsequent *Green Lantern* series). Kyle Rayner is positioned in a very interesting way within the *Rebirth* series as the most recent Green Lantern, presumably someone who would have to be replaced in order for Jordan to return as the Green Lantern (as Jordan's return was promised by series pre-publicity). Self-consciously playing with expectations, Johns makes Rayner aware of the immanent return of Parallax, supposedly the villain that Jordan had become. Moreover, he plays with series tropes in a way that demonstrates a sense of the referential possibilities of elements that have become cliché. At the beginning, a spaceship crash-lands on earth, piloted by Rayner on the verge of death and trying to give his power ring to a teenager who finds him; he says to the teenager, "Don't be afraid" (Johns, *Green Lantern: Rebirth* 14). This recalls the beginning of Jordan's experience as the Green Lantern with Abin Sur's crash-landing and the search for a fearless new bearer of the ring (which turns out to be a seemingly unworthy earthling). The story begins in the middle of things in a way characteristic of superhero comic book stories but also very much in line with the traditional and digital experiences of art. Based on past tropes established within the Green Lantern story, Rayner would have to die (or at least be significantly incapacitated) in order to necessitate another bearer for

8. Eternal, Self-Conscious Recurrence (or More Revision)　199

The situation, role, and words of Kyle Rayner (a narrator presumed to soon be dead) recalls Hal Jordan and Abin Sur before him (from *Green Lantern: Rebirth*, p. 12).

the ring (opening the door for Jordan's return). Most significant in this string of events is that Rayner serves as the narrative voice, the digital age singer that the audience knows is dead but somehow is still alive. (This death motif is continued as Jordan and Sinestro are reanimated in the course of *Rebirth* and most of the "dead" DC universe is brought back in the later Green Lantern story *Blackest Night*.) Rayner provides some of the explanatory linkages between events, including the explanation that makes the series not just a continuation but a major retelling of the origin of Jordan (and the Green Lanterns in general). Now sharing psychic space with the consciousness of the Spectre, Jordan proves that Rayner was well informed, and an image of himself as Parallax returns, fighting for control of Jordan's consciousness. After Hal Jordan was qualitatively excluded as a member of the Green Lantern corps by his own actions, any valid attempt to restore him would require significant changes for a superhero readership that loves variation but might not accept the restoration of Green Lantern status for a villain of his degree. The answer to this problem comes from Rayner, and his explanation causes the narrative to circle back on itself to provide an explanation for all that has taken place in the Green Lantern mythos (a method that resembles the movement of epic poems and the experience of most internet users). In ancient times, a monster named Parallax, made out of pure fear (represented by the color yellow), terrorized the universe; the Guardians created a central power battery, based on the power of their will, that contained the monster within it, thus explaining the yellow "impurity" of the rings subsequently crafted. Finding a "spiritual" way out through the subsequently created power rings, Parallax infected Jordan and steered him on a course that destroyed the Green Lantern Corps and almost the entire universe. This revisionary move on the part of Johns is motivated by a self-conscious agenda, but it works together with existing mythology in a way that seems organic. This bricolage characteristic of all mythic expansion would resonate with the audience who signaled their support in the form of sales of the subsequently relaunched *Green Lantern* series. In this way, the system is restored with new information patches that explain in a nearly seamless way how the dead come back to life. However, this is not to say that Johns does not subtly call attention to the process by which he generates this new chapter to the old epic of Jordan as the Green Lantern (expanding the mythology and narrative technique to account for divergent readings).

Although he is not aware of connections between superhero comic books and new traditional culture in an academic sense, Johns, like Gardener Fox and Alan Moore, demonstrates an awareness of the complex relationship of the medium to its own conventions. The choice to destroy time made by Jordan as Parallax in *Zero Hour* was quickly glossed over as evil even though he had become a god-like being that intended to rebuild it better than it had been. Informed at least in part by literate culture's devotion to a singular time line, the reason why fans would want to see Jordan return is questioned by his arch-rival, Sinestro (who claims Jordan is either as moral or immoral as he is).[18] In a confrontation between Sinestro and Jordan's former partner, Green Arrow, Sinestro states:

> Had he not interfered in my sector, I would never have crossed over into his. I am called [my home planet's] greatest villain by my own people. That is my place in history. Now on your homeworld, the very memory is spit on by its heroes. He shares my pain. Even you betrayed him with your bow. He has no one left to believe in him. No one to help him [Johns, *Green Lantern: Rebirth* 99].

To which, Green Arrow, now wearing Jordan's old power ring replies, "Yes, he does." At this point in DC history, Johns would be part of the process of reestablishing the multiple earths with the *Infinite Crisis* and *52* series. Sinestro's repositioning of Jordan as evil is interesting because he is evil in *Zero Hour* largely for wanting to create a variation, something clearly no longer as problematic at DC; it's also interesting because this segment features a clever "cheat" to the audience, as Sinestro turns toward Green Arrow who is, relatively, in the reader's position.[19] This is not the only cheat, as Rayner stares at the audience when saying, "Don't be afraid," and Jordan looks at the audience as he witnesses his father's death and the first appearance of Sinestro; in this way, the reader is invited to participate in the ethos and trauma of the Green Lantern (while the cheats do not disrupt the spatial principles established in the story). Regardless, this may be the most significant cheat, as alternating panels draw us closer and closer to Sinestro and Green Arrow until Sinestro becomes only a mouth and Green Arrow only an eye. In many ways, if the return of Jordan as Green Lantern is to work, the reader, internalizing the *spoken* words of Sinestro via the *visual* conventions of comic books, is Green Arrow and must decide how to respond to Sinestro's "He has no one left to believe in him."

It could be argued that our response is wholly prescribed for us in Green Arrow's response to Sinestro but other plot developments suggest otherwise. Since his foremost weapon is fear, Batman is set up as having a grudge against Jordan as a fearless man (and therefore, someone against whom he has no leverage). Nevertheless, still in character as a skeptic, Batman remains sympathetic to the reader, who may have encountered the story of Jordan as Parallax in *Zero Hour*. This comes to the final interaction in the series between Jordan and Batman; darkness hides all of Batman's face except for his eyes, and, like Green Arrow, he becomes the reading eyes of comic book audience, saying, "Do you expect me to believe this? That you were influenced? Possessed? Is that what Parallax was? An outside force that—" and Jordan replies, "I don't expect you to believe anything." Jordan faces the reader in a manner similar to his double Sinestro and likewise serves as the text itself by saying, "And quite honestly, I don't care [what you believe]" (Johns, *Green Lantern: Rebirth* 151). In addition to making new links in the old story through Rayner (a potentially unreliable, certain-to-be-dead character), the skeptical reader is reminded that the unity of the text ultimately resides with the reader; the implied "center" of the text, Hal Jordan as the Green Lantern, could care less what is believed. This story is a "re"-birth, only as important as it is relatively important to other Green Lantern stories. In addition, Jordan may be the main character but he isn't the exclusive center of the text, as Rayner doesn't die and remains a ring-bearing Green Lantern as well. In fact, joining the larger body of the Green Lantern corps are not only Jordan and Rayner but also the other previous earthling Green Lanterns, John Stewart and Guy Gardner.[20] By nodding to all eras and incarnations of the Green Lantern over the decades, Johns creates for the audience an open-ended project of interpretation in which one might choose favorite Green Lanterns as well as favorite stories as touchstones for understanding. There is a reveling in the individual Green Lantern's styles as they band together (an important superheroic cliché) to defeat the newly released Parallax, now in possession of a Guardian. After all the activity of the rings serve well as a metaphor for individual choices as it uses light to create solid constructs of anything the bearer has in mind. Similarly, the green lantern is a physical object used to recharge the rings but also is a symbol worn on the chests of the Green Lantern, a symbol that again become real in later issues as a brand on Sinestro's back or more literally, the shape of the prison that holds him (and so on). The lantern is something that can be anything: representing the world like Achilles's shield, working in Scott McCloud's terms like an icon, and serving as a gateway to a larger activity like a computer icon.[21]

The entirety of the series has a nonlinear structure, beginning in the middle of things (as would be mandated by the notion of a continuing series) but moving back in time at certain points to clarify, explain, and illustrate. While a printed text cannot offer the multimedia, linking possibilities of the internet, it can approximate the same experience that someone would have as user. The nonlinear structure varies in duration and depends upon narrative context: quite notably, it contains a number of false starts that do not uncover false information but indicate that the search is different for different people and perhaps that the search should be refined. For instance, Jordan asks Carol Ferris whether she remembers their first time on the Ferris Aircraft landing strip; she thinks about (and we see) Jordan asking her on a date, and, thereafter, he thinks about (and we see) their childhood viewing of his father's tragic test flight (Johns, *Green Lantern: Rebirth* 43–46). The last few pages of the series are a return to the origin of Jordan as the Green Lantern, ending at the beginning and demonstrating that the beginning has changed because of our paths into Jordan's "future"; the ending provides a slight variation on crash-landing of Abin Sur that accentuates the accumulated mythology of the Green Lantern and the themes of *Rebirth*. The last page features a large panel with Abin Sur turning to Jordan (and the reader) to hold out the power ring and ask, "Do you accept this duty?" (although our straight line of sight to Abin Sur is disrupted by the back of Jordan's head in the foreground). In a column on the right, five panels are stacked, with the first three representing Jordan's face and the last two representing Abin Sur's face: unchanging scenes in each case excepting the word balloons. The first (with Jordan) contains no words, the second "Buddy, if I'm not dreaming—," the third "Absolutely," the fourth (with Abin Sur) "An earthman ... heh ... I never thought I'd live to see the d—," and fifth contains no words (161). In addition to creating variation within the same visual input by providing different words and a different place in the sequence, this is an ironic and anti-heroic conclusion; it has the potential to connect the reader who knows not only the long-standing bias in the Green Lantern Corps against earthlings but also Jordan's future successes and failures as the Green Lantern. And again, with the last panel, the emphasis on death and the dead man speaking once again returns.

Judging from the popularity of *Rebirth*, readers responded to Sinestro's statement like Green Arrow by asserting that they believed in Hal Jordan, self-consciously making a choice to join a tribe of fans. With the Green Lantern series restarted for the fourth time, Jordan's "Secret Origin" was retold in a way that had no alibi such as Jordan asking Carol Ferris whether she remembers this or that. However, it functions like traditional art in that this disruption to linearity is connected to what comes before and what follows. In particular, it makes the "Blackest Night" prophecy a central part of what drove Abin Sur to be outside his sector and in a spaceship that crash-lands on earth. Aside from this current variation and elaboration of the origin story, supplementing and supplanting the old versions (one of which is Johns's own), the story is narrated in parts by handwritten text from Jordan's journal. In this way, we seem to have an author in charge of his own story, but the story itself reveals his consistent attempt to subvert authority. This occurs with Ferris Aircraft, the Guardians, and most significantly with himself, as events (and not text) reveal his fearlessness is an overcompensation for the fear he's felt since he saw his father die in a test flight. The Blackest Night prophecy expands the Green Lantern mythology to include other color lanterns (completing the rainbow's color spectrum, with each one representing a different character trait). Eventually, the discovery of these other lantern communities that the Guardians' had tried to suppress would lead to a great war and the "Blackest Night." In order to explain this prophecy absent from Green Lantern mythos to this point, he uses the Guardians attempt to keep secret the last chapter of the their holy book, the book of Oa (a physical book that greatly resembles a comic book or tablet computer in design, as portrayed in *Green Lantern: The Sinestro Corps War*). Eventually, the worst fears of the Blackest Night are realized, as black power rings resurrect the dead and use them as their evil corps, a story told in many regular series and limited series as a major crossover event.[22] Before the Blackest Night begins, Hal Jordan has a conversation with Barry Allen, the recently resurrected Flash, that reveals the self-conscious sense of a story line that brings the dead back to life in superhero comic books. Since both heroes were brought back from the dead, the Flash argues, "Death isn't necessarily the end. Not In this line of work." After providing a list of characters who have returned from the dead (often the case in superhero comic books that want to tell variations on the same stories), the Green Lantern eventually says, "Everything changed when you disappeared, Barry. The world got more dangerous. Our jobs more deadly." The Flash has the last word on the issue expressing his hope for the return of heroes recently killed like Batman, Aquaman, and the Martian Manhunter (Johns, *Blackest Night* 9–10). While his hope is ironically realized by the resurrection of those heroes in the zombie-like forms of Black Lanterns, their conversation also demonstrates the way Johns walks a line between telling his story and revealing his self-conscious understanding of superhero comic books. As a practitioner of new traditionality, his work comments on resurrection, a trope central to superhero comic books (and also the grim and gritty tradition of superhero violence traced back to 1985, the year Barry Allen died in *Crisis on Infinite Earths*).

One of the most important aspects of the Johns's Green Lantern saga is that it is not self-contained; this claim applies not only to the simultaneous publication of related titles like *Green Lantern* and *Green Lantern Corps* but also to the way Green Lantern exists in a superhero universe. The DC universe (or multiverse, if you will) and the Marvel universe are a series of related superhero stories that often cross over with one another and in the Modern Age, are punctuated by major event crossover series like *Blackest Night*. This sort of interrelated narrative creates individual reader experiences rather than a cohesive narrative, much like linking on the internet or reading as described by postmodern theory. In his article, "Postmodern Narrative, the Marvel Universe, and the Reader," Carl Silvio describes the Marvel universe as postmodern because it was based on individual comic book titles whose stories were constantly subject to one another's influence. Using Patricia Waugh's definition of metafiction, he suggests that the interrelated narratives of the Marvel universe self-consciously call attention to themselves and therefore, intentionally or unintentionally, raise questions about the relationship between fiction and reality and concomitantly questions about authority (39). In an earlier article, "Who Owns Our Myths? Heroism and Copyright in an Age of Mass Culture," Neil Harris expresses anxiety about corporate ownership of superhero stories, our modern day myths; while everyone knows and has access to superhero stories to some degree, corporate control seems to limit the open-ended possibilities offered by traditional mythic stories (266–267). Without referring directly to Harris, Silvio acknowledges this apparent contradiction to the openness he describes but identifies that there are things that the industry thinks that it controls that it doesn't.[23] In addition to encouraging a participatory fan culture with related but varied superhero products from other industries, Marvel Comics cannot control the order or way that related stories are consumed, creating an active and critical consumer; no story is a self-contained and the coherent whole is not subject to the control of just one creator or consumer.

It seems important to me to note that the postmodernity that Silvio describes predates the Marvel universe and has its origins in DC crossovers like the *Justice Society of America* and *World's Finest* team-ups. While the self-conscious questions about the relationship between fiction and reality would be famously posed in stories like that of *Fantastic Four* #10 in 1963 (featuring Stan Lee and Jack Kirby as characters), a more clearly postmodern take on superheroes would appear several years earlier with Gardener Fox's "Flash of Two Worlds" (see chapter 6). By acknowledging the retcons that have now become standard practice in the superhero industry (with the Barry Allen Flash breaking the fourth wall), the story undermines many industry practices designed to encourage consumption and control the popular understanding of its characters. One of the most famous editorial intrusions of the Silver Age would be references back to past issues to clarify events in the most recent issue ("as seen in *Flash* #110"). However, as time passed and further retcons became necessary and more frequent, these references became archaic and irrelevant archeological markers of things that never happened. As the traffic between the Silver Age Flash's Earth-1 and the Golden Age Flash's Earth-2 became more frequent with Justice League and Justice Society team-ups, imaginary pasts seemed to be as real as the canonically approved presents. The exciting possibilities of this fan-approved intertextual process (that the industry could not control but decided to continue) reaches a new height with multiverse-spanning event series like Marvel's *Secret Wars* and DC's *Crisis on Infinite Earths*. This type of open universe crossover model was replicated within subsequently created superhero lines by publishers, such as Eclipse and Wildstorm, and has been conceptually examined by Alan Moore's *League of Extraordinary Gentlemen* (which creates porous boundaries between major adventure stories drawn from about five centuries of British literature). Curiously, this reader-centered intextuality extended across company lines between DC and Marvel thought by many insiders never to be crossed with intercompany team-ups such as *Superman vs. Spider-Man* (1976), *Batman vs. the Incredible Hulk* (1981), and *The Uncanny X-Men and the Teen Titans* (1982). These crossovers exist in the real time and space of comic book worlds (as if a Superman/Spider-Man team-up was always possible) but are also in the no-man's-land of the imaginary story (never to be again referred to as part of standard continuity by either company).

As I argued in chapter 2, the capitalist designs of the industry, which would seem to immediately rule out superhero comic books as traditional art, actually leads to certain pronounced aspects that make it traditional. Likewise, a crossover series is often regarded as the publisher's crass money grab, requiring readers to buy the series plus all the tie-in issues in order to comprehend the story as a whole. This was notable from the start with *Secret Wars* and *Crisis on Infinite Earths*, series that promised big changes in all superhero titles that would be incomprehensible without buying *Secret Wars* and *Crisis on Infinite Earths* and all related titles. However, it required a new way of linking texts, not just by buying issues as they appeared on the stands but by putting pieces together subsequently. In *Secret Wars*, heroes were whisked away by a mysterious force one month, and, in the next month, they returned fundamentally changed; Spider-Man appeared in a new costume and the Thing left the Fantastic Four (among other developments), and the reasons why only became apparent months later as Secret Wars continued its regular monthly publication schedule. The Modern Age crossover series is the standard that led from the retcon as regular but imperceptible occurrence to the retcon as the frequent and self-conscious norm fundamentally shaped by the audience. While every issue fits together chronologically, the type of subsequent linking that works outside the boundaries of chronology is also accentuated by the complicated choices now made by publishers collecting monthly series. Take for instance, *Blackest Night*, *Green Lantern: Blackest Night*, *Green Lantern Corps: Blackest Night*, etc., each collecting parts of a crossover event meant to be read in a specific order as each issue hit the stands but later published as a collected run of each of the titles. As much as publishers would like consumers to buy all related titles, almost all do not and almost all read them in different orders. In short, the crossover in its basic form creates links between series that do not have integrity in their own terms but also cannot force the audience to connect any one series to any other series. With the intercompany crossovers especially, a new space is created by acknowledging the potential linkages between everything but ultimately allowing the reader freedom of how to understand the crossover as "real," "imaginary," or something else (something else being the most likely choice).

As had been suggested in other parts of this study, I hope this reversal of industry intentions offers us another opportunity to rethink the definitions that we have established for traditional cultures (rather than simply say that the early American comic book industry only produced something vaguely like traditional culture). If I agree with Foley that many different types of oral cultures exist, as do oral cultures alongside literate cultures, I think it's justified to also say that traditional cultures might proceed from centralized sources of authority in ways that we do not expect. The superhero comic book industry is the center that does not hold and this non-center has become one of the best representations of new traditionality, digital culture, and postmodernism. Earlier in this chapter, I made reference to several theories of digital culture to support Foley's claim about the connection between the psychology of traditional and digital cultures; I also sought to further and/or modify it by identifying digital culture more discretely as new traditionality. Now, I want to take those theories about digital culture and more clearly, build a bridge to postmodern theories, the two representing integrally related paradigms. In *Digital McLuhan*, Levinson initially worked his way through one of McLuhan's frequent assertions about new media: "The user is the content" (39). This claim was made about television with the idea that the CBS eye looks back at us, but, as Levison explains, the assertion is much more clearly understood in relation to digital culture; it might as well be applied to superhero comic books as a foremost representation of digital age with the retcon and crossover creating a relative sense of history and reality that depends upon the reader. Likewise, in *Writing Space*, Bolter analyzes the reading of hypertext novels, a more specific extension of the conceptual experience of internet links and states, "there is no story at all; there is only readings" (125). Despite intrusive advertising and attempts by the government to restrict content (20), the "reading" experience of comic books and subsequently, the internet remains fundamentally beyond authorial control, and this is celebrated by self-conscious creators who present ideas often labeled "postmodern." This connection between the technology, its philosophical basis, and the general field of postmodern theory is a large part of Landow's *Hypertext 3.0*.

When discussing the type of readership created by the internet and digital culture, Landow uses several examples from outside the digital age, beginning with rewritings of Victorian novels like *Jane Eyre* as revised in *The Wide Sargasso Sea*. As he notes, novels such as *The Wide Sargasso Sea* are curious cases as they are unconventional texts that require very active reading but are distributed by major publishers and taught in college classrooms (7). Landow continues with examples that lead more directly into the art of the digital age such as fanfaction, like that produced and distributed by *Star Trek* fans (before and after the advent of the internet). While Star Trek may be Landow's example, we can easily substitute superhero comic books as the basis for fanfaction. As profiled in chapter 6, fan writers of the early comic book convention scene regularly rose to be the new creators within the superhero industry. The influence of such fan writers has increased exponentially with ready access to computers and internet, as fans produce internet-based fiction, criticism, films, and of course, comic books. Whether it is direct by hiring the fans or indirect by incorporating fan ideas, the boundary between the reader and the writer is slim. The mediums predictive of hypertext function like hypertext in many ways, "blur[ing] the boundaries between reader and writer and therefore instantiates ... [a] quality of Barthes's ideal text" (4); the idea set forth by Barthes in *S/Z* is that "the goal of literary work (of literature as work) is to make the reader no longer a consumer, but a producer of the text" (Barthes, *S/Z* 4). Moving into an era in which such a relationship with a text is more likely, Landow notes that anxiety about postmodernism dates back to Thomas Carlyle's fears about the flood of cheaply printed materials mass produced by machines (Landow 47–48). While Jean Baudrillard made an argument connecting digital technology and postmodernism, he drew his examples of the digital from analog technology (44); his examples are not so retrospective as to include comic books, but the point still holds that digital culture predates digital technology per se. Although still technically analog, comic books would eventually contribute to that flood identified by Carlyle and lead to the postmodern shape of new traditionality more definitively than almost any other analog artform. Before more fully dealing with the connections that Landow draws between digital culture and postmodern theory, the technology that enables our movement through the visual interface of the computer internet must be mentioned. At the beginning of his monograph, Landow profiles various types of linking that involved various combinations of moving from and to lexias and strings combined with unidirectional and bidirectional movements; eventually, he profiles the one-to-many movement that he believes to be the ultimate realization of the hypertextual model. This compares roughly with Scott McCloud's description of various types of transitions between panels in a comic book with the space between panels (the gutter) as interpretative space (*Understanding* 74). These sorts of links are predetermined for the reader but often open to interpretation in interesting ways (86) that McCloud sees as the ultimate end of comic books in the digital age (*Reinventing* 226–229).

Even though Landow's express focus has often been with hypertext as the connection between digital theories and postmodern theories, it would be wrong to give him exclusive credit for the connection between these theories. Bolter examined similar issues in *Writing Space* and described the experimental style of Jacques Derrida's writing (which reorganizes typographical space) as well as his content as nonlinear and digital. In another point that helps me build another bridge from Foley's work to postmodernism, Bolter summarized part of *Of Grammatology* in this way: "Nonlinear writing had been suppressed, although never eradicated, by linear writing. Nonlinear writing resurfaced in the writing of the 20th century, when it seemed that the modern experience could not be recorded in a liner way" (Bolter 109). In order to make the transition from the readerly text in literature to the readerly text in digital media, Landow begins his book in this way: "When designers of computer software examine the pages of *Glas* or *Of Grammatology*, they encounter a digitized, hypertextual Derrida.... Statements by theorists concerned with literature, like those theorists concerned with computing, show a remarkable convergence" (1).[24] From this point, he shows how digital technology works to give the reader control over the text and to demonstrate the loss of author(ity) over the text and he links this to the emerging trend in postmodern theory, indicating just such a change "in the writing of the 20th century." In addition to moving toward the death of the author described by Michel Foucault and Roland Barthes, he includes Claude Levi-Strauss as part of this emergence:

> [Claude Levi Strauss's] mythological works demonstrated for a generation of critics that works of powerful imagination take form without an author.... Levi-Stauss's presentation of mythological thought as a complex system of transformations without a center turns it

into a networked text — not surprising since the network serves as one of the main paradigms of synchronous structure [128–129].

Levi-Strauss's sense of mythology would be synchronic as the thing all around and ever present rather than as the thing that develops through the linear progression of history. As the source of 20th-century studies of the "savage" mind, Levi-Strauss is one last important link in the bridge built from undomesticated to postmodern or in terms more particular to this study, from oral to digital, from traditional to new traditional. Landow points out Foucault's suggestion that changes have occurred that make it more difficult to retain literary notions of the author because "the unboundedness of the new textuality disperses the author" (128).[25] Likewise, Landow shows Barthes has a digital age interest in exploring the new absence of authority in the following way: "Hypertext and contemporary theory ... both agree in configuring the author of a text as text. As Barthes explains in his famous exposition of the idea, 'this "I" which approaches the text is already itself a plurality of other texts, of codes which are infinite'" (126).

In "The Writer's Audience is Always a Fiction," Walter Ong would again clarify a difference between oral and literate cultures, arguing that the writer works differently from the speaker who deals more directly with an audience; the writer always constructs an imaginary audience, and the reader adjusts him or herself to the expectations set for that imaginary audience. Both Foucault and Barthes would describe the writer, or more generally the author, as something else in the contemporary era beyond the strict confines of the literate era. When describing the "author-function" in "What Is an Author?," Foucault shows how unimportant the author is as principle of unity that is supposed to bind together a text, a group of texts, or the ideas associated with a group of texts: "there was a time when these texts which we now call 'literary' (stories, folk tales, epics, and tragedies) were accepted, circulated, and valorized without any question of the validity of the author." (125). Likewise, in his argument against the vanity of textual criticism in "The Death of the Author," Barthes states: "in ethnographic societies the responsibility for a narrative is never assumed by a person but a mediator, shaman, or relater whose 'performance'— the mastery of a narrative code — may possibly be admired but never his 'genius'" ("The Death" 142). Foucault demonstrates how the author cannot be considered a unified subject any more than author might be a unifying principle, since criticism re-creates the author separate from the real existence of the human being known by the author's name ("What" 129). The writer's text works in a very particular way, "primarily concerned with creating an opening where the writing subject endlessly disappears" (116). Also focusing on recent writers (both Foucault and Barthes identify Stéphane Mallarmé), Barthes argues "that writing is the destruction ... of every point of origin" ("The Death" 142) and the frustration of certain meaning (144). In this estimation of writing as it now exists, writing is no longer "recording" but "a performative, a rare verbal form ... the *I sing* of very ancient poets" (145–146); as a consequence, the author is in fact a text composed of many sources, and the unity can only be provided by the reader: "a text is made of multiple writings, drawn from many cultures and entering into mutual relations of dialogue, parody, contestation, but there is one place where this multiplicity is focused and that place is the reader, not as hitherto said, the author" (148). With a very similar sense of the author in mind, Foucault ends his essay with questions of the old sense of the author as compared with the new. The old include, "Who is the real author?" and "Have we proof of his authenticity and originality?," and the new include, "Where does it come from; how is it circulated; who controls it?" and "Who can fulfill these diverse functions of the subject?" ("What" 138). These "new" questions have served as the basis of my study and will be seen as part of the open-ended works I will profile in the remainder of this chapter.

Postmodernism and the Post-Superhero Superhero Comic Book: The Reader and the Archeology of Thought

Geoff Johns serves as a good starting point as a creator who is aware of his playful connection to the mythology of superheroes but chooses not to fully expose the workings of his text; in this way, Johns subtly develops a new sense of the readership in the digital era but also maintains a somewhat organic feel of more traditional superhero comic books. However, other superhero comic book creators choose to more obviously expose the workings of the text and subvert its authority. The key components are the way their works decenter authority, removing the author from the author's traditional place and elevating the reader as the maker of the text.[26] Significantly, these comic books also accentuate how the reader's task of providing unity to the text is nearly impossible. This type of comic book has increased in prominence in recent years, and my starting point for this examination is with superhero comic books that take the action and even presence of superheroes away from the center. When the collector's bubble burst in the 1990s, sales of one particular title remained relatively untouched: Neil Gaiman's *Sandman*, a title published under Vertigo, DC's line of comics for adult readers. Although Gaiman's god-like protagonist exists in the DC universe (meeting the Swamp Thing, the original Sandman, and Batman among others), the new Sandman (or Morpheus) lives outside the action that drives conventional superhero plots. In fact, most of the stories about Morpheus take place in dreams, the realm that he governs as one of the seven god-like beings called the Endless.[27] As a consequence, plots were often developed in unconventional fashions, working outside the logic associated with the realism of 19th-century novels in the industrial world. Perhaps more significant would be Gaiman bringing Dave McKean to mainstream comics as cover artist for *Sandman*; in addition to working in his usual surreal style with multimedia collages, McKean argued that Morpheus not be featured on every cover (as sometimes he was only a minor part of the stories therein). Although at times seemingly unrelated to superhero comic books, *Sandman*, first published in 1989, was at the forefront of a new trend that made superheroes relatively minor components of superhero comic books.[28] Although the decentering of superheroes in this way is often traced back to *Watchmen*, Moore's story still focused on superheroes, despite making them fairly unlikable (and ordinary humans a relief from their presence).[29] The most definitive starting point for the trend would be in 1994 with Kurt Busiek and Alex Ross's *Marvels*, a comic book series that examines the history of the Marvel universe from the perspective of an ordinary reporter. Busiek used Phil Sheldon, a reporter, as a device to revisit the supposedly canonical history of the Marvel universe but to subvert its conventional meaning. Initially a supporter of superheroes, popularizing them with a coffee-table book he writes, Sheldon pulls away from them after the death of Spider-Man's Gwen Stacy. Ironically, even with the power he has as a "reader" to make sense of superheroes, Sheldon turns away from them and toward humanity, ending his career with a photograph of the newspaper boy. He assumes the boy to be a nice, ordinary boy, but his name indicates to the comic book reader that he will grow up to be Ghost Rider, another Marvel superhero; even though a reader might provide unity to a text, there are still details that the reader cannot conveniently reconcile. Ross's painting is an interesting factor in this project, as his Norman Rockwell-like realism evokes nostalgia but also increases the irony as the narrative stops short of the type of comfortable meaning that Rockwell's paintings always provided.

In the next year, Kurt Busiek would follow up *Marvels* with the Image title, *Astro City*, a series doing something similar with a wholly original superhero universe, also focusing more on the alter egos of superheroes. In this vein, even more significant would by the work of Brian Michael Bendis, with *Powers* (also published by Image in 2000) and *Alias* (set in the Marvel universe in 2001). Bendis would begin his career as a crime comics writer with titles like *Jinx* and *Goldfish* and would be brought into the fold at Image by Todd McFarlane (who had founded Image comics largely with a grim and gritty synthesis of superhero and crime comics). Shortly thereafter, Bendis would be recruited by Marvel and would simultaneously write *Powers* (an original creator-owned title), *Daredevil* (a Marvel Knights title, darker in tone but in the mainstream Marvel universe), *Alias* (a MAX title in a slightly alternate R-rated Marvel universe), and *Ultimate Spider-Man* (a Marvel Ultimate title set in the Marvel Ultimate universe); he would eventually write *The Avengers* (the most significant superteam in the Marvel universe) and serve as the architect for many supposedly paradigm-shifting crossover events (like *House of M*, *Secret War*, *Dark Reign*, etc.). While this overview demonstrates that Bendis has little directly invested in a canonical version of the Marvel universe, it also demonstrates his sense of how Marvel titles change and interact in relationship to one another. *Powers* and *Alias* decenter the superhero by foregrounding the strange synthesis of crime and superhero stories, focusing on more conventional crime story motifs that just happen to be situated in a superheroic world. *Powers* is the story of a police unit devoted to investigating superhero-related crimes, and *Alias* is the story of a private investigator, who is a former superhero and honorary member of the Avengers. Since *Alias* takes place in a Marvel universe, the decentering that takes place is more obvious, and the liberties Bendis takes are more significant, as the "properties" with which he works are not owned by him.

Jessica Jones is the alias of the title, no longer with a superhero identity but making a living as a private investigator with seedy cases worthy of film noir. While Jones did not exist in the Marvel universe before Bendis created her, his story begins with her already retired, with a past that necessarily rewrites Marvel mythology (as she has interacted with the Avengers and other Marvel A-list heroes before the start of the series). In general, the tone is one of irreverent commentary, as Jones has rejected the calling of anyone with superpowers (putting on a costume to fight crime). In the first panel of a scene that depicts her lunch with Carol Danvers (Ms. Marvel), Jones states, "So, I said to him, I said: well, if that's true, shouldn't you shoot the webs out of your ass?" (Bendis, *Alias* 110). With a joke clearly made at the expense of Spider-Man, Jones continues her conversation with Danvers, both critiquing his costume and eventually, their own (with their own as products of a flashy 1980s fashion sensibility). Of course, Ms. Marvel's costume has a "real" history in Marvel comic books, and Jones costume (as the superhero called Jewel) was invented specifically for the *Alias* series. In addition to denying the authoritative history of the Marvel universe with a sort of bricolage style mythology, Jones, more than *Marvels'* Sheldon, approximates the role of the fan with a devotion and disdain for the official version of things. Jones takes cases that continue to draw her into the fringes of Marvel's superhero universe, such as when she is hired to find Rick Jones (no relation to Jessica Jones), the ordinary kid who served as a sidekick for the Hulk, Captain America, and the Avengers. After reading Rick Jones's bargain bin autobiography, she tracks him down and returns him to his girlfriend; only after discussing with him how she related to his ideas in the autobiography does she discover that this man has merely assumed the identity of Rick Jones, the everyman famous only for his association with superheroes. In addition to providing full pages from the autobiography as an alternative text for the reader, the series undermines this Rick Jones and Jessica Jones as pretenders who have trouble maintaining a clear sense of self (much less culture) within this endlessly complex world.

The contrast between the crime fiction world of Jones as a private investigator and the superhero world of Jones as Jewel is accentuated by the contrast between the rendering of her world and the photographs of her in costume with the Avengers. Illustrated by Michael Gaydos, with realistic figures drawn with heavy lines, deep shadows, and muted colors, the pictures on the wall are rendered in a way that capture the traditional brightness of Benday coloring. An extreme contrast, the picture also represents Jewel in a bad costume, with pink hair, and she's so short the photographer cuts off the heads of Thor, Iron Man, and the Vision in order to center her head. Seeing her in these two ways, the reader has the job of reconciling visual motifs that seem hopelessly different. When Bendis moves into the origin of Jessica Jones (not at the beginning but three quarters of the way through the series), the artistic style shifts to a composite of Michael Gaydos and Steve Ditko (the first page of the origin being a variation on the first page of the first Spider-Man story in *Amazing Fantasy* #15). Since Peter Parker as the nerdy high school student is always seen as a double for the comic book reader of the 1960s, it's even more pointed that Jones is a nerdy high school student in love with Parker. Unfortunately, he doesn't realize she exists, and she masturbates in her room in front of a poster of Johnny Storm, the Human Torch. The dissonance between the Ditko-like style of the art of the origin story and the sexual content is extreme but is no different for readers in terms of what they as readers who reconcile the Silver Age and Modern Age do by habit. While the series thereafter returns to Gaydos's style, it also temporarily uses a style like that of early Todd McFarlane, typical of the 1980s, to represent the short career of Jewel as a superhero. She ended that career shortly after she was possessed by the mind-control power of the lascivious Killgrave, something from which she was only completely freed with the help of Jean Grey of the X-Men (the episode with Grey in yet another style, a 1990s manga-influenced depiction).[30] The reader is likely shocked like Jones, with the illustration intensifying the effect (moving the reader from visual associations with the relative innocence of the Silver Age to the grim and gritty world of the Modern Age). Yet, it still seems that the task for the reader is to provide unity to the text that creators intentionally do not provide.[31]

It might seem a stretch to read her possession by Killgrave as a commentary on a superhero industry trying but unable to control its readers, but subsequent plot points open up this possibility. With the encouragement of law enforcement and the superhero community, Jones tries to tries complete a investigative assignment, and she visits Killgrave in order to obtain information about victims of his crimes. Jones is to interview him through a video screen that looks like a comic book panel and when Jones first arrives in his line of sight, he says, "Jessica Jones. If it isn't my favorite comic book character of all time" (Bendis, *Alias: The Secret* 113). Like a good reader of the comic book world she inhabits, she repeatedly tries to complete her assigned plot-driven task, but Killgrave keeps interrupting with a formal analysis of their situation within the medium; in the transition from a panel featuring him (on the screen) to a reversal shot of Jessica, he says, "Tight shot on Jessica. She stares ahead blankly ... trying not to give Killgrave the satisfaction of how much this confrontation is getting to her" (116). And the next panel looks that way that he describes it. Later, he begins to set up events to come in the story as if their life were in a comic book and he says, "Oh, so we're going to pretend you don't really know what's going on? You don't want to embarrass yourself in front of your readers" (117). When Jones asks him, if "we're all just characters in a comic book," why doesn't he just walk out of the prison, he replies, "I'm not the writer.... But you know what we both share. You were there for the flashback!... You're the biggest whore in the history of the medium" (118–119). When she walks away, he yells,

"Jessica, whatever you do ... don't contradict the continuity!" (120). In this sequence, Killgrave is featured in panels in which he almost always directly faces the reader (like the newscasts in *The Dark Knight Returns*). In addition to having a special relationship with Jones, he also has a special relationship with the reader. While he mentions the writer, he also mentions the reader and the reader's expectations; perhaps most notable is the mention of continuity, the invention of a history that will be canonical. Ironically, the master of mind control identifies conventions of the work in front of readers in a way that frees them from the realism of literacy and forces the reader to recognize their role as the constructor of a reality. Other characters assume that Killgrave's rants are another means to disorient Jones, and the story returns to the crime fiction/superhero world of *Alias*. However, even after his ultimate defeat, his comments haunt the reading to the point that they reconfigure a common phrase used in the literate age that closes the series. After Jones reveals to Luke Cage (Power Man) that she is pregnant with his child, she says, "Alright then. New chapter" (*Alias: The Secret Origins*). (Her story continues in the new series *The Pulse*.) In this way, Bendis's self-conscious effacement of himself as the writer cleverly exposes the essential nature of the comic book reading process: the reader's role in making seamless a tapestry that incorporates various, almost hopelessly different pieces of cultural mythology.

Two other intensely self-conscious writers have worked in veins so similar that they often mirror one another throughout the 1990s and 2000s: Grant Morrison and Warren Ellis. Grant Morrison was part of a British influx to the American comic book industry invasion that most notably included Alan Moore. Like Moore with *Swamp Thing*, he was allowed to prove his talent in the late 1980s with historically underperforming heroes like *Animal Man* and *Doom Patrol*. In short order, he became a fan favorite, eventually working with major DC superheroes and designing major crossover events like *52* and *Final Crisis*.[32] Along the way, he became known as a challenging writer who left much to the discernment of the reader, most famously with *Arkham Asylum: A Serious House on a Serious Earth* and his run on Batman that led to the death of the character. However, the first famous self-conscious and perhaps postmodern move made by Grant Morrison in superhero comic books would be the end of the arc that he developed with *Animal Man*. Initially, seeming to work like an animal-rights screed, the title quickly became something else with the main character, Buddy Baker, detecting something beyond his frame of reference that seems to control him. Initially, he assumes it to be the aliens who gave him his animal powers, but it becomes clear that something more far-reaching was at work. During a drug-induced vision quest, reality begins to break down for Animal Man, represented by the break down of traditional panel structure. Within his vision, he revisits his origin with an overly formal use of the six-panel page titled "Who's Who in the DC Universe," and eventually the panels disappear and the white space in between the panels surrounds Animal Man. In a splash page, he turns to the reader and exclaims, "I can see you!" (Morrison, *Animal Man: Des Ex Machina* 41). The Native American friend who helped him reach this dream state still exists within the panels, and a close up of Animal Man (still outside panels) overlaps with the panel containing his friend, and he sees Animal Man's hand as enormous. Eventually, Animal Man's search leads him to the Psycho Pirate, one of the only characters in *Crisis on Infinite Earths* scripted to have a memory of the crisis. As a consequence, Animal Man's story crosses over the stories of other characters in the post–Crisis universe but also of characters obliterated during the crisis and removed from the DC universe; these other characters also include variations of no longer existent superheroes that Morrison creates for the *Animal Man* series. After creating porous boundaries between what *Crisis on Infinite Earths* has determined is real and is not, the series leads to Animal Man's discovery that he is a comic book character. In a rather heavy-handed move, Animal Man meets Grant Morrison in the pages of the comic book that we are reading and Animal Man's interaction with Morrison is somewhat long and pedantic.[33]

Nevertheless, the run culminates with several great moments, including the point at which Morrison breaks from his conversation with Animal Man in order to encourage the reader to join PETA (222); he also thanks editors and friends as Animal Man fights some new villains in the background (221). As they walk, Animal Man asks to where they are walking and Morrison responds with a playful commentary on the conventions of the medium and a standard superhero trope: "[We're going] nowhere. Just walking. I don't suppose you ever notice how easy it is to travel just by cutting from one panel to the next. Maybe that's why superheroes never grow old — they save up all their time cutting from one place to another" (214). Moreover, the Morrison character represents the control that Animal Man should have over his life and does not and also the control Morrison should have over Animal Man's life and does not. At one point, Animal Man becomes furious because he realizes that Morrison is responsible for the death of his family, and he kills Morrison. In the next panel, Morrison reappears unscathed and declares, "I made you do that too. I can make you do anything. I mean, you're not really violent, are you? You've never really been one of those horrible characters with a gun in every pocket and too much testosterone" (210). Swayed by a continuity-based argument, Animal Man reflects on his identity and resumes his conversation with Morrison who thereafter explains something in potential contradiction with his supposed ultimate control: "You live in a world created by committee. Someone else writes your life when you're with the Justice League. Hadn't you noticed?" (213). Of course, a sense of contradiction between "individual" creators on a committee only exists within a literate mindset; the Morrison character breaks out of a literate mindset in some ways (claiming that Animal Man is pre-existent and more real than he is) and adheres to it in others (insisting he can't violate the rules of consistency and bring back Animal Man's family). However, at the end of the story, Animal Man returns to his comic book world and finds his family alive, showing how the author is choosing to remove himself from the literate mindset and acquiesce to desires of the fans and his character; from what he said, it's possible he was not responsible for the retcon. Almost two decades later, Morrison would return to the relative lack of control a writer has over what is written within superhero comic books in a more refined way; *All Star*

Morrison speaks to the reader, he ignores the drama around him, and panel integrity begins to break down again (from *Animal Man* #26, p.16).

Superman is a series that even further displaces the writer, this time by elevating the importance of the superheroic character. The All Star line is DC's invitation to creators to develop stories that are completely free of DC continuity (resulting in series not even related to one another like Marvel's Ultimate line). At the same time, the creators who've worked in this line have no choice but to borrow extensively from the mythology of characters in play, and *All Star Superman* synthesizes Superman stories from all major comic book ages. The series begins with a plan by Lex Luthor that results in Superman having only a year to live. In order to determine how the world might survive without him, Superman creates a self-contained universe, and we are offered a glimpse of the hand of presumably Joe Shuster drawing a Golden Age version of Superman with the words: "I really think this is it ... third time lucky. This is the one ... this is going to change everything" (Morrison, *All Star Superman, Vol. 2* 105). By making the world of Superman primary, Morrison reverses the traditional order of creation given to the creative genius in the literate world and robs the claim of authority from the author. In fact, the reader seems to be in a vastly superior position, not only as one who knows a large piece of the accumulated mythology of Superman but also as the only one who catches a glimpse of this event (something even the Superman of *All Star Superman* does not know).[34]

What we can recognize with the work of Bendis and Morrison is a motivated interest in the spaces between things (panels, issues, series, creative teams, ages, etc.) and the way those spaces are filled by the reader. The author has very little authority, and the reader is implicated in the meaning-making process, exposed to a sense of multiple realities that are open to interpretation. Warren Ellis demonstrates a motivated interest in those and many other aspects that lead to the openness in superhero comic books, ranging from the industry's ineffectual attempt to control its own creations to the new creation of equally viable realities by unsanctioned creators and consumers. Although his most famous work has been done outside the mainstream American superhero industry, he not only frequently returns to work with publishers like Marvel Comics but also uses mainstream superhero tropes as a referent for his most popular and successful work outside the big two. His work with Marvel has been an interesting exploration of the porous membranes between variants. He helped to craft the Ultimate universe with Brian Michael Bendis and Mark Millar and one of his most popular Ultimate Fantastic Four stories deals with the Ultimate universe Reed Richards contacting another Reed Richards in a parallel universe. While this other Richards seems very much like the Richards in the mainstream Marvel universe, he is a zombie Richards in a world overrun with a zombie virus (a story that has led to Marvel's popular *Marvel Zombies* series). Even more extreme is Ellis's *Ruins*, which provides a variation on *Marvels* but has Phil Sheldon explore a world where most superpowers have led to tragedy and destruction. But as Brendan Riley argues in "Warren Ellis Is the Future of Superhero Comics: How to Write Superhero Stories that Aren't Superhero Stories," Ellis prefers to build a meaningful margin outside the big two that doesn't lose sight of the mainstream.

In regard to Ellis's well-known *The Authority*, that repositions superheroic characters in relation to the powers-that-be, the borrowing from the big two is significant and intentional. Ellis took over the Wildstorm title *Stormwatch* and built the groundwork for *The Authority*; in his run, the Stormwatch superhero team chooses to subject itself to no earthly power, as no prince or principality can overpower them. In addition, the Stormwatch team discover "the Bleed," a space between different dimensions, a space through which the Authority regularly traveled.[35] The transition from *Stormwatch* to *The Authority* is much lauded by Geoff Klock who demonstrates Ellis's love of the in-between. While some characters move from *Stormwatch* to *The Authority*, most are killed in *WildC.A.T.S./Aliens*, an inter-company crossover, featuring another Wildstorm superteam and the aliens from the Aliens film and comic book franchise. Significant members of Stormwatch are not depicted but reported killed in another team's one-shot comic book, and in a one-shot comic book that cannot be reprinted because of copyright restrictions that accompany the crossover (Klock 146–150). From what will forever be a gap for most readers comes *The Authority* that takes the superhero team to what might be called its logical end: "The Authority is the zenith of the superhero qua power fantasy, and the degree to which readers enjoy the title is the degree to which they participate in the genre for precisely this reason" (137). Filled with double splash pages of the Authority reigning righteous violence on those they deem to be villains, the series seems to celebrate the power of the vigilante superhero. At the same time, Ellis is clearly stating that he is aware of this trope and informs the reader by making everything an excessive variation on superheroes in the mythology shared by the big two. Apollo (an obvious variation on Superman) and the Midnighter (an obvious variation on Batman) are gay lovers, and one of the last missions that Ellis scripts for *The Authority* is to kill God (like a pop culture version of Nietzsche's superman). Rather than heighten a straightforward visceral enjoyment of the panoramic action depicted within each issue, these near-parodies encourage the reader to question and reread the authority of the Authority.

However, *The Authority* serves as a prelude to Ellis's more fully realized series, *Planetary*, a work which furthers the radical openness suggested by the standard practices of mainstream superhero comic books. Klock describes the series in this way: "Planetary ... is the height of the revisionary superhero narrative. Planetary is the comic book as literary critic" (153).[36] Self-conscious in a way that goes beyond trendy inside jokes for fans, *Planetary* critiques the futile attempt of the superhero industry to control its creations by demonstrating that the industry's core practices (like retcons and crossovers) create porous membranes between various superhero characters, plotlines, and ideas. The openness of *Planetary* works against a particular notion of authority: a master narrative that postmodern theorists state often serves as a tool of oppression. *Planetary* is a comic book series about the Planetary group, an organization with the set archeological goal of writing the "secret history" of the 20th century. Since the history they seek is unknown to most (and based on popular culture), it resides outside the boundaries set by the canon; while archeologists might be seeking to affirm an existing paradigm by making certain additions to an exhibit or canon, the Planetary group's discoveries and methodologies suggest otherwise. The history actually stretches back to the 19th century and into the 21st, including characters like Sherlock Holmes and Dracula, Axel Brass and Bret Leather (variations on pulp fiction's Doc Savage and the Shadow), and Dr. Randall Dowling and Kevin Sack (variations of comic books' Mr. Fantastic and Kazar); this is a short list in a series that initially seems to revel in the group's supposed archaeological project, merely scratching the surface of a culture filled with the often buried but related artifacts of pulp fiction, comic books, and B-movies.[37] As an institutional practice, archeology is regularly associated with an Enlightenment mindset that seeks to catalogue items for a museum exhibit and thereby establish for display the authoritative version of history. While working under the supposed auspices of scientific objectivity, such projects have been critiqued by the politically-minded in the post–Enlightenment world as imposition of a master narrative on history for the particular gain of one group over another. As central to the complicated arc of *Planetary*, Ellis explores the standard practice of a group that undoes its own authority, whether that be archaeologists or more metaphorically, superhero comic book producers. The Planetary group ultimately seems to be less interested in museum exhibits and more interested in what Ong describes as "the archeology of thought" capable of resisting monolithic perspectives.

At the start, Elijah Snow, capable of psychically manipulating temperature, is recruited to be the third man in a Planetary team that also consists of the super-strong and nearly invulnerable Jakita Wagner and the inter-technology communication savant "The Drummer." The fourth man is unknown to everyone on the team but provides them with their assignments and nearly unlimited funds to realize their information-gathering purposes. On his first Planetary assignment, Snow discovers Axel Brass, the Doc Savage type hero of a past generation, a sort of archeological artifact himself, buried alive since 1945. Formerly leader of a super-team that consisted of heroes (and villains) similar to the Shadow, Blackhawk, and Fu Manchu among others, the team discovered the snowflake, visually like a chaos theory fractal that represents not only all realities but the continuous creation of new realities: "The snowflake rotates. Each element of the snowflake rotates. Each rotation describes an entirely new universe. The total number of rotations equals the number of atoms making up the earth. Each rotation creates a new earth. This is the multiverse" (Ellis, *Planetary: All Around* 16). (Quite significantly, this three-dimensionality resembles Levi-Strauss's description of the workings of "the savage mind," Levison's understanding of McLuhan's acoustic space, and Espen Aarseth's mapping of digital genres.) The attempts of Brass's group to manipulate the snowflake for the supposed greater good of their earth resulted in releasing a desperate group of superbeings, trying to save their own earth. Klock notes that this group resembles Golden Age superheroes (157), suggesting the unintentional way pulp heroes gave birth to superheroes. Brass's team fought them and won with the result being his own burial underground as the guardian of the snowflake. Of course, "multiverse" is a term used often in DC superhero comic books, and, as *Planetary* continues, movement between parallel realities becomes as likely a possibility as in the DC multiverse. In "Strange Harbors," the Planetary team learns about a human being who is enhanced in order to pilot a shiftship through the Bleed (the space between parallel realities); the human complies because "it's the right thing to do" (93). At the end, it seems like Jakita will walk away from the pilot in need of resources so that she may record just another oddity in human history. But then, Snow abandons the role of the objective observer and actively shapes the situation, declaring, "We'd be delighted to provide you with whatever you need, for as long as you need it. It's time Planetary stopped watching things and started doing things" (Ellis, *Planetary: All Around* 93). Unseen by Snow, the Drummer turns toward Jakita and gives her a sly wink. Several things of significance occur in short order within the series, with the snowflake representing endless possibilities and the bleed representing that ability to travel between possible realities. The continuing Planetary project represented through the breadth of the series gives us stories that are variations of H.P. Lovecraft's horror fiction, Jack Kirby's *New Gods* and *Eternals* comics, Japanese giant monster movies, and the list goes on (however, the list is more heavily populated with superhero comic book variations than anything else). The general interest and practice of the series itself seems to set forth an argument for the creation and production of endless variations that may supplant the original. However, it metaphorically and more directly deals with the openness of superhero comic book narrative with the devices of the snowflake and the shiftship.

One of the most interesting aspects of Snow's decision to aid the new pilot of the shiftship is that the ethical imperative for doing so is left almost entirely implicit, the assumption being that such travel is inherently important. With such travel, the center will not hold, and apparently, in Snow's estimation, that is a good thing. Also, if the archeological mission of Planetary has some parallel with the archeological mission of the superhero industry beginning in the Silver Age, we see that an objective view of history is impossible. Ultimately, it will be influenced by the supposed truth-teller in ways often determined by one's cultural unconscious. In *Planetary*, it seems the best way to deal with the situation is to not claim the truth as obvious or ordinary but to maintain the idea that reality is uncanny. As Snow says, "It's a strange world. Let's keep it that way" (Ellis, *Planetary: All Around* 23). Also, as Snow becomes an activist rather than a traditional archeologist, he disavows the Enlightenment faith that any record might be objective and embraces the postmodern claim to bias as inevitable but productive when recognized as what it is. In short order, Snow encounters the story of the villainous exploits of Randal Dowling and his three fellow space travelers, an evil variation of the Fantastic Four. (Of course, the Fantastic Four would be the starting point in the retroactive history of the Marvel universe written by Stan Lee, recounting how Marvel superhero comic books were more appealing to the literate sensibilities of a refined reader.) In the sixth issue, he hears these words from William Leather, an evil variation of the Human Torch: "We were reborn in the exploding heart of the multiverse. We are explorers, scientist gods, heroes of a world that doesn't deserve us... We were given the world in 1961... We are the secret history of the planet — for we are its secret chiefs" (139). Within the context of the series, his rhetoric is villainous not for his sense of egotism and entitlement but for his sense of authority over history; *Planetary* reveals not only that objective distance is a fiction but also that there can be no authoritative version of a story. To make a long story short (and it is a long and intentionally convoluted story), Snow discovers his memories of his unnaturally long life have been wiped as a consequence of his conflict with Dowling, and that he is Planetary's fourth man; in essence, if any traditional approach to archeology remained in the series, it falls apart as his own lost memories become part of the secret history of the 20th century. In the thirteenth issue, "Century," he remembers an encounter with Sherlock Homes and Holmes's secret conspiracy with Dracula (as well as other fictional characters from the Victorian era). In addition to rewriting Enlightenment history (the overall intent of a series that disrupts the culture of the museum, the canon, and literacy), Ellis rewrites Moore's *The League of Extraordinary Men*: a rewriting of both Victorian adventure fiction and the teams that were part of an open-ended superhero comic book history practically from the start. While this may seem to line up with pointless intertextual jokes characteristic of many modern superhero comic books, this is not ever Ellis's intention with his work: "My approach is really to take in as much information as I can, from as many different sources as I can, and let it all kind of distill and fester in the back of my brain.... There's something to be said for questioning the discourse [but] my problems with avowedly postmodern fiction is that that is usually reduced to an excuse for an ironic gag" (McBride).

If we take Ellis at his word, there is purpose for the play that he enacts in *Planetary*. The mechanics of the story has revealed that the mysterious industry control behind the Planetary project is actually the somewhat hapless recruit, a reader of the situation who exerts more and more control as the story progresses. And as Snow enters his end game against Dowling, he not only demonstrates an inability to separate himself from the history he is meant to record but also articulates a new way for his new order to be installed. Dowling is destroyed with the activation of the shiftship and much to Jakita's dismay the typical end of a superhero story is lost: "That's it? I didn't even get to hit anything, Elijah" (Ellis, *Planetary: Spacetime* 173). In addition to identifying popular culture's "influence" as the unacknowledged backbone of mainstream culture, Ellis ultimately makes a potent postmodern statement, seeking to reposition popular culture, leaving no master or master narrative intact. What takes place in the morality set forth by *Planetary* is essentially in opposition to the morality set forth in *Zero Hour*, because the heroes of *Planetary* identify as evil those who want to create a single time stream under the control of one authority; one's relationship to time is objectively determined in *Zero Hour* but subjectively produced in Planetary. In fact, after the *Planetary* series seems to come to its logical end (with Dowling's destruction), another issue features Snow seeking to revisit the past to save a partner who died (bringing back the dead being an essential trope of superhero comic books). The Drummer previously explained the possibility of time travel as follows:

> The furthest point back you can go is the point where the first time machine was switched on.... You and everybody else [would go back and look at that]. Everyone from the entirety of future history arriving at once, the second after you flipped the switch. Therefore, the whole of the future can be said to have happened at once. And you can't change it because it's already happened [181–182].

Initially, The Drummer's explanation seems to be informed by scientific thought that implies there is a single time stream, but, in fact, it is informed most fully by the thought experiment on parallel realities known as "Schrodinger's cat." Asserting that the act of observation changed the situation observed, Erwin Schrodinger asked a question about an observer's experience of an unpredictable situation. Will an observer find the cat in a container with an unstable radioactive substance dead or alive (and do the variant possibilities exist together in some way for the observer)? The quantum mechanics thought experiment is an unanswerable paradox that the Drummer anxiously suggests will result in "an infinite number of dead cats arriving on your doorstep at once" (183). Based on Schrodinger's speculation, other physicists offered their opinion on what would be eventually known as the "many-worlds interpretation" of the experiment. All prominent discussions of the thought experiment involve the observer and whether the observer experiences a distinct reality or a synthesis of possible realities (and whether an observer experiencing the synthesis would be able to separate this synthesis into its component parts). In this thought experiment, we can see issues central to the working definitions that have for traditionality (in which the observer would not be aware of the synthesis) and new traditionality (in which the observer would).

Elijah Snow, who is entrenched in his many-world mythic sense of reality is comfortable with the loss of history the Drummer describes, insists that the experiment move forward. The time-travel device and the act of time travel itself causes endless multiples of Snow, Jakita, and the Drummer to appear. After their long-lost comrade, Ambrose Chase, is brought back to the land of the living, the series ends with a splash page that features the Planetary group in the foreground with endless groups of their multiples in the background. Frost states: "It's taken a long time to get here, but you and me and her and him — we're just getting started" (202). The indefinite pronouns used by Frost could refer to the immediate group but they could also be applied to any other Planetary group; moreover, they could be applied to Planetary fans who waited a long time for the conclusion of the series (as Ellis fell ill during its publication and the series was long delayed). Regardless, the boundaries between realities has been broken in many ways, and the conclusion is remarkably open-ended. In developing a new sense of archeology separated from established power, *Planetary* also revises itself in several DC crossover one-shots with some of the potent statements about series set within the imaginary space of clearly non-canonical texts. In "Night on Earth," the Planetary group tracks Batman only to slide between realities and find Bob Kane's Batman, Adam West's Batman, Frank Miller's Batman, and so on with no clear sense of the "real" Batman. In "Terra

The final image in Planetary features Elijah Snow speaking to other characters that include multiples of himself and his audience (from *Planetary* #27, p. 28).

Occulta," Ellis presents an insidious version of the Planetary group out to destroy a Superman, Batman, and Wonder Woman who are unlike any other versions of Superman, Batman, and Wonder Woman (Ellis, *Planetary: Crossing*). Consequently, these one-shots become part of the "secret history" of the Planetary multiverse to be uncovered by the reader. Considering Ellis's activist orientation toward postmodern theory and the motivation of Snow as a protagonist, *Planetary* becomes a more clearly political work against the imposition of master narratives that seek to negate the reader. The argument against the master narrative is implicitly undergirded by various postmodern theories but can be best represented by Jean-Francois Lyotard's sense of the postmodern project as an effort to "resist the network of exchanges in which cultural objects are commodities." According to Lyotard, the obsession with mastery has led us to a point in human history in which we find a crisis in politics, philosophy, and human interaction; the desire for mastery makes the philosopher "a secret accomplice" of oppressors who seek to justify their oppression through "a constituting order that gives meaning to the world" (Olson). Although it may be quite contrary to the conscious intent of the superhero comic book industry, the openness of the created superhero universes prevents any one creator, law, or institution from limiting narrative possibilities.[38] Even (and perhaps especially) with retcons encouraged by an industry seeking to erase past variations, the industry leaves endless traces and loses more control than they gain through the act that keeps superheroes young and relevant; as more versions are created, control is less viable and the openness of superhero worlds is more notably represented. *Planetary* revels in that situation and uses it to create a politically motivated work of postmodern comic book art.

When I use the term *postmodern*, I think also of the term *digital* and want you to think of the term *new traditional*. The express goal of this chapter is to demonstrate the connection of self-conscious traditionality to digital and postmodern theories as represented in superhero comic books of the 1990s and 2000s. As the inseparable cultures of digital and postmodern theories have changed the way we think about the creator, text, and audience, the self-conscious aesthetics of superhero comic books have assumed a comfortable place in culture. With major architects of superhero comic book universes invested in the practices of new traditionality, the psychology of new traditional culture is even more fully presented and represented. Their self-conscious practices may mean that the future of superhero comics lies with more radical variants such as Steven T. Seagle and Teddy Kristiansen's *It's a Bird* (about the writing of a Superman story rather than a Superman story per se). Such moves lead many to call the trends in superhero comic books increasingly insular, but, in the literate world, tribal and postmodern culture has also been identified in this way as well. We do see superhero fans forming their own tribal groups at conventions and on the internet (a self-conscious choice not available to members of orthodox traditional cultures), groups not swallowed by the industry as wholly as the industry might like. Such groups do require some level of knowledge from its members but demonstrating your ability to navigate the retcon (the pathways to knowledge) is much more important. The type of readership that encourages self-conscious tribalization and fragmentation is threatening to the literate mindset, especially when it translates to some sort of political activism. However, the pleasure of reading is different for the new traditional mind, self-consciously moving from originality to variation, from certain knowledge to open endings. With the history of superhero comic books in mind, superheroes may be one of the most certain emblematic figures of the postmodern/digital age that we have. Regardless, this connection makes superhero stories one of the most, if not the most, important genres in the medium, integrally tied to its conventions and its emerging culture.

Conclusion

Everything Old Is New Again (and Again and...):
An Open Invitation to an Open Ending

When I first saw the film *Superman II*, I loved that Lois Lane finally saw through Clark Kent's glasses and recognized him as Superman; in turn, I hated that Lane's knowledge of Kent's secret identity was erased at the end of the film by Superman's barely explained ability to wipe her memory. At the time I saw the film, I was much more entangled within the preoccupations of literate culture and saw the end as a cheat. Now, I not only appreciate the way that the film participates in the long tradition in superhero comic books, returning to an origin point so that clichés may seem to remain the same[1]; I'm also thrilled with the fact that more than one version of the film exists on DVD (the theatrical release credited to the replacement director, Richard Lester and the director's cut by the original director, Richard Donner, who was fired for creative differences with the producers).[2] Respectively, these two aspects of *Superman II* invoke the more orthodox traditionality of early superhero comic books and the self-conscious new traditionality of later superhero comic books. Of course, superheroes were a major multimedia phenomenon long before *Superman II*, and this was just one of my entry points to the genre. Nevertheless, it is one of the indicators of how superheroes have successfully migrated to other mediums; with the superhero's dramatic growth in popularity around the world (perhaps traced back to this film franchise), the conventions of new traditionality have at least in part accompanied the superhero. Admittedly, the successful export of superhero media and merchandise (not just comic books) may say much about the cultural capital and trade power of the United States in certain parts of the world. However, I don't want to make an argument like that of Scott McCloud in *Reinventing Comics* and suggest that cultural desire is more often than not shaped by corporate power; this Marxist reading of culture doesn't allow for the dynamic interplay between various forces that shape culture. In the conclusion to my last chapter, I argued that the superhero is emblematic of the rebirth of traditionality in the dawning of the digital age (if not emblematic of traditionality and the digital age itself). I think that the superhero speaks to the postindustrial world because the superhero (particularly in its original context, the comic book) speaks to something in the way the world is taking shape.

Many have played with some of the essential features of the superhero, so well identified by Richard Reynolds in *Superheroes: A Modern Mythology*.[3] As I did in chapter 3, I'd like to narrow those features from Reynolds's seven to discuss the three I consider most centrally descriptive to the superhero: seeking justice outside the law, experiencing an orphan status, and wearing a disguise that leads to a dual identity. Seeking justice outside the law is a necessary part of the way most postmodern thinkers would suggest that justice is realized, as the law cannot produce justice in a postmodern world. Experiencing an orphan status is a fair description of the people who have grown up in a digital world and now feel estranged from the high-culture arguments of a literate world. And wearing a disguise that leads to a dual identity is a phenomenon so common in an age of online gaming and social networking that the description of the activity as such seems far too artificial to describe what now comes so naturally to so many. Many would take issue with the idea that this is what the superhero was necessarily describing in the early 20th century, and so would I; instead, I argue that the superhero is unintentionally created in order to accommodate the particular characteristics of the American hero as well as the basic characteristics of the epic hero and therefore, the basic characteristics of the digital hero. (This argument is purposefully based on the extensive argument throughout the course of my book.) Regardless, I would like to more forcefully return to my argument that the more orthodox traditionality of superhero comic books in the United States was necessarily leading to new traditionality — this term that represents a culture in which people act ritually not because there is no other option but because they self-consciously choose to think in act in such ways. The age of new media and what some people are now calling hypermedia has people much more aware of their own practices, and it has made necessary studies like this that analyze media not just as a thing unto itself but also through its community and transmission. The medium of comic books appealed to younger readers because of its content, but its content is highly determined in early years by its form, something that approximated the technological and theoretical changes of the digital age through its appearance and speed of production. In the United States and in many places around the world, young readers chose and continued to choose superhero comic books over other mediums like film and television that participated in large part and in relatively short order with the principles of high culture. It wasn't until the advent of the video game that comic books lost its youth audience (but famously matured for an older audience as the principles of digital culture were no longer wholesale accepted as bad art).

An ad for 2011 reboot of DC comic books that begins the simultaneous paper and digital publication of all titles and adds another layer of variation by retelling superhero origin stories again (from a DC Comics promotional flyer, cover detail).

Even though we may see comic books as a representation of technological manifestations in digital culture, the technology that drives Windows operating systems, internet webpages, and video game platforms makes comic books look terribly analog. However, with its inherent leanings toward traditionality, comic books are not nearly as analog as the novel, a quintessential product of literate culture, and the novel is far from extinction. It continues to sell in its print form and has been successfully remediated with the Kindle and Nook,[4] very successfully approximating the aesthetics of the digital age. With its approximation of digital aesthetics from the start, it needs much less in the way of remediation than the novel, and McCloud has argued that the spread of comic book pages is naturally predisposed to reading on the screen.[5] Although slow to heed McCloud's call for digital comics in the early 2000s, creators have produced digital comics at an exponentially increasing rate in the late 2000s, and the superhero genre seems to be alive and well in that context. Moreover, Marvel entered the digital world with its traditional comic books by putting selections from their back catalogue on CD-ROM (starting with *40 Years of the Amazing Spider-Man* in 2004) and eventually making most of their back catalogue available on the internet by subscription. Marvel continued to innovate with the first comic book published simultaneously in print and digital form (*Spiderwoman* in 2009), and DC made the huge jump into the digital age in 2011 with their reboot of their entire line; all of their comic books restarted with issue #1, revised the origins for their superheroes, and were published simultaneously in print and digital form. Thinking of the quick transition from the newsstand to the direct market, exclusive digital publication can't be far behind. This digital publication may result in a resurgence of the monthlies with monthly comics existing again in an easily accessible and shared form; in addition, with no physical form, they could be regarded as more ephemeral than the four-color pamphlet-like book. As the art of the superhero comic book merges with technology more appropriate to the art, there undoubtedly will be changes to superhero comic books as they are now known. More needs to be written on the medium, with the best now written by Will Eisner (*Comics and Sequential Art*), Scott McCloud (*Understanding Comics*), and Thierry Groensteen (*The System of Comics*) with a good collection by Jeet Heer and Kent Worcester (*A Comic Studies Reader*). And much more needs to be written on the medium as part of digital culture, with the best now written by Scott McCloud (*Reinventing Comics*)—but McCloud tends to focus on distribution and marketing at the expense of other more theoretical issues. I hope that this work is a decisive step in that direction with the idea of new traditionality encouraging a new perspective on old readings of superhero comic books. However, in this regard, my work is far from over, and I look forward to writing more on aforementioned changes in the artform as they are realized with the superhero comic book in the digital world. If that writing takes shape as a new edition to this work, I know that, in keeping with the tenets of new traditionality, additional chapters will necessitate a revision to the whole; with the future being what it is, that new edition might be in the form of a printed book, an ebook, or a website (where the argument might become more distinctly your own). Regardless, I hope this study has served its purpose and more fully identified Superman as the man of tomorrow, with superhero comic books as the both a product and reboot of a culture leading to the digital age.

Chapter Notes

Chapter 1

1. I insert the qualifiers within this sentence because there are always exceptions to this rule. As I will try to make clear throughout this chapter, the canonical tenets are only stable as long as the variation of the story is less popular than the canonical story. And I chose the focus of the superhero's eternal youth, because this links it with the typical heroic stories that are part of oral tradition.

2. In addition to some personal encounters dealing with this subject in general, this very well represents the beginning of roughly one half of the blog reviews on the book I edited called *The Amazing Transforming Superhero*.

3. Perhaps, the best evidence of this would be that few people actually know the creators of either Superman or Batman; even avid readers of Superman and Batman comic books rarely work their way back to the original adventure of these characters developed by Jerry Siegel and Joel Shuster, and Bill Finger and Bob Kane, respectively.

4. See Brownstein's *Eisner/Miller*.

5. This quotation was relayed to me by a colleague who connected with Eisner several times. While he wrote it down verbatim, he is unable to specify the exact occasion. Although this makes it a bit dicey to include as a quotation, I trust the colleague and love the quotation too much to not include it.

6. The idea of copyright will be discussed further in chapter 2, but I will mention here that it works in both ways, protecting the intellectual property of the conglomerate and that of the individual. Furthermore, while being a financial protection, the practices of selling characters and stories further disseminates characters and stories and encourages the desire to "own" those characters and stories in licit and illicit ways.

7. A good example of a similar historical overview can be found in Geoff Klock's *How to Read Superhero Comics and Why*. While his history is not inaccurate, it is certainly succinct and therefore selective, designed to set up his interpretation of the Modern Age of superheroes. As Kenneth Burke has claimed, the selection of one reality is the deflection of another.

8. I should also acknowledge the curious paradox of being able to refer to various historical texts within a work that suggests the superhero industry is creating an oral-culture sensibility; after all, within oral tradition, the most recent version of history is usually the standard. Nevertheless, this is a luxury that I have within a literate culture (whether or not the culture is in transition and may be in the last stages of literate development).

9. Many theorists and critics of graphic literature have included these past items as flashpoints to demonstrate the long history of combining words with pictures, of putting pictures in a sequence to tell a story (see Scott McCloud's *Understanding Comics* and Robert Harvey's *The Art of the Comic Book*). Considering the overall direction of my argument, I rather like these ideas but do not feel confident in identifying them as indisputable facts.

10. It should be noted that limestone lithography was invented by Alois Senefelder in 1796, but I choose the 19th century as a reference point because the presses based on his prototype were not in common use until the end of the 19th century.

11. I use the phrase "firmly" established because conventions such as word balloons predate the comic strips seen in these newspapers, but it was through these newspapers that such conventions became essential parts of popular reading experience.

12. I'm characterizing superheroes by choosing three of the seven characteristics of the superhero established by Richard Reynolds in his superhero monomyth: (1) the costume and secret identity, (2) justice above the law, and (3) orphan status. The other four are not as fully descriptive and as universal as Reynolds suggests them to be: (1), (2), (3), and (4). I mention the ideals of the time period, because many authors have made arguments about the success of Superman and Batman based on how they represent the American psyche at the time period. The best resources on this would be:

13. As previously mentioned, the readership for superhero comic books (like comic books in general) was much more mixed demographically during the early history of the medium (Wright). Also, the term I use here to describe the standard superhero plot ("power fantasy") is one that has become part of typical understandings of the superhero and is one that I will use subsequently with more explanation. The popu-

larization of this term in reference to discussions of the superhero is due in large part to Scott McCloud's *Reinventing Comics*.

14. In other places, I will also refer to Bill Finger as the creator of Batman, as all accounts seem to rightfully give him equal credit with Bob Kane; nevertheless, DC Comics has only ever given Bob Kane credit, and Kane argued for his sole credit in an account made only subsequent to Finger's death: *Batman and Me*.

15. This company would later be merged with DC Comics.

16. During World War II, this was something done across the board with superheroes including those least likely, such as the much more locally focused Batman; however, while this change would be lasting for Superman, Batman tended not to maintain the patriotic tenure as well during or after World War II. Many suggest that while Superman's origin story support it (Superman as the ultimate immigrant), Batman's story doesn't (Batman as the victim of the bankrupt American dream).

17. Despite the popularity of war comics in the 1950s, the end of World War II would be the end of popularity for Captain America, who publishers tried to keep afloat with no real success by finding a new enemy (*Captain America, Commie Smasher*) and by later borrowing from the popular genre of horror (*Captain America's Strange Tales*).

18. Some speculate that the younger audience who provided the largest segment of superhero readership was being lured away by television (although this is hard to support entirely, as television of the time did not offer the immediate satisfaction of the comic books — or in years to come, video games).

19. This is very similar to the Production Code used to ease public fears about the dangerous influence of Hollywood films. This would later be replaced by the rating system, an approach which was also put in place in years to come for television and video games after Congressional hearings were held on those other mediums as well. Currently, very few comic book publishers submit to the Comics Code authority, and most have abandoned the ratings systems meant to replace the Comics Code.

20. This slump in the sales of superhero comic books should not imply that the superhero was fading from national consciousness, as evidenced by the television of *The Adventures of Superman* starring George Reeves from 1952–1958. (The same could be said for superheroes in recent years as superhero comic book sales fall to an all-time low, and, yet, superhero films are consistently top earners at the box office.)

21. Although the Marvel superheroes do represent a significant revision (and some would say revolution) to the superhero, it's important to note that initial sales for many of these titles were modest, and interest developed over time. However, it should also be noted that with Marvel's interest in continuity, this later interest in on-going titles probably created a greater interest in back issues and began to develop a collector culture (see Matthew Pustz's *Comic Book Culture*).

22. In many ways, Marvel Comics' stories were set up with dynamic action traditional of earlier comic books that traditionally drew younger readers. However, while the individual issues could stand alone, the plots were undeniably enhanced by knowledge of past issues (a difference seen in the change from Television 1. (such *Perry Mason* in the late 1950s and early 1960s) to Television 2. (such as *Magnum, P.I.* in the 1980s). Moreover, in short order, the individual issues of Marvel comics would often be incomprehensible to someone without knowledge of past issues (perhaps representing a third stage in the development of television series with a show such as *The X-Files* in the 1990s). This all took place within the Marvel comics of the 1960s.

23. See Pustz's *Comic Book Culture*.

24. While never a top-seller within the Marvel lineup, *What If?* has been published for various long stretches through to present day (remembered by current industry professionals with much greater affection than the sales might indicate).

25. Anticipating the upcoming reference to blaxploitation films, it should also be mentioned that the choice to revive these genres (usually low-budget productions that appealed to the male target demographic for comic book publishers) may have had much to do with their success at the box office: Hammer horror, Harryhausen fantasy, and badly dubbed kung fu films.

26. This brings to mind Alan Moore's introduction to the supposedly ground-breaking *The Dark Knight Returns*: "Everything is exactly the same, except for the fact that it's all totally different."

27. In his treatment of the "Death of Superman" story in 1992, Richard Reynolds suggests that Superman's replacement by four imposters might seem to suggest the obsolescence of the original Superman, but, with his temporary absence, "the primacy of the original is strengthened" (Reynolds 123).

28. Thomas Andrae's argument is very Marxist through his awareness of the corporate ability to rob art of its integrity (taking Superman from the writer Jerry Siegel and blacklisting him) and his assertion about the irrelevance of history to the time scheme of a mythic story (making Superman into a eternally youthful character who engages the same situation endlessly):

> The disintegration of time in Superman stories has ominous psychosocial implications. It exemplifies what Theodor Adorno described as the key attribute of mass culture, its substitution of mythic repetition for historical development.... To paraphrase later Marxists, one could argue that the destruction of time undermines the individual's capacity to become a self-constituted subject — the ability to emancipate oneself from the inhibitions and distortions of the past and to create a future that authentically expresses the individual's needs and desires. It promotes a psychologically regressive state in which the reader is reduced to a condition of impotence and passivity ... [Andrae 135].

29. Neil Harris's "Who Owns our Myths?" treats the idea of universally accepted myth as a function of corporate culture. Referencing the Siegel and Shuster

case to regain control of Superman, the article shows how the corporation protects itself at the expense of the individual. Teasing out what it might mean to say, a mythically resonant story makes meaning for everyone but belongs to the corporation, Harris identifies Superman's story as "post-industrial folklore" (Harris 242): stories which are presented to people as profound mythology largely so that properties will remain viable and continue to sell.

30. John Shelton Lawrence and Robert Jewett's *The Myth of the American Superhero* demonstrates how the stories of superheroes (and American heroes in general) fundamentally disconnect from the democratic ideals enshrined within the U.S. Constitution. Significant not only because it treats the transhistorical, crosscultural notion of the monomyth as suspect, their book suggests that most people lack a general awareness of influence and meaning of their corporately produced myths.

31. This is an idea best represented in the early chapters of Lord's *The Singer of Tales* and Ong's *Orality and Literacy*.

32. This is an idea best represented in the later chapters of Ong's *Orality and Literacy* and McLuhan's *The Gutenberg Galaxy*, and throughout Bolter's *Writing Space*.

33. This is a shift in terminology best represented in Davis's "Agon and Gnomon."

34. Of course, no scholarly work is the result of spontaneous inspiration but rather grows from the work which preceded it. In the case of Milman Parry, he was reacting to many trends in linguistics that typified oral culture and interpreted the epic poem. And he was encouraged to pursue his course of study by his teacher, Antoine Meillet. For a full account, see John Miles Foley's excellent overview of the field, *The Theory of Oral Composition*.

35. These articles would be published posthumously as a collection: *The Making of Homeric Verse*.

36. Within *Ramus, Method, and the Decay of Dialogue* and *The Presence of the Word*, Ong would argue that the growing visual culture (which posits that the visual is the reliable means to reach the real world) works against oral-culture sensibilities. Although I do not dispute this entirely, my reading of the current cultural situation causes me to read Ong's ideas with even more nuance. This will be more fully addressed in chapter 4.

37. This would be the previously mentioned residual orality.

38. A possible historical basis for this argument can be found in Eric Havelock's *Preface to Plato* in which he argues that Plato's argument against poets is an argument against orality. As the Western world has accepted Platonic thought, the Western world seems to have also accepted his bias against orality. Therefore, arguing against new media that may have resemblances to oral tradition may actually be a defense of thought fundamentally shaped by Platonic doctrine.

39. As mentioned in the previous paragraph, epic poems were produced in literate eras as well, and this goes beyond residue to conscious repetition. This is a good parallel for the postmodern age of comic books (chapter 8), but, nevertheless, I argue that the "orality" of superhero comic books is also a return of repressed residue made possible through the industry and the medium.

40. In the literate world, traditional heroes in line with the stories of epic poetry have been consigned to genres such as science fiction, fantasy, and the superhero story, receiving limited critical respectability; the pressures of literate sensibilities on the mind of the critic may go far to explain why.

41. This claim about visual culture is made by Ong, very prominently, in one of his earliest works on orality and literacy: *Ramus, Method, and the Decay of Dialogue*.

Chapter 2

1. These scholars include Scott McCloud and Thierry Groensteen, among others. Film is another medium that was initially treated as an outgrowth literature, drama, painting, and/or photography until theorists like Sergei Eisenstein and Andre Bazin suggested it was something other than an outgrowth of any one form, or a simple synthesis. However, this suggestion was made much earlier in the case of film history than of comic books, and, therefore, film now has a much richer body of scholarship but also has been conceptualized by critics in terms more specifically literary.

2. At this point in the text, Lord also makes a case against "popular." While I agree that the term may still carry some negative connotations, I think the broad meaning of the term has enough usefulness as to outweigh such connotations. In addition, the negativity of the connotations associated with *popular* has changed and lessened since the time at which he wrote *The Singer of Tales*.

3. It's important to note that the Homeric question often raised before Parry was whether Homer was in fact a singular author (the Unitarian approach) or a name given to the collective composition of his epics (the Analyst approach). Nevertheless, despite this slightly broader approach, Parry would still avoid the either/or trap of the Homeric question and instead posit a more nuanced response.

4. Even though Ong highlights the advent of literacy in a dramatic way, he's also concedes that writing was not the sole cause of this psychic shift: "The shift from orality to writing intimately interrelates with more psychic and social developments.... Developments in food production, in trade, in political organization, in religious institutions, in technological skills, in educational practices, in means of transportation, in family organization, and in other areas of human life all play their distinctive roles" (*Orality* 172).

5. The major works that preceded this text and from which most of its ideas are drawn are *Ramus, Method, and the Decay of Dialogue*, *The Presence of the Word*, and *Interfaces of the Word*.

6. Ong comments extensively on how listening creates a sense of interiority (*Orality* 70–73).

7. At a conceptual level, a statement like this is a point of contention for Jacques Derrida in *On Grammatology*. The relevance of Derrida's work will be discussed in chapter 8, because George Landow makes connections between the digital revolution and deconstruction.

8. In terms of the general principle of enacting orality within a literate world, a precedent has been set in studies of oral conventions within literature (Foley, *The Theory* 38; Zumthor 27).

9. The criticisms not worth taking into account are those entrenched in the ideas of literate culture that argue that epics like Homer's *Odyssey* could only be the product of individual genius rather than cooperative work.

10. While this is a reliable generalization, there are exceptions to this rule, such as when orality continues to exist alongside literacy, and the orality is practiced by those who have superior socio-economic status. Of course, even in such a case, this orality is new, modified by its coexistence with literacy, and not the same as the "pure" orality that preceded it.

11. Throughout my treatment of comic books (particularly in historical and visual terms), I will be using very specific terms to describe them. As many critics (but most notably Scott McCloud in *Understanding Comics*) have noted, comic books are very hard to define in exact terms (a complaint made about most of new media forms). Nevertheless, words create our perceptions, and I'll try to be as specific as possible, incorporating various definitions (most prominently those from McCloud and Groensteen).

12. This is important to note in order to highlight the awkward transition seen between strip and book. When published in book form, collected strips suffered as a book-length reading experience, because the pace was designed to build to a slight climax at the end of every strip. In addition, because of the dimensions of the page, an entire strip regularly could not fit entirely across a page, and, therefore, the panels were re-cut (disrupting even the recreated experience of reading a large series of strips at one sitting).

13. Will Eisner is the creator of *The Spirit*, a superhero newspaper insert that dramatically, thematically, and stylistically superseded much of previous work done in the genre. With a neo-realist style, he would return to the form years later, championing comic books as art, inventing the term "graphic novel," and producing classics such as *A Contract with God* (fiction) and *Comics and Sequential Art*.

14. As will be discussed in the next chapter, Superman's powers were much more limited upon his debut; he accumulated his innumerable powers over the course of years.

15. In large part, this sentence refers to Ong's very famous essay, "The Writer's Audience Is Always a Fiction."

16. Along these lines, it's worth noting that John Miles Foley's overview of the field, *The Theory of Oral Composition: History and Methodology*, makes no reference to McLuhan. I do not intend this to suggest Foley, one of the most important contemporary scholars in the field, has made an error in judgment. As this chapter will acknowledge, there is often thought to be good reason to exclude McLuhan from such an overview. Nevertheless, with my perspective on orality and literacy (admittedly unorthodox), I feel he belongs. And it should be noted that he taught at Saint Louis University from 1937 to 1944, and some claim he inspired Ong to pursue his research in orality and literacy.

17. Of course, the title of the work itself explains why so many scholars of literacy have a problem with McLuhan. First, he distinguishes between the state of mind produced in scribal cultures from that in typographic cultures; second, he ascribes to Johannes Gutenberg (and Gutenberg alone) a typographic shift that has cross-cultural global consequences.

18. McLuhan devoted a chapter of *Understanding Media* to comic books but focused on *Mad* magazine rather than superhero comic books.

19. McLuhan actually understood the technology of new media and the media produced by that technology as remarkably similar to one another in his "extension of the senses" argument.

20. I do not intend to shy from connections that might be made to other forms of new media but do feel that there are trends in other forms of new media that cause those other forms to be pointing less uniformly to McLuhan's global village. Therefore, I choose to refer to new media less generically than McLuhan.

21. Consciously or unconsciously, the standard model embraced by the literate world for the development of time (a character-driven plot with a climax) is the one set forth by Aristotle in his *Poetics*. Even though Aristotle differed from Plato in his estimation of art, his overall philosophical viewpoint favored the literate world in a way very similar to that of his teacher. And Plato's outright bias toward literacy is the subject of Havelock's *Preface to Plato*.

22. The pathological return to the origin story (in order to set up new action) is best exemplified by a hero created in the Bronze Age: Wolverine. Incredibly long-lived and with a faulty memory, his character is set up in such as way as to allow for the constant return to his starting point.

23. Since Bill Finger and Bob Kane had an investment in claiming Batman as their creation, their accounts of clear intentions for Batman's origin must be regarded as suspect — especially in Kane's case who claimed Batman was his idea most vociferously after Finger's death (famously in Kane's *Batman and Me* but before that as well). I contend that it is unlikely; as both were rushing to produce another superhero during the early years of the Superman craze, the character was much more likely to have been developed later. This was a standard approach to characters who debuted in anthology titles, and whose stories only continued with positive reader response.

24. *Detective Comics* #235 was published in 1956, and, some would argue, is part of the Silver Age.

25. Andrae and Wright have been most articulate in this respect, and Andrae was the earliest to do so.

26. All of this would hold true until the development of the comic culture in the 1980s, which changed reader's estimation of the comic book by identifying the comic book on a widespread basis as a collectible. The industry would respond in kind by producing the comic books on high-quality paper with better printing processes and by embracing the concept of the "graphic novel."

27. Based on anecdotal evidence, those comic books were often thrown out by the owners but also sometimes, to the owners' dismay, by their mothers.

28. Theoretically, the copyrights owned by corporate entities can be extended far beyond the original creator's death, as the company is still "alive" and actively producing material based on those characters.

29. In terms of the suit's failure, Siegel and Shuster sued for five million and the rights to Superman. In addition to not regaining their rights, "[a] settlement was arranged in which the pair received $100,000 for signing a quitclaim to both Superman and Superboy.... In a shockingly short time, the partners found themselves just about out of the comics business, with most of their money eaten up by legal fees and their bylines removed from the Superman comic books and newspaper strips" (Daniels, *Superman* 73). In recent years, Jerry Siegel's family has overturned this decision in a rather significant way, winning many of the rights to Superman. However, the opinion that settled the case was unusually complicated, parsing out what Siegel created from what a multitude of other artists contributed to the Superman mythology.

30. For more on his case, see Mark Evanier's *Kirby: King of Comics*.

31. This is a position that he takes frequently in one of his last interviews, a book-length conversation with Frank Miller titled *Miller/Eisner*.

32. Throughout the early years of Superman's existence, Siegel and Shuster were provided creators credit (even though they were not listed as writer and illustrator on the Superman stories that they produced); this practice was ended with the failure of their lawsuit to reclaim their rights to the character.

33. It should also be noted that Kirby's primary work done for DC was done on the *New Gods* titles, on which he had unprecedented creative control (DC's concessions to retain the services of one of Marvel's founding creators); however, the New Gods were Kirby's original creations and not established characters within the DC universe. Moreover, DC would cancel all of Kirby's *New Gods* titles, in short order, because of poor sales, thus responding to the market (or one could say the larger community dynamic as an oral culture might). The New Gods characters were then made part of the DC universe and produced in various incarnations by other writers and illustrators.

34. Even if completely accepted, the idea that superhero readership changes quickly can only work to a limited degree as an excuse for the rapid reinvention of Superman in comic books and various other mediums; ultimately, some of that young reading audience would be present during any one of those periods of reinvention, and, as historically implied by levels of readership, no reinvention resulted in a massive drop in readership. A conclusion to be drawn is that, from the start, reinvention of superheroes was a norm expected by the audience.

35. Probably the best representation of this can be found in Frank Miller's *The Dark Knight Returns*, in which Batman and Superman are pit against one another, not because they are tricked by a supervillain but because they are ideologically opposed to one another. I do not include this in the main text of this chapter, because it takes the argument too far from the Golden Age.

36. It's important to note that this is not unique to comic books, predated by on-going stories in newspapers and pulp fiction and radio serials.

37. As will be mentioned further in later chapters, this tribal organization has accelerated with the advent of the internet, an essential component of creating the secondary orality known best as "the global village," McLuhan's international tribe.

38. This should not be read as a suggestion by Ong that literate culture ultimately ends conflict but tends to regard ideas and intellectual interplay in fundamentally different ways; for more on Ong's sense of competition grounded in individual psyche, see Ong's *Fighting for Life: Contest, Sexuality, and Consciousness*.

39. Feiffer is also making a commentary on the strip versus the book, but the irony remains relevant nevertheless.

40. In addition to pitting superhero comic books against the ideological pressure of literate culture, Feiffer also provides an answer to Marxist critics who might suggest that such art is part of an industrial culture and, therefore, is designed (intentionally or not) in order to keep the status quo intact. Adding to Feiffer's claim about the alternative reading experience provided by superhero comic books, it can be said that the Marxist decries the illusory power of art; that illusion might prevent the individual from thinking beyond the art in order to reach self-conscious awareness. In most Marxist estimations, art creates the illusion of reality that reinforces the ideology supporting the superstructure and distances one's self from the real world. Therefore, the solution would be either to expose the illusion of the art or to create practical art oriented to basic needs within the human lifeworld. While Superman and Batman may encourage readers to buy war-bonds, they break the fourth wall to do so; on the whole, their stories defy realism not only in their fantastic elements but, more importantly, in their disregard for the rules of literary and pictorial realism. In addition, while their activist stories are based in the ability to do the fantastic, they are always based on the physical action taken to address the perceived need of the exploited. Of course, there is great variety within the stories of all superheroes, and, as often as superheroes undermine the status quo, many superheroes act as agents of the state and support the superstructure. However, I would argue that this is always offset by the way the stories refuse to adhere to narrative and visual conventions of realism.

41. The intent here is not to ignore other comic

book traditions, most notably the manga flourishing in Japan (and now marketed around the world). However, despite the diversity of genre and the lack of a uniform presence of "heavy" heroes of epic poetry within manga, I would argue that the illustration style is more uniform and more uniformly connected to traditional artwork of ancient Japan. In this way, the style compensates for the lack of uniform content and still makes manga very oral or traditional in nature. For more on the importance of illustration style in superhero comic books, see chapter 4.

42. I do not intend to gloss over the fact that the popularity of the superhero seemed to be waning in the early 1950s and that factors external to the industry eliminated the competition (see chapter 5). Nevertheless, superheroes seem indelibly tied to oral characteristics of the medium and (although this is hopelessly speculative) I believe they would have survived regardless.

43. I will also refer to non-superhero traditions in chapter 8, showing how specific content has become less relevant in more recent comic books that represent secondary orality, a new traditionality in the digital age.

44. An objection that might be raised here with the use of the term "folk," for reasons previously mentioned. However, I choose to use it for the sake of its widely recognized denotative meaning.

Chapter 3

1. In his enthusiastic introduction to *Superman: From the Thirties to the Seventies*, E. Nelson Bridwell moves in this direction: "[Superman] was superpowerful. One of the oldest stories known is the *Gilgamesh Epic*, of ancient Babylonia. Gilgamesh, part mortal, part god, was the first recorded superhero. Ancient Greece knew countless superbeings, including Herakles (Hercules to the Romans).... Besides Herakles, there was Zetes and Kalais, who flew; Euphemos, the super-speedster; Kaineus, who was invulnerable; and even Lynkeus, who, we are told, could see things underground — yes, X-ray vision in ancient Greece!" (8). He is just one of countless who do so, and many critics have joined them in works of scholarship such as Don LoCicero's *Superheroes and Gods: A Comparative Study from Babylonia to Batman*.

2. I do not want to expand my argument too far abroad, as compelling as I find some of McLuhan's arguments about new media technology and the global village. I recognize that some cultures are still untouched and/or resistant to new media technology. And I also want to acknowledge the sociology of a world power like the kind held by the United States, a country that exports its culture around the world in an aggressive way (whether or not that culture is truly wanted).

3. If the reference to iconography in regard to comic book art is unclear, "iconographic" is a term employed by Scott McCloud in *Understanding Comics* that only tangentially refers to the long history of visual icons. This will be discussed further in chapter 4.

4. Although very insightful about the general appeal of superheroes, Reynolds spends a great deal of time with this explanation that, again, works only in part: "Budgetary considerations make the superhero particularly suitable for the comics medium. Parallels can be drawn between the comic book and the cinema, but in one respect the two media are totally unalike. Film is an expensive art form.... Comics are cheaper, and they are cheaper just where the cinema is most expensive. It costs DC no more to have John Byrne draw Superman replacing a space station in orbit or bathing on the surface of a star, than to show Clark Kent crossing the street on his way to the office" (Reynolds 17).

5. Since the anxieties that McLuhan demonstrates seem to be squarely grounded in the fears of literate culture, speculating about how his later ideas on Superman might soften is worthwhile. Of course, a tribal perspective is not a fascist perspective; there is a difference between the tribal thought of oral culture and the groupthink of fascism. But it is my feeling that McLuhan sees something in Superman stories that might be tempered by the perspective on oral culture set forth in *The Gutenberg Galaxy*.

6. Following the previous footnote, I cannot argue uniformly that superheroes never act as fascists (in the true political sense of the word) and some of the best comic books of the Modern Age have seemingly been written to address this concern: Frank Miller's *The Dark Knight Returns*; Alan Moore's *Watchmen*; and Warren Ellis's *The Authority*.

7. It's worth noting that "faster than a speeding bullet" and other prominent epithets associated with Superman (such as "truth, justice, and the America way") came from the radio and television show and were later incorporated into the comic book. This demonstrates the porousness of the various new media forms the superhero inhabits, the oral basis for some of the most famous epithets associated with Superman, and the comic book form's almost immediate recognition of the importance of said epithets.

8. For more on the American shape of superheroes, see Lawrence and Jewett's *The Myth of the American Superhero* and for more on the American shape of Superman, see Andrae's "From Menace to Messiah," Engle's "What Makes Superman So Darned American?," and Chang's "Superman Is about to Visit the Relocation Centers."

9. Jaynes works against conventional dating of Homer's *Iliad* and *Odyssey* and places the *Odyssey* one hundred years later than the *Iliad*.

10. Although not characterized in the same way, Lord includes interesting commentary on the disguise as both hiding the self and part of the self in the contemporary oral epics central to *The Singer of Tales* (103–104).

11. Jerry Siegel remarked, "I'm lying in bed counting sheep and it hits me. I conceive a character like Samson, Hercules, and all the strong men I heard tell all rolled into one. Only more so" (Friedrich 66).

12. It's important to recognize that not all superheroes had such consciously developed mythic paral-

lels (such as Batman and the Green Lantern). Nevertheless, most did in ways central (the Spectre as the hand of God) and tangential (the Flash whose costume is based on visual depictions of Mercury).

13. In his effort at "Defining the Field" in *Oral Poetry: An Introduction*, Paul Zumthor describes the baggage that accompanies studies of folk art and popular culture and demonstrates why such study is still on the fringes of academic respectability.

14. It's worth noting that Ong is not as antagonistic toward ideas about the unconscious as McLuhan. Within the larger body of Ong's work, he returns to the concept of the unconscious many times as his explanation for a language awareness that transcends one's own experience, most concertedly in *The Presence of the Word*. McLuhan is not always as antagonistic to psychoanalytic theories and is sometimes sympathetic to psychoanalytic theories of the unconscious.

15. Part of Lord's work would be the philologist's reconstruction of the identity of oral cultures in a world whose awareness of knowledge itself was seemingly forever changed by the continued ramifications of the printing press. As a consequence of this reconstruction, some critics now feel that Lord's treatment of oral tradition is too romantic (with Lord longing for the stories and storytelling practices of bygone times) and too schematic (with Lord implying that the oral world is lost forever excepting for the things that we can reconstruct within scholarly tomes). Although I disagree with this claim for the most part, it is important to recognize that some of this sentiment may exist, inherited in part from Milman Parry as suggested in Adam Parry's collection: "In a sense Parry is one of the lovers of the exotic in our century.... His historical sense led him to distinguish sharply between Homeric style and that of his own era" (Parry xxvi-xxvii). Likewise, at points within *The Singer of Tales*, Lord does argue against the presence of orality within the literate world: "It is worthy of emphasis that the question we asked ourselves is whether there can be such a thing as a transitional *text*.... I believe the answer must be in the negative, because the two techniques are mutually exclusive. Once the oral technique is lost, it is never regained" (129). I feel these acknowledgments are important to make in a work such as this that applies theories of orality to a contemporary medium (and before reviewing basic ideas of oral tradition to be applied even more particularly to Superman). Nevertheless, if this tendency did exist, Lord did not allow this tendency to fundamentally color his work as a whole and established undeniably important and lasting precepts about the nature of oral culture.

16. D. H. Lawrence's notion of the round characters (complex characters that drive the plot) versus flat characters (simple characters that serve a plot function) is clearly an innovation of the literate world.

17. As of yet, I am not trying to historicize aspects of oral culture or suggest linear development by dealing with examples from the Superman canon in a largely historical order (this is more part of the analysis within chapters 7 and 8). Instead, this approach simply provides some more clarity and ultimately. still works very well; examples could be drawn from any era of Superman's "life" to exemplify the characteristics of the epic.

18. Lawsuits filed in recent years have changed this general ignorance to a certain extent. During the production of the first Superman film with Christopher Reeve, Jerry Siegel filed a lawsuit against DC to again try to claim ownership of Superman and related properties. Modestly successful in an era that might have been more sympathetic to the individual creator than the corporation, the lawsuit ensured that Siegel and Shuster would always be identified as Superman's creators. However, this line in the credits does not provide a true historical or narrative sense of Superman in the Siegel and Shuster era. Incidentally, during the production of *Superman Returns*, Siegel's widow renewed the legal fight with DC and Warner Bros. in order to claim more control and financial restitution (with even greater success).

19. In particular, see *Thus Spoke Zarathustra*.

20. Although "The Reign of the Superman" is not a comic book story, it is a short story with illustrations. Considering the importance of the illustrated form to the content of the comic book story (to be covered more fully in chapter 4), it would be interesting to speculate on the oral characteristics of picture books. In addition to most literate adults considering picture books to be material only for children (who live a more "oral" existence), written forms of folk and fairy tales are often relegated to picture books for children (despite violent content and sexual themes). This may imply that something about how the interaction of narrative and related image activates something like the experience of oral tradition.

21. Both of these characters continue to exist as peripheral characters in the DC universe, maintained in essence but often changed in subtle ways by new back stories.

22. One of the most notable exceptions to this statement would be Mayer's *Superfolks*, often regarded as a forerunner for comic book works like *Watchmen*.

23. In recent years, many scholars have been working to recover this personal history and read Superman as a Moses figure more than a Christ-figure. See Weinstein's *Up, Up, and Oy Vey!* and Fingeroth's *Disguised as Clark Kent*. Of course, while this argument is important, it hardly contradicts previous readings of Superman as a metaphorical Christ-figure; since the medieval period, Christians have consistently read Moses as a prefiguration of Christ.

24. Within my introduction to *The Amazing Transforming Superhero*, I referred to this phenomenon as *critical* revisionism. "[T]hese are interpretive positions taken by critics of popular culture, interpretive positions that ultimately have an impact on the way that superhero stories are told" (22). In reference to Superman, I note the curious fact that Superman is quite clearly a Christ-figure in *Superman Returns*, a film directed by Brian Singer (a high profile filmmaker who is Jewish and probably earned the director's chair for the project on the basis of his work on the X-Men films, which uses mutant culture to explore Jewish is-

sues). Of course, it's also possible that this need not be regarded as either Siegel and Shuster's self-effacement or Singer's acceptance of the dominant culture's interpretation of Superman; they could be thinking of Superman as the fulfillment of the messianic promise.

25. For further discussion of this historical framework of the Superwoman and Supergirl stories, see Beritela's "Super-Girls and Mild Mannered Men: Gender Trouble in Metropolis."

26. Even though Umberto Eco describes the mythos of Superman with different principles in mind, his characterization works in a way that is roughly parallel and highlights this same movement/lack of movement: "The mythological character of the comic strips finds himself in this singular situation: he must be an archetype, the totality of certain collective aspirations, and therefore he must necessarily become immobilized in an emblematic and fixed nature which renders him easily recognizable (this is what happens to Superman); but since he is marketed in the sphere of a 'romantic' production for a public ... he must be subjected to a development that is typical" (110).

27. During the first thirty-some years of Superman's "life," he is often identified through the artists who give him his various looks in those first three decades; respectively, that would be Joe Shuster, Wayne Boring, and Curt Swan.

28. In case we needed further proof that these stories were in the vein of oral tradition and therefore backward and forward looking simultaneously, it seems the grand plan to update the resurrected Superman's look was to change his hair by giving him a mullet (popular in the 1980s but out of style in the 1990s).

29. The Superman-Red and Superman-Blue storylines would also become part of the real world of Superman in 1998, but these were less well received because of the new costume and new powers that seemed to stray too far from the Superman story for most fans.

30. Two notes in this regard: (1) The conspiracy theories that developed around George Reeves death could be read as an alternate and perhaps more subtle manifestation of this idea. (2) This resistance to the human vulnerability of a Superman actor would be echoed many years later, as letters came to Christopher Reeve after his horseback riding accident; many were produced by distressed letter-writers who couldn't understand how Superman could be paralyzed.

31. Of course, *the* writer touted and clearly associated with the project was the scribe of *The Godfather*, Mario Puzo. Together with Marlon Brando, he was thought to bring respectability to the pulp fiction icon.

32. This would be reinforced in many places in years to come, including Mark Waid's *Birthright*, Grant Morrison's *All Star Superman*, and the television series *Smallville*.

33. Geoff Klock begins *How to Read Superhero Comics and Why* by arguing that *Crisis on Infinite Earths* was a spectacular failure in its clean-up of the DC multiverse.

34. Gary Engle explores Superman as the immigrant with American ideals in his excellent essay, "What Makes Superman so Darned American?"

35. Jeph Loeb served as the creative consultant for *Smallville*, which regularly juggles motifs from grown-up teen dramas, such as *The O.C.*, with homespun family dramas of the past, such as *The Waltons*.

36. Although somewhat distinctive, this new relationship between Clark and Luthor is undoubtedly inspired by younger years of friendship portrayed in *Smallville*.

37. Subsequently released would be three new Superman origin stories: *Superman: Secret Origin*; *Superman: Earth One*; and the 2011 DC universe reboot of *Superman*.

38. Incidentally, Wildstorm has been acquired by Warner Bros. and the DC publishing group.

39. See Ong, *The Presence* 25.

40. Incidentally, as evidence of Superman being part of "multi-media interaction which feeds itself" (mentioned earlier), Kurt Busiek's *Up, Up, and Away* coincided with the release of *Superman Returns* and presented a variation on the film's story (while still preserving the relative continuity of the series and making several important alterations, such as subtracting Superman's son).

41. In fact, this forgetfulness would be seen most forcefully in the outraged reactions of film bloggers who felt that *Superman Returns* tarnished the idea of a morally upright Superman with an illegitimate child; of course, the physical consummation of the relationship between the unwed Superman and Lois Lane had taken place 25 years earlier in *Superman II*.

42. Much has been written on the responsiveness of comic book writers to the insistent letters of devoted fans, printing and responding to letters in pre–chat room era comic book letters pages (Putz 167–169); more on this will be covered in chapter 5.

43. This seems to be a curious bit of self-loathing and perhaps a strange sort of comic book nihilism: our superhero comic book reading world doesn't even survive the crisis. However, oral-culture stories suggest that the most recently told story is the most real to us.

44. Will Eisner comments on what he considers to be the new significance of writers and artists to the comic buying public in a conversation with Frank Miller: "People are buying your stuff because it's Frank Miller, not because it's comics. They're buying me because it's me, not because it's comics" (Brownstein 140).

45. It's worth noting that McFarlane's sales of superhero action figures made his company much of its money. However, his business practices were very similar to those of the big two, marketing their comic books to collectors in the 1990s. By producing strange variants of the product that required collectors to buy many of the same product, the wider consumer base was quickly exhausted.

46. These authors, especially Ellis, will be discussed more extensively in chapter 8.

Chapter 4

1. Ong describes "the archeology of thought": "an excavation into intellectual history to expose the often

nonabstract underpinning — social, technological, and other — of abstract thought" (*Ramus* vii).

2. In my reference to the images within superhero comic books, I will be primarily using the term "illustration," which I acknowledge is rejected by some creators in the field — the idea being that illustration describes secondary art produced in response to other art (such as illustrations provided for a picture book version of *Gulliver's Travels*). Although I recognize the existence of that perception, I do not define the term in this way and choose to use it for two reasons. The first is that referring to the images within superhero comic books as the art or artwork begs the question of what we have in the written script (making the work of scriptwriters secondary or more appropriately, preliminary). The second is that I understand illustration as companion art (not secondary art), and this fits the codependence of word and image in comic books much better.

3. Although appreciative of his work, Ong takes exception to Derrida's notion of writing; see *Orality and Literacy* (163–164).

4. Ong makes the claim that the movement toward hypervisualism was inevitable because it appealed to the general progress of the human mind toward "the modern scientific and technological world" (*Interfaces* 128).

5. Even though a very appropriate quotation, it would be remiss not to note that the term "literal" could present problems in the midst of a discussion of orality and literacy; regardless, this is the term McLuhan chooses for better or worse.

6. At this point, it would only be fair to note that Havelock's ideas have been much more widely accepted by people like me (scholars of literature) than they have been by scholars of philosophy (and Plato in particular) who approach Plato with different concerns in mind.

7. Of course, this art would lead to the hieroglyphic art that works as a sort of picture-writing; however, rather than making my case problematic, I believe it enhances my case in that it leads to a visual codependence of word and image.

8. Another interesting point by McLuhan is made in reference to field research of nonliterate cultures; he argues that nonliterate man rejects the three-dimensional representations of the world found in photography and film (and realistic painting) but that he accepts two-dimensional representation of the world found in cartoons (animated films) (*The Gutenberg* 39). This is worth mentioning because art associated with animation is very similar to art associated with comic books. However, there is also great variety represented in the styles of each medium. In addition, this idea is also relegated to an endnote, because his argument is made as part of his distinction between film and television (with cartoons solely associated with television). The sharp distinction made between film and television is no more supportable than the firm association of cartoons with television. Last but not least, McLuhan also makes a potentially offensive assertion that the appeal of cartoons for "natives" is the same as the appeal of cartoons for "our children."

9. Another interesting point by McLuhan is made in reference to his short study of *King Lear* in *The Gutenberg Galaxy*; he argues that *King Lear* represents the "first verbal manifestation" of the third dimension (15–17). Again, McLuhan's assertion is problematic for several reasons, including unclear literary interpretation and a leap in logic that borders on informal fallacy (citing something as first would require knowledge of everything that precedes it).

10. Ong also indicates that there is a connection between the vocal performance of a work and the handwritten recording of a work, each quite distinctive to the performer (unlike the uniformity of typography); although not quite the same since a letterer handwrote text for multiple comic books, it may be worth mentioning that this handwriting convention persists in comic books.

11. Of course, the term *tradition* has a long history in various critical discourses, and it would be Milman Parry himself would begin to recharacterize the word as part of the discussion of orality and literacy.

12. I have chosen to use *orality* and *literacy* thus far (and will continue to do so in combination with *traditionality*) because of their still more recognizable place within the scholarly discourse.

13. The subtitle of his book is "The Invisible Art," which works on several levels. To begin, he works against a certain type of cultural bias that still regards comic books as kid's stuff and something other than art. Also, if comic books are written well, they do not call attention to themselves as art but rather fundamentally connect with the reader; I will explain this further in the body of this chapter but want to add that this is similar to the experience of oral poetry that is not regarded by an oral culture as art so much as a fundamental part of one's life.

14. In his *System of Comics*, Groenstein refers to McCloud somewhat derisively; Groenstein suggest that he has to cover some ground similar to McCloud because McCloud fails to fully engage ideas outside his own work.

15. Ironically but not surprisingly, this format has been somewhat off-putting to those not currently in this field of study who are beginning to wonder whether graphic literature deserves their attention. I believe McCloud's approach is wholly valid and regret that most of my quotations will be limited to the language in his book; as with most comic books, the words only make complete sense with the compliment of the visuals with which they are presented.

16. Of course, as Ong would consistently state, literate culture never works wholly in terms of literacy and is always haunted by its past as oral culture.

17. In an intentionally humorous sequence, McCloud runs through the difficulty of accurately defining the medium. He begins with "sequential art" and in response to a heckler in the crowd makes it more specific. He thereafter tries out several other possibilities, always proceeding onto greater specificity until the definition is too cumbersome to be useful: "juxtaposed pictorial and other images in deliberate sequence." The initial term is used by Will Eisner to

describe the medium in his work, *Comics and Sequential Art*.

18. At times, this is strategic but in the following quotation, it does not seem very well calculated.

19. At the outset, I will mention that McCloud's use of the term "icon" may be somewhat related to Gombrich's use of the term caricature but I am reluctant to push this connection too far. Gombrich spends much time discussing the caricature used in 20th-century comic books and animation but as David Carrier notes, Gombrich regards comic books as a lesser art form for "illiterates." (69).

20. McCloud's reference to icons ties to Bolter's analysis in concept but in focus as well. McCloud works extensively with the digital future of comics (but still not computer icons) in *Reinventing Comics*.

21. In his world history of images used to tell stories, McCloud is correct in suggesting iconographic art exists at the same time as the highly literal epic poems and that realistic art necessarily rose with the advent of print (*Understanding* 141–145). Moreover, he is further correct in his description of abstract art in the 20th century as not the same thing as iconographic art, rejected by most people as irrelevant and incomprehensible. "Unfortunately for comics, no sooner had the fine arts rediscovered the link between words and pictures — than modern art itself became virtually incomprehensible to the average viewer. [Image of people in gallery arguing over a Joan Miro painting]" (*Understanding* 150). This type of abstraction would appear to a limited degree with artists like that of Bill Sienkiewicz and Dave McKean in the post-1980s boom in the diversity of artistic styles used in superhero comic books.

22. Even if objectivity of Platonism gives rise to structuralism, we have to remember that there are degrees of subjectivity and objectivity. If we return to Ong's continuum, which begins with touch and moves on to taste, smell, hearing, and sight, we recognize that the aural culture of traditionality doesn't suggest complete subjectivity in relation to art. Ultimately, one of the things that could be said about the sign, in slight opposition to Ong's comment, is that the degree to which signifier and signified are separated is different, much less in oral culture than in literate culture. In addition, it's worth mentioning that Gombrich's text was prominently answered by Norman Bryson's *Vision and Painting*, which took a much more structural approach to the subject.

23. In *Reinventing Comics*, McCloud questions whether superhero comic books have now reached their maturity or their senility; his general tone suggests he sides with the latter idea. (It's important to note that McCloud is thinking of the genre via a standard of the literate world: linear progression.) The significant problem that McCloud identifies with superhero comic books is that they seem suited to explore only one theme: power. According to McCloud, the resolutions always rely upon the adolescent desire to have power (114). I would concede this is a somewhat accurate critique but ultimately too simplistic.

24. These are the three primary terms that Mc-Cloud uses to characterize comic book art in *Understanding Comics*. He positions each term at a point of a triangle and places all comic art in the space therein.

25. However, I do believe that McCloud's call for diversity in comic books and graphic novels is more justified than most. While I do believe that the traits of the early industry (both in terms of technology and the general business model) predispose creators to produce superhero stories, McCloud is inclined to change both technology and the business model. He is both an advocate for digital comic books (the "infinite canvas" of the internet) and a proponent for creators' rights (one of the originators of the "Creator's Bill of Rights"). For more on both these issues, see McCloud's *Reinventing Comics*.

26. Another aspect of early comic books that brought added revenue to the publishers and kept comic book costs low were advertisements. This is certainly something to take into consideration as it introduces a commercial aspect to superhero comic books that do not exist per se in oral epics. At the same time, while the advertisements are now interesting assessments of comic book audiences, the reading practices of superhero comic book culture indicate that advertisements were largely ignored upon first reading of the comic book. It was only on repeated readings that they were noticed, and thus the superhero became subject not so much to commodification (in this case) as to an increasing awareness of "background noises." These advertisements are the equivalent of sidebar advertisers on contemporary websites whose advertising value has often been questioned.

27. Again, Will Eisner illustrated in at least four different styles as a fill-in artist to imply that his company was filled with many artists capable of working in various house styles; this act suggests a certain impressive level of technical skill and virtuosity.

28. Although I'd like to stick with Superman initially, Bob Kane provides an even better example of this almost manic transitions for one panel to the next (consider the first six panels of "Batman Versus the Vampire" in *Detective Comics* #31), which entirely reverses perspective six times. This makes the action difficult to follow, and it creates a disorienting effect, perhaps adding to the atmosphere of noirish paranoia; of course, this disorientation would probably not be registered by someone in a traditional culture.

29. As Kirby and Ditko are discussed, their contributions to the creative process cannot be underestimated, as they worked within what was subsequently called the "Marvel method" (which meant Lee provided artists with a general outline, and those artists worked out specific plot points).

30. Many argue that their contributions to the creation of Marvel superheroes (and their continuing stories) were substantial, providing fully outlined plots as well as designs (requiring Lee to merely write dialogue).

31. Although it should be noted that his representations of enemies of the allied cause do not squarely fall into the category of the completely obvious and offensive stereotypes often employed in wartime comic books — but of course, in literate culture, the line be-

tween what is offensive and what is not in this regard is debatable. In traditional culture, the villains are often represented with all the offensive imagery that an artist can muster as villains are often considered to be uniformly and irredeemably "other."

32. See chapter 5 for a more extensive discussion of the Marvel "revolution."

33. This would especially be the case with the otherworldly setting seen in Thor, with Asgaard and other realms of the gods, which were made to look otherworldly to evoke a mythic sensibility.

34. Thor may be the hero of most prominent interest to this study, as it seems to bridge the gap between the oral epic and superhero mythology. More will be said on Thor in chapter 5 but primarily on Thor as a predecessor for Kirby's *New Gods* series. For a good study of Thor as a mythic superhero, see Reynolds's *Superheroes: A Modern Mythology*.

35. Like Kirby with Thor's Asgaard and perhaps even more so, Dr. Strange would regularly enter netherworlds that defied conventions of three-dimensional space.

36. In the case of Kirby and Ditko, they would have been especially likely to have been recognized as such, as Marvel was one of the publishers that broke from standard practice in the comic book industry, providing credit to creators working on any comic book on its title page. Interestingly, no creators (writers or illustrators) who moved away from the "classic" superheroes in the Golden and Silver Ages found success that equaled that of their earlier work.

37. McLuhan makes a very important use of the flag as an icon representing the mentality of traditional culture in the following quotation. "Suppose that, instead of displaying the Stars and Stripes, we were to write the words 'American Flag' across a piece of cloth and to display that. While the symbols would convey the same meaning, the effect would be quite different. To translate the rich visual mosaic of the Stars and Stripes into written form would be to deprive it of most of its qualities of corporate image and of experience, yet the abstract literal bond would remain the same. Perhaps the illustration will serve to suggest the change the tribal man experiences when he becomes literate. Nearly all the emotional and corporate family feeling is eliminated from his relationship with his social group. He is emotionally free to separate from the tribe and to become a civilized individual, a man of visual organization who has uniform attitudes, habits, and rights with all other civilized individuals" (McLuhan, *Understanding* 118). Unfortunately, the argument becomes somewhat muddled by his too general use of the term "visual" at the end (when he really is just referring to the visual sensibilities of literate man). But otherwise, this statement sets up well McCloud's broader sense of iconographic art.

38. Both of these heroes have symbols drawn more directly from the human lifeworld (the bat and spider, respectively) but the stylizations of these symbols render them as imprintable, such as Superman's "S." I also think Captain America's costume is worth mentioning at this point, as it is clearly tied to a certain type of national identity in the United States (basically just a variation on the American flag). The limitations of such symbology were clearly marked by the commercial failure of his series after the end of WWII. However, upon his resuscitation in the 1960s, Captain America was resituated as symbol of American ideals much more than as an American soldier, giving the costume a much more ambiguous, imprintable nature. See the above endnote for the potential richness in the flag as an icon. Nevertheless, Captain America has yet to become as popular as his fictional companions outside the United States.

39. As indicated in chapter 2, I'm not arguing for a uniformity among Golden Age and Silver Age superheroes but in this case, I am arguing for a similar flexibility in their iconographic representation that makes them not unlike one another in basic conception.

40. For the Hulk, I'm thinking primarily of his colored skin and musculature and for Wolverine, I'm thinking about his claws, hair, sharp-edged costume, and often sported "X."

41. In addition, Ross is very far removed from the industrial model of the early comic book illustrators; his process of painting is very time intensive, and he may labor more than a year on a single work.

42. It should be noted that Superman's costume is remarkably similar to the one debuted in *Action Comics* #1, but the current incarnation of the shield differs slightly from the original design; originally, it was less clear in detail and color (a red "S" against a black background) but was refined within the first few years of comic book publication.

43. One of my favorites outside the medium of comic books is featured in *Superman Returns* because it accentuates the transhistorical nature of the image within a modern context; Superman "rescues" an associate of Lex Luthor in a runaway car, and the exact pose of Superman (like that of *Action Comics* #1) is only revealed in a cameraphone snapshot.

44. I do want to acknowledge that this was Kirby's general tendency at the time but this panel design/arrangement grew from his sense of growing import of every story he created to the universe of that comic book.

45. However, that background detail is far from complete and at times in the past timeframe, Miller provides no background detail, choosing instead to isolate figures. As will be noted in chapter 7, Miller often hearkens to the realism of Neal Adams as an early inspiration but even Miller's early work is highly traditional and iconographic.

46. For more on this, see chapter 5.

47. This attitude certainly explains the uphill battle that Will Eisner fought not only with the public but also with industry professionals to establish comic books as art; most professionals understood comic books as oral poets would understand their work and certainly not as high literates would understand art.

48. For a profile of the many uses of the gutter, see McCloud's *Understanding Comics* where he identifies the movement from panel to panel in the six following

ways: moment-to-moment, action-to-action, subject-to subject, scene-to-scene, aspect-to-aspect, and non-sequitur (70–72). Incidentally, I like this list very much but, like some other readers, take issue with the non-sequitur, questioning whether any two elements in a sequence within a narrative or poetic context can ever truly be disconnected.

Chapter 5

1. The most prominent anecdotal explanation is that the designations came from a letter published in a DC comic book separating Golden Age superheroes from their 1950s revivals or in a Marvel comic book separating the DC and Marvel superheroes.

2. Although the story elements related to a distinctly modern genre (dependent upon the 20th-century invention of the teenager), the illustration of Archie comics was a very distinctive house style that can be readily identified as iconographic.

3. Even though more famous as strips than as collections in comic books, the two most prominent examples of each would be *Flash Gordon* and *Prince Valiant*; curiously, while the story conventions largely adhered to those of the epic, the illustration of each tended to be more realistic than that of the contemporaneous superhero comics.

4. The film noir anti-hero is a symbol of the anti-institutionalism, regarding the assimilation of industrial society as a threat to his individualism. Clearly unlike the hero of the oral epic whose story always extolled the values of the tribe over the self, this anti-hero is well described by Wright in his overview of crime comic books (including the neo–Freudian fear of the female likely to destroy male individualism): "There were few positive role models in the crime comic books for males or females. Police rarely figured prominently in the stories, and their dutiful service to the law was almost always overshadowed by the exciting criminals who flouted it. The grinding wheels of justice appeared slow, inefficient, and susceptible to manipulation by criminals with only average intelligence.... [Often] the law only caught up with the criminals after they had allowed themselves to be distracted by women" (Wright 84).

5. In addition to noting this as a shift in the industry, it is worth mentioning that this shift would have registered at a personal level, as Bill Gaines was the son of Max Gaines, who published superhero comic books including *Wonder Woman*.

6. Using collective fears of the culture is an interesting approach to take for someone who considered himself a socially conscious liberal. Moreover, it could also be noted that Wertham's analysis of art is very Marxist (art as a product of industrial culture that undermines individuality). And in turn, I suppose it could be argued that this grew out of his youthful interest in Fabian socialism and that his participation in Cold War rhetoric was an unintentional reaction formation.

7. Although I'm very open to gay readings of the dynamic duo in the wake of Comics Code comic books and the campy television series, Wertham's reading of the homosexual encouragement offered by Batman and numerous other superhero titles seems to say more about Wertham than the titles. Although Wertham's book was written in a time where standards for social science research were quite different, even the most generous readers have found fault with tenuous nature of the following speculations: "At home they lead an idyllic life. They are Bruce Wayne and 'Dick' Grayson.... It is like a wish dream of two homosexuals living together. Sometimes they are shown on a couch, Bruce reclining and Dick sitting next to him, jacket off, collar open, and his hand on his friend's arm. Like the girls in other stories, Robin is sometimes held captive by the villains and Batman has to give in or 'Robin gets killed'" (Wertham 190–191); Wertham would go on to give a similarly framed lesbian reading to Wonder Woman. Wertham's views seem to be characteristic of the growing suspicion of homosociality, noted by Eve Sedgwick as an increasing part of masculine identity in the modern Western world (in both *Between Men* and *Epistemology of the Closet*). For a slightly different, worthwhile alternate take on Wertham's attitude on homosexuality, see chapters 2 and 3 of Brooker's *Batman Unmasked* (a portion of which is quoted in endnote 9).

8. This quotation provides a good opportunity to comment on some issues central to the epic, which would be virtues within a tribal context but morally problematic within a global context. For instance, threats to the tribe were regularly stereotyped in oral epics, not only made into sub-men but sometimes made into monsters (the ultimate others). In an oral framework, the tribe is the world and anything that threatens the tribe is evil; concomitantly, extreme violent action taken to protect the tribe and destroy threats would be portrayed as imminently justifiable and justified. In a global context where alliances with nations very unlike your own are a matter of course, this sort of "othering" and the violent attitudes it encourages would be counterproductive at best. While I do not seek to justify the practice of stereotyping or the use of violence, I do recognize it as a characteristic of a culture that thinks in more traditional terms.

9. Nyberg notes that Wertham's work is much more complex than most of his critics give him credit for being; in addition, his ideas were grounded in the intellectual tenure of his time: "Wertham shared many of the concerns of the scholars of the Frankfurt School who settled in the United States in the 1930s and whose critique of American mass culture was quite influential in the intellectual community. Wertham was no stranger to their ideas and philosophy; he knew Theodor Adorno well and was familiar with the work of other critics in the same tradition" (Nyberg 86–87). In a much more colloquial fashion, Brooker strikes this sympathetic note on Wertham and his project: "It is a worthless exercise ... to set him up as Aunt Sally and deride him as an idiot or an ogre by the standards of our own very different culture.... [His case

about homosexuality] is simply an exaggeration, and an irresponsible one, for it misrepresents the original text for the sake of making a point more easily.... Most of us would, if fully appraised of Wertham's views, fall pretty much into accord with his attitudes toward racism and toward the depiction of nudity in adult magazines.... I have little doubt, bearing in mind his political leanings during the 1950s, that were he alive today Wertham would have fundamentally reconsidered the views on homosexuality he expresses in *Seduction of the Innocent*" (Brooker 110, 111, 115). Undoubtedly, the most generous of readers would be Reibman, as Wertham's biographer who writes this about Wertham's work in his introduction to *Seduction of the Innocent*: "This legacy is ... for all those who are deeply concerned with the violent nature of society. The response to a new generation of violent crime and horror comics is part and parcel of a culture inured by increased racial tension, economic dislocation, tabloid television news, and a virulent species of degrading, violent film and video images.... Fredric Wertham embodied the fundamental principles of a humane psychiatrist" (Reibman xxxvii). While I find myself wanting to disagree with Reibman in some respects, my own views on Wertham are tempered primarily by his later work on fanzines that revisit comic book readership in a much more carefully argued and affirmative fashion (*The World of Fanzines: A Special Form of Communication*); in fact, his claims about the activity of fanzines as an expression of imagination, control, and ownership are not completely out of line with some of my own ideas about fanzines.

10. Fredric Wertham worked with Clarence Darrow, among others, to be one of the first psychiatrists to regularly offer expert opinion in court cases and this part of his reputation also contributed to his prominent presence at the hearings.

11. In fact, DC established "its own rigorous editorial code" in 1941 (Wright 182). For more details on the internal code, see Nyberg (75–76).

12. In many ways, Gaines used humor to do much the same thing as he used horror to do: question American ideals. Although it may not have direct relevance, I think it's worth quoting Patti Smith who said, "After *Mad*, drugs were nothing."

13. Other genres were also revived by publishers other than DC and Marvel (who will be showcased in following paragraphs as the big two superhero publishers). Interestingly, the war story became a central part of Dell and Charlton's lineup, and these stories came complete with authority-affirming, anti-communist stories. However, in comparison with Marvel and especially DC's new superhero lineup, these titles sold poorly. See Wright (187–199).

14. As Hollywood answered the challenge of television with grander epics and grittier subject matter, comic books had lost much of their competitive edge, thanks to the Comics Code, in the general market and teen market (then captivated by juvenile delinquent films and paperback novels put out in the 1950s) (Wright 181).

15. However, he is inspired by a superhero comic book named *The Flash*; I will deal more with this reflexive move in chapter 6.

16. Of course, parceling out the oral, literate, and secondary oral aspects of comic books is the most difficult part of my study, and I acknowledge that some things that I call *oral* may be counter-argued as *literary* or *secondarily oral* by others. However, this is not unlike the way in which scholars in the literate world have had to struggle with oral *texts* like the *Iliad* and *Beowulf*.

17. I use the word *establishment* because many work with the mistaken perception that Marvel superheroes were a sales bonanza from the start; in fact, it took some time for the new vision of Lee and Kirby (and Ditko) to catch the interests of consumers.

18. Many have speculated on the origin of this outsider viewpoint, and some have ascribed it to the Jewish background of Lee and Kirby (shared with other creators such as Siegel, Shuster, Finger, Kane, Simon, Eisner, etc.) and some have simply ascribed it to producing artwork looked down upon by most of America. While their worldviews are different from one another and cannot be credited to any one factor, these things are undoubtedly contributing elements.

19. I certainly don't want to fall into the trap of some who study oral culture who romanticize this lost culture. At one level, I suppose the temptation isn't as great with comic books, as not as much has been lost. Nevertheless, it is still very important to acknowledge that quality at the beginning stages of an art form (even if derived from other art forms) will be lesser that the art produced by those who inherit the lessons learned from beginners. And it should also be mentioned that quality will vary in every art form, from one creator to another, whether that creator be a singer, writer, or illustrator.

20. I intend "the wide spread of literate culture" to be vague enough to accommodate a variety of different theories about the dating of Homer's work and the nature of orality and literacy at the time he composed his epics; I do not want to be connected just to narrower notions of the composition, as represented in works like Barry Powell's *Homer and the Invention of the Greek Alphabet*.

21. This story is recounted in Lee's *Origins of Marvel Comics* (16–17), a book which is part history and part reprint collection. I include the story here because it has been corroborated elsewhere and certainly seems more reliable than some of Jack Kirby's later recounting (when motivated by his cause to retrieve his original artwork from the Marvel vault). Nevertheless, I will not use this resource too extensively, as Lee engages more in colloquial retellings than presenting critical histories; in addition, the book was published in 1974 and seems to me to be more influenced by the idea of Marvel superheroes as they came to be rather than what they were at their inception.

22. However, Marvel comic books would credit the creators on title pages, working in opposition to Golden Age anonymity but not in the sense of shared ownership and participation; later in this chapter, I will describe how this new practice of crediting the

creators was used well by Lee to develop a new and perhaps fuller sort of community formation between the creators and the audience.

23. Of course, in a literate world that recognizes the individual more clearly than the group and assigns monetary value to one's "original" creations, the ambiguity inherent within the Marvel method has led to some fairly ugly sniping between Lee, Kirby, and Ditko (i.e., who "really" created the Fantastic Four, the Hulk, Spider-Man, etc.).

24. The distinction between these two terms (*worker* and *artisan*) is much more meaningful to a literate culture than an oral culture.

25. In fact, issue #2 would give the readers a story that grew directly out of the popular culture of the Cold War, with stories like *Invasion of the Body Snatchers*, which portrayed the ease and insidiousness of foreign invasion in implicit forms. In "The Fantastic Four Meet the Skrulls from Outer Space," the shape-changing Skrulls assume the form and powers of the Fantastic Four and quickly turn public opinion against them. However, it could be argued that this story may be representing fears of McCarthyism as much as fears of the Red Menace, with the Fantastic Four charged with crimes that they did not commit. Nevertheless, with the introduction of the Red Ghost (a communist supervillain) in issue #13, Marvel would demonstrate that the story was not propelled by an explicit political philosophy but rather by generalized cultural anxiety. On this point, Kirby's reflected that he may have disliked McCarthy's tactics but feared communism as radical and dangerous (George, *Jack Kirby* 32).

26. This is the corollary to the large number of incredible creators in the field of comic books before the Modern Age who refused to call comic books an art form because comic books seemed to be lacking in terms established by literate culture.

27. The responsiveness of writers to their fans (or at least the promise of it) can be seen by looking at almost any of the early letter pages in Marvel comic books where fans are assured that their ideas are incorporated whenever possible.

28. Lee's position against costumes may be seen to be voiced by the Thing in *The Fantastic Four* #3, where the costumes are introduced and he complains, "Bah! Costumes — tights — that's kid's stuff! Who need's em? ... I ain't gonna where this fool outfit!" (7). And he does tear off the mask and shirt before his costumed debut.

29. Lee would have been better served to indicate various speech patterns of characters such as the Thing, who speaks in a dialect influenced by Bronx usages and in celebrity realms, Jimmy Durante (McClelland 72). However, this was like other Marvel innovations, slow to be realized. Consider the formal tones of some of the prosaic language used by the Thing in the issue #1: "Why must the doorways they build be so narrow? ... His first shot missed because he was so nervous! But he'll not get another chance! ... I have gone far enough! I should be under my destination by now!" (Lee 4).

30. The scientist hero is part of the Silver Age as instituted by DC and with an orientation toward logos, the scientist may seem to necessarily be an indicator of the literate age. However, the scientist heroes of Marvel comics are less indicative of this than the simpler renderings of DC heroes thanks to the previously mentioned worldview that seemed to be shared by Lee, Kirby, and Ditko. Rather than understand the scientist as a means to save all from the old and antiquated ways, Marvel scientists failed as often as they succeeded, discovering that some places should never be explored. With Reed Richards, it's significant that an accident he couldn't fully predict led to their powers, and he is never able to reverse the permanent change to Grimm (which Grimm considers a curse). Other things worth mentioning along these lines are that Richards's greatest discovery is the Negative Zone (which released one of their greatest enemies, Annihilus), and the other great scientist in the Marvel universe is Bruce Banner (whose grandest experiment led to him becoming the destructive force of the Hulk).

31. Although authors like Bradford Wright assert that the Invisible Girl is emblematic of a new feminist ideal and would attract female readers (204), a cursory read of the first few years of *The Fantastic Four* proves her to be otherwise: regularly requiring rescue, staying behind on missions, and becoming an object of romantic contention between Mr. Fantastic and the Sub-Mariner.

32. Despite Lee's initial decision to not to use previous superheroes owned by Atlas/Marvel, Lee and Kirby brought back several, most notably Sub-Mariner (more clearly an anti-hero and villain) and Captain America. Although still a relatively flat character, Captain America avoided being completely "friendly" with others, because he was a man out of time and felt at odds with the less patriotic 1960s culture. Incidentally, the collision of different time periods is clearly seen as the super–Nazi, the Red Skull, is brought into the different tenor of the Marvel universe; his dated anti–American rhetoric is out of place, and even his new articulation of himself in *Tales of Suspense* #80 is comical: "The War had never ended — and never been won! It was only the first battle we lost! So long as evil lives — to muster the forces of bigotry, greed, and oppression — the fight goes on!" (Lee 8).

33. Although a clear intention to do so from the start could be questioned, as Johnny reads an issue of *The Incredible Hulk* in *The Fantastic Four* #5, I will discuss this more later in the chapter to refute the over self-consciousness of the early Lee and Kirby comic books, but here it is worth mentioning, as the Hulk (who later crosses over with the Fantastic Four) only seems to exist for Johnny as a character in a comic book (Lee 2).

34. More will be presented on this universe model in chapters 6 and 8, with particular attention paid to Carl Silvio's description of this design as postmodern in chapter 8.

35. In fact, the creators were also dubbed with epithets such as Stan *the Man* Lee and Jack *King* Kirby. Of course, this practice might have further erased anonymity and contributed to the creation of the author in superhero comic books, pushing comic books toward literacy.

36. Although this could simply read as self-aggrandizing, this statement from Lee is at least worth including in an endnote: "I like to think that anything I write will sound good when it's read aloud.... Many English teachers have told me that [the comic books] scan as poetry" (McLaughlin 51).

37. Along these lines, EC had their "Fan-Addict Club," and, in the wake of the senate hearings, Bill Gaines appealed to these loyal fans to make their voices heard in the midst of the crushing blow of the code era; ultimately and perhaps obviously, this appeal was unsuccessful (Pustz 39–42).

38. The original letter points out that Bruce Banner has changed into the Hulk by will, only at night, and only with the help of a machine.

39. This pagination reflects that the letters page is two pages after the most recently numbered page of the comic book (preceded by an advertisement). Only comic book story pages are numbered.

40. Rather than subscribe to the ideas of high art developed in literate culture (that suggests that art should be based on ideals held by the educated few), Lee tends to argue that art should be based upon the ideas of culture in general. Since Lee is often a salesman and spokesperson, the following segment may be more representative of his true feelings, as it is drawn from a contentious debate with Harvey Kurtzman (arguing for the future of comic books as high art): "It's only the people who are away from norm, who are doing things on their own who are doing any good ... that's the biggest crock I've ever heard in my life! There are inspired comic books ... If people didn't enjoy today's comic books, we wouldn't have these conventions. You're talking as though we're discussing a field that had nothing good in it and that nobody likes, and why don't we do something good" (McLaughlin 43–44).

41. The famous exception to this would be *The Amazing Spider-Man* #96–98, which undoubtedly caused publishers to reconsider the code in general. Although an anti-drug storyline, these issues had references to drugs and depictions of drug paraphernalia (both strictly prohibited by the code) and had to be run without the code's seal of approval. Several revisions to the code followed in 1971, and the success of these issues also made publishers question its general necessity.

42. One of the ways that Marvel would make this distinction most dramatically would be through lampooning the competition (and sometimes themselves) in the comic book, *Not Brand Eech*. More than a marketing scheme, the type of parodic humor contained within indicated not only awareness of but also distance from superhero conventions and therefore, some tendencies toward literacy's self-awareness.

43. This may or may not have been a bid for greater cultural respectability for superhero comic books. I tend to think it's much more of a practical decision for Marvel, trying to reach a demographic then largely untapped by DC. This would better explain why Lee is reaching out to an older and supposedly more discerning audience and yet feels the way he does in the rant quoted in the earlier endnote.

44. Expanding on comic books as better equipped to deliver fantasy than television, Lee states: "When comic artists want something far out, we can drawn whatever we dream ... I think of our stories as fairy tales for people who have outgrown conventional fairy tales ... I think we all have a warm spot in our hearts for the Grimm or Anderson stories, the Oz books, Br'er Rabbit, things like that.... Then suddenly you discover that comic books have what you've been looking for. Everything is bigger than life. There's an element of magic. There's a tremendous amount of fantasy running through them. Anything goes!" (McLaughlin 48–49).

45. The idea of continuity has already been addressed as something that takes the superhero story to an epic length and therefore positions the repeated stories and themes more clearly as the episodic repetition of an epic poem. However, the episodes were printed and catalogued by many collectors who treated back issues like historical documents and used precedent evidence for the "no prize." Along these same lines, the editor would often cite the source for references to the past made by characters or the narrator by adding text to the panels in which references were made (usually reading something like "As seen in issue #5!"). This served a practical purpose by creating a sense of loss in readers who did not own the issue mentioned (and therefore, would likely collect all subsequent issues in order to better understand such subsequent references). However, this practice certainly catered to a desire among fans influenced by the practices of literate culture to preserve and tabulate.

46. Of course, this would be the argument of Alexis de Tocqueville about the paradox of American democracy trying to balance individualism and community, which leaves the country ready to surrender collective power to the strong leader because he theoretically represents the strong whole of the country. This ideal is discussed more by Tim Blackmore as a means to analyze a specific comic book text, Miller's *The Dark Knight Returns*, in his article, "The Dark Knight of Democracy."

47. The typical story is that Lee was so unsure about this unique new superhero that he put Spider-Man's first story in the last of issue of the poorly selling anthology title (Wright 210). While this may have some truth, it may also be hyperbole to sell Spider-Man as radically new and different (as many of Marvel superheroes were sold).

48. Thierry Groensteen also has incredibly perceptive ideas about the speech and thought balloon but limits his speculations more specifically to ideas that are clearly grounded in semiotics.

49. In recent years, the overriding attitude of Marvel has been to regard their superhero comic books as raw material for their film productions (that create much more profit for the company). This fact is mentioned because their line of comic books (that sells much less than in their various heydays) has been a safe space to continue to work as they have in the past, varying themes, changing formulae, etc. Even though this is a different way of identifying comic books as

Chapter 6

1. This term is not exclusive to DC comic books, and many think it was coined by William James in *The Will to Believe*. As will be noted in other ways within this chapter, the appearance of such a concept in this 1895 (and subsequently its discussion in theories of physics and its frequent employment as science fiction motif) is not coincidentally tied to the advent of certain new media forms. I contend that this new fascination with variation has much to do with secondary orality: a perspective encouraged by new media (with James's ideas predating Ong's sense of secondary orality).

2. Regardless of the way that McLuhan labels it, the understanding of the unconscious against which he rails seems to be more the Jungian notion of the unconscious than the Freudian notion of the unconscious.

3. As will be noted in a few lines, Ong works much more specifically with Freudian concepts in his early work. However, the reference here to "the unconscious or subconscious" indicates that he is probably using the more general sense of the unconscious used by a wider variety of psychologists ("subconscious" being coined by Pierre Janet before Freud and necessarily used in less psychoanalytic ways).

4. Although Freud's psychological studies almost always ventured into some general claims about humankind, his first orthodox venture into cultural critique would probably be the essays that comprise *Totem and Taboo*; in addition to representing less mature thought by Freud, these essays also have the tendency to work with a somewhat simplistic, exaggerated, and speculative notion of the primitive as "other."

5. It is worth suggesting that Ong's path would eventually resemble that of Freud's before him (in that both see civilization as crowding out the basic functions of the unconscious). In *Fighting for Life*, Ong seems to be more squarely in Freud's camp, seeing civilization as potentially dangerous to the natural development of the human psyche. However, Ong's writings on orality and literacy were always more conservative in this regard, working analytically to describe the different shape of human thought. In addition, as a devout Jesuit, Ong would remain notably out of line with Freud's sweeping statements about religion as a cultural institution. (Freud identifies religion as collective neurosis in his *The Future of an Illusion*.) In addition to discussions of religion in other works, Ong deals extensively with the implications of orality and literacy to the understanding of the Christian Word in his aforementioned "analytically" oriented writings.

6. More will be written about this era to contextualize *Crisis on Infinite Earths*, and much more will be written about this era in chapter 7. This is not to suggest that serious collectors did not exist before the 1970s, but the phenomenon was not widespread. Exceptions include the avid fans of Marvel mobilizing in the 1960s, mentioned in chapter 5, and the DC fans like Jerry Bails to be mentioned in this chapter.

7. This is an interesting statement about the momentum toward variation within the short history of the superhero comic book industry, greatly surpassing anything seen in the natural evolution of conventional oral culture.

8. Although I don't think this is the sole reason, Bradford Wright suggests that superheroes were not written in a way that addresses the atomic era. "Comic book writers accustomed to dealing in simple solutions frankly did not know how to deal with the reality of the atomic age any better than the rest of the population did. This raised some serious questions about the continuing ability of superheroes to speak to the concerns of their audience" (Wright 72). Of course, this is something that Marvel superheroes would be built to address.

9. This situation actually brings up an interesting copyright question for a company that had used copyright so often in order to maintain and expand its market dominance. Since DC would undoubtedly feel that the new Flash is merely an update of the old, they would continue to have actionable cases against imitators. However, if the copyright system were set up by application like trademark, would DC need a separate trademark for the new Flash? This is an especially thorny question as Barry Allen becomes not just an update of Jay Garrick but a separate character on another world (as set up in "Flash of Two Worlds"). This mention is necessary to show how the legal measures used to protect the intellectual property in the literate world cannot fully contain the repetition-with-a-difference ideal of oral culture (primary or secondary).

10. In interviews and lectures that followed the publication of *Orality and Literacy*, Ong felt the need to maintain the discrete nature of his terminology so that their application would not become too general; he did so by occasionally using the terms *secondary literacy* and *secondary visuality*.

11. In terms of a politics that might allow for a global village in the midst of such a variety of viewpoints, Lyotard identifies a recognition of difference as a prerequisite that establishes a fundamental connection — another postmodern paradox.

12. I refer to Jameson with some hesitation, as his work on postmodernism was initially analytical and therefore nonjudgmental, but subsequent work more clearly articulates his position as an opponent to the basic tenets of postmodernism. Nevertheless, *Postmodernism, or, the Cultural Logic of Late Capitalism* still presents some of the more cogent ideas about postmodernism's use of pastiche.

13. These superheroes include Ultraa, with an origin very similar to Superman, who decides that Earth-Prime is not ready for superheroes and relocates to Earth-1. Also included is another version of Superboy, whose story is told in an issue of *DC Comics Presents* (supposedly just one of a spate of consequence-free,

end-of-the-story-line stories told immediately before *Crisis on the Infinite Earths*).

14. Quantum physicists have developed many multiverse theories in the last three decades based primarily on the theories of Albert Einstein (presented to a limited degree as part of the discussion of *Planetary* in chapter 8). Therefore, the idea of the multiverse became part of the popular imagination before there were theories to support it.

15. Before Bails and his work, other fans had been writing about superhero comic books but had done so within the confines of science fiction fanzines like Dick and Pat Lupoff's *Xero* (which contained essays eventually collected in *All in Color for a Dime*).

16. In 1976, the magazine was titled *The Nostalgia Journal* and only became known as *The Comics Journal* in 1977. It competed primarily with an adzine turned fanzine turned professional magazine known as *The Buyer's Guide to Comic Fandom*, which debuted in 1971 but really only became a professional magazine in 1983 (when its title changed to *Comic Buyer's Guide*). However, Gary Groth, the editor of *The Comics Journal*, would quickly establish an identity for the magazine that separated it from its competitor.

17. This reference to "magazines" actually refers primarily to *The Comics Journal*, which takes a hostile position to the market dominance of the superhero genre in American comic books. *The Comics Journal* tends to find fault in superhero comic books in the same way that literate culture tends to find fault in epic poetry.

18. Like many at Marvel comics, Wolfman would resist the constraints of the Comics Code, and his most often made argument against it as a facile list of rules would be that the strict adherence to the code forbade listing his last name in comic book credits.

19. After the end of the series, Wolfman would produce the *History of the DC Universe*, a two-issue history book that presents the new post–*Crisis* history of the DC universe (not multiverse), erasing variations and contradictions. This would be accompanied by a new version of the series *Secret Origins* in which origins were not reprinted (as in past incarnations of the series) but retold to fit post–*Crisis* continuity. The final issue of the 1980s series featured a retelling the "Flash of Two Worlds" with Jay Garrick's Keystone City stolen by villains and forced to vibrate at another frequency that practically erased it from the memories of everyone else in the world.

20. This may actually represent the way culture at large understands the conventions of traditionality versus the conventions of literacy (as potentially implied by the adult bias against superhero comic books described in previous chapters). Therefore, with its quick move from traditionality to new traditionality, DC may have been missing out on the older audience that Marvel so aggressively pursued (an audience more enmeshed in culture at large and therefore, more literate). From the late 1960s to the early 1980s, DC would lag behind Marvel in sales of comic books to a buying public consistently skewing older.

21. The "Crisis" in the title is taken from the repeated use of "Crisis" in the titles of the multiverse crossover stories between the Justice League and the Justice Society (a bit of evidence in the split Wolfman feels between employing the clichés of the past and avoiding clichés in the future). Also, it's worth noting that DC rejected the limited series idea in 1970, arguing that a 12-issue limited series wouldn't be profitable. Sales of new series were always low and at best, sales picked up somewhere around the sixth issue (Wolfman 5). DC's willingness to go forward with this idea indicates that the editors felt the temperament of the market had changed. In addition to the growing direct market that encouraged collection, they may have also been influenced by independent creators like Dave Sim, who survived only because of the direct market and understood his comic book storytelling in terms shaped by literate culture (Loosely following the Aristotelian formulation for storytelling, he insisted that his series, *Cerebus*, would be limited [at 300 issues!] and have a clear sense of passing time with a discrete beginning, middle, and end.).

22. In the intervening period, Marvel would release two relatively uninspired super team-up limited series: *Contest of Champions* (3 issues in 1982) and *Secret Wars* (12 issues in 1984). A 15-issue encyclopedia-type series called *The Official Handbook of the Marvel Universe* would be published in 1982 with entries for superheroes and supervillains which, like the *History of the DC Universe*, would recon origin stories and eliminate contradictions.

23. As is appropriate with a traditional culture, some stories survive and others do not based on the sense that readers have of the authentic treatment of the central characters and mythology (usually a combination of the creators adhering to cliché and yet making the stories relevant). The final Superman story (by Alan Moore) is now considered "classic" and the final Wonder Woman story is largely forgotten (seen as the wrong way to end the story of a liberated woman). Nevertheless, the marriage to Trevor is interesting as it only came about through the existence of the multiverse and several retcons. In the early 1970s Trevor was killed but eventually returned as a double from one of the parallel earths; this connection to a parallel earth was later written out but is fun to note nonetheless.

24. Also interesting is that Grant Morrison restored Earth-Prime (renamed as Earth-Q) in a rather pristine, superhero-less form in *All Star Superman* #10 complete with Joe Shuster drawing *Action* #1; while the DC All Star series is supposed to be free from the past mythology and overlapping continuities of DC multiverse/universe stories, Morrison is very intentionally employing many of the conventions associated with such DC stories.

25. *The Kingdom* is a sequel to *Kingdom Come*, a series co-plotted and illustrated by Alex Ross. In the future, most classic superheroes of the DC universe have retired, and the world is now run by notably less moral metahumans. In most readings, the return of Superman and crew to battle the metahumans is understood as Waid and Ross's rejection of the nihilistic superheroes of the Modern Age in favor of the classic

superheroes of the Golden and Silver Ages (the metahumans metaphorically represent Modern Age superheroes like Wolverine, the Punisher, Lobo, and Spawn). Therefore, we can speculate that *The Kingdom* is Waid's second step in restoring what he probably considers to be central superhero comic books: moving from moral values to endless variation.

26. In post–Crisis years, Elseworlds had become the official designation for stories outside the normal DC continuity, which in its label harkens more to the multiverse concept than the imaginary story concept.

27. But never fear, true believers! Kara Zor-El, the Supergirl from Krypton, would return to regular DC continuity in years to come within one of Jeph Loeb's Superman/Batman team-up series. (I apologize for borrowing a phrase more clearly associated with Marvel to describe a DC event but I couldn't resist.)

28. This series was preceded the year before by another crossover series titled *Identity Crisis*. While the scope of *Identity Crisis* is not of the universe-saving level, and it does not directly address the multiverse, it is worth a mention as it was published the year before *Infinite Crisis* and seems to address some issues central to the discussion. Within the series, when Dr. Light uncovers secret identities of the Justice League, he rapes the Elongated Man's wife and promise to do more of the same. In a nearly split vote, the superheroes vote to have Zantana wipe Dr. Light's memory and then do the same to Batman (who was unaware of the vote and opposed it afterwards). Their choice leads to significant problems but also turns out to not have anything to do with the mystery to be solved in the series: the murder of the Elongated Man's wife. In many ways, we could see this as a commentary on the memory-wiping intended of *Crisis on Infinite Earths*, but since it is not clearly an intentional commentary, I will not pursue it further.

29. DC's publications made this acknowledgment as well with a six-volume series of collections beginning its publication schedule before *Infinite Crisis*. The collections were titled *Crisis on the Multiple Earths* and contained classic multiverse stories including "Flash of Two Worlds" and many others.

30. With this stated, I must also say that the multiverse of *52* has some limitations in that the number not only indicates the number of weeks of publication for the series but also the number of parallel universes in existence. Limiting the number of universes is somewhat curious in that it recognized some non-continuity stories with their own universe but not others. While not a compromise between literacy and new traditionality, it may be understood as displaying some of the reticence toward unlimited variation seen within the literate mind. However, it may also be understood as displaying some of the reticence toward unlimited variation seen within the traditional mind; after all, primary oral cultures are characterized through their conservatism.

31. In 2003, Mark Waid's *Superman: Birthright* was published with references to it as the new Superman origin story or a story to be combined with John Byrne's *Man of Steel* to form the whole origin story. All of the story elements of two series cannot be combined without some contradiction, and this sense is very much in line with secondary orality (which picks and chooses to create the best cliché). And more significantly, after *Infinite Crisis*, it was revealed that both were to be set aside for a yet-to-be-told story (it turned out to be Geoff Johns's *Superman: Secret Origin*. Of course, that story couldn't differ radically from these two past versions, as the current Superman series have used elements of each in their current stories. Regardless, I can't think of a better example of new traditionality in action: the stories that you are reading are based on a variation of an origin yet to be published.

32. Along these lines, two trends are worth noting. First, some Marvel creators wanted to explain all aspects of Captain America's history including those parts most fans wanted to forget (such as his "commie smasher" years); however, this often was done by putting another spin on those years (with the commie smasher being a wholly different Captain America, not Steve Rogers). For more on this see Jason Dittmar's "Retconning America: Captain America in the Wake of World War II and the McCarthy Hearings." While this seems to indicate a compromise between traditionality and literacy, other times the dynamics of memory related to traditionality become more pronounced with certain other retcons. After the murder of Steve Rogers as Captain America, the recently revived Bucky Barnes took up the Captain America identity with a gun at his side; this led to outrage from many fans who believed it violated Captain America's integrity (a character that had been written as anti-gun in more recent years). Of course, this conveniently forgets his regular use of firearms in the original run of the series. For more on this see Phillip L. Cunningham's "Stevie's Got a Gun: Captain America and his Problematic Use of Force."

33. Thomas used the first letters page space in issue #1 to introduce the *What If?* concept to Marvel readers. Comparing it the "imaginary" stories popular in DC comics, he engaged in the standard Marvel practice of suggesting that Marvel had discovered a better way to do the thing that had become old and tired at DC. Therefore, *What If?* would feature stories that were not imaginary but that took place in parallel universes much like parallel universe stories told in previous issues of *The Fantastic Four* and *The Avengers*. Of course, Roy Thomas the Marvel promoter would have to disassociate himself from Roy Thomas the fanzine producer who would have been very well aware of the DC multiverse stories (told at the same time as the DC imaginary stories). In addition, he promised that *What If?* would be the only title to tell alternative universe stories from that point forward, but this promise would be broken quickly and often.

34. The first series ran from 1977 to 1984, and the second series ran from 1989 to 1998. Subsequently, the series has been revived several times for limited runs.

35. Subsequently, most alternate earths in the Marvel omniverse have been numbered, including the alternate earths of the *What If?* series.

36. In *The Official Handbook to the Marvel Universe*, alternative universe have their own special section.

37. *Marvel Zombies* is a title that also playfully refers to a description given in the past to extremely loyal Marvel fans. Incidentally, a fan at a convention suggested that his superhero horror series be followed with another genre combination between superhero stories and science fiction (represented by the *Planet of the Apes* series); Marvel obliged with *Marvel Apes*, once again demonstrating the close relation between creators and audience in the superhero comic book industry.

38. Within *Universe X*, vol. 1, the omniverse is introduced by Captain Britain, with a direct nod to Alan Moore, who first numbered the Marvel universe as 616 in a story about Merlin, who protected the omniverse. However, more important is the visual representation of the omniverse that includes a pastiche/bricolage of images from comic books of the past in their various artistic styles (much like the visual representation of Hypertime in *The Kingdom*). Although it may only be in part intended, the series as a whole has a variety of artists working in a variety of styles — giving a pastiche-like feel to the work as a whole.

39. Despite the way in which *Earth X* approximates the workings of new traditionality with such accuracy, it should be noted that Alex Ross has a marked preference for Golden and Silver Age and has expressed anxiety about straying too far from the source of inspiration. And yet while his work does evoke the inspiration and sentiment of pastimes, his projects have almost always provided self-conscious variations of those heroes often in dystopic worlds.

40. However, only some of the series feature crossovers between worlds (like the Justice League and Avengers team-up) while others simply work with the idea that the superheroes always lived in the same world (like the Superman and Spider-Man team-up).

Chapter 7

1. They are important foci for the analyses of the Modern Age in Richard Reynolds's *Superheroes: A Modern Mythology*, Geof Klock's *How to Read Superhero Comics and Why*, and Richard Wright's *Comic Book Nation* (among many others).

2. Dave Sim and Scott McCloud are an interesting pairing as creators of the Creator Bill of Rights. Sim was (and is) most well known for the self-published title, *Cerebus*, a bitterly satirical take on fantasy and superhero stories, and McCloud was most well known for the Eclipse published title, *Zot*, a nostalgic and somewhat self-conscious take on science fiction and superhero stories (McCloud would eventually be much better known for his nonfiction comic books such as *Understanding Comics*). Their personalities and politics were very different, but their partnership demonstrated how creators of different stripes were pulled together at this time (even if some were only drawn in order to have a bigger slice of the corporate pie).

3. Also previously cited in chapter 5, this quotation from Ong describes most of the less sophisticated superhero comic books that preceded the Modern Age (as well as those with more sophistication). However, it also describes a point that will be more fully analyzed by Miller and Moore (in particular, with Moore's *Watchmen*).

> Contest between heavily laden type figures is a central operation in an oral-culture's retention of its articulated knowledge and its sense of identity. The old oral world had to keep everything as formulaicly fixed as possible, and violent external conflict had been the principle ploy to make a story interesting. The old oral world will be recognized as the one in which little children still want their stories told: typed heroes and gore — though the sophistication of great epics is wanting in children's tales, as it is in the regressive Westerns and whodunits on television [Ong, *Interfaces* 210–211].

4. Although the term "teenager" had been in place for some time by the 1970s, I would argue that it wasn't until then that the idea of teenage rebellion had been enshrined as a cultural imperative. For instance, *The Catcher in the Rye* was published in 1951 and had limited appeal for some time, and *Rebel without a Cause* was released in 1955 but was considered controversial. However, after a period of censorship in the 1960s, *Catcher in the Rye* became enshrined as a classic on high school reading lists in the 1970s and with the film school boom of the 1970s, *Rebel without a Cause* achieved a similar status. Together with the late 1960s turn against anti–Communists, segregationists, big government, and big business, reading stories of outsiders became much more fashionable within popular culture for teenagers and even for adults.

5. Wright situates Wolverine more squarely in terms of his historical framework:

> Wolverine was one of many tough, right-wing antiheroes who emerged in popular culture to reflect the antigovernment attitudes generated by the Vietnam War, Watergate, and the reaction against the rights revolution of the 1960s. Unencumbered by bureaucratic technicalities or liberal sensibilities, Wolverine dispensed justice with righteous violence. John Byrne imagined him as "'Dirty Harry' with a Canadian accent" [265].

At the same time, Spider-Man was involved in a similar but more occasional debate with the violent moralist known as the Punisher. The Punisher asked Spider-Man why he threw criminals in a prison from which they would undoubtedly escape rather than kill them. The Punisher's origin was a variation of the story of another icon of the 1970s action film, Charles Bronson's *Death Wish* character. And when Frank Miller re-creates Batman in *The Dark Knight Returns*, he would frequently compare his Batman to Dirty Harry.

6. Frank Miller acknowledges several influences including Gil Kane but highlights the importance of Will Eisner: "I've studied Eisner's work in particular ... I find ... his storytelling to be crucial to an understanding of the form" (George, *Frank Miller* 23).

7. It is interesting to note that Miller is best known

for blending superhero story with crime fiction, as crime fiction is an outgrowth of the mystery. Ong identifies the mystery as quintessentially literate because of the sense of closure created by the genre's narrative arc. However, Ong understood the mystery through the rather narrow lens of late 19th- and early 20th-century English mysteries and the Enlightenment ideal of logic held in such high esteem by Sherlock Holmes. Doyle's mysteries and the English parlor room mysteries were quite different from the post–WWI mysteries and crime fiction that inspired Miller, such as the work of Dashiell Hammett and Mickey Spillaine. In addition to directly implicating the detective in the mystery, their stories were violent and conspiratorial. Often episodic, the line between truth and falsehood was regularly put into question; the objective distance between the hero and the crime was lost, and elements of cases or entire cases sometimes were left unsolved. In short, this type of crime fiction worked against the sense of closure offered by the traditional mystery.

8. Moore's *Marvelman* story is a fascinating case of being the one of the most influential superhero stories that most people have never read — a sort of Beowulf, temporarily lost due to circumstances. While I suppose I could then make a case for its ephemeral nature, it is really the trappings of literature culture that make it so obscure. L. Miller and Son published reprints of *Captain Marvel* until stopped by the original publisher Fawcett (Fawcett being the publisher sued by DC who claimed that Captain Marvel imitated Superman). L. Miller and Son then published *Marvelman*, Mick Anglo's variation on Captain Marvel (much more closely resembling Captain Marvel than Captain Marvel resembled Superman). *Marvelman* ceased publication in 1960 and L. Miller and Son sold the plates to Alan Class, Ltd. When the series began in *Warrior*, Dez Skinn claimed to have purchased the rights and to have split them between himself, Moore, and Leach, but he never did so. *Warrior* was canceled before the series was completed and Eclipse (an American publisher) bought the reprint rights from Skinn. The series was retitled *Miracleman* in order to avoid legal wrangling with DC (who bought Captain Marvel from Fawcett). Moore completed the series with Eclipse and, when Neil Gaiman took over the title, Moore gave him his supposed share in Miraclemen. Eclipse went bankrupt before Gaiman completed his run, and Todd McFarlane bought all Eclipse characters for Image comics (which he assumed included Marvelman/Miraclemen). This led to about two decades of legal wrangling that may now be resolved with Marvel's purchase of Marvelman/Miraclman. Regardless, the series was kept out-of-print and unread by many, with its relevance to the Modern Age of superhero comic books existing largely as a mythic story.

9. Although there is no grand critical point to be made, both Miller and Moore made their breakthrough in American superhero comics by synthesizing superhero stories with crime stories and horror stories, respectively — crime comics and horror comics being the dominant concern of Fredric Wertham's campaign against comic books. As the Comics Code became less relevant, adult sensibilities shaped superhero comics using conventions that Wertham had deemed most threatening to the young comic book reader.

10. This is a bit of an extremist position on Superman, as several stories in the history of Superman make overtures in this direction, with the earliest, best example of this being Eliot S. Maggin's "Must There Be a Superman?"

11. One of Moore's first works with the man of steel would be story in *DC Comics Presents*, a "team-up" between Superman and the Swamp Thing. Although not radically innovative, it is an interesting story that features Superman infected with a Kryptonian fungus. Without an antidote, he retreats to a remote location and begins to go insane in the presence of the Swamp Thing. He attacks the Swamp Thing, but the creature convinces Superman that "it is ... the fighting ... that is killing you" (Moore, *DC Universe* 147). Superman is "cured" by succumbing to the Swamp Thing's green world. Although not overtly critical of superhero tropes like *Watchmen*, the idea that the fighting is killing the superhero is nevertheless introduced.

12. For the specific and eventual outcome of the movement that really gained footing in the 1980s, "A Bill of Rights for Comic Creators" can be seen at Scott McCloud's website.

13. All of these articles stray outside the realm of superhero graphic novels intended for adults with references to *American Flagg, Cerebus, Maus*, and *American Splendor*. And while all entertain the notion that Miller and Moore deserve serious critical attention, several dismiss aspects of their work or their works entirely with little critical qualifications. In Lloyd Rose's "Comic Books for Grown-Ups" in *The Atlantic Monthly*, Miller's "draftsmanship is weak" (77). In Peter S. Prescott's "The Comic Book (Gulp!) Grows Up" in *Newsweek*, the criticism is more scathing with the claim Miller's "Batman reads like a story board for the Bernhard Goetz School of Social Work" (71). (Prescott seems to miss the rather obvious parody of Bernhard Goetz in *The Dark Knight Returns*.) In addition, with more serious consideration, Prescott states "Moore's *Watchmen* if even more overreaching ... soon sinks beneath the weight of it pretentions..." (71).

14. Jay Cocks in the previously mentioned *Time* article discussed *Watchmen*'s "cinematic" perspectives and thus associated comic books with a then-respectable but once questionable art form. However, in his conclusion, he mentioned the problem with adapting *Watchmen* for the big screen: "But a book of this scope can only be scaled down and confined on the screen, no matter how lavishly it is adapted. Graphic novels are cinema for the page, but they are already outsizing the medium they have learned so much from" (Cocks and Gallagher). Although a backhanded compliment, graphic novels are clearly portrayed as something other than other high art forms to which they might be conveniently compared.

15. It's clear from the overall tone and the conclusions of the *Comic Book Nation* that Bradford Wright loves superheroes but at times feels guilty for doing so

(particularly with the Modern Age). The following portion of the last quotation used in text was removed as potentially distracting, but it demonstrates his occasional acknowledgment of superhero comic books as an inferior art form: "Comic books remained essentially the domain of superheroes and male adolescent fantasies.... The institution of creators' rights, in effect, encouraged comic book makers to better accommodate the tastes of young people, for whom violence, cynicism, and moral ambiguity were the cultural commodities most in demand" (262).

16. It should also be mentioned that Lois and her husband had been exchanging romantic banter, and he seems to be closing the door to their bedroom. In this way, Superman's question seems to also ask about the consummation of a relationship that remained unconsummated for decades.

17. The move toward this adult content and prestige format is quite intentional as noted by Miller, discussing his relationship with Dick Giordano, DC's editor-in-chief: "I discussed every aspect of the series with Dick Giordano, who's editing it, before I started, and I was very nervous about how they might react to some of the things I wanted to do. It really is a much more severe view of the character. But it turns out this is what Dick has been wanting" (George 36). Although DC Comics is generally credited with a move toward a clearly adult audience with content and format, the move began earlier with other works and also with Marvel; the rival comic book publisher put out its first glossy superhero "graphic novel" in 1982 (*The Death of Captain Marvel*) and its first line of "adult" comic books in the same year (Epic Comics). More on this shift will follow in this chapter.

18. Miller flatly states, "Dark Knight was really the beginning of a much more conscious approach to the craft" (wiater 225); in reference to working with past stories, Miller opines, "What I was after was the feeling I had when I was 6 years old and I first saw a Batman comic. That memory is a lot more vivid than most of my real life as a child.... When I was doing Dark Knight, I was essentially trying to evoke that same feeling, but to an older and more sophisticated audience" (Robinson, "Frank Miller").

19. Miller has often suggested that he tried to bleach out the post–Wertham, Technicolor gleam of a happy world associated with Batman thanks comic books and the 1960s television series: "In this perfect world of comic books, which it was back them, why would people dress up in tights to fight crime? ... It was 1985 when I started working on this, and I thought, 'What kind of world would be scary enough for Batman?' And I looked out my window" (Robinson, "Frank Miller").

20. In Tim Blackmore's article, "The Dark Knight of Democracy," he makes a similar point but with a different critical paradigm (with Batman as the individual); using Tocqueville as a starting point, he suggests that Batman begins the story as the individual rather than part of a collective:

> The individual gives up Old Testament justice in exchange for a court system which fails him. As the court system fails him, he attempts to reclaim physical power from the centralized one. Miller "stress[es] that Superman and Batman are enemies ... Batman has tremendous contempt for Superman because he's such a 'good boy,' because he takes orders from the President" (Borax 40). Miller outlines Tocqueville's fear: there is a national power (Superman) who works for the "common good," as opposed to the individual power (Batman) who works for the "particular good" [Blackmore 39].

21. Considering Miller's feelings about the McCarthy era and its influence on comic books publishing, this portrayal of the United States in the 1980s might also be part of Miller's self-conscious commentary on the medium: "Do we want the protection of the first amendment, and are we going to fight for it? Our self-contempt is our biggest problem, that and the absolute cowardice the publishers have since the McCarthy era" (63).

22. Citations for *Watchmen* include chapter number and page number within the chapter (each chapter an issue in the series).

23. Both Miller and Moore would regret the way that their works were understood as a prescription for the grim and gritty superhero stories that followed in the 1990s with retooled heroes such as the Punisher and Wolverine, and also with new heroes such as Spawn, Cable, and Lobo. Miller states:

> Since *Dark Knight*, very cynical editors have hired artists to trace off pages of the *Dark Knight*, and they've hired writers to repeat what they think they understand about *Dark Knight*, which essentially is that it is very brutal, and that includes little TV panels. Of course, all this misses the point of the whole thing, so what we're seeing is a lot of third-rate imitations [Sharrett 35].

And Moore states:

> I kind of hoped that after we'd done *Watchmen* people would have looked at it and not said, "Oh wow, we can do superheroes but with more violence and sex and swearing." I really hoped that they would look at it and think, "Hey, there's interesting story possibilities here..." We were trying to say that, "There's a world of storytelling possibilities out there. *Watchmen* is just us exploring one of those possibilities." That there's a world of possibilities and everybody should explore their own. But instead, you got these retreads of *Watchmen*. People trying to graft dark sensibilities upon characters that had never been designed to carry those kinds of sensibilities. Any poor wretched innocent Golden Age character — it was pretty certain that they were going to be re-imagined as a sort of dark, psychopathic monster from the edges of human rationality [Khoury 120].

24. Alan Moore states: "[I]f you equate [an incredibly powerful superhero] with the atom bomb, the atom bomb doesn't have to take over the world, but by being there it changes everything" (Groth and Fiore 100).

25. Jack Goody's primary criticism of Levi-Strauss is that *The Savage Mind* reinforces this dichotomy

despite its attempt to undermine it; for more on this, see Goody's *The Domestication of the Savage Mind*.

26. In fact, *The Dark Knight Returns* would lead to a sequel tilted *The Dark Knight Strikes Again*. As I note in my essay, "Frank Miller Strikes Again and Batman Becomes a Postmodern Anti-Hero," this sequel was part Miller's plans from the start for his future-version of Batman. However, as I also note in the essay, *The Dark Knight Strikes Again* ultimately functions less as an orthodox sequel and more as a parody of the grim and gritty superhero trend that it inspired.

27. Blackmore states, "Miller's unprecedented 16-panel grid works cinematically to produce a dark, claustrophobic world. The use of the confining screen also reveals Miller's view of the TV generation: they can be convinced of anything with ease. The regular, unbreakable grid is a symbol of how ordered and small the lives of people are" (43).

28. Nash states, "Media interviews with men and women in the street highlight the absence of innocence and the problematic nature of democratic or popular approval of Batman's vigilante actions" (42).

29. Other forms of technology like transportation and weapons technology are also included and fare even more poorly in both works. Both creators are operating with a post–Enlightenment sense of technology, no longer believing that increasing technology is a marker in our march toward utopia.

30. Van Ness makes a case that the intended realism of *Watchmen* was limited by technology of its time; subsequent collections of *Watchmen* were recolored with a more muted color palate, with a greater distinction between colors used in the "real" world and in *Tales of the Black Freighter*. Of course, revisions are a fascinating part of the mix in this study, but the original color scheme is not radically altered (40–41).

31. For instance, the cover of chapter III features a nuclear symbol surrounded by the words "Fallout Shelter." Due to smoke that rises from the street, certain letters are obscured and the words are then also "all hel" (with tendrils of smoke seeming to form the profile of a skull).

32. It would take considerably longer for *Watchmen* to reach the screen since it did not contain marketable characters and since various directors (such as Terry Gilliam) considered it more difficult to adapt. Eventually, it would be adapted in 2009 by Zack Snyder and was considered too faithful to the source material. For instance, *Tales of the Black Freighter*, a comic book specific element, was adapted as an animated film. (It was not included in the theatrical release but in a subsequent DVD version; *Watchmen* had three different edit variations on DVD, a case where technology encourages variation within a commodity system.)

33. Marvel stocks were traded on stock market in 1991 (Wright 254), and the *Wall Street Journal* deemed superhero comic books to be a good investment. This good investment collector's market was to be short lived, as superhero comic book publishers exploited the collectors by printing variations on the same popular issue (gold foil covers were favorites). In short order, the consumers exhausted their resources and became frustrated with the publishers ultimately self-defeating grab for more cash.

34. Wildstorm and Image are related companies with Wildstorm being one of a group of companies that formed Image. However, Wildstorm remained relatively independent within the Image corporate structure.

35. On *Talk of the Nation*, Miller states:
We're constantly told all cultures are equal, and every belief system is as good as the next.... For some reason, nobody seems to be talking about who we're up against, and the sixth century barbarism they actually represent. These people saw people's heads off. They enslave women, they genitally mutilate their daughters, they do not behave by any cultural norms that are sensible to us. I'm speaking into a microphone that never could have been a product of their culture, and I'm living in a city where three thousand of my neighbors were killed thieves of airplanes they never could have built.... we've been kind of fighting a war on the side, and sitting like a bunch of [Athenians and] Romans complaining about it (Miller, "Writers").

36. Groth and Fiore refer to Miller's politics as that of a "mugged liberal" (59), and I might refer to him as a former member of the US civilization and current member of a US tribe. While my general analysis of Miller's current approach is one that is less self-conscious and more earnest, he does create interesting bits of parody within works that otherwise avoid variation: see *Batman to Strikes Again* (spoofing DC characters and using them in earnest), *All Star Batman and Robin* (interacting with Grant Morrison's contemporaneous run of the regular *Batman* title), and *Sin City 7: Hell and Back* (the psychotic dream vision of pop culture, Miller's past work).

37. *Promethea* is also an interesting and obvious way that Moore enacts his expanding study of variation in superhero comic books. The protagonist is a student studying Promethea (a mythic heroine) who is chosen to be the new Promethea. After a Shazam-like transformation into Promethea, she is able to travel to a realm where she can interact with a multitude of Promethea incarnations from the past.

38. *Postmodern* is a term often used to describe *The Dark Knight Returns* and *Watchmen* (see Reynold's highly influential *Superheroes: A Modern Mythology*). I also call them postmodern but regard them as works that have postmodern characteristics that are utilized in an effort to critique postmodernism. In "Deconstructing the Hero," Iain Thomson makes an interesting statement that works fairly well for me: "In the end, *Watchmen*'s postmodern ambivalence concerning the hero places it somewhere between the Enlightenment rejection of, and the existentialist commitment to, the idea of the hero.... For, even if one believes that there is something admirable in the desire to live without heroes, the problem remains that we have not woken up and walked with our eyes wide-open into the clear light of the post-heroic tomorrow" (116).

Chapter 8

1. For a description of the romantic treatment of cyberspace and digital culture, see Vincent Mosco's *The Digital Sublime: Myth, Power, and Cyberspace*.

2. This means that the stories lose their original racially and politically charged context and need to find a new reason to have tension in the relationship.

3. This is a generally true statement, excepting the last few minutes of the last episode.

4. Other rivals do exist within the comic book world with publishers of superhero comic books like Image and Dark Horse, but, relatively, they claim only a small share of the market in comic book stores, traditional bookstores, and online subscriptions.

5. While this has been my contention for quite a while, I was pleased to hear others sharing the sentiment in a panel on which I presented at the 2011 Popular Culture Association Conference; in particular, Garret Castleberry spoke insightfully on the retcon (with the idea that the retcon is the new norm); his paper was "Introducing a Theory of Rhetcon in Postmodern Superhero Storytelling: An Analysis of Green Lantern: Rebirth." (Unfortunately, because of limitations of time, he was unable to spend much time with the chosen text itself.)

6. *Kick-Ass* might seem an exception to the characterization of "non-superhero," but it walks a strange line between the superhero as real and as fiction.

7. There is no internal monologue in oral culture as it is known in literate culture. The self-consciousness of new traditionality in the digital age provides technology that is something like internal monologue but is public and therefore, erases the interiority of the text. Consider the quick and ready exchange of ideas through texting, Twitter, and internet comment strings; this is also seen in other mediums and technologies with reality television's "confessional" booth and Bluray's feature that allows users to create their own commentary about films.

8. In *The Language of New Media*, Lev Manovich explores the radical step forward from written narrative to video game narrative, with a particular focus *Doom* and *Myst*. In particular, he demonstrates how the narrative/description dichotomy in literature is replaced the narrative/exploration codependence in video games. I would suggest this digital age replacement is prefigured in comic books and harkens back to some of the basic tenets of traditional art.

9. In *The Savage Mind*, Levi-Strauss graphs the model of thinking that he describes (268). Although he doesn't use these terms, he demonstrates how the undomesticated mind does not work in linear or analog terms. In some ways, this model is in line with the idea of the "ergodic" literature used by Espen Aarseth to describe cyberspace in *Cybertext* (although I have the same reservations toward Aarseth's claims as George Landow in *Hypertext 3.0* [325–326]).

10. In *Digital McLuhan*, Levison's essential argument is that McLuhan's theories anticipated digital culture and that the technology that he used to exemplify his theories didn't represent them as well as more recent computer age technology. He also suggests that McLuhan thinks in ways that are fundamentally tied to digital culture, with *The Gutenberg Galaxy* written with pages that resemble webpages (31).

11. Before moving into his description of the reader in the digital age, Bolter gives a pointed overview of the 19th-century practice that immediately predates the new media transformation leading to the digital age:

> The goal of this exacting scholarship [textual criticism] was to determine letter by letter what Plato, Euripides, or the Church fathers "really" wrote: to apply the standards of printed accuracy to the manuscript tradition of ancient and medieval authors. Textual criticism set out to establish a little canon for each author—a definitive list of works and a definitive edition of each work in which all scribal deviations were relegated to the footnotes. Print also provided dignity and distance for works of the canon, placing authors in writing space not available to other literate men and women. By ensuring that the reader cannot enter into the space that the text occupies, printing still remains the appropriate technology for those who wish to encourage worshipful reading [167–168].

12. Bolter points out an irony about texts like mine, critiquing a medium in another medium that may be ill-suited to do so (and therefore, perhaps identifying the appropriateness of a work like the *Pathways Project*):

> The success of the World Wide Web derives from the ways in which it borrows from and reforms not only print, but also graphics design, photography, film, and television. Although we do not seem to regard the Web as a place for a new kind of essay, we do think of it as a space for multimediated writing with high visual appeal. This very appeal tends to devalue the Web for many scholars in the Humanities.... The field of cultural studies examines the cultural iconography of television and magazine ads, and film studies and art history take as their objects of study visual or audiovisual media. Yes even these disciplines produce essays and monographs. Although scholars are aware that popular culture is using new media to renegotiate the relationship between the verbal and the audiovisual, they continue to write about this renegotiation in printed essays, often without images [113].

Base on this issue alone, Scott McColud's *Understanding Comics* trilogy may be considered one of the most appropriate critical responses to the critical discussion of comic books.

13. In addition to the bringing the Green Lantern back from the dead with *Green Lantern: Rebirth*, Johns has done something similar with the similarly titled *Flash: Rebirth*. He has also added to that the subsequently developed *Green Lantern: Secret Origin* and *Superman: Secret Origin*, somewhat comically titled. These limited series were named after the DC *Secret Origins* series that existed in three different incarnations, initially reprinting past DC origins and then retelling origins in the 1980s to fit post–*Crisis* continuity. More to the point, while "secret origin" refers

to the subtle way in which origins were developed (and redeveloped) in previous superhero ages, every retelling of superhero origins in the Modern Age calls attention to itself (despite Johns's potential for subtlety).

14. Some might take exception with this characterization, citing Denny O'Neil's Green Lantern/Green Arrow team-ups of the 1970s. I would agree in part, but O'Neil maintained Jordan's personality as a variation on their pro-establishment heroes.

15. Demonstrating Mark Waid's other perspective on the matter, an updated Rip Hunter, the Silver Age member of this Modern Age team, works against the Linear Men in order to restore the infinite timelines of infinite earths (or hypertime) in Waid's *The Kingdom*.

16. One of the most awkward applications of linear time to a story that wants to work in others ways is to indicate a countdown to Parallax's destruction of the linear timeline as it now exists. As superheroes travel to different points in time to confront our time-traveling villain, narrative boxes indicate the location and amount of time that remains: "Earth. 21 hours, 38 minutes ago" (Jurgen 38). That reference is to present day earth, but the countdown is still used as superheroes travel to the past and the future and most awkwardly, even to the vanishing point (supposedly "beyond the passage of time") (2).

17. This is a nice metaphor for someone who respects the superhero comic book fan but doesn't operate like a collector (someone who doesn't take his toys out of the box, puts them on the shelf, and never plays with them).

18. Sinestro has long been a double for Green Lantern much as the Joker has been for Batman, but Sinestro is much more morally ambiguous (as a rebel Green Lantern); he has long been a fan-favorite villain and serves as the central character in 2011 DC reboot Green Lantern. More on the 2011 DC reboot will follow in the conclusion.

19. I borrow the term "cheat" from theater because Sinestro is not really breaking the fourth wall. Instead, this hint of self-consciousness in the text seems to be part of Johns's strategy to enact self-consciousness in a way that does not entirely disrupt the narrative as narrative.

20. Johns did something similar in *Flash: Rebirth*, maintaining and further developing the Flash superhero family (a practice very reminiscent of the Golden and Silver Ages).

21. Bolter comments on the relationship between words and the visual components that surround them on the computer screen: "Indeed, even the words on the screen, set above, beside, of beneath images, serve as visual units and enter into the larger spatial structure ... in all picture writing before and after literacy, the element that exist at the margin between linguistic and pictorial meaning" (63).

22. To reinforce John's love of variation as practiced in new traditionality, I'll mention his very next major crossover event series, *Flashpoint*, in which the current DC universe is radically altered with only a few heroes noticing the difference.

23. Silvio also uses Linda Hutcheon's idea of postmodernism as inherently contradictory to also explain this problem, but this seems less compelling than his other, less abstract explanation.

24. With references now made in this chapter to the resemblances between the writing of both McLuhan and Derrida to internet webpages, I feel it's necessary to also mention the resemblances between comic book pages and the basic design of both a computer display with windows and internet webpages. Comic books regularly approximate these even more effectively with their creative use of visuals and their encouragement of the reader to move in unconventional ways. With the connection Landow makes between digital and postmodern culture in mind, I will also refer to Ronald Schmidt's interesting observations about the basic conventions of comic books in general as a postmodern reading experience in "Deconstructive Comics": "Rather than two stable texts (words and pictures) juxtaposed, the comic book is a form of self-inflicted 'double-writing,' collapsing traditional strategies for reading word and picture texts" (158).

25. Although not referring to Foucault (and not as extreme as Foucault), Will Eisner thinks that comic books are part of such 20th-century changes: "This is a medium that requires intelligence on the part of the reader. It requires a contribution, a participation.... You participate, your reader contributes to it, and you have a sort of dialogue with the reader" (Robinson, "Will Eisner").

26. Like some other new media, comic books would seem to have a natural tendency to decenter the author, as comic books are usually the product of combined talents (like film and animation projects). This hasn't stopped people from imposing the models of literacy on new media, perhaps most famously with Francois Truffaut's auteur theory of film (with the director as the authority). Often, comic book studies have fallen into that trap, and, unfortunately, I share that tendency, often explicitly referring to the writer as the author.

27. In "The Death of the Author," Barthes identifies the dream-work of surrealism as one of the ways in which 20th-century art was working to frustrate certain meaning (144).

28. In Gaiman's *1602*, Peter Parquagh spends the entire story as Peter Parquagh and never becomes a *1602*-version of Spider-Man. Incidentally, a *1602*-version of Mr. Fantastic makes this claim about the universe in which they live: "I posit that we are in a universe which favors stories. A universe in which no story can ever truly end; in which there can only be continuances" (156).

29. Perhaps, it could be argued that superhero as decentered could be even backdated to the *X-Men* series with young people treated as outsiders because their powers came from their genetic identity as mutants.

30. Bendis chooses to do this elsewhere, such as in the child's comic book stylings that interrupt the flow of *Daredevil: Wake Up* and the use of depictions of the Avengers from the 1960s at the end of *Avengers: Disassembled*.

31. This approach that puts the onus on the reader is similar to that of 20th-century collage artists ranging from Pablo Picasso to Jean-Michel Basquiat. The iconographic style that Picasso implemented in his paintings seems to have been connected to his exposure to tribal masks seen most clearly in *Les Demoiselles d'Avignon* (an early example of his cubism and collage). Although some might resist this comparison between 20th-century movements in comic book art and high art, this has been done elsewhere by E. H. Gombrich (334–358) and Scott McCloud (*Understanding* 144–150).

32. It's only fair to mention that Morrison also wrote the somewhat tiresome version of "Flash of Two Worlds" in *Secret Origins* that squared the story with post–*Crisis* continuity. Despite its somewhat pedantic purpose, the clever construction saves it from being a rote story, with its multiple narrators (most notably a child, causing the reader to piece the story together and question its veracity).

33. Shortly after this, the title character of *Cerebus* (known well for its parodies of superheroes) met his "creator," Dave Sim, in a culmination of a long story arc.

34. For another take on the "real" existence of Superman as predating the creation of Superman as a comic book character, also see Rick Veitch's surreal *The Maximortal*.

35. When DC acquired Wildstorm, the Bleed was identified as a means by which DC characters could visit the Wildstorm universe and vice versa.

36. However, Klock's high esteem for *Planetary* is the result of reading the series quite differently than I do (as a full exposure of Harold Bloom's *Anxiety of Influence* at work).

37. Klock states:

The hidden road, the road the critics knows, is the hidden road of influence, the backroad connecting the superhero narrative with its own history, its tradition, its influence and effects. That is why Planetary covers not simply superhero history but also the places where superhero narrative intersects with other media and stories [170].

38. In "'This is the Authority: This Planet is Under Our Protection'—An Exegesis of Superheroes' Interrogations of Law," Jason Bainbridge states:

[T]he superhero presents an alternative or corollary to modernity, a process of estrangement by which to highlight the inadequacies in the present system in the same way a test case might highlight the inadequacies of law.... It suggests that modernity is limited, it is only one of what Lyotard would term "the grand narratives" or ways of seeing the world open to us [462–463].

Conclusion

1. In addition the rich Silver Age tradition of such revelations followed by quick and convenient rewrites of history and memory, this type of practice continues in the supposedly more realistic Modern Age. In addition to various other reboots of Spider-Man in recent years, I was a not surprised or outraged (like some fans) by the way Marvel threw out years of continuity with 2007's Spider-Man story, "One More Day." Within the arc, the demon Mephisto saved Aunt May's life, and in exchange he took Peter Parker's marriage to Mary Jane and his secret identity, exposing him to the public (nicely returning Spider-Man to a state known to not just comic book readers but also the public at large). Incidentally, Peter and Mary Jane remained married in the Spider-Man comic strip.

2. Richard Donner also worked with Geoff Johns to produce *Superman: Last Son*, a graphic novel that could very easily be read as a sequel to his director's cut.

3. The other person who has done good work in this area is Peter Coogan with *Superhero: The Secret Origin of a Genre*.

4. For a fascinating study of the new media and new technology practice of remediation, see *Remediation: Understanding New Media* by Jay David Bolter and Richard Grusin; their argument is much broader and more nuanced than my quick reference to remediation might suggest. For more, particularly on the novel in the digital age, also see Janet Murray's *Hamlet on the Holodeck* and N. Katherine Hayles's *Electronic Literature*.

5. This is also argued by Mario Saraceni in chapter 6 of *The Language of Comics*.

Works Cited

Books marked with an asterisk are merely the first of a larger series cited as a whole.

Aarseth, Espen J. *Cybertext: Perspectives on Ergodic Literature*. Baltimore: Johns Hopkins University Press, 1997. Print.

Adventures of Superman. Motion Pictures for Television, 1952–1958. Television.

Andrae, Thomas. "From Menace to Messiah: The History and Historicity of Superman." *American Media and Mass Culture: Left Perspectives*. Ed. Donald Lazere. Berkeley: University of Berkley Press, 1987. 124–138. Print.

Azzarello, Brian, and Jim Lee. *Superman: For Tomorrow, Vol. 2*. New York: DC Comics, 2006. Print.

Bainbridge, Jason. "'This Is the Authority. This Planet Is Under Our Protection'—An Exegesis of Superheroes' Interrogations of Law." *Law, Culture, and the Humanities* 3.3 (2007): 455–476. Print.

Barnes, Dave. "Time in the Gutter: Temporal Structures in Watchmen." *Kronoscope* 9.1–2 (2009): 51–60. Print.

Barthes, Roland. "The Death of the Author." *Image-Music-Text*. Trans: Stephen Heath. New York: Hill and Wang, 1977. 142–148. Print.

_____. *S/Z*. Trans. Richard Miller. New York: Hill and Wang, 1974. Print.

Bates, Cary, and Ross Andru. "Flash: Fact or Fiction?" *Flash* 1.179. *The Greatest Flash Stories Ever Told*. New York: DC Comics, 2007. 103–125. Print.

Bates, Cary, Eliot S. Maggin, and Dick Dillon. "Avenging Ghosts of the Justice Society." *Justice League of America* 1.124. *Crisis on the Multiple Earths, Vol. 4*. New York: DC Comics, 2006. . [n. pag.?] Print.

_____, _____, and _____. "Where on Earth Am I?" *Justice League of America* 1.123. *Crisis on the Multiple Earths, Vol. 4*. New York: DC Comics, 2006. [n. pag.?] Print.

Bates, Cary, and Irv Novak. "The Day I Saved the Flash." *Flash* 1.228 (August 1974). Print.

Batman. Dir. Tim Burton. Warner Bros., 1989. Film.

Batman. 20th Century–Fox Television, 1966–1968. Film.

Batman Begins. Dir. Christopher Nolan. Warner Bros., 2005. Film.

Batman Returns. Dir. Tim Burton. Warner Bros., 1992. Film.

Baudry, Jean-Louis. "The Apparatus." *Camera Obscura* 1 (1976): 104–126.

Bendis, Brian Michael, and Michael Gaydos. *Alias*. New York: Marvel Comics, 2004. Print.

_____, and _____. *Alias: The Secret Origins of Jessica Jones*. New York: Marvel Comics, 2004. Print.

Bendis, Brian Michael, and David Mack. *Daredevil: Wake Up*. New York: Marvel Comics, 2003. Print.

Bendis, Brian Michael, and Michael Avon Oeming. *Powers: The Definitive Collection, Vol. 1*. New York: Marvel Comics, 2006. Print.*

Bergengren, Ralph. "The Humor of the Colored Supplement." *Arguing Comics: Literary Masters on a Popular Medium*. Ed. Jeet Heer and Kent Worcester. Jackson: University of Mississippi Press, 2004. 9–12. Print.

Beritela, Gerard F. "Super-Girls and Mild Mannered Men: Gender Trouble in Metropolis." Wandtke, *The Amazing Transforming Superhero*. 52–69. Print.

Binder, Otto, and Pete Costanza. "The Sivana Family Strikes at the Marvel Family." *The Marvel Family* 1.10. *Shazam! From the 40's to the 70's*. New York: Harmony, 1977. 172–209. Print.

Binder, Otto, and Dick Sprang. "The Girl of Steel." *Superman* 1.123. *The Greatest Superman Stories Ever Told*. New York: DC Comics, 1987. 67–92. Print.

Blackmore, Tim. "The Dark Knight of Democracy: Tocqueville and Miller Cast Some Light on the Subject." *Journal of American Culture* 14.1 (1991): 37–56. Print.

Bolter, Jay David. *Writing Space: Computers, Hypertext, and the Remediation of Print*. Mahwah, NJ: Lawrence Erlbaum, 2001. Print.

Bolter, Jay David, and Richard Grusin. *Remediation: Understanding New Media*. Cambridge, MA: MIT Press, 1999. Print.

Bridwell, E. Nelson. "Introduction." *Superman: From the Thirties to the Seventies*. New York: Crown, 7–15. Print.

Brooker, Will. *Batman Unmasked: Analyzing a Cultural Icon*. New York: Continuum, 2001. Print.

Brownstein, Charles. *Eisner/Miller*. Milwaukie, OR: Dark Horse, 2005. Print.

Bryson, Norman. *Vision and Painting: The Logic of the Gaze*. New Haven: Yale University Press, 1989. Print.

Busiek, Kurt, and Stuart Immonen. *Superman: Secret Identity*. New York: DC Comics, 2004. Print.

Busiek, Kurt, Geoff Johns, and Pete Woods. *Superman: Up, Up, and Away*. New York: DC Comics, 2007. Print.

Busiek, Kurt, and Alex Ross. *Marvels*. New York: Marvel Comics, 2004. Print.

Byrne, John. *The Man of Steel*. New York: DC Comics, 1993. Print.

Campbell, Joseph. *The Hero with a Thousand Faces*. Princeton: Princeton University Press, 1973. Print.

Carrier, David. *The Aesthetics of Comics*. University Park: Pennsylvania State University Press, 2000. Print.

Castleberry, Garret. "Introducing a Theory of Rhetcon in Postmodern Superhero Storytelling: An Analysis of *Green Lantern: Rebirth*." PCA/ACA Conference, San Antonio, April 23, 2011. Address.

Chabon, Michael. *The Amazing Adventures of Kavalier and Clay: A Novel*. New York: Random House, 2000. Print.

Chang, Gordon H. "'Superman Is about to Visit the Relocation Centers' and the Limits of Wartime Liberalism." *Amerasia Journal* 19.1 (1993): 37–60. Print.

Claremont, Chris, and John Byrne. *X-Men: The Dark Phoenix Saga*. New York: Marvel Comics, 2006. Print.

Claremont, Chris, and Frank Miller. *Wolverine*. New York: Marvel Comics, 2009. Print.

Cocks, Jay, and John E. Gallagher. "The Passing of Pow! And Bam!" *Time* 25 Jan. 1988: 65–66. Print.

Conway, Gerry, and Don Heck. "Of Gods and Men." *Wonder Woman* 1.329 (Feb. 1986). Print.

Conway, Gerry, and Gil Kane. "The Night Gwen Stacy Died." *Spider-Man* 1.121. *40 Years of the Amazing Spider-Man*. TOPICS Entertainment, 2006. DVD-ROM.

Coogan, Peter. *Superhero: The Secret Origin of a Genre*. Austin: MonkeyBrain, 2006. Print.

Cooke, Darwyn. *DC: The New Frontier, Vol.1*. New York: DC Comics, 2004. Print.*

Cooke, John B. "Toasting Absent Heroes: Alan Moore Discusses the Charlton-Watchmen Connection." *Comic Book Artist* 9. TwoMorrows Publishing. 5 Oct. 2000. Web. 29 Jan. 2002.

Cunningham, Phillip L. "Stevie's Got a Gun: Captain America and his Problematic Use of Force." *Captain America and the Struggle of the Superhero*. Ed. Robert G. Weiner. Jefferson, NC: McFarland, 2009. 176–189. Print.

Daniels, Les. *Batman, the Complete History*. San Francisco: Chronicle, 1999. Print.

_____. *Superman, the Complete History*. San Francisco: Chronicle, 1998. Print.

The Dark Knight. Dir. Christopher Nolan. Warner Bros., 2008. Film.

David, Peter, and Ed Benes. *Supergirl: Many Happy Returns*. New York: DC Comics, 2003. Print.

Davis, Adam Brooke. "Agon and Gnomon: Forms and Functions of the Anglo-Saxon Riddles." *De Gustibus: Essays for Alain Renoir*. Ed. John Miles Foley. New York: Garland, 1992. 110–150. Print.

Dean, Michael. "Fine Young Cannibals: How Phil Seuling and a Generation of Teenage Entrepreneurs Created the Direct Market and Changed the Face of Comics." *The Comics Journal*. 277 (July 2006): 49–59. Print.

Deppy, Dirk. "Suicide Club: How Green and Stupidity Disemboweled the American Comic-Book Industry in the 1990s." *The Comics Journal*. 277 (July 2006): 69–75. Print.

Dido, Dan. "Introduction." Johns and Jimenez 5–6. Print.

DiLiddo, Annalisa. *Alan Moore: Comics as Performance, Fiction as Scalpel*. Jackson: University Press of Mississippi, 2009. Print.

Dittmer, Jason. "Retconning America: Captain America in the Wake of World War II and the McCarthy Hearings." Wandtke, *The Amazing Transforming Superhero* 35–51. Print.

Dorfman, Leo, and Curt Swan. "The Amazing Story of Superman-Red and Superman Blue." *Superman* 1.162. *The Greatest Superman Stories Ever Told*. New York: DC Comics, 1987. 207–230. Print.

Duncan, Randy, and Matthew J. Smith. *The Power of Comics: History, Form, and Culture*. New York: Continuum, 2009. Print.

Eco, Umberto. "The Myth of Superman." *The Role of the Reader: Explorations in the Semiotics of Texts*. Bloomington: Indiana University Press, 1979. 107–124. Print.

Eisner, Will. *Comics and Sequential Art*. Tamarac, FL: Poorhouse, 1990. Print.

Ellis, Warren, and John Cassaday. *Planetary: All Over the World and Other Stories*. New York: DC Comics, 1999. Print.

_____, and _____. *Planetary: Crossing Worlds*. New York: DC Comics, 2004. Print.

_____, and _____. *Planetary: Spacetime Archeology*. New York: DC Comics, 2009. Print.

Ellis, Warren, and Bryan Hitch. *The Authority: Relentless*. New York: DC Comics, 2000. Print.*

Ellis, Warren, and Tom Raney. *Stormwatch: Force of Nature*. New York: DC Comics, 1999. Print.

Engle, Gary. "What Makes Superman So Darned American?" *Superman at Fifty: The Persistence of a Legend*. New York: Macmillan, 1987. 70–87. Print.

Englehart, Steve, and Sal Buscema. "The Coming of the Nomad." *Captain America*. 1.180. *Captain America—The Complete Comic Collection*. GIT Corporation, 2007. DVD-ROM.

Evanier, Mark. "Introduction." Kirby, *Jimmy Olsen* 3–5. Print.

_____. *Kirby: King of Comics*. New York: Abrams, 2008. Print.

Feiffer, Jules. *The Great Comic Book Heroes*. Seattle: Fantagraphics, 2003. Print.

Finger, Bill, and Wayne Boring. "The Origin of Superman." *Superman* 1.53. *The Greatest Superman Stories Ever Told*. New York: DC Comics, 1987. 57–66. Print.

Finger, Bill, and Bob Kane. "The Case of the Chemical Syndicate." *Detective Comics* 1.27. *Superman: From the Thirties to the Seventies*. New York: Crown, 20–25. Print.

_____, and _____. "The Legend of the Batman — Who He Is and How He Came to Be." *Batman* 1.1. *Batman: From the Thirties to the Seventies*. New York: Crown, 1971. 26–27. Print.

_____, and _____. "The Origin of Batman." *Batman* 1.47. *The Greatest Batman Stories Ever Told*. New York: DC Comics, 1988. 66–78. Print.

Finger, Bill, and Sheldon Moldoff. "The First Batman." *Detective Comics* 1.235. *The Greatest Batman Stories Ever Told*. New York: DC Comics, 1988. 109–118. Print.

_____, and _____. "Prisoners of Three Worlds." *Batman* 1.153. *Batman From the 30's to the 70's*. New York: Crown, 1971. 272–296. Print.

Fingeroth, Danny. *Disguised as Clark Kent: Jews, Comics, and the Creation of the Superhero*. New York: Continuum, 2007. Print.

Foley, John Miles. *How to Read an Oral Poem*. Urbana: University of Illinois Press, 2002. Print.

_____. "The Impossibility of Canon." *Teaching Oral Traditions*. Ed. John Miles Foley. New York: Modern Language Association, 1998. 13–33. Print.

_____. *The Pathways Project*. n.d. Web.10 April 2010.

_____. *The Theory of Oral Composition: History and Methodology*. Bloomington: Indiana University Press, 1988. Print.

_____. *Traditional Oral Epic: The Odyssey, Beowulf, and the Serbo-Croatian Return Song*. Berkeley: University of California Press, 1990. Print.

Foucault, Michel. "What Is an Author?" *Language, Counter-Memory, Practice: Selected Essays and Interviews*. Trans. Donald F. Bouchard and Sherry Simon. Ithaca: Cornell University Press, 1977. 113–138. Print.

Fox, Gardner, and Carmine Infantino. "Flash of Two Worlds." *Flash* 1. 123. *Crisis on the Multiple Earths: The Team-Ups, Vol.1*. New York: DC Comics, 2005. 5–30. Print.

_____, and _____. "Vengeance of the Immortal Villain!" *Flash* 137. *Crisis on the Multiple Earths: The Team-Ups, Vol.1*. New York: DC Comics, 2005. 58–82. Print.

Fox, Gardener, and Bob Kane. "Batman Versus the Vampire." *Detective Comics* 1.31–32. *The Greatest Batman Stories Ever Told*. New York: DC Comics, 1989. 17–36. Print.

Fox, Gardener, and Mike Sekowsky. "Crisis on Earth-Three!" *Justice League of America* 1.29. *Crisis on Multiple Earths: The Team-Ups, Vol.1*. New York: DC Comics, 2005. [n. pag.?]. Print.

Fox, Robin. *The Tribal Imagination: Civilization and the Savage Mind*. Cambridge, MA: Harvard University Press, 2011. Print.

Freud, Sigmund. *Civilization and Its Discontents*. New York: W.W. Norton, 1961. Print.

_____. *Three Essays on the Theory of Sexuality*. New York: Basic Books, 2000. Print.

_____. *Totem and Taboo*. New York: W.W. Norton, 1990. Print.

Friedrich, Otto. "Up, Up, and Awaaay!: America's Favorite Hero Turns 50, Ever Changing but Indestructible." *Time* 14 Mar. 1988: 66–73. Print.

Gaiman, Neil, and Sam Keith. *The Sandman, Vol. 1: Preludes and Nocturnes*. New York: DC Comics, 2009. Print.*

Gaiman, Neil, and Andy Kubert. *1602*. New York: Marvel Comics, 2007. Print

"Gaiman, Neil, v. McFarlane, Todd." *Seventh Circuit Court of Appeals*. 24 Feb. 2004. Web. 9 Jan. 2008.

George, Milo. *Frank Miller: The Interviews, 1981–2003*. Seattle: Fantagrpahics, 2003. Print.

_____. *Jack Kirby: The Comics Journal Library, Volume One*. Seattle: Fantagraphics, 2002. Print.

Gombrich, E.H. *Art and Illusion: A Study in the Psychology of Pictorial Representation*. London: Phaidon, 1959. Print.

Goody, Jack. *The Domestication of the Savage Mind*. Cambridge: Cambridge University Press, 1977. Print.

Gordan, Ian, Mark Jancovich, and Mathew P. McAllister. *Film and Comic Books*. Jackson: University Press of Mississippi, 2007. Print.

Gorla, Stefano. "Interview with Will Eisner." "From the Desk of Will Eisner." *WillEisner.com*. 17 Dec. 2001. Web. 15 Mar. 2004.

Groensteen, Thierry. *The System of Comics*. Trans. Bart Beatty and Nick Nguyen. Jackson: University Press of Mississippi, 2007. Print.

Grossman, Lev. "Top 10 Graphic Novels." *Time*. n.d. Web. 20 Nov. 2009.

_____, and Richard Lacayo. "The 100 Best English-Language Novels from 1923 to the Present." *Time*. 16 Oct. 2005. Web. 20 Nov. 2009.

Groth, Gary. "Black and White and Dead All Over." *The Comics Journal* 277 (July 2006): 61–67. Print.

_____, and Robert Fiore. *The New Comics*. New York: Berkley, 1988. Print.

Hamilton, Edmond, and Dick Sprang. "The Jungle Cat-Queen." *Detective Comics* 1.211. *The Greatest Batman Stories Ever Told*. New York: DC Comics, 1989. 97–108. Print.

Harris, Neil. "Who Owns Our Myths? Heroism and

Copyright in an Age of Mass Culture." *Social Research* 52.2 (Summer 1985): 241–267. Print.

Harvey, Robert C. *The Art of the Comic Book: An Aesthetic History*. Jackson: University Press of Mississippi, 1996. Print.

Havelock, Eric A. *Preface to Plato*. Cambridge, MA: Harvard University Press, 1982. Print.

Hayles, N. Katherine. *Electronic Literature: New Horizons of the Literary*. Notre Dame, IN: University of Notre Dame Press, 2008. Print.

Heer, Jeet, and Kent Worcester. *Arguing Comics: Literary Masters on a Popular Medium*. Jackson: University of Mississippi Press, 2004. Print.

_____, and _____. *A Comics Studies Reader*. Jackson: University Press of Mississippi, 2009. Print.

James, William. *The Will to Believe and Other Essays in Popular Philosophy and Human Immortality*. Seaside, OR: Watchmaker, 2010. Print.

Jameson, Fredric. *Postmodernism, or, The Cultural Logic of Late Capitalism*. Durham: Duke University Press, 1997. Print.

Jaynes, Julian. *The Origin of Consciousness in the Breakdown of the Bicameral Mind*. New York: Mariner Books, 2000. Print.

Johns, Geoff, Dave Gibbons, Ivan Reis, and Ethan Van Sciver. *Green Lantern: The Sinestro Corps War: Volume 1*. New York: DC Comics, 2008. Print.

Johns, Geoff, and Phil Jimenez. *Infinite Crisis*. New York: DC Comics, 2008. Print.

Johns, Geoff, and Ivan Reis. *Blackest Night*. New York: DC Comics, 2010. Print.

_____, and _____. *Green Lantern: Secret Origin*. New York: DC Comics, 2008. Print.

Johns, Geoff, and Ethan Van Sciver. *Green Lantern: Rebirth*. New York: DC Comics, 2010. Print.

Jones, Bruce, and Brent Anderson. "Children of the Damned." *Kazar* 3.11 (Feb. 1982). Print.

Jones, Gerard. *Men of Tomorrow: Geeks, Gangsters, and the Birth of the Comic Book*. New York: Basic, 2004. Print.

Jurgens, Dan. *Zero Hour: Crisis in Time*. New York: DC Comics, 1994. Print.

Jurgens, Dan, Karl Kesel, Jerry Ordway, Louise Simonson, and Roger Stern. *A World Without a Superman*. New York: DC Comics, 1993. Print.

Jurgens, Dan, Karl Kesel, Louise Simonson, and Roger Stern. *The Return of Superman*. New York: DC Comics, 1993. Print.

Jurgens, Dan, Jerry Ordway, Louise Simonson, and Roger Stern. *The Death of Superman*. New York: DC Comics, 1993. Print.

Justice League. Warner Bros. Television, 2001–2004. Television.

Justice League Heroes. By Snowblind Studios. Warner Bros. Interactive, 2006. Video game.

Justice League Unlimited. Warner Bros. Television, 2004–2006. Television.

"Justice League Movie Planned Without Bale and Routh." *The Guardian*. 23 Aug. 2007. Web. 29 Aug. 2009.

Kane, Bob. *Batman and Me*. Forestville, CA: Eclipse, 1989. Print.

Khoury, George. *The Extraordinary Works of Alan Moore*. Raleigh, NC: TwoMorrows, 2003. Print.

Kirby, Jack. *Forever People*. New York: DC Comics, 1998. Print.

_____. *Jimmy Olsen: Adventure by Jack Kirby, Vol.1*. New York: DC Comics, 2003. Print.

_____. *The New Gods*. New York: DC Comics, 1998. Print.

Kirk, G. S. *The Songs of Homer*. Cambridge: Cambridge University Press, 2005. Print.

Klock, Geoff. *How to Read Superhero Comics and Why*. New York: Continuum, 2002. Print.

Knowles, Chris. *Our Gods Wear Spandex: The Secret History of Comic Book Heroes*. Newburyport, MA: Weiser Books, 2007. Print.

Krueger, Jim, and Alex Ross. *Justice, Vol.1*. New York: DC Comics, 2008. Print.*

_____, _____, and Doug Braithwaite. *Paradise X*. Vol. 2. New York: Marvel Comics, 2007. Print.

_____, _____, and _____. *Universe X*. Vol. 1. New York: Marvel Comics, 2006. Print.

Landow, George P. *Hypertext 3.0: Critical Theory and New Media in an Era of Globalization*. Baltimore: Johns Hopkins University Press, 2006. Print.

Lawrence, John Shelton, and Robert Jewett. *The American Monomyth*. Lanham, MD: University Press of America, 1988. Print.

_____, _____, and _____. *The Myth of the American Superhero*. Grand Rapids, MI: Eerdmans, 2002. Print.

Lee, Stan. *Origins of Marvel Comics*. New York: Simon and Schuster, 1974. Print.

Lee, Stan, and Steve Ditko. "Spider-Man!" *Amazing Fantasy*. 1.15. *40 Years of the Amazing Spider-Man*. TOPICS Entertainment, 2006. DVD-ROM.

_____, and _____. "Spider-Man Versus Dr. Octopus." *Spider-Man* 1.3. *40 Years of the Amazing Spider Man*. TOPICS Entertainment, 2006. DVD-ROM.

Lee, Stan, and Gil Kane. "And Now, the Goblin!" *Spider-Man* 1.96. *40 Years of the Amazing Spider-Man*. TOPICS Entertainment, 2006. DVD-ROM.*

Lee, Stan, and Jack Kirby. "Behold! A Distant Star!" *The Fantastic Four*. 1.37. *44 Years of the Fantastic Four*. GIT Corporation, 2007. DVD-ROM.

_____, and _____. "The Coming of Galactus." *The Fantastic Four*. 1.48. *44 Years of the Fantastic Four*. GIT Corporation, 2007. DVD-ROM.

_____, and _____. *The Fantastic Four*. 1.1. *44 Years of the Fantastic Four*. GIT Corporation, 2007. DVD-ROM.

_____, and _____. "The Fantastic Four Versus the Red Ghost and his Indescribable Super-Apes." *The Fantastic Four*. 1.13. *44 Years of the Fantastic Four*. GIT Corporation, 2007. DVD-ROM.

_____, and _____. "The Menace of the Miracle

Man." *The Fantastic Four.* 1.3. *44 Years of the Fantastic Four.* GIT Corporation, 2007. DVD-ROM.

____, and ____. "Prisoners of Dr. Doom." *The Fantastic Four.* 1.5. *44 Years of the Fantastic Four.* GIT Corporation, 2007. DVD-ROM.

____, and ____. "The Return of Dr. Doom." *The Fantastic Four.* 1.10. *44 Years of the Fantastic Four.* GIT Corporation, 2007. DVD-ROM.

____, and ____. "Skrulls from Outer Space." *The Fantastic Four.* 1.2. *44 Years of the Fantastic Four.* GIT Corporation, 2007. DVD-ROM.

____, and ____. "Vs. the Metal Master." *The Incredible Hulk.* 1. 6. *The Incredible Hulk—The Complete Comic Collection.* Marvel Entertainment, 2004. DVD-ROM.

____, and ____. *The X-Men.* 1. 1. *44 Years of the X-Men.* GIT Corporation, 2005. DVD-ROM.

Lee, Stan, and George Mair. *Excelsior! The Amazing Life of Stan Lee.* New York: Fireside, 2002. Print.

Lee, Stan, and John Romita, Sr. "Spider-Man No More!" *Spider-Man* 1.50. *40 Years of the Amazing Spider-Man.* TOPICS Entertainment, 2006. DVD-ROM.

Levi-Strauss, Claude. *The Savage Mind.* Trans. George Weidenfeld. Chicago: University of Chicago Press, 1967. Print.

Levinson, Paul. *Digital McLuhan: A Guide to the Information Millennium.* New York: Routledge, 1999. Print.

Locicero, Don. *Superheroes and Gods: A Comparative Study from Babylonia to Batman.* Jefferson, NC: McFarland, 2007. Print.

Loeb, Jeph, and Tim Sale. *A Superman for All Seasons.* New York: DC Comics, 1999. Print.

Lois and Clark: The New Adventures of Superman. Warner Bros. Television, 1993–1997. Television.

Lord, Alfred B. *The Singer of Tales.* New York: Antheneum, 1968. Print.

____. *The Singer Resumes the Tale.* Ithaca: Cornell University Press, 1995. Print.

Lupoff, Dick, and Pat Lupoff. *All in Color for a Dime.* Iola, WI: Krause Publications, 1997. Print.

Lyotard, Jean-Francois. *The Postmodern Condition: A Report on Knowledge.* Trans. Geoff Bennington and Brain Massumi. Minneapolis: University of Minnesota Press, 1984. Print.

Maggin, Eliot S., and Curt Swan. "Must There Be a Superman?" *Superman* 1.247. *The Greatest Superman Stories Ever Told.* New York: DC Comics, 1987. 255–271. Print.

____, and ____. "Year of the Comet." *DC Comics Presents* 1.87 (Nov. 1985) Print.

Manovich, Lev. *The Language of New Media.* Cambridge, MA: MIT, 2001. Print.

Marz, Ron, and Bill Willingham. *Green Lantern: Emerald Twilight.* New York: DC Comics, 1994. Print.

Mayer, Robert. *Superfolks.* New York: St. Martin's, 2005. Print.

McBride, Melanie. "The Transmetropolitan Condition: An Interview with Warren Ellis." *Mindjack: The Beat of Digital Culture.* 2002. Web. 26 Mar. 2010.

McClelland, Jeff. "From Jimmy Durante to Michael Chiklis: The Thing Comes Full Circle." Wandtke, *The Amazing Transforming Superhero* 70–86. Print.

McCloud, Scott. "A Bill of Rights for Comics Creators." ScottMcCloud.com. n.d. Web. 23 Jan. 2011.

____. *Making Comics: Storytelling Secrets of Comics, Manga, and Graphic Novels.* New York: HarperCollins, 2006. Print.

____. *Reinventing Comics: How Imagination and Technology Are Revolutionizing an Art Form.* New York: HarperCollins, 2000. Print.

____. *Understanding Comics: The Invisible Art.* New York: HarperCollins, 1994. Print.

McLaughlin, Jeff. *Stan Lee: Conversations.* Jackson: University Press of Mississippi, 2007. Print.

McLuhan, Marshall. *The Gutenberg Galaxy.* Toronto: University of Toronto Press, 2000. Print.

____. *The Mechanical Bride: Folklore of Industrial Man.* Corte Madera, CA: Ginko, 2002. Print.

____. *Understanding Media: The Extensions of Man.* Cambridge, MA: MIT Press, 1998. Print.

McLuhan, Marshall, and Quentin Fiore. *The Medium is the Massage: An Inventory of Effects.* Corte Madera, CA: Ginko, 2001. Print.

McLuhan, Marshall, and Wilfred Watson. *From Cliché to Archetype.* New York: Pocket, 1970. Print.

Meltzer, Brad, and Rags Morales. *Identity Crisis.* New York: DC Comics, 2005. Print.

Metz, Christian. *Film Language: A Semiotics of the Cinema.* Trans. Michael Taylor. New York: Oxford University Press, 1974. Print.

Millar, Mark, and Dave Johnson. *Superman: Red Son.* New York: DC Comics, 2004. Print.

Millar, Mark, and Tom Peyer. *The Authority: Transfer of Power.* New York: DC Comics, 2002. Print.

Miller, Frank. *The Dark Knight Returns.* New York: DC Comics, 1996. Print.

____. *The Dark Knight Strikes Again.* New York: DC Comics, 2002. Print.

____. "Roulette." *Daredevil: Visionaries: Frank Miller, Vol. 3.* New York: Marvel Comics, 2001. 207–229. Print.

____. *Sin City: Hell and Back.* Milwaukie, OR: Dark Horse, 2005. Print.

____. "Writers, Artists Describe State of the Nation." *Talk of the Nation.* 24 Jan. 2007. Web. 14 Nov. 2008.

____, and Jim Lee. *All Star Batman and Robin, the Boy Wonder.* New York: DC Comics, 2008. Print.

Moore, Alan, Stephen Bisette, and Rick Veitch. "The Anatomy Lesson." *The Saga of the Swamp Thing.* New York: DC Comics, 1987. 1–24. Print.

Moore, Alan, and Brain Bolland. *The Killing Joke. DC Universe: The Stories of Alan Moore.* New York: DC Comics, 2006. 256–303. Print.

Moore, Alan, and Dave Gibbons. "For the Man Who

Has Everything..." *DC Universe: The Stories of Alan Moore.* New York: DC Comics, 2006. 9–50. Print.

———, and ———. *Watchmen.* New York: DC Comics, 1987. Print.

Moore, Alan, and Gene Ha. *Top Ten: Book One.* La Jolla, CA: America's Best Comics, 1999. Print.*

Moore, Alan, and Gary Leach. *Miracleman: The Dream of Flying.* Forestville, California: Eclipse Comics, 1990. Print.*

Moore, Alan, and Kevin O'Neill. *The League of Extraordinary Gentlemen, Vol. 1.* New York: America's Best Comics, 2002. Print.*

Moore, Alan, and Curt Swan. "Whatever Happened to the Man of Tomorrow." *DC Universe: The Stories of Alan Moore.* New York: DC Comics, 2006. 167–214. Print.

Moore, Alan, and J. H. Williams III. *Promethea, Book 1.* La Jolla, CA: America's Best Comics, 2000. Print.*

Morrison, Grant, and Mike Parobeck. "Flash of Two Worlds." *Secret Origins* 3.50 (Aug. 1990): 9–24. Print.

Morrison, Grant, and Frank Quietly. *All Star Superman, Vol. 2.* New York: DC Comics, 2009. Print.

Morrison, Grant, and Chas Truog. *Animal Man: Deus Ex Machina.* New York: DC Comics, 2003. Print.

Mosco, Vincent. *The Digital Sublime: Myth, Power, and Cyberspace.* Cambridge, MA: MIT Press, 2005. Print.

Murray, Janet H. *Hamlet on the Holodeck: The Future of Narrative in Cyberspace.* New York: The Free Press, 1997. Print.

Nash, Jesse W. "Gotham's Dark Knight: The Postmodern Transformation of Arthurian Mythos." *Popular Arthurian Traditions.* Ed. Sally K. Slocum. Bowling Green, KY: Bowling Green University Popular Press, 1992. 36–45. Print.

Nietzsche, Friedrich. *Thus Spoke Zarathustra: A Book for Everyone and No One.* Trans. R. Hollingdale. New York: Penguin, 2003. Print.

Nyberg, Amy Kiste. *Seal of Approval: The History of the Comics Code.* Jackson: University Press of Mississippi, 1998. Print.

Oehlert, Mark. "From Captain American to Wolverine: Cyborgs in Comic Books: Alternative Images of Cybernetic Heroes and Villains." *The Cybercultures Reader.* Ed. David Bell and Barbara M. Kennedy. New York: Routledge, 2000. 112–123. Print.

Olson, Gary A. "Resisting a Discourse of Mastery: A Conversation with Jean-Francois Lyotard." *The Theory Project.* Illinois State University, 2007. Web. 3 Feb. 2011.

Ong, Walter J. *Faith and Contexts, Vol 1: Selected Essays and Studies, 1952–1991.* Tampa: University of South Florida Press, 1991. Print.

———. *Fighting for Life: Contest, Sexuality, and Consciousness.* Ithaca: Cornell University Press, 1981. Print.

———. *Interfaces of the Word: Studies in the Evolution of Consciousness and Culture.* Ithaca: Cornell University Press, 1977. Print.

———. *Orality and Literacy: The Technologizing of the Word.* London: Routledge, 1982. Print.

———. *The Presence of the Word: Some Prolegomena for Cultural and Religious History.* Minneapolis: University of Minnesota Press, 1967. Print.

———. *Ramus, Method, and the Decay of Dialogue: From the Art of Discourse to the Art of Reason.* Cambridge, MA: Harvard University Press, 1958. Print.

———. "The Writer's Audience Is Always a Fiction." *PMLA.* 90.1 (1975): 9–21. Print.

Owsley, Jim, Keith Giffen, Gerard Jones, and M. D. Bright. *Green Lantern: Emerald Dawn.* New York: DC Comics, 1991. Print.

Parry, Milman. *The Making of Homeric Verse: The Collected Papers of Milman Parry.* Ed. Adam Parry. New York: Oxford University Press, 1987. Print.

Pearson, Robert E., and William Uricchio. *The Many Lives of Batman: Critical Approaches to a Superhero and his Media.* London: Routledge, 1991. Print.

Plato. *The Republic.* Trans. Desmond Lee. New York: Penguin, 2007. Print.

Powell, Barry. *Homer and the Invention of the Greek Alphabet.* Cambridge: Cambridge University Press, 1996. Print.

Prescott, Peter S. "The Comic Book (Gulp!) Grows Up." *Newsweek* 111. 3 (18 Jan. 1988): 70–71. Print.

Pustz, Matthew J. *Comic Book Culture: Fanboys and True Believers.* Jackson: University Press of Mississippi, 1999. Print.

Reibman, James E. "Introduction." *Seduction of the Innocent.* By Fredric Wertham. New York: Main Road, 2004. Print.

Reynolds, Richard. *Superheroes: A Modern Mythology.* Jackson: University Press of Mississippi, 1994. Print.

Rhoades, Shirrel. *Comic Books: How the Industry Works.* New York: Peter Lang, 2008. Print.

Riley, Brendan. "Warren Ellis Is the Future of Superhero Comics: How to Write Superhero Stories that Aren't Superhero Stories." Wandtke, *The Amazing Transforming Superhero* 129–148. Print.

Robinson, Tasha. "Frank Miller." *The Onion A.V. Club.* 5 Dec. 2001. Web. 23 Mar. 2005.

———. "Will Eisner." *The Onion A.V. Club.* 27 September 2000. Web. 20 June 2003.

Rose, Lloyd. "Comic Books for Grown-Ups." *Atlantic* 258. 2 (Aug. 1986): 77–80. Print.

Ross, Alex. *Mythology: The DC Comics Art of Alex Ross.* New York: Pantheon, 2005. Print.

Sabin, Roger. *Comics, Comix, and Graphic Novels: A History of Comic Art.* London: Phaidon, 1996. Print.

Saraceni, Mario. *The Language of Comics.* New York: Routledge, 2003. Print.

Savage, William W. *Comic Books and America, 1945–1954.* Norman: University of Oklahoma Press, 1990. Print.

Schelly, Bill. *The Golden Age of Comic Fandom.* Seattle: Hamster Press, 1999. Print.

Schmitt, Ronald. "Deconstructive Comics." *Journal of Popular Culture* 25.4 (spring 1992): 153–162. Print.

Seagle, Steven T., and Teddy Kristiansen. *It's a Bird.* New York: Vertigo, 2005. Print.

Sedgwick, Eve. *Between Men: English Literature and Male Homosocial Desire.* New York: Columbia University Press, 1985. Print.

_____. *Epistemology of the Closet.* Berkeley: University of California Press, 2008. Print.

Shooter, Jim, and Mike Zeck. "The Reign of the Superman." *Science Fiction* 3. (Jan. 1933). Print.

_____, and _____. *Secret Wars.* New York: Marvel Comics, 2008. Print.

Siegel, Jerry, and Paul Casidy. "Superman Versus Luthor." *Superman* 1.4. *The Greatest Superman Stories Ever Told.* New York: DC Comics, 1987. 17–29. Print.

Siegel, Jerry, and Leo Nowak. "The Machinations of the Light." *Superman* 1.13. *Superman: From the Thirties to the Seventies.* New York: Crown, 77–89. Print.

_____, and _____. "Superman Versus the Archer." *Superman* 1.13. *The Greatest Superman Stories Ever Told.* New York: DC Comics, 1987. 30–42. Print.

Siegel, Jerry, and George Roussos. "Lois Lane, Superwoman." *Action Comics* 1. 60. *Superman: From the Thirties to the Seventies.* 186–197. New York: Crown, 7–15. Print.

Siegel, Jerry, and Joe Shuster. *Superman* 1.1 *Superman: From the Thirties to the Seventies.* New York: Crown, 38–50. Print.

_____, and _____. "Superman, Champion of the Oppressed." *Action Comics* 1. 1. *Superman: From the Thirties to the Seventies.* New York: Crown, 20–37. Print.

_____, and _____. "What If Superman Ended the War?" *Look* 17 February 1940. *The Greatest Superman Stories Ever Told.* New York: DC Comics, 1987. 43–44. Print.

Siegel, Jerry, and Curt Swan. "The Death of Superman." *Superman* 1.149. *The Greatest Superman Stories Ever Told.* New York: DC Comics, 1987. 182–206. Print.

Siegel, Jerry, and Ira Yarbrough. "The Mysterious Mr. Mxyztplk." *Superman* 1.30. *The Greatest Superman Stories Ever Told.* New York: DC Comics, 1987. 45–56. Print.

Silvio, Carl. "Postmodern Narrative, the Marvel Universe, and the Reader." *Studies in Popular Culture* 15 (1994): 39–50. Print.

Sim, Dave. *Cerebus.* Kitchener, Ontario: Aardvark-Vanaheim, 1992. Print.*

Simon, Joe, and Jack Kirby. "Meet Captain America." *Captain America Comics* 1.1. *Golden Age Captain America.* New York: Marvel Comics, 2005. 3–10. Print.

Smallville. Warner Bros. Television, 2001–2011. Television.

Spiegelman, Art. *Jack Cole and Plastic Man: Forms Stretched to their Limits.* San Francisco: Chronicle, 2001. Print.

Stock, Brian. *Listening for the Text: On the Uses of the Past.* Philadelphia: University of Pennsylvania Press, 1996. Print.

Superman II. Dir. Richard Lester. Warner Bros., 1980. Film.

Superman II: The Richard Donner Cut. Dir. Richard Donner. Warner Home Video, 2006. DVD.

Superman III. Dir. Richard Lester. Warner Bros., 1983. Film.

Superman IV: The Quest for Peace. Dir. Sidney J. Furie. Warner Bros., 1987. Film.

Superman: Doomsday. Warner Home Video, 2007. DVD.

Superman Returns. Dir. Brian Singer. Warner Bros., 2006. Film.

Superman Returns. By Electronic Arts. Warner Bros. Interactive, 2006. Video game.

Superman: Shadow of Apokalips. By Infogrames. Warner Bros. Interactive, 2002. Video game.

Superman: The Animated Series. Warner Bros. Television, 1996–2000. Television.

Superman: The Man of Steel. By Circus Freak Studios. Atari, 2002. Video game.

Superman: The Movie. Dir. Richard Donner. Warner Bros., 1978. Film.

Thomas, Roy, Sal Buscema, and Neal Adams. *The Avengers: The Kree-Skrull War.* New York: Marvel Comics, 2000. Print.

Thomas, Roy, and Jim Craig. "What If Spider-Man Joined the Fantastic Four." *What If?* 1.1. *What If? Classic Vol. 1.* New York: Marvel Comics, 2004. 5–39. Print.

Thomson, Iain. "Deconstructing the Hero." *Comics as Philosophy.* Ed. Jeff McLaughlin. Jackson: University Press of Mississippi, 2006. 100–129. Print.

Toohey, Peter. *Reading Epic: An Introduction to Ancient Narratives.* New York: Routledge, 1992. Print.

Van Ness, Sara J. *Watchmen as Literature: A Critical Study of the Graphic Novel.* Jefferson, NC: McFarland, 2010. Print.

Veitch, Rick. *The Maximortal.* West Townsend, VT: King Hell, 2005. Print.

Wagner, Matt. *Trinity.* New York: DC Comics, 2005. Print.

Waid, Mark. "Introduction." *Crisis on the Multiple Earths: The Team-Ups, Vol. 1.* New York: DC Comics, 2005. 1–4. Print.

Waid, Mark, and Ariel Olivetti. *The Kingdom.* New York: DC Comics, 2000. Print.

Waid, Mark, and Alex Ross. *Kingdom Come.* New York: DC Comics, 1997. Print.

Waid, Mark, and Leinil Francis Yu. *Superman: Birthright.* New York: DC Comics, 2004. Print.

Wandtke, Terrence, ed. *The Amazing Transforming Superhero: Essays on the Revision of Characters in Comic Books, Film, and Television*. Jefferson, NC: McFarland, 2007. Print.

_____. "Introduction: Once Upon a Time Once Again." Wandtke, *The Amazing Transforming Superhero* 5–32. Print.

Weinstein, Simcha. *Up, Up, and Oy Vey!: How Jewish History, Culture, and Values Shaped the Comic Book Superhero*. Baltimore: Leviathan, 2006. Print.

Wertham, Fredric. *Seduction of the Innocent*. New York: Main Road, 2004. Print.

_____. *The World of Fanzines: A Special Form of Communication*. Carbondale: Southern Illinois University Press, 1973. Print.

Wilson, Nathan. "An Interview with Geoff Johns, Part 2." *The Comics Journal*. 8 Feb. 2011. Web. 19 June 2011.

Wolfman, Marv. *Crisis on Infinite Earths*. New York: Ibooks, 2005. Print.

_____, and George Perez. *Crisis on Infinite Earths*. New York: DC Comics, 2001. Print.

Wright, Bradford W. *Comic Book Nation: The Transformation of Youth Culture in America*. Baltimore: Johns Hopkins University Press, 2001. Print.

Zumthor, Paul. *Oral Poetry: An Introduction*. Trans. Kathryn Murphy-Judy. Minneapolis: University of Minnesota Press, 1990. Print.

Index

Aarseth, Espen 215, 247
Achilles 82, 118–119, 121, 127, 201
Action Comics 34, 62, 64, 92, 99–100, 153, 155, 235, 241
Adams, Arthur 96, 185
Adams, Neal 96, 128, 162, 165–166, 185, 235
Adorno, Theodor 236
Alias 191, 209–211
The All Star line 21, 26, 212–213, 246
The All Winners Squad 94, 114, 118
Alter Ego 146
Amazing Fantasy 113, 124, 210
Andrae, Thomas 23, 226, 228, 230
Animal Man 211–212
Aquaman 203
The Atlantic Monthly 170, 186
The Atom 112, 138
The Authority 22, 26, 75, 78, 192, 213–214, 230
The Avengers 119, 120, 128–129, 159, 209, 242, 248

Bails, Jerry 146, 156, 240, 241
Bainbridge, Jason 249
Barnes, David 182
Barr, Mike 152
Barthes, Roland 111, 206–207, 248
Basquiat, Jean-Michel 249
Bates, Cary 145
Batgirl 18
Batman 1, 4, 9–10, 11–13, 14, 16, 17, 20, 22, 34, 38–39, 44, 48, 55, 68–69, 93, 97, 98, 106, 109, 111, 112, 124, 127, 137–138, 145, 149, 151–152, 153–154, 159, 168, 171–172, 173, 176–180, 181, 184, 185, 189, 192, 195, 196, 201, 203, 204, 208, 211, 214, 217, 219, 225, 226, 229, 230, 231, 236, 239, 242, 245, 246; *Batman Begins* 13; *Batman Returns* 13; *The Dark Knight* 13, 20, 98

Batwoman 18
Baudrillard, Jean 206
Baudry, Jean-Louis 86
Bazin, André 227
Beck, C.C. 58, 93
Bendis, Brian Michael 191, 209–211, 213, 248
Benes, Ed 153
Benson, Larry 32
Beowulf 4, 24, 29, 32, 56, 131, 162
Bergengren, Ralph 50
Beritela, Gerard F. 232
Berkley, George 82
The Black Panther 19
Blackmore, Tim 184, 239, 246
Bloom, Harold 23, 193, 249
Bolter, Jay David 86, 195, 205, 206, 247, 248, 249
Bond, James 14
Boring, Wayne 45–47, 93, 232
Brando, Marlon 232
Bridwell, E. Nelson 230
Brontë, Charlotte 137
Brontë, Emily 137
Brooker, Will 236, 237
Bryson, Norman 234
Buffy the Vampire Slayer 11
Burke, Kenneth 225
Burton, Tim 11, 13
Busiek, Kurt 73, 76–77, 127, 208, 232
Byrne, John 72–73, 96, 99, 151, 164, 166, 185, 196, 230, 242, 243

Cage, Luke 19
Campbell, Joseph 56
The Cantos 24
Captain America 17, 22, 34, 93–94, 106, 114, 128, 129, 156, 173, 192, 209, 226, 235, 238, 242
Captain Marvel 17, 18, 34, 47–48, 58, 93, 97, 106, 111, 119, 124, 128, 244
Carlson, K.C. 197
Carlyle, Thomas 206
Carrier, David 86, 129, 234
Cassidy, Paul 45
Castleberry, Garret 247

Chang, Gordon H. 230
Claremont, Chris 164–165, 196
Cocks, Jay 244
Comics Code 17, 19, 68–69, 106, 110–111, 123, 131, 138, 168, 185, 226, 236, 237, 239, 241, 244
The Comics Journal 146
Contest of Champions 20, 241
Coogan, Peter 249
Crime Does Not Pay 107
Crisis on Infinite Earths 5, 20, 21, 72, 76, 132, 134, 136, 147–155, 157, 158, 160, 165, 168, 196, 197, 203, 204 211–212, 232, 240, 241
Cunningham, Phillip L. 242
Cyclops 164–165

Daredevil 96, 102, 165–167, 171, 185, 189, 209, 248
Darrow, Clarence 237
David, Peter 153
Davis, Adam 85, 227
Davis, Alan 168
Dazzler 3, 187
The Death of Captain Marvel 245
Deppey, Dick 187
Derrida, Jacques 206, 228, 233, 248
Descartes, René 82, 175
Detective Comics 16, 34, 38–39, 228
Dick Tracy 16, 34
Dido, Dan 138
Ditko, Steve 93, 95–96, 105, 106, 113–114, 119 125, 127, 128, 210, 234, 235, 237, 238
Dittmar, Jason 242
Dobrotka, Ed 45
Dr. Strange 95, 119, 120
Donenfeld, Harry 34, 99
Donner, Richard 221, 249

Earth X 99, 134, 158–159, 243
Eco, Umberto 22, 23, 39, 40, 120, 172, 232
Einstein, Albert 241

259

Eisenstein, Sergei 227
Eisner, Will 14, 34, 43, 44, 102, 103, 223, 228, 229, 232, 233, 234, 235, 237, 243, 248
Elliot, T.S. 190
Ellis, Warren 26, 78, 191, 193, 211, 213–219, 230, 232
Elseworlds 78, 153, 159, 241
Engle, Gary 230, 232
Englehart, Steve 128
Entertainment Weekly 186
Erikson, Erik 135
Evanier, Mark 229

Famous Funnies 34
Fantastic Four 1, 18, 72, 94–95, 114–120, 124, 127, 128, 130, 131, 156, 157, 159, 164, 204, 213, 214, 216, 238, 242, 248
Feiffer, Jules 22–23, 50–51, 170, 229
52 134, 156, 211, 242
Finger, Bill 68, 111, 151, 225, 226, 228, 237
Fingeroth, Danny 231
The Flash 5, 17, 18, 106, 112, 138–141, 142–145, 149–150, 155, 157, 171, 196, 203, 204, 231, 240, 241, 248, 249
Flash Gordon 15, 34, 236
Flinton, Ben 138
Foley, John Miles 25–26, 32–33, 85, 170, 173, 183, 188, 193–194, 195, 198, 205, 206, 227, 228
Foucault, Michel 111, 206–207, 248
Fox, Gardner 5, 138–141, 142–145, 146, 147, 156, 161, 174, 196, 200, 204
Fox, Robin 175, 177
Freud, Sigmund 57, 135–136, 142–143, 175, 240

Gaiman, Neil 21, 77, 193, 208, 244, 248
Gaines, Bill 108, 110, 236, 237, 239
Gaines, Max 34, 236
Galactus 94, 95, 119, 127, 159
Gaydos, Michael 210
Gibbons, Dave 168, 185
Gilliam, Terry 246
Giordano, Dick 173, 245
Gombrich, E.H. 84, 87, 88, 92, 234, 249
Goodman, Martin 93, 114
Goody, Jack 175, 245–246
Gordon, Ian 86
Green Arrow 96, 198, 200–201, 202, 248
Green Lantern 17, 18, 22, 38, 96, 106, 112, 138, 145, 148, 152, 156, 157, 191, 195–203, 231, 247–248

Groenstein, Thierry 87, 223, 227, 228, 233, 239
Groth, Gary 187, 188, 241, 246
Grusin, Richard 249

Haire-Sargeant, Lin 137
Hamlet 124
Hammett, Dashiell 244
Harris, Neil 23, 203, 226, 227
Harvey, Robert 102, 166, 225
Havelock, Eric 82–83, 227, 228, 233
Hawkman 112, 138
Hayles, Janet 249
Hearst, William Randolph 33
Heer, Jeet 23, 223
Hitch, Bryan 96
Hogarth, William 87
Homer 49, 52, 57, 75, 94, 113, 114, 118, 120, 131, 162, 227, 228, 230, 237
Howe, Irving 85, 86
The Hulk 18, 73, 95, 119, 120, 121, 122, 124, 128, 204, 209, 235, 238, 239
Hutcheon, Linda 248

Identity Crisis 134, 242
The Iliad 82, 94, 114, 118, 230
Infinite Crisis 134, 153–156, 158, 242
Iron Man 4, 95, 119, 120, 121, 210

James, William 240
Jameson, Fredric 142, 240
Janet, Pierre 240
Janson, Klaus 185
Jaynes, Julian 57
Jewett, Robert 23, 180, 227, 230
Jimenez, Phil 153
Johns, Geoff 153, 155, 191, 195–196, 197–203, 242, 248, 249
The Joker 1
Jones, Gerard 43
Jones, Rick 128–129
The Journal American 33
Joyce, James 142
The Justice League of America 13, 94, 112, 114, 116, 118, 120, 145, 147, 148, 152, 159, 192, 204, 241
The Justice Society of America 22, 48, 112, 138, 144, 145, 146, 147, 148, 241

Kane, Bob 16, 93, 151–152, 203, 204, 217, 225, 226, 228, 234, 237
Kane, Gil 243
Kazar 158, 214
Kipling, Rudyard 107
Kirby, Jack 5, 18, 43, 44, 52, 93, 96, 102, 103, 105, 106, 113–121, 127, 128 130, 143, 146, 156, 158, 164, 185, 188, 204, 215, 229, 234, 235, 237, 238
Kirk, G.S. 32, 40
Klock, Geoff 22, 23, 150–151, 181, 213–214, 215, 225, 232, 243, 249
Knowles, Chrisopher 53
Krazy Kat 16
Kristiansen, Teddy 219
Krueger, Jim 158–159
Kubert, Ada 99
Kurtzman, Harvey 239
Kyd, Thomas 137

Lacan, Jacques 136
Landow, George 195, 205–206, 228, 247, 248
Lane, Lois 2, 9, 10, 19, 63, 67, 69, 72, 73, 76, 150, 159, 171, 221
Lawrence, D.H. 231
Lawrence, John Shelton 23, 180, 227, 230
Leach, Gary 168
The League of Extraordinary Gentlemen 189, 204, 216
Lecter, Hannibal 14
Ledger, Heath 13
Lee, Jim 21, 77, 96, 185, 188, 189
Lee, Stan 5, 18, 52, 93, 102, 105, 106, 113–128, 130–131, 143, 146, 149, 156, 162, 165, 166, 188, 204, 216, 234, 237, 238, 239
Lester, Richard 221
Lévi-Strauss, Claude 174–176, 195, 206–207, 215, 245–246, 247
Levinson, Paul 195, 205, 216, 247
Lichtenstein, Roy 128
Liebowitz, Jack 34
Lilifield, Rob 189
Little Nemo in Slumberland 16, 34
LoCicero, Don 230
Loeb, Jeph 73, 232, 242
Look 66
Lord, Albert 24–25, 29–30, 32, 33, 36, 37–38, 45, 48, 49, 51, 59, 75, 101, 102–104, 134, 137, 193, 226, 230, 231
Lovecraft, H.P. 215
Luthor, Lex 19, 69–70, 71, 72, 73, 75, 76, 92, 99, 151, 153, 154, 155, 159–160, 213, 232
Lyotard, Jean-François 142, 219, 240, 249

MacKenzie, Roger 165
Mad 110, 228, 237
Maggin, Eliot S. 76, 244
Mallarmé, Stéphané 207
Manovich, Lev 247
Marble, Anne Russell 85

Index

Marston, William Moulton 58
The Martian Manhunter 203
The Marvel Method 114–115, 116
Marvelman (Miracleman) 77, 167–168, 244
Marvels 127, 208, 209, 213
Marx, Groucho 6
Mayer, Rober 231
Mazzucchelli, David 151–152
McCloud, Scott 77, 86–91, 92, 97, 99, 102, 103, 141, 163, 185, 201, 206, 221, 223, 225, 226, 227, 228, 230, 233, 234, 235, 243, 247, 249
McFarlane, Todd 21, 77, 97, 152, 188, 189, 209, 210, 232
McGinness, Ed 97, 99
McKean, Dave 208, 234
McLuhan, Marshall 6, 25, 32, 36–37, 42, 43, 49, 55, 57, 59, 60, 65, 75–76, 79, 82, 83, 84, 86, 88, 92, 104, 134–135, 141, 184, 195, 215, 227, 228, 229, 230, 231, 233, 235, 240, 247, 248
Meillet, Antoine 29, 227
Meltzer, Brad 193
Metz, Christian 8, 86
Millar, Mark 78, 159–160, 193, 196
Miller, Frank 5, 11, 14, 20, 26, 70, 97, 98, 102, 105, 151, 160, 161–162, 165–167, 169, 170, 171–174, 176–180, 184–187, 188 189–190, 196, 198, 217, 229, 230, 232, 235, 239, 243, 244, 245, 246
Milton, John 135, 160
Miró, Juan 234
Moebius 185
Moore, Alan 5, 20, 26, 72, 77, 98, 105, 152, 157, 160, 161–162, 165, 167–169, 170, 171–174, 180–187, 188, 189–190, 198, 200, 204, 211, 226, 230, 241, 243, 244, 245
The Morning Journal 15
Morrison, Grant 152, 196, 211–213, 232, 241, 246
Mosco, Vincent 247
Murray, Janet 249
Mxyzptlk, Mr. 17

Nash, Jesse 176, 246
New Gods 102, 120, 215, 229, 235
Newsweek 170, 186
Nicholson, Jack 13
Nietzsche, Friedrich 61–62, 158, 214
Nightwing 154
Nixon, Richard 174
Nolan, Christopher 13
Nyberg, Amy 108, 109, 111, 237

O'Connor, Bill 138
Odysseus 4, 55–58, 66, 111
The Odyssey 24, 29, 32, 52, 114, 131, 194, 228, 230
Oehlert, Mark 195
O'Neil, Denny 96, 151, 248
Ong, Walter 3, 9, 25, 27, 28, 31–32, 33, 36, 37, 38, 41, 42, 43, 44, 49–51, 53–54, 55, 57, 59–61, 65, 71, 76, 79, 80, 81–82, 83, 84–85, 86, 87, 88, 90, 101, 103, 104, 105, 113–114, 131, 134–136, 137, 141–143, 160, 164, 165, 173, 191, 193, 207, 215, 227, 228, 229, 231, 233, 234, 240, 243, 244
Overstreet Comic Book Price Guide 146

Paradise Lost 24, 160
Parker, Bill 58
Parry, Milman 24–25, 29–30, 32, 33, 36, 37, 49, 51, 134, 227, 231, 233
pastiche 142, 153, 155
The Pathways Project 170, 194, 247
Pearsall, Derek 103
Perez, George 97, 147, 149, 153
Peter, Harry 93
The Phantom 16, 34
Picasso, Pablo 249
Picoult, Jodi 193
Pirandello, Luigi 142
Planetary 26, 191, 214–219
Plato 83–84, 85, 136, 228, 233; "The Allegory of the Cave" 83
Poe, Edgar Allan 168
Postman, Neil 191
Powell, Barry 237
Prescott, Peter S. 244
Prince Valiant 16, 34, 236
Pulitzer, Joseph 33
Punch 15, 33
Pustz, Matthew 109, 122, 226, 232
Puzo, Mario 232

Quesada, Joe 97, 157
Quietly, Frank 97

Ramus, Peter 81
Reagan, Ronald 177
Reeve, Christopher 71, 231, 232
Reeves, George 11, 71, 99, 226, 232
Reibman, James 110, 237
Reynolds, Richard 22, 23, 53, 55–56, 164 186, 221, 225, 226, 230, 235, 243
Rhys, Jean 137
Riley, Brendan 213
Robin 16, 106, 109, 178, 180, 236
Rolling Stone 186

Romero, Caesar 13
Romita, John 96, 125, 127
Rose, Lloyd 170, 244
Ross, Alex 71, 99, 134, 158–159, 208, 235, 241, 243

Sabin, Roger 186
Sandman 21, 208
Saraceni, Mario 249
Sartre, Jean-Paul 175
Saussure, Ferdinand de 90
Savage, William W. 54
Schelly, Bill 121, 146
Schmidt, Ronald 248
Schrödinger, Erwin 217
Schwartz, Julius 138, 144, 169
Seagle, Steven T. 219
Secret Wars 20, 204, 241
Sedgwick, Eve 236
Seligman, Kurt 84
Senefelder, Alois 35
Shakespeare, William 137
Sheena 107
Shuster, Joe 16, 41, 43, 45–47, 58, 60–62, 64, 65–67, 92, 99, 103, 185, 213, 225, 226, 229, 231, 232, 237, 241
Siegel, Jerry 16, 40, 41, 43, 58, 60–62, 64, 65–67, 103, 111, 225, 226, 229, 230, 231, 232, 237
Sienkiewicz, Bill 234
Sikela, John 45, 102
Silver Surfer 1, 94
Silvio, Carl 203
Sim, Dave 77, 90, 163, 241, 243, 249
Simon, Joe 93
The Simpsons 2
Sinestro 196, 197, 200–202, 248
Singer, Bryan 232
1602 21, 248
Smith, Kevin 193
Snyder, Zack 246
Spawn 22, 77, 189, 191
Spider-Man 2, 4, 7, 14, 18, 22, 95, 96, 98, 124–127, 129, 131, 156, 159, 165, 174, 204, 209, 223, 238, 239, 243, 248, 249
Spiegelman, Art 90, 186
Spillane, Mickey 244
The Spirit 14, 228
Spock, Benjamin 108
Stacy, Gwen 2, 126, 129, 208
Starlin, Jim 20
Steranko, Jim 95
Stock, Brian 33
Straczynski, Michael J. 193
Strange Tales 119
Supergirl 10, 67, 71, 149–150, 153, 189, 242
Superman 2, 4, 5, 7, 9, 10–11, 16, 17, 18, 19, 22, 34–35, 38, 39, 40–41, 43, 44, 46–48, 51, 54–56, 58–78, 91, 92–93, 97–100,

102, 103, 106, 111, 112, 137–138, 145, 149, 150, 151, 152, 153–155, 159–160, 168–169, 171, 172, 177–180, 189, 192, 196, 204, 212–213, 214, 219, 221, 223, 225, 226, 227, 229, 230, 231, 232, 235, 240, 242, 243, 244, 245; *Lois and Clark* 73; "The Reign of the Superman" 61–62; *Smallville* 11, 192, 232; *Superman II* 11, 72, 221, 232; *Superman III* 11, 76; *Superman IV* 11, 76; *Superman: Doomsday* 71; *Superman Returns* 11, 72, 76, 192, 231, 232, 235; *Superman: The Animated Series* 192; *Superman: The Movie* 19
Swamp Thing 168, 208, 211, 244
Swan, Curt 69, 93, 151, 169, 185, 232

Tales from the Crypt 108
Tarzan 16, 34
The Teen Titans 19, 204
Teenage Mutant Ninja Turtles 187
The Terminator 14
Thomas, Roy 128–129, 146, 147, 151, 156, 242
Thomson, Iain 246
Thor 95, 119, 120, 158, 210, 235
Time 170, 186
Timm, Bruce 71

Toohey, Peter 119
Töpffer, Rodolphe 87
Truffaut, François 248

The Ultimate line 14, 21, 26, 78, 157, 213

Van Ness, Sara J. 170, 182, 246
Varley, Lynn 176
Veitch, Rick 249

Wagner, Matt 99
Waid, Mark 70, 73, 152, 232, 241, 242, 248
Warhol, Andy 128
The Watcher 19, 156, 158
Watchmen 5, 20, 23, 119, 161–162, 164, 165, 168, 169, 171, 172–174, 179, 180–187, 189, 192, 195, 208, 230, 243, 244, 245, 246
Waugh, Patricia 203
Wein, Len 168
Weinstein, Simcha 231
Weisinger, Mort 68
Wertham, Fredric 5, 17, 50, 68, 105–106, 108–111, 131, 138, 163, 168, 245
West, Adam 10, 18, 180, 217, 236, 237, 244
What If? 19, 134, 156–157, 226, 242
Whedon, Joss 193
Wheeler-Nicholson, Malcolm 34

Wolfman, Marv 5, 134, 147–150, 196, 241
Wolverine 98, 158, 164–165, 173, 228, 235, 241, 243
Wonder Woman 17, 34, 58, 93, 97, 106, 112, 119, 120, 150, 152, 153–155, 159, 189, 219, 236, 241
Wood, Robert 29
Worchester, Kent 23, 223
The World 15, 33
Wright, Bradford 33, 54–55, 56–57, 107–108, 114, 124, 128, 162, 163, 169, 170–171, 225, 228, 236, 238, 240, 243, 244, 246

X-Men 3, 19, 20, 22, 95, 119, 120, 121, 157, 164–165, 204, 210, 231, 248; Dark Phoenix Saga 3, 165

Yarbrough 45
The Yellow Kid 33
YouTube 14
Yu, Leinil Francis 99

Zero Hour 152–153, 196, 197–198, 201, 217
Zorro 38, 62
Zumthor, Paul 76, 231

www.ingramcontent.com/pod-product-compliance
Ingram Content Group UK Ltd.
Pitfield, Milton Keynes, MK11 3LW, UK
UKHW050537150426
5217IPUK00026B/1979